The Splendid
Blond Beast

Also by Christopher Simpson

Blowback: *America's Recruitment of Nazis and Its Effects on the Cold War*

The Splendid Blond Beast

Money, Law, and Genocide in the Twentieth Century

CHRISTOPHER SIMPSON

GROVE PRESS
NEW YORK

Published by Grove Press
A division of Grove Press, Inc.
841 Broadway
New York, New York 10003-4793

Published in Canada by General Publishing Company, Ltd.

Library of Congress Cataloging-in-Publication Data

Simpson, Christopher.
  The splendid blond beast : money, law, and genocide in the
twentieth century / Christopher Simpson.
      p.   cm.
  Includes index.
  ISBN 0-8021-1362-1
  1. United States—Foreign relations—20th century. 2. Armenian
massacres, 1915–1923. 3. Holocaust, Jewish (1939–1945)
4. Genocide—History—20th century. I. Title.
E744.S5636   1993
327.73—dc20   92-16783
                                                      CIP

Manufactured in the United States of America
Printed on acid-free paper
Designed by Jules Perlmutter/Off-Broadway Graphics
First Edition 1993
  10 9 8 7 6 5 4 3 2 1

For Susan

Acknowledgments

I AM GRATEFUL for assistance in United States archives to Brewster Chamberlain and the U.S. Holocaust Memorial Museum, Dennis Bilger of the Harry S Truman Library, to the research staffs at the U.S. National Archives, the Franklin D. Roosevelt Library, Library of Congress, and the McKeldon Library at the University of Maryland. I am especially grateful to Marilla Guptil of the United Nations Archives, who helped with research in the United Nations War Crimes Commission archives, and to Senator Claiborne Pell and Benjamin Ferencz, who permitted access to important collections of private papers.

My special thanks for assistance in German archives and for assistance in translations to Konrad Ege, Mike Fichter, Thomas and Rena Giefer, Bernd Greiner and the Hamburger Institut für Sozialforschung, Monika Halkort, Katharina Hering, Anke Mackrodt, David Marwell and the Berlin Document Center, Oliver Rathkolb, Ludger Wess, and the Bundesarchiv Koblenz. I am especially grateful to Gabrielle Körner and the Gedenkstatte Deutscher Widerstand, whose enthusiasm and research skills became essential to this project.

Thanks also to Rouben Adalian and the Armenian Assembly,

Eddy Becker, Chip Berlet, Bernard Bernstein, Kai Bird, Tracy Brandt, Noam Chomsky, Arthur Macy Cox, Ann Coyle, Vakahn Dadrian, Rebecca Daugherty and the Reporters Committee for Freedom of the Press, Carolyn Eisenberg, Richard Falk, Mika Fink, John Friedman, John Gimbel, Sue Goodwin, Jean Hardesty and Political Research Associates, Richard Hovannisian, Radu Ionid, Mary Kaufman, Earl Kintner, Mel Leffler, Mark Levy, Louis Madison, Jonathan Marshall, Marc Mazurovsky, Pat Merloe, Marcel Ophuls, Mark Pavlick, Vladimir Pechatnov, Robert Pehle, David Preston, Kate Porterfield, John Prados and Jill Gay, Marc Raskin, Jan Philipp Reemstsma, Alti Rodal, Steven Rogers, Eli Rosenbaum, Hans Safrian, Neal Sher, the Simon Wiesenthal Center, Bradley F. Smith, Ervin Staub, John Stevenson, Telford Taylor, George Wheeler, Murat Williams, and George Willis.

My special thanks to those whose editing, patience, and business acumen made this book possible: Walt Bode, Gail Ross, and John Herman (who should have been thanked last time, but wasn't).

My most special gratitude goes to Bruce and Caroline Simpson, Susan Coyle, and Konrad Ege, who stuck with me through the whole thing.

Contents

*There has always been
a certain conflict between justice and the law.*

HERBERT PELL

The Splendid
Blond Beast

1

The
Splendid Blond Beast

FRIEDRICH NIETZSCHE called the aristocratic predators who write
society's laws "the splendid blond beast" precisely because
they so often behave as though they are beyond the reach of elementary morality. As he saw things, these elites have cut a path toward
a certain sort of excellence consisting mainly of the exercise of
power at the expense of others. When dealing with ordinary people, he said, they "revert to the innocence of wild animals. . . . We
can imagine them returning from an orgy of murder, arson, rape
and torture, jubilant and at peace with themselves as though they
had committed a fraternity prank—convinced, moreover, that the
poets for a long time to come will have something to sing about and
to praise."[1] Their brutality was true courage, Nietzsche thought,
and the foundation of social order.

Today genocide—the deliberate destruction of a racial, cultural,
or political group—is the paramount example of the institutionalized and sanctioned violence of which Nietzsche spoke.
Genocide has been a basic mechanism of empire and the national

state since their inception and remains widely practiced in "advanced" and "civilized" areas.[2] Most genocides in this century have been perpetrated by nation-states upon ethnic minorities living within the state's own borders; most of the victims have been children. The people responsible for mass murder have by and large gotten away with what they have done. Most have succeeded in keeping wealth that they looted from their victims; most have never faced trial. Genocide is still difficult to eradicate because it is usually tolerated, at least by those who benefit from it.

The Splendid Blond Beast examines how the social mechanisms of genocide often encourage tacit international cooperation in the escape from justice of those who perpetrated the crime. It looks at the social underpinnings and day-to-day dynamics of two mass crimes, the Armenian Genocide of 1915–18 and Hitler's Holocaust of the Jews, as well as the U.S. government's response to those tragedies.

According to psychologist Ervin Staub, who has studied dozens of mass crimes, genocidal societies usually go through an evolution during which the different strata of society literally learn how to carry out group murder. In his book *The Roots of Evil*, Staub contends that genocidal atrocities most often take place in countries under great political, economic, and often military stress. They are usually led by authoritarian parties that wield great power yet are insecure in their rule, such as the Nazis in Germany or the *Ittihad* (Committee of Union and Progress) in Turkey. The ideologies of such parties can vary in important respects, but they are nonetheless often similar in that they create unity among "in-group" members through dehumanization of outsiders. Genocidal societies also show a marked tendency toward what psychologists call "just-world" thinking: Victims are believed to have brought their suffering upon themselves and, thus, to deserve what they get.[3]

But the ideology of these authoritarian parties and even their seizure of state power are not necessarily enough to trigger a genocide. The leading perpetrators need mass mobilizations to actually implement their agenda. For example, the real spearheads of genocide in Germany—the Nazi party, SS, and similar groups—by themselves lacked the resources to disenfranchise and eventually murder millions of Jews. They succeeded in unleashing the Holocaust, however, by harnessing many of the otherwise ordinary elements of German life—of commerce, the courts, university scholarship, religious observance, routine government administration, and so on—to the specialized tasks necessary for mass murder. Not surprisingly, many of the leaders of these "ordinary" institutions were the existing notables in German society. The Nazi genocide probably would not have been possible without the active or tacit cooperation of many collaborators who did not consider themselves Nazis and, in some cases, even opposed aspects of Hitler's policies, yet nonetheless cooperated in mass murder. Put bluntly, the Nazis succeeded in genocide in part through offering bystanders money, property, status, and other rewards for their active or tacit complicity in the crime.

The actions of Nazi Germany's business elite illustrate how this works. Prior to 1933, German business leaders did not show a marked impulse toward genocide. Anti-Semitism was present in German commercial life, of course, but was often less pronounced there than in other European cultures of the day.[4] Among the Nazis' first acts in power, however, was the introduction of incentives to encourage persecution of Jews. New Aryanization laws created a profitable business for banks, corporations, and merchants willing to enforce Nazi racial preferences. Tens of thousands of Germans seized businesses or real estate owned by Jews, paying a fraction of the property's true value, or drove Jewish competitors out of business.[5] Jewish wealth, and later Jewish blood, provided an essential lubricant that kept Germany's ruling coalition intact throughout its first decade in power. By 1944 and 1945, leaders of major German companies such as automaker Daimler Benz,[6] electrical manufacturers AEG and Siemens,[7] and most of Germany's large mining, steelmaking, chemical, and construction companies found themselves deeply compromised by their exploitation of concentration camp labor, theft, and in some cases complicity in mass murder. They committed these crimes not so much out of ideological conviction but more often as a means of preserving their influence within Germany's economy and society. For much of the German economic elite, their cooperation in atrocities was offered to Hitler's government in exchange for its aid in maintaining their status.

A somewhat similar pattern of rewards for those who cooperate in persecution can be seen in other genocides. During the Turkish genocide of Armenians, the *Ittihad* government extended economic incentives to Turks willing to participate in the deportation and murder of Armenians.[8] During the nineteenth century, the U.S. government offered bounties for murdering Native Americans and, perhaps more fundamentally, provided free farmland and other business opportunities to settlers willing to encroach on Native American territories.[9] A similar process continues today, particularly in Central and South America.

Thus, in genocidal situations, mass violence can become entwined with the very institutions that give a society coherency. This has important implications for how perpetrators and their collaborators are treated once most of the killing is over. By the time the genocide has ended, it is usually clear that the ordinary, integrative institutions of society remained centers of power during the killing and shared responsibility for it.

These institutions usually hold on to some measure of authority in the wake of any economic or political crisis of legitimacy created by their actions. Even if the regime is brought down by a military defeat, as was the case in Turkey and in Nazi Germany, the residual power of these institutions means that there are likely to be factions among the victors, and even among the victims, who perceive an interest in allying themselves with the old power centers. Such cliques will conceal the old guard's complicity in crime and exploit their relationship with the old power centers for political or economic advantage.

During the two genocides examined in this book, international law obstructed bystanders from rescuing victims of mass crimes and, in some cases, from punishing the perpetrators. The biases in international law that favored the powerful and prosperous also tended to protect and encourage persecutors, especially when these groups intertwined or overlapped. In fact, the social mechanisms of genocide—that is, how it works, how it is actually carried out—aborted the development of international laws and precedents that might otherwise have restricted genocides, particularly after World War I. Thus, the law and the crime became caught in a cycle in which the law facilitated the crime and the crime, in turn, helped institutionalize a form of law with which it could coexist. The losers in this vicious circle were the ordinary people, children, and rebels who have always borne the brunt of tyranny.

This symbiotic evolution of world order, on the one hand, and the destruction of innocent people, on the other, can be seen in the international treaties and legal precedents prior to World War II concerning war crimes and crimes against humanity. The body of war crimes law in effect during those years was written mainly by the United States and the major powers of Europe to favor themselves and to stigmatize rebellions by indigenous peoples or colonized countries. Understanding the complex and sometimes contradictory effects of these precedents is often difficult, however, because the very concept of war crime may seem paradoxical. The object and method of war would seem at first glance to be the destruction of other societies through murder, pillage, or any other means at hand. "War consists largely of acts that would be criminal if performed in time of peace—killing, wounding, kidnapping, destroying or carrying off other people's property," said Telford Taylor, the chief U.S. prosecutor at the second round of the Nuremberg trials. Often such conduct is not regarded as criminal if it takes place in the course of war, Taylor continued, "because the state of war lays a blanket of immunity over the warriors."[10]

But under international treaties this immunity for warriors is not absolute. Its boundaries are marked by what are known as the laws of war. The widely accepted Hague conventions on war crimes and the Geneva conventions on treatment of prisoners of war set limits on the conduct of commanders and soldiers during war, for example. Legally speaking, "enemy soldiers who surrender must not be killed, and are to be taken prisoner," Taylor noted. "Captured cities and towns must not be pillaged, nor 'undefended' places bombarded; poisoned weapons and other arms 'calculated to cause unnecessary suffering' are forbidden." Further, "When an army occupies enemy territory, it must endeavor to restore public order, and respect family honor and rights, the lives of persons, and private property, as well as religious convictions and practices."

For most of this century, the protection of these treaties has extended almost exclusively to members of professional armies, fighting in uniform, with the authorization of their nation's leaders. Insurgents who resisted official armies were only rarely protected by these treaties—in fact, they were often considered to have committed a war crime when they rebelled against prevailing authorities. Nazi leaders used that legal precedent to enlist German military support for the extraordinarily brutal antipartisan campaigns integral to the Holocaust.[11] Allied forces meanwhile took advantage of a similar loophole to authorize bombing campaigns against German cities that even Franklin Roosevelt had condemned as a war crime as recently as 1939.[12] Thus international law typically provided protection for the powerful and ruthless rather than for their victims.

The fact is that no clear international ban against crimes against humanity existed prior to 1945, due in large part to U.S. opposition. Unlike war crimes, crimes against humanity* are usually something a government does to its own people, such as genocide, slavery, or other forms of mass violence against civilians. Although such crimes were defined in detail at the International Military Tribunal at Nuremberg and in later United Nations action, even today they remain a relatively new concept in international law and often run counter to more established legal custom. Crimes against humanity remain considerably harder to prosecute than war crimes, narrowly defined, in part because criminal nation-states are unlikely to prosecute themselves, and because international diplomatic practice—particularly by the United States—has blocked the creation of an international criminal court that would have jurisdiction to try perpetrators of these atrocities. Even the most horrific cases of human rights abuses are often protected from international justice.

Can different genocides and episodes of mass political violence be compared with one another or even jointly discussed within the covers of a single book? This question becomes particularly acute when studying the Nazi Holocaust side by side with other mass crimes. At least four legitimate concerns are sometimes raised

---

* A good definition for these terms can be found in the Allied Control Council Law No. 10, promulgated at Berlin in December 1945.

War crimes, that text said, are "atrocities and offenses . . . constituting violations of the laws or customs of war," such as murder or ill treatment of prisoners of war, plunder, wanton destruction, or devastation that is "not justified by military necessity."

Crimes against humanity on the other hand, include "atrocities and offenses including but not limited to murder, extermination, enslavement, deportation, imprisonment, torture, rape, or other inhumane acts committed against any civilian population," or "persecution on political, racial or religious grounds whether or not in violation of the domestic laws of the country where perpetrated."

Finally, *crimes against peace* are defined as "initiation of invasions of other countries and wars of aggression in violation of international law and treaties," including the planning of such wars.

when authors identify common elements among the Holocaust and other crimes. The first and most basic of these concerns is that the Holocaust may be denigrated, cheapened, or exploited by comparison to other events. The second concern is that the events of the Holocaust were factually so different from the events of any other suffering—in the scope of the Nazi crime, its sophistication, and its absolute determination to exterminate Jews as such—that for strictly scientific reasons it may be impossible or inappropriate to compare the Holocaust with other genocides. Third, there is a belief that the positivist scientific method used by most historians and authors is not adequate for understanding the Holocaust, that the limits of this method will inevitably reduce attempts at understanding to banalities. Finally, some people are convinced on religious or philosophical grounds that the Holocaust was unique, separate from all other human history, and that it cannot be rationally understood, but instead must be contemplated on a spiritual or even mystical plane. These concerns are realistic and are sometimes based on bitter experience.

But to claim that study of the Holocaust must be separate from all other inquiries "romanticize[s] evil and gives it mythic proportions," contends Ervin Staub, who is himself a survivor of the Jewish ghetto at Budapest. "It discourage[s] the realistic understanding that is necessary if we are to work effectively for a world without genocides and mass killings and torture. Only by understanding the roots of evil do we gain the possibility of shaping the future so that it will not happen again."[13]

Extreme evil such as genocide defies comparisons of magnitude. The Holocaust is clearly not the same as the Armenian Genocide, nor are these atrocities equal in some hackneyed sense. Each has terrible, distinctive features that set it apart.

The tendency in some quarters to mystify the Holocaust can actually rob it of significance, according to Yehuda Bauer, head of the Institute of Contemporary Jewry at Hebrew University. If the Holocaust is reduced to an event outside of any historical context, the world can then neither understand it in itself nor learn from it as a warning for the future. Discussion of the Holocaust with other atrocities does not mean they are simplistically equivalent, Bauer insisted.[14] Instead, it is appropriate to compare events accurately, including instances of genocide, and to discern the differences among them on the basis of facts.

Sociologist Helen Fein, author of *Accounting for Genocide* and the director of the Institute for the Study of Genocide in New York, made a similar point in a recent discussion of the various understandings of the uniqueness of the Holocaust. For Fein, comparative studies should probe not only the singular features of the Holocaust, but also those elements that it had in common with other crimes.[15] Other noted scholars contend that historically based, scientific studies of the Holocaust and other instances of genocide are not only appropriate, but are also morally imperative.[16]

The Turkish murders of Armenians and the Nazi Holocaust are more deeply linked than simply being two examples of genocide. The international failure to halt the Armenian Genocide or to bring its perpetrators to justice was in part a product of the then-existing structure of international law and international relations. That failure was not inevitable, but it was in a certain terrible sense the logical result of a mass murder committed within the context of international law as it then stood.

That tragedy in turn helped shape Hitler's ambition to exterminate Jews. Hitler repeatedly pointed to the Turkish race-murder of Armenians as an example for his own thinking.[17] Meanwhile, the reasons of state that had obstructed international efforts to rescue Armenians carried through to World War II largely intact, so that by the 1940s the Allied refusal to rescue Jews also seemed to key U.S. officials of the day to be reasonable and "appropriate," even in situations where rescue would have been relatively simple and inexpensive.[18]

The account that follows traces how leaders of the United States and the major European powers intentionally frustrated the "immediate demands of justice" for the victims of World War I, as U.S. Secretary of State Robert Lansing put it,[19] in the hope of reestablishing a world order that would favor them in the aftermath of the war.

During the 1920s, this shaky new order gave birth to a coterie of bankers, international lawyers, and diplomats who specialized in the complex tasks of U.S.-European trade, investment, and geopolitics. For simplicity's sake, this book focuses on U.S.-German relations, though of course the United States established substantial new economic and political ties with almost every European country, Japan, and leading Asian nations.

Hitler's seizure of power in Germany presented U.S. and German business groups with complex opportunities and challenges. The Nazi-sponsored Aryanization campaigns, clandestine rearmament, industrial bailouts, and public-works programs created a gold rush for businesses favored by the Nazi government. The chauvinistic Nazis tended to view U.S.-based multinational companies with suspicion, but encouraged them to invest in Germany when it seemed to be in their interest to do so. Soon U.S. corporate investment was expanding more rapidly in Hitler's Germany than in any other country in Europe, despite the worldwide economic depression.[20]

During World War II, the structure of international law established in the wake of World War I not only obstructed efforts to rescue European Jews, but it also became a tool in the hands of factions in Washington and London who favored making a separate peace with the Nazis at the expense of the USSR. They contended that Hitler's crimes inside Axis countries were legal, technically speaking, and that Hitler himself was immune from prosecution because of his status as head of state. The Allies should avoid making too much of an issue of Nazi crimes, argued British Foreign Minister Anthony Eden and the U.S. State Department's chief legal advisor, Green Hackworth, because doing so would undermine political initiatives to settle the war through negotiations; in addition, most atrocities would be impossible to prosecute.[21] Tragically, these same factions often controlled the U.S. State Department's day-to-day implementation of policy concerning Jewish immigration and refugee relief.

This "legalist" faction was opposed by President Franklin Roosevelt and his secretary of the treasury, Henry Morgenthau, Jr., by U.S. War Crimes Commissioner Herbert Pell, by British Prime Minister Winston Churchill, and, for somewhat different reasons, by Soviet Premier Josef Stalin. These groups within the Allied camp fought tough legal and political battles over the extent of the authority of the United Nations War Crimes Commission (UNWCC); over the USSR's massacre of Polish officers at Katyn; and, perhaps most importantly, over the Allies' postwar plans for reconstruction of Germany.

Meanwhile, much of the economic, political, and social elite in

Germany, Vichy France, and most of the Nazi-occupied territories cooperated with the Nazis throughout their rule, only to lose confidence in Hitler's government late in the game. De Gaulle's France, the USSR, and some U.S. leaders favored harsh treatment of these corporate collaborators after the war, particularly in Germany. The U.S. and British foreign ministries strongly disagreed, as will be seen, as did leading corporate interests in the West.

Both Allied factions acknowledged that much of Germany's business elite had directly participated in the Holocaust, but they drew quite different conclusions from this fact. For Allied hard-liners, the business elite's participation in Hitler's extermination-through-forced-labor program rekindled their argument that new precedents must be set in international law by bringing such people to justice. In contrast, the foreign ministries insisted that most of the German elite's activities had not been illegal under existing international agreements. Capitalism had grown terribly fragile in Europe owing to depression and war, they contended, and removing national elites from power would only strengthen the hand of native revolutionaries.

The careers of John Foster Dulles and Allen Dulles, who were to become U.S. secretary of state and director of the CIA respectively, were archetypes of the complex paths traveled by international economic elites during the first four decades after World War I. Their stories are emphasized in the pages that follow as an illustration of broader trends.

In the wake of World War I, the Dulles brothers helped construct the international treaties and legal definitions that shut down efforts to bring mass murderers of that time to justice.[22] Between the wars, both were active in U.S.-German trade and diplomatic relations, particularly in developing ornate corporate camouflage intended to frustrate efforts to increase public accountability of major companies. Like many other corporate leaders in the United States, the two brothers also disagreed for a time on how best to respond to the new war unfolding between Germany and Britain. They did agree, however, on what was to them the pivotal issue: the preservation of the influence of European business and diplomatic elites, including that of Germany, when the conflict was over.

Allen Dulles exploited his post in the Office of Strategic Services

(OSS) to quash war crimes prosecutions of senior Nazi officials and German business leaders who cooperated with him in a series of clandestine schemes to secure U.S. advantage in Central Europe. He personally intervened to ensure the escape from prosecution of major German bankers and industrialists complicit in the Nazis' extermination-through-labor program, according to archival records brought to light here for the first time.[23] Dulles also protected SS *Obergruppenführer* Karl Wolff, the highest-ranking SS officer to survive the war and one of the principal sponsors of the Treblinka extermination camp, as well as a number of Wolff's senior aides, who were alleged to have been responsible for deportation of Jews to Auschwitz and massacres of Italian partisans.[24]

Meanwhile, John Foster Dulles helped forge consensus on Wall Street and in the Republican party in favor of an "internationalist" U.S. foreign policy based on rebuilding the German economic elite into a renewed bulwark against revolution in Europe. As will be seen, a key element in his effort was the extension of a de facto amnesty to most of Germany's business leadership, regardless of their activities during the Third Reich.

Herbert Pell's UNWCC became one of the first targets for the Allied factions favoring clemency for Axis notables who had collaborated in Nazi crimes. State department legal chief Green Hackworth succeeded in engineering Pell's dismissal in early 1945, then in shutting down the UNWCC altogether within thirty-six months after the end of the war. Then a U.S. intelligence agent named Ivan Kerno, who had worked with Allen Dulles since the 1920s and who served as senior legal counsel to the new United Nations Organization,[25] sealed the UNWCC records, keeping them off-limits to war-crimes investigators for more than forty years. It took the scandal surrounding the wartime career of UN Secretary General Kurt Waldheim to break these files open at last.

The issue of personal and institutional responsibility for these events raises complicated questions of evidence and justice that are discussed more fully in the pages that follow. But one point is clear: There is no guarantee that the mere good faith of military victors or of a postgenocidal government will be adequate to come to grips with the crime of genocide or with similar systemic violence. The tendency, in fact, will be quite the opposite. The overall drift will be to forget, to compromise, and to walk away from injustice.

But that is getting ahead of the story. To understand why the postwar efforts to bring Nazis to justice turned out the way they did, it is first necessary to go back to an earlier generation's experience with slaughter, when the international community tried for the first time to bring the perpetrators of genocide to justice.

2

"The Immediate Demands of Justice"

PUNISHMENT OF defeated powers for war crimes and crimes against humanity was the first item on the agenda of the peace conference that opened in Paris in 1919. The previous year had seen extraordinary changes in world affairs. Three world empires that had stood for centuries all finally collapsed. In czarist Russia, Communists seized power in late 1917 and took that country out of the European war a few months later, though a civil war continued in the East. The Ottoman Empire in the Middle East disintegrated, and Republican governments supplanted the old monarchy in what once was Austria-Hungary. Armies mutinied in Germany and serious attempts at revolution exploded in Berlin and Budapest. Nations such as Czechoslovakia and Yugoslavia that had long been subordinate territories of old regimes could see independence on the horizon. Existing countries wanted their borders redrawn at the expense of the defeated powers of World War I.

The governments that waged the war had killed at least seven million soldiers, but that was only the official estimate, and it was almost certainly low. Czarist Russia alone lost about 1.7 million soldiers; Germany, a much smaller country, lost 1.6 million; France, about a million. The United States, which entered the war after much of the killing had already taken place, suffered over 120,000 dead.[1] It was by far the most deadly conflict in history up to that time.

Civilians sacrificed the most. In Turkey, the ruling junta attempted to exterminate that country's largest minority group, the Armenians, through pogroms, mass murder, and deportation. They killed about one million people between 1915 and 1918. More than half of the dead were children, and almost all the casualities were civilians.[2] In Europe, civilian suffering became desperate even where there was no genocide. There is no reliable accounting of these losses, but some insight can be gained from the fact that in Europe new forms of starvation diseases were discovered during the war. These took the name hunger edema—hunger swelling—and were believed to be "a species of dropsy first noticed in 1916," according to contemporary reports, "which specially affected the old, the overworked, and inmates of institutions."[3] Epidemics of tuberculosis and influenza during the war killed at least three times as many people as did the fighting itself, and most of the afflicted were children and the elderly. Cholera and typhus ripped through civilian populations, particularly in southeastern Europe, despite improvements in public health measures among soldiers.[4]

The U.S. Federal Reserve Board found that by the spring of 1918 the belligerents had spent about $140 billion on the execution of the war, with the expectation that another $20 billion would be spent before the year was out. This was strictly for soldiers' pay, military hardware, and other direct costs. These were almost unimaginable outlays for that era, representing the bulk of existing productive capacity of all Western society.[5]

When the 1919 Paris Peace Conference opened, most of the victors believed that the defeated Central Powers—Germany, Austria-Hungary, Turkey, and Bulgaria—should be compelled to pay reparations to cover the winners' war costs, and that the defeated military leaders should be punished. If Germany had instigated World War I (as the victors agreed) and had been criminal during the war's execution, then Germany's rulers and the country generally should be forced to pay heavy damages for the destruction that had flowed from these acts. If, in the process, Germany should be eliminated as a commercial rival in the postwar world, so much the better.

The 1919 conference was the forum at which these demands were to be made concrete. Officially, this was a gathering of the successful Entente, or Associated Powers—Great Britain, France, Italy, the United States, and several smaller countries—to decide the peace terms to present to Germany in what would become known as the Treaty of Versailles. The conferees made a self-conscious effort to bring defeated war criminals to justice as one element in a broad endeavor to redress the grievances left by the war.

The issue of punishment for wartime atrocities played a much greater part in these peace talks than it had in any previous conflict, for at least three reasons.

First, public opinion had been a more important factor in the conduct of war than previously, and public opinion strongly favored harsh punishment of those who had perpetrated atrocities. When fighting broke out in 1914, there had been plenty of nationalist enthusiasm among the citizens of the belligerents. But this support diminished as the number of casualties mounted and the futility of the fighting became apparent. Pacifist and Communist arguments that blamed the war on an imperial squabble among the rich won a widening audience as the months passed. By 1916, European governments on both sides of the conflict faced increasing difficulties mobilizing their populations to fight.

War administrations in each country turned to atrocity stories, promises of revenge, and inspiring tales about fallen heroes as a means of bolstering public enthusiasm for continued fighting. A tight, symbiotic relationship soon emerged between the national media and the intelligence services of each major power, as both groups had an interest in wide dissemination of moving stories that demonized the enemy and sanctified each country's own war effort. Dozens of men who later emerged as prominent journalists and public relations specialists, among them Walter Lippmann and Arthur Sweetser of the United States, pioneered modern tactics for organized media campaigns, early radio broadcasting, staged events, and other war propaganda.[6] Some of the stories were myths or deliberate disinformation, of course. But there were no shortages of real atrocities, or of real heroes, in this war. As the fighting drew to a close, potent public sentiment emerged in the victorious Associated Powers to punish the Central Powers not only for allegedly initiating the conflict but also for a long list of atrocities that their forces had perpetrated. Popular demands for trials of the German kaiser and his high command became key election issues in both Britain and the United States.[7]

The second reason why wartime atrocities became an important issue at the 1919 peace conference was that for the first time there were reasonably specific agreements concerning what was to be considered a war crime. Each of the major belligerents had signed the Hague conventions of 1899 and 1907 and the Geneva conventions of 1864 and 1906 (also known as the Red Cross conventions), which set basic standards for military conduct during wars. The governments had formally agreed not to destroy one another's hospitals or hospital ships, for example, and had banned use of poison gas and deadly expanding (dumdum) bullets. They had also accepted measures regarding the honorable treatment of navies and of merchant ships.[8]

The Hague and Geneva conventions reflected a compromise between the national security strategies of the world's principal powers and the antiwar idealism of the era. The conventions rhetorically committed the signatories to peace, and peace activists of the day welcomed the treaties warmly. As a practical matter, however, the Hague conventions often proved to be measures to more rationally manage military conflicts on the European continent. Both Hague conferences had come about largely because of an acute need on the part of the declining European monarchies to restrict the contemporary arms race, which had already begun to bankrupt empires. Most of their actual provisions were derived from European commercial treaties on naval seizure of goods. The terms reflected the conviction of a number of business leaders of the day, notably Andrew Carnegie, that stable international commerce was the most effective means of maintaining peace among nations. Just in case, though, most of the major powers included loopholes intended to immunize themselves from the conventions when they chose to do so. The United States, for instance, specifically exempted anything it might choose to do in Central and South America and the Philippines from the terms of the Hague agreements.[9]

The treaties aimed to make war a "professional" matter conducted between regular armies and navies fighting according to mutually accepted rules of engagement. They sought to protect (European) civil commerce and civilians from war and to set ground rules for the treatment of war prisoners, conduct under a flag of truce, and so on. All wars were supposed to be formally declared—no sneak attacks—and there were provisions encouraging rivals to negotiate before beginning an armed conflict.

At the same time, the main military powers quite openly sought to use the conventions to stabilize Europe and buttress their authority over shaky colonial empires. They formally banned fighting by guerrilla groups, revolutionaries, and unauthorized armies, which had increasingly become a problem for imperial powers worldwide. The military and legal doctrine known as "reprisal" authorized countries that had signed the treaties to legally commit what would otherwise clearly be crimes—shooting hostages, mistreating prisoners of war, etc.—to punish enemies during wartime for their (alleged) war crimes, so as to deter them from further violations.[10] This meant that rebellions could "legally" be met with extraordinary savagery, in part because the basic revolutionary tactic of guerrilla fighting by irregular troops had itself been declared to be a war crime.

The colonies and subjugated countries that attended the Hague meetings were in many cases represented by European or American attorneys whose salaries had been paid by foreign business interests. U.S. diplomat John Foster, who had been U.S. secretary of state in 1892–93, represented the crumbling Chinese imperial government at the 1907 Hague conference, for example. Foster's grandson John Foster Dulles, then still in college, was the "Chinese" delegation's recording secretary.[11]

Nevertheless, the Hague conventions and the Geneva conventions did provide an early legal framework under which nations could seek redress for some types of atrocities, particularly in Europe. They provided an important reference point establishing that the major powers accepted some formal limitations on war, at least among themselves.

Third, the issue of German war crimes became closely bound up with the debate over war reparations. Even the defeated powers agreed in principle that some form of restitution should be paid to the victims of war crimes, though exactly who fit into that category was subject to bitter dispute. By 1919, millions of people had been

killed or maimed by poison gas, aerial bombing, submarine attack
on civilian shipping, or mistreatment as prisoners of war—all
actions that appeared to be in violation of the Hague or Geneva
conventions. The final cost of paying damages to these people
would run to tens of billions of dollars, depending in important
part on how the term *war crime* was defined and how responsibility for such offenses was allocated.[12] In this way, the international response to the atrocities of World War I acquired a
substantial economic aspect, in addition to its more widely recognized moral, political, and judicial dimensions.

War crimes and crimes against humanity thus emerged at the
Paris Conference as a pivotal issue, both in symbolic and practical
terms. This was more than simply an important judicial matter; it
became a focus of a wide-ranging debate over what sort of society
Europe would build in the wake of the war.

The destruction of the old European order carried with it new
political and economic opportunities, many of which greatly favored the United States. That in turn spurred the careers of a
generation of scholars, attorneys, and executives on both sides of
the Atlantic who specialized in U.S. political and business relations abroad. Each of the belligerent countries gave new promi-
nence to its small cadre of experts on international affairs,
intelligence, propaganda, and economic warfare. As the war
wound down, many of these experts went on to become professionals in newly emerging aspects of international trade, banking,
and legal affairs.

John Foster Dulles and Allen Dulles were archetypical of the
group of U.S. specialists on European affairs that was to shape
American relations with the Continent for the next fifty years. The
Dulles brothers were the grandsons and the nephews, respectively,
of two U.S. secretaries of state. John Foster Dulles's ambition, even
as a child, had been to become a corporate lawyer, as his grand-
father had been. Allen wasn't quite sure what he wanted, except
that it had to include adventure and conquest.[13] Both were to get
their wish.

John Foster Dulles grew up squint-eyed, square-shouldered, and
wound so tightly, his detractors joked, that if he sat on a lump of
coal he could turn it into a diamond. His family connections

helped him win a position in 1911 as a junior attorney with the prestigious Wall Street law firm of Sullivan & Cromwell. Except for a handful of short adventures in government service, John Foster Dulles was to remain at Sullivan & Cromwell for the next forty years. "This was to be his real career, the one at which he spent most of his life," Dulles's biographer Ronald Pruessen has written, "and it was to affect greatly almost everything else he ever did."[14]

Dulles specialized in international legal services for banks, corporations, and syndicates of wealthy investors. His law firm had pioneered the practice of international legal support for multinational companies back in the last quarter of the nineteenth century,[15] and Dulles's personal efforts consisted in large part of ensuring that such services continued to develop throughout the first half of the twentieth. His first clients in his early years at Sullivan & Cromwell included a powerful German-American pharmaceutical company, Merck & Co., French banks investing in Brazilian railroads, U.S. and British banks buying up Nicaragua, and a syndicate of major U.S. investors who had pooled their funds to invest in European stocks and bonds.[16]

John Foster Dulles's government service during World War I became closely intertwined with his business aspirations. President Woodrow Wilson appointed Dulles's Uncle Bert, Robert Lansing, U.S. Secretary of State, and Foster Dulles joined the State Department in 1917 as a specialist in political-economic affairs. He soon undertook negotiating assignments for the War Trade Board, where he organized the exchange of American raw materials for Danish shipping facilities, agreements with Spain for exclusive U.S. purchasing of Spanish horses and mules— important to the war effort in those days—and similar measures that marked the dawn of modern economic warfare. He then spent a few months in U.S. military intelligence before becoming, at age thirty-one, one of the State Department's most important representatives at the 1919 Paris Peace Conference—all in less than three years.[17]

His brother Allen, meanwhile, entered the U.S. Foreign Service, the career staff of the U.S. State Department, and was posted as a junior intelligence officer in Bern, Switzerland, in early 1917. Switzerland was neutral in the European war, and Bern became an informal center where shifting groups of nationalist rivals, emigré insurrectionists, and international businessmen could meet. It was at Bern "where I learned what a valuable place Switzerland was for information, and when I became interested in intelligence work," Dulles remembered later.[18] He was assigned responsibility for liaison with representatives of the various Central European liberal-nationalist groups rebelling against the disintegrating Austro-Hungarian Empire. Through Slovak lawyer and diplomat Ivan Kerno, Dulles met and befriended prominent Czech national-ist leaders such as Jan Masaryk and Eduard Beneš, and many Central European diplomats[19] he was later to cultivate as sources of intelligence and influence during his subsequent work, particu-larly at the U.S. Office of Strategic Services (OSS) during World War II and the Central Intelligence Agency after the war.

Allen joined his brother at the 1919 Paris peace conference, where John Foster Dulles served as an assistant to the chief U.S. negotiator, Norman Davis, and specialized in German war repara-tions and related financial matters.[20] Officially, Allen became a member of the Czech Boundary Commission, which carved the new Czechoslovak state out of Germany's Sudetenland and pieces of the defunct Austro-Hungarian Empire. He was simultaneously in charge of the U.S. delegation's political intelligence efforts in Central Europe.[21] He was twenty-five years old.

By most standards, Allen Dulles was a junior member of the Foreign Service, the low man on the totem pole. But with Uncle Bert as secretary of state, Allen Dulles could seek and at times did gain the ear of the President of the United States. When the 1919 Communist revolution broke out in Budapest, Hungary, for exam-ple, Dulles's recommendations for measures to "isolate the Hun-garian Revolution from Russia and prevent its spread to neighboring countries" made its way to President Wilson's desk; it is found today among Wilson's papers. Dulles's comments even at this early age were consistent with those that were to mark his geopolitical concerns for the next four decades. Among his points for President Wilson: Send U.S. gunboats to "control the situation in Budapest"; encourage the Czechs, Romanians, French, and Slov-enes (each of whom had territorial claims against Hungary) to seize Hungarian rail lines, mountain passes, and other strategic points; distribute U.S. food aid on the condition that the Hun-garians establish a "responsible" (i.e., counter-revolutionary) gov-ernment; and begin aid and propaganda measures to shore up the traditional structures of power in surrounding countries.[22]

As things turned out, Wilson did not send gunboats to Budapest, but the Czechs and Romanians did indeed invade Hungary, and with their help Hungarian admiral Miklós Horthy established a new administration in Budapest favored by the West. In the meantime, the threat of Communist rebellions in Budapest and Berlin helped push the conferees at Paris toward a more accommodating settlement with the new German government, which many saw as a bulwark against further insurrections in Central Europe.

The Paris Conference broached the issue of war crimes as its first official act. It created a "Commission on the Responsibility of the Authors of the War and the Enforcement of Penalties" that was to decide who was to be held responsible for initiating the war and on the mechanisms for prosecuting alleged war crimes. The U.S. representatives to this War Crimes Commission were Secretary of State Robert Lansing and James B. Scott, a senior legal advisor to the State Department. Lansing became the commission's chairman.[23]

Lansing viewed agreements such as the Hague conventions and Geneva conventions as infringements of U.S. national sovereignty. He strongly opposed any trials for war crimes or atrocities beyond those that the defeated powers might choose to carry out against their own military officers. "Lansing exhibited one curious state of mind," observed presidential advisor Edward House during an earlier debate over the U.S. response to the sinking of the *Lusitania*. "He believes that almost any form of atrocity is permissible provided a nation's safety is involved."[24] When House asked Lansing who should best determine the level of atrocity appropriate to protect the nation, Lansing replied, "the military authorities of the nation committing the atrocities."[25] Thus, the leaders of the armed forces accused of committing a crime should be the final judge of whether the act was justified in the interests of the nation. Lansing believed that any new precedents set by the Paris conference against war crimes would probably endanger the United States in a future crisis, and he insisted that his government exempt itself from international commitments that might limit its freedom of action.

Lansing contended that punishment oi German leaders was undesirable for political and economic reasons as well. "[H]ow far

should we go in breaking down the present political organization
of the Central Empires or by military operations render them ut-
terly impotent?" Lansing wrote during the negotiations. "We have
seen the hideous consequences of Bolshevik rule in Russia, and we
know that the doctrine is spreading westward. The possibility of a
proletarian despotism over Central Europe is terrible to contem-
plate. . . . The situation must be met. . . . We must look to the future,
even though we forget the immediate demands of justice. Reprisals
[against Germany] and reparations are all very well, but will they
preserve society from anarchy and give to the world an enduring
peace?"[26] Lansing lobbied influential friends before and during the
conference, historian James Willis reports, arguing that "any
breakdown of authority in Germany must be avoided to prevent the
spread of Bolshevism."[27]

But there was strong sentiment among the European delegates on
the War Crimes Commission for tough action. The majority called
for trials of Kaiser Wilhelm and other German leaders. Their resolution indicated that "abundant evidence" had already been collected of "outrages of every description committed on land, at sea,
and in the air, against the laws and customs of war and the laws of
humanity" by Germany and its partners. It described the Central
Powers' wartime rule as "a system of terrorism . . . aided by all the
resources of modern science" that had been created for the purpose
of suppressing all resistance. They cited thirty-two specific
crimes, including massacres of civilians, torture and massacres of
prisoners, use of human shields, mass requisition of private property, destruction of hospital ships, aerial bombardment of undefended cities and towns, religious persecution, deliberate
starvation of civilians, manipulation of currencies, destruction of
industries in German-occupied zones for the purpose of "pro-
mot[ing] German economic supremacy after the war," pillage, rape,
and forced labor. They contended that Germany and the Central
Powers were solely responsible for initiation of the war and the
criminal activities that flowed from it.[28]

In an important departure from tradition, the commission singled out Turkish massacres and deportations of Armenian civilians
as being so grotesque that—although they had not been specifically
banned by the Hague and Geneva conventions—these actions were
inherently criminal under the most elementary norms of human
behavior. This was, they said, a "crime against humanity."[29]

Lansing strongly objected to any introduction of the concept of "laws of humanity" and to trials of foreign leaders before any foreign or international court. International law, he contended, regulated relations among nations; it had no jurisdiction over what a state chooses to do to its own people. International efforts to set human rights standards could never be enforced, he continued, and their failure would undermine compliance with treaties that could be enforced, such as treaties concerning international commerce, which remained fragile despite their relative success during the previous century. Lansing voiced similar opposition to the demands that Kaiser Wilhelm and other leaders be tried before an international court. A leader should be responsible to the "political authority of his country," not to an international court, Lansing contended. The kaiser should be forced from power but not tried.[30]

Germany floated its own proposals concerning war crimes in letters to the conference and in press statements. (Germany remained an enemy power at this stage, barred from presenting delegates.) The German government claimed to support an independent commission to study the question of war guilt, offering to submit cases of accused German criminals to an international court of neutral jurists if the Associated Powers would do the same. However, Germany wanted to retain the authority to retry Germans who were found guilty. The delegates at Paris viewed the proposals as efforts to sidestep responsibility and never formally considered them.[31] Indeed, the fact that the Germans had made these recommendations tended to cut short discussion of somewhat similar French overtures favoring creation of an international criminal court. To some delegates the French proposals were too much like the German plan.

Despite opposition from Lansing and the U.S. delegation, the War Crimes Commission passed a resolution by a large majority condemning enemy violations of what they termed "laws of humanity," particularly the Turkish persecution of Armenians. This opened the door to international trials of Turkish *Ittihad* leaders and perhaps to trials of other Central Powers leaders who were alleged to have committed lesser acts of persecution in Europe. Importantly, the commission's findings required that specific clauses be included in any peace treaty to force the defeated powers to turn over war-crimes suspects and evidence to the courts of the victors.[32]

But Robert Lansing, as commission chairman, refused to transmit the resolution to the highest council of the Paris conference, thus effectively vetoing it. That dispute soon spilled over into the personal discussions among the "Big Four" leaders—U.S. President Wilson, British Prime Minister David Lloyd George, French Premier Georges Clemenceau, and Italian Premier Vittorio Orlando. For a time, the U.S. delegation's opposition to war crimes trials threatened to derail the Paris Conference.

As Lansing saw things, he had important allies in his efforts to block the resolution, despite the lopsided vote against him in the commission. Lansing thought that "the British [delegation] knew the practical impossibility of the action" against war criminals, but "they were forced by public opinion to advocate [measures against criminals] and were depending upon the United States to block it," historian Arthur Walworth has written.[33] President Wilson also supported Lansing on this point and argued in private meetings that a trial of the kaiser would make a martyr of him, perhaps leading to a restoration of the recently overthrown Hohenzollern dynasty in Germany. Wilson preferred to sidestep the issue of war crimes altogether and leave it unresolved in any treaty ending the war.

But Lloyd George, Clemenceau, and Orlando each insisted on strong provisions concerning war crimes and the related issue of war reparations in any peace treaty with Germany. "This question [of war crimes trials], with that of reparations, is one that interests English opinion to the highest degree," the British prime minister told Wilson, "and we could not sign a peace treaty that left it without solution."[34] In time, Wilson softened (though Lansing did not), and the Big Four approved a compromise that watered down the War Crimes Commission's original proposals. Wilson believed that the compromise language would mollify public opinion and divert attention from the war crimes issue. "In withdrawing his opposition to the war-crimes clauses," Walworth commented, "Wilson recognized that they were too ineffectual to warrant any determined resistance to them. When asked by [U.S.] Ambassador [to Great Britain John W.] Davis whether he expected to 'catch his rabbit', [Wilson] said no, 'it was all damned foolishness anyway.'"[35]

3

Young Turks

I N THE END, the delegates at the Paris peace conference insisted on including in the 1919 Treaty of Versailles provisions that required the German government to admit responsibility for instigating the war and to turn over war crimes suspects and evidence to military courts of the Associated Powers for trial. Lansing's views concerning "crimes against humanity" prevailed, however, and that phrase is not found in the peace treaties with Germany or the other Central Powers.

The concept of a crime against humanity was not well defined at this point, even by its advocates. But the definition had at least two important elements that set it apart from earlier understandings of war crimes, which were limited to acts that a government might take against the population or troops of a foreign power.

First, crimes against humanity included atrocities that were criminal not only under civil law but also under the most elementary morality, yet were not technically war crimes. The new definition included domestic campaigns to exterminate a particular ethnic or religious group as well as institutionalized slavery, even though neither of these was considered a war crime under the Hague or Geneva covenants.

Second, many (though not all) atrocities committed by a government against its own people were defined as crimes against humanity.

It was the Turkish government's attempted genocide of that country's large Armenian population that had led to the demand for a clear international ban on crimes against humanity. Turkey was the center of the Ottoman Empire, and the Armenians were a large minority group whose ancestral home clustered around Mount Ararat in eastern Turkey. During the last decades of the nineteenth century, Turkish religious extremists and security forces seeking racial and religious purity in Turkey had repeatedly instigated pogroms, murdering tens of thousands Armenians.[1] One result was that militant Armenians took up arms and began pressing for political independence.

Shortly before World War I, a secretive and disciplined cabal of young Turkish military officers known as the *Ittihad* took power in Turkey and brought the country into an alliance with Germany. These were the original "Young Turks," and their capacity for cruelty and violence still reverberates in that phrase today.

In the first months of World War I the Young Turks instigated a national effort to exterminate the Armenian population under the guise of modernization, suppressing domestic dissent, and securing Turkey's borders. The *Ittihad* bent the power of the Turkish state to their purpose. Beginning in late 1914 and accelerating over the next three years, the Turkish government rounded up Armenian men for forced labor, worked many to death building a trans-Turkish railway for German business interests, then shot the survivors. The government then secretly ordered mass executions of Armenian intellectuals and political leaders in the spring of 1915. The state also uprooted Armenian women and children from their homes and drove them into vast resettlement camps that were barren of supplies or shelter. When the camps became full, the Turks expelled the people into the deserts of what is today Syria and Iraq.[2] Hundreds of thousands of Armenians died from shootings, starvation, exposure, and disease.

The state declared that all the property of deported Armenian families had been "abandoned," then confiscated it and used it to reward *Ittihad* party activists and others who participated in the

extermination process.[3] Many Turks prospered by liquidating
Armenians' businesses, stealing their stocks, and seizing Armenian farms and real estate.

The genocide was particularly cruel to Armenian women and
girls, who became the objects of a pervasive, tacitly sanctioned
campaign of rape. Turkish police encouraged gangs of thugs to
prey upon the deportees as a means of humiliating and destroying
these women. Meanwhile, some Armenian girls were able to escape deportation by announcing a religious conversion to Islam,
and in this way some Turkish men secured Armenian concubines
and house slaves.[4]

Surviving Turkish, German, and U.S. documents establish that
the *Ittihad* expected to strike quickly, to keep the deportations and
massacres secret, and to exterminate the Armenians as a race
before the outside world learned of the atrocities. The *Ittihad* also
persecuted substantial numbers of Greeks, Jews, and other minority groups, in some cases deporting them along with the Armenians. The Turkish government made a careful effort to explain
away leaks that appeared in the press as nothing more than exaggerated accounts of the usual casualties of war.[5]

But the *Ittihad* miscalculated. Their empire was primarily Is-
lamic, and the Armenians were largely Christians. When the
genocide began, a number of Western diplomats and Christian
missionaries in Turkey (including a German, Pastor Johannes Lepsius) made determined efforts to record the massacres and deportations and to mobilize world opinion against Turkish actions.
The U.S. ambassador to Turkey, Henry Morgenthau, and several
U.S. consuls publicly protested the deportations and began to aid
refugees—an unusually courageous gesture by diplomats, who
ordinarily make a point of washing their hands of such matters.[6]
These efforts struck a responsive chord in the countries of the
Western Alliance and, to a lesser degree, inside Germany as well.
Publicity against the atrocities became particularly strong in
countries where the news media remained hungry for wartime
atrocity stories involving Germans and their clients and were
willing to give full play to deeply rooted Christian prejudices
against Muslims.[7]

Tragically, Armenia could supply an almost unlimited number
of such accounts. Unlike some war propaganda, most of the stories
were true. In the end, however, the Armenians and their supporters

failed to mobilize enough international support to halt the mass killings and deportations, although they did succeed in placing the crime of genocide clearly on the public agenda for the first time in modern history.

At the height of the pogroms in 1915, the governments of France, Great Britain, and czarist Russia issued a joint declaration denouncing the mass killings of Armenians as "crimes against humanity and civilization" and warning the leaders of the Turkish government that they would be held "personally responsible."[8]

But too often there was little of substance behind the indignant rhetoric. At the height of the genocide, a factional split among the Young Turks opened the possibility that Turkey might put an end to the massacres in exchange for an agreement from the Associated Powers to abandon their claims on Turkey and the Ottoman Empire. Djemal Pasha, a member of the triumvirate that ruled Turkey, had settled into Damascus and exercised local control over much of what is today Syria, Jordan, and Israel. In late 1915, while Turkish efforts to exterminate Armenians were at their height, Djemal sought out an Armenian emissary and convinced him to carry an offer to the governments of the Associated Powers. If czarist Russia, France, and Britain would back him, Djemal promised, he would undertake a coup d'état against his Young Turk rivals, end the massacres, and take Turkey out of the war. Djemal himself would then emerge as sultan.

The price for the plan was that the European powers would abandon imperial claims to what is today Iraq and Syria and provide reconstruction assistance to Djemal's government after the war. Djemal, for his part, was willing to concede control of Constantinople and the Dardanelles to Russia.

"Djemal appears to have acted on the mistaken assumption that saving the Armenians—as distinct from merely exploiting their plight for propaganda purposes—was an important Allied objective," writes David Fromkin, a historian specializing in Ottoman affairs. The Russians favored Djemal's plan and for a time assured him that the other Associated Powers would cooperate. But in early 1916, France rejected Djemal's offer and claimed southern Turkey, Syria, and parts of Iraq. Great Britain followed suit, claiming Iraq on behalf of a local "Iraqi" government created by London. "In their passion for booty," Fromkin writes, "the Allied governments lost sight of the condition upon which future gains were predicated: winning the war. . . . Djemal's offer afforded the Allies their one great opportunity to subvert the Ottoman Empire from within"—and to save innocent lives—"and they let it go."9 Nor did the Allies exploit Djemal's attempted betrayal of his colleagues for propaganda or intelligence purposes. As far as can be determined, the other Young Turks never learned of Djemal's secret correspondence with the enemy, and he remained part of the ruling triumvirate for the remainder of the war.

The pro-Armenian publicity may not have changed the West's basic policy toward Turkey, but it did have a significant impact on public opinion in the Associated Powers. By the time the Paris Peace Conference began, there was widespread sentiment among the victorious nations that justice required some form of trial and punishment for those who had perpetrated atrocities in Turkey.

The *Ittihad* dictatorship crumbled as the war drew to a close, and a new, Western-backed Turkish government signed an armistice with the Associated Powers in late October 1918. Two days later, most of the senior *Ittihad* leaders fled their country for Germany, which granted them asylum. They left behind many who had collaborated in the genocide, however, including state and local administrators, party activists, Turkish businessmen and farmers who had seized Armenian property, policemen, and a variety of specialists in mass violence. The new Turkish government arrested several hundred former party leaders who were suspected of direct roles in the mass deportations and killings, and began to prepare cases against them for murder, treason, theft, and similar offenses under Turkish law.

The new Turkish authorities carried out a series of such trials during 1919 and 1920, placing on the public record an important collection of confessions by former *Ittihad* leaders, secret state and party papers concerning the tactics of deportation and mass murder, and an evidentiary outline against several hundred *Ittihad* leaders who had been instrumental in the crime. Much of this evidence was published in the official Turkish parliamentary gazette, *Takyimi Vekayi*.10

The trials were strongly opposed by a rising Turkish nationalist movement, however, which regarded the prosecutions as a symbol of foreign efforts to dismember Turkey. Led by military strongman Mustapha Kemal (later known as Ataturk), the new movement welcomed *Ittihadists* to its ranks and placed some party veterans in leading posts. Kemal's movement enjoyed great influence in the postwar Turkish military, interior ministry, and particularly the police. Kemalist sympathizers systematically delayed and obstructed Turkey's criminal prosecutions, destroyed evidence, organized escapes, and sparked large demonstrations and public protests against the trials.[11]

Importantly, Britain, France, and the United States were at that time vying with one another to divide up the vast oil and mineral wealth of Turkey's Ottoman Empire. Kemal skillfully played the three powers against each other and insisted on amnesty for the *Ittihadists* as part of the price for his support in the division of the defunct empire.[12]

Though often overlooked today, the Ottoman holdings were of extraordinary value, perhaps the richest imperial treasure since the European seizure of the New World four centuries earlier. The empire had been eroding for decades, but by the time of the Turkish defeat in World War I, it still included most of what is today Turkey, Iraq, Saudi Arabia, Syria, Lebanon, Israel, Jordan, and the oil sheikdoms of the Persian Gulf. The European governments sensed that the time had come to seize this rich prize.

The British had been the dominant foreign power in the Middle East prior to World War I. Their Anglo-Persian Oil Company (later known as British Petroleum, or BP) and the Turkish Petroleum Company effectively controlled most of the oil reserves in the region. But the French acquired an important mandate in the area during the war, and by 1919 they were seeking substantial concessions from the British. Both countries preferred to keep the U.S.-backed Standard Oil Company of New Jersey (today known as Exxon) out of the area.[13] The U.S. government meanwhile opposed many aspects of the European colonial rule in the Middle East, preferring instead what it termed "open-door" policies—those that facilitated U.S. penetration of new markets and acquisition of new sources of supply.

Senior officials of all three Western powers became preoccupied with oil politics in the Middle East. It even led to an awkward new term, "oleaginous diplomacy," that was used for years to refer to government initiatives on behalf of oil companies. "Oil," said French Premier Georges Clemenceau, "is as necessary as blood."[14]

For a short time after the war, the three allies pressed the new

Turkish government on two fronts: First, they supported tough punishment for *Ittihadist* criminals, payment of damages to Armenians and Greeks for the lives and property lost during the massacres, establishment of an independent Armenian republic in northeastern Turkey, and transfer to Greece of the port city of Smyrna. Second, they demanded that the Turks surrender all claims to the resources of the former Ottoman territories outside of Turkey proper, particularly the Mosul oilfields in what is today northern Iraq. Although many Turks saw these terms as humiliatingly onerous, the first postwar Turkish government agreed to them in the Treaty of Sèvres, signed in August 1920. That agreement was hailed at the time as the formal conclusion of World War I.[15]

But the Associated Powers could not agree among themselves on the terms of the division of the Mosul oilfields, and new fighting broke out between the Armenian nationalists, who sought to establish the republic they believed they had been guaranteed at Sèvres, and the Turkish Kemalists, who still regarded Armenia as a part of Turkey. Kemal's embrace of the *Ittihadists* contributed to an escalating cycle of revenge killings and renewed massacres in Turkey.

By the end of 1920, the Kemalists were clearly in the ascendance, having established a rival government at Ankara, in the center of the country. The increasingly shaky Turkish government at Istanbul, under intense Kemalist pressure to abrogate the Treaty of Sèvres, abruptly shut down the criminal trials of *Ittihadists*. The Western allies then stepped up their jockeying for influence in the Kemalist camp.

The U.S. High Commissioner to Turkey was Admiral Mark L. Bristol, a man with a reputation as a bigot and a determined advocate of U.S. alliance with Mustafa Kemal. "The Armenians," Bristol wrote, "are a race like the Jews—they have little or no national spirit and poor moral character."[16] It was better for the United States, he contended, to jettison support for the Armenian republic as soon as possible, stabilize U.S. relations with the emerging Turkish government, and to enlist Kemal's support in gaining access to the oilfields of the former Ottoman Empire. Bristol's argument found a receptive audience in the new Harding administration in Washington, whose affinity for oil interests eventually blossomed into the famous Teapot Dome bribery scandal.[17]

As High Commissioner to Turkey, Bristol had considerably more power than might be enjoyed by any conventional ambassador. As the civil war unfolded inside Turkey, Bristol barred newspaper reporters from access to areas where renewed massacres of Armenians were taking place, purportedly to avoid inciting further atrocities against civilians.

His correspondent at the State Department in Washington was Allen Dulles. After the Paris conference, Dulles had served briefly as chief of staff to Bristol, then moved on to Washington to become chief of the State Department's Near East desk just as "oleaginous diplomacy" was reaching its heyday.

Dulles supported Bristol's initiatives. "Confidentially the State Department is in a bind. Our task would be simple if the reports of the atrocities could be declared untrue or even exaggerated but the evidence, alas, is irrefutable," Dulles wrote in reply to Bristol's requests for State Department intervention with U.S. publishers to shift the tone of news reports still dribbling out of Turkey and Armenia. "[T]he Secretary of State wants to avoid giving the impression that while the United States is willing to intervene actively to protect its commercial interests, it is not willing to move on behalf of the Christian minorities." Dulles went on to complain about the agitation in the U.S. on behalf of Armenians, Greeks, and Palestinian Jews. "I've been kept busy trying to ward off congressional resolutions of sympathy for these groups."[18]

The change in the U.S. government's response to the Armenian massacres presents an acute example of the conflicts that often shape U.S. foreign policy. From 1914 to 1919, the U.S. government and public opinion sharply condemned the Turkish massacres. Ambassador Henry Morgenthau repeatedly intervened with the Turkish government to protest the killings, raised funds for refugee relief, and mobilized opposition to the genocide. A close review of the declassified State Department archives of the period shows that much of the government's internal reporting on Turkey was strongly sympathetic to the Armenians throughout the war and the first months after the war.[19]

The Western press, too, was overwhelmingly favorable to the Armenians and hostile to the Turkish government. One recent study by Marjorie Housepian Dobkin found that between April and December of 1915, the *New York Times* published more than 100 articles concerning the massacres when the killings were at their height. All of the *Times* coverage was sympathetic to the Armenians, and most of the news stories appeared on the front page or the first three pages of the newspaper. A roughly similar pattern can be found in publications such as the *New York Herald Tribune*, *Boston Herald*, and *Atlantic Monthly* and in the journals of various Christian missionary societies.[20] The volume of news coverage rose and fell with events over the next five years, but on the whole it remained strongly sympathetic to the Armenians.[21]

Yet a remarkable shift in U.S. media content and government behavior took place as the new Harding administration established itself in 1921. "Those who underestimate the power of commerce in the history of the Middle East cannot have studied the postwar situation in Turkey between 1918 and 1923," Dobkin writes. "There were, of course, other political factors that proved disastrous for the Armenians . . . but the systematic effort (chiefly by the Harding administration) to turn U.S. public opinion towards Turkey was purely and simply motivated by the desire to beat the [rival Associated] Powers to what were thought of as the vast, untapped resources of that country, and chiefly the oil."[22]

"It was not possible to bring about the desired change in public opinion without denigrating what the Armenians had suffered," she continues. Retired U.S. Admiral William Colby Chester joined Admiral Mark Bristol as a leading public spokesman for reconciliation with Turkey. Chester was not a disinterested party. The Turkish government had granted him an oil concession in Iraq that was potentially worth hundreds of millions of dollars. Writing in the influential journal *Current History*, Chester contended that the Armenians had been deported not to deserts, but to "the most delightful and fertile parts of Syria . . . at great expense of money and effort"—a claim that went well beyond even what the Kemal government was willing to argue.[23] Dobkin reports that missionary leaders such as Cleveland Dodge and George Plimpton, who had once been instrumental in documenting the genocide, began to lend their names to publicity insisting that the reported Turkish excesses had been "greatly exaggerated."[24]

By mid-1923, the complex and interlocking challenges created by the demands for justice in the wake of the Armenian Genocide, on the one hand, and U.S. political and commercial interests in Turkey, on the other, had been settled in favor of a de facto U.S. alliance with the new Kemalist government. The day-to-day details of the U.S. diplomatic shift in favor of Kemal were handled by Ambassador Joseph Grew (who will reappear later in this narrative as acting secretary of state during a pivotal moment in World War II) and the chief of the Near East desk at State, Allen Dulles. The U.S., which had been the principal international supporter of the nascent Armenian Republic, withdrew its promises of aid and protection. Mustafa Kemal soon succeeded through force of arms in suppressing Armenia and in establishing a new Turkish government at Ankara. In July 1923, the Turks and the European allies signed a new agreement, replacing the aborted Treaty of Sèvres with the Treaty of Lausanne.[25] Western governments agreed to new Turkish borders, officially recognized Kemal's government, abandoned any claim on behalf of an Armenian republic, and specifically agreed to an amnesty for all *Ittihadists* who had been convicted in the earlier trials.[26]

As things turned out, many of the top *Ittihadists* who fled Turkey in 1918 were assassinated by Armenian commandos. Talaat, the minister of internal affairs and grand vizier of the *Ittihad* state, was shot in Berlin on March 15, 1921. Behaeddin Sakir (Chakir), a senior member of the "Commission of Supply," which had coordinated much of the extermination campaign, and Djemal Azmy, military governor during the height of the killings in Trebizond, were killed in Berlin on April 17, 1922. Enver, the former minister of war, is said to have been killed by the Soviet army in Bukhara in 1922, though many of the details of his death remain uncertain. Djemal, who with Talaat and Enver had constituted the ruling triumvirate of the *Ittihad* state, was gunned down in July 1922 in Tiflis. He was on his way to a trade conference in Berlin, where he was to buy weapons for the Afghan army.[27]

Armenians lost a great deal under the terms of the Lausanne treaty while Western commercial interests prospered. The new Turkish leader Kemal agreed to relinquish all claims on the territories of the old Ottoman Empire outside Turkish borders, thus formally opening the door to the Anglo-American control of Middle East oil that was to continue with minimal change for the next fifty years. This was not a simple quid pro quo, of course. The agreement also involved other important elements, notably a settlement of most reparation claims against Turkey and an agreement between Greece and Turkey to repatriate thousands of ethnic Greeks and Turks to their respective countries of origin. There were to be several more years of squabbles before the U.S.-European disputes over the Mosul oilfields were finally settled.

The point was nonetheless clear. Western governments had discarded wartime promises of action against the *Ittihadists* who had murdered about a million people in order to help their political maneuvering over oil concessions in the Middle East. The dominant faction in Turkish society never accepted Armenian claims as legitimate, despite the strong evidence of genocide established by Turkey's own courts. In fact, the Turkish government even today continues to refuse to acknowledge *Ittihadist* responsibility for the Armenian massacres, and has instead in recent years financed a large and sophisticated publicity campaign aimed at rewriting the history of the war years.[28]

As the Western powers sparred over Middle East oil, a series of events was unfolding in Germany that would test the Associated Powers' commitment to punish war crimes. The Berlin government was hostile to the war crimes clauses that had been approved by President Wilson and the rest of the Big Four at the Paris Conference. Inside Germany, only the radical left wing favored trials of the leaders of the old regime. The German military elite, who were the main targets of the war crimes and war guilt clauses of the peace treaty, strongly opposed any cooperation with the Associated Powers in this matter. Because the newly established republican government in Germany was heavily dependent upon even lukewarm support from the military to avoid a coup, it too resisted cooperation, though it continued to seek an armistice. Most German politicians and the press referred to the war crimes provisions of the Versailles Treaty as the *Schamparagraphen*—the shame paragraphs[29]—and contended that these provisions would open the way to harsh reparations.

"In the manner of waging war," German Foreign Minister Ulrich von Brockdorff-Rantzau told the delegates at Versailles, "Germany was not the only one who erred." The Associated Powers' blockade of German ports had continued after the armistice, prolonging the extreme food shortages in some German cities and killing hundreds of thousands of noncombatants, Brockdorff contended.

Although he overestimated the number of dead and the effectiveness of the blockade, the suffering was real enough. The blockade of food had been carried out "coolly and deliberately after our opponents had won a certain and assured victory. Remember that," he told Western leaders, "when you speak of guilt and atonement."[30] Meanwhile, the new German government created its own legal commission to refute each Allied war crimes charge, even enlisting the famous sociologist Max Weber in an effort to find a means of sidestepping responsibility for the war.[31]

This conflict over war crimes nearly led to the collapse of the armistice and a return to open warfare. In mid-June 1919, the Associated Powers gave the German government seven days to sign the treaty drawn up at Paris or face an invasion by Allied troops. The German cabinet refused to acquiesce, and the ruling coalition collapsed. The German defense minister warned that he had met with a group of army officers, many of whom were prepared to overthrow the government and renew the war if the treaty was signed with the *Schamparagraphen* intact. The Catholic Center party managed to tack together a new government on the basis of a French envoy's promise—subsequently retracted—that the war guilt clauses would be cut from the treaty. The Vatican attempted to intervene on Germany's behalf, but without success. Western governments then issued a new ultimatum, stating that unless the treaty was signed as it stood, their troops would march into Germany in less than twenty-four hours. Germany signed only minutes before the deadline.[32]

Over the next several months, the Associated Powers drew up a list of 901 Germans whom they accused of war crimes. In most instances, the offenses were quite specific: The British charged one German submarine captain, Lieutenant Commander Karl Neumann, with the deliberate sinking of the hospital ship *Dover Castle* on May 26, 1917—seemingly a direct violation of the Hague convention. (Neumann's defense was that he had been ordered by his superiors to sink the ship.) They also brought an indictment against the U-boat captain responsible for the destruction of the hospital ship *Llondovery Castle* in June 1918, in which 234 soldiers and nurses were killed. The German captain was said to have acted in violation of direct orders not to attack the ship and was further accused of shelling the survivors' lifeboats in order to conceal what he had done. Other cases involved gross mistreatment of prisoners and similar offenses.[33]

But despite the provisions of the recently signed treaty, the German government refused to turn the suspects or evidence over to military courts of the victorious powers. After much negotiation, the Allies agreed to let Germany try the accused criminals in its own courts, in a special proceeding at Leipzig.[34]

The Leipzig trials were a farce. Roughly half of the defendants simply "escaped," and the court acquitted the U-boat captain, Neumann. The handful who were convicted of serious crimes, including the mass murder of unarmed prisoners, received prison sentences of less than ten months. In the *Llondovery Castle* case, the German court convicted two junior officers of offenses under Germany's own military code and handed down four-year sentences. But both prisoners escaped from jail with the connivance of their guards less than six months later, made their way to asylum in Switzerland, and were hailed as heroes by the German press.[35]

"Thus ended the Leipzig trials," records a United Nations report on the event. "The net result of the trials was that out of a total of 901 cases of revolting crimes brought before the Leipzig court, 888 were acquitted or summarily dismissed, and only 13 ended in a conviction; furthermore, although the sentences were so inadequate, those who had been convicted were not even made to serve their sentence. Several escaped, and the prison wardens who had engineered their escape were publicly congratulated."[36]

Meanwhile, Lansing's (and Wilson's) position prevailed with respect to a trial for the former German monarch, Kaiser Wilhelm II. The Associated Powers had agreed at Paris to a compromise provision in the Versailles Treaty calling for an arraignment of the kaiser for "a supreme offense against international morality and the sanctity of treaties"—that is, for instigating the war. This was, in truth, perhaps the weakest of the plausible charges against Wilhelm; the claim that he alone should bear responsibility for beginning the war was obviously suspect even in 1919. Be that as it may, the charges against the kaiser outlined in the treaty were offenses against moral as distinct from legal sensibilities, and there were no mechanisms for punishing him even if he was convicted. In any event, Wilhelm fled to Holland and gained asylum with the tacit cooperation of the British Foreign Office. The other Associated Powers buried their demands for a trial of the kaiser within months after having announced them.[37]

Taken as a whole, world experience with atrocities showed that even though these crimes were highly politicized during the war, exploited for their propaganda value, and often condemned (or justified, depending upon a government's relationship to the atrocity) largely for political effect, governmental attitudes changed rapidly after the war. The definitions of the offenses, the selection of courts used for trying suspects, and the punishments meted out to perpetrators each became charged political issues capable of igniting new wars.

This was at least in part because of the mass nature of many of the atrocities themselves. The genocide of Armenians involved thousands of perpetrators and tens of thousands of beneficiaries of looted Armenian property. Thus, even Turkey's own postwar government found it difficult to try individual ringleaders without putting the country itself on trial. Each detail of legal interpretation, even in cases of seemingly extreme and obvious atrocities, became for many Turks a matter upon which national honor or even survival seemed to depend.

Importantly, the pressures against justice came not only from the defendants but also from a coalition of both victorious and defeated powers. Secretary of State Lansing's actions at Paris and the U.S.-British-French squabble over the Mosul oilfields indicate that, only months after the war had drawn to a close, powerful factions among the victors were willing to sacrifice the most elementary standards of justice in the name of national security or economic expediency.

The victors' inability or unwillingness to investigate offenses by their own forces also undermined efforts to make sanctions against atrocities work. "The French suggestion to establish an international criminal court associated with the League of Nations was scarcely given a hearing," legal historian James Willis points out. "The German offer to submit cases of accused war criminals to preliminary judgment of an international court of neutral jurists, if the [Associated Powers] would do the same, was not considered at all. . . . If there had been a thorough debate of the problem of war crimes committed by the Allies as well as the crimes of the Germans, it is possible that the peace conference could have made provisions for punishment of war crimes a permanent part of international relations."[38] As it was, serious consideration of international sanctions against atrocities was largely forgotten until the height of the Nazi Holocaust, when the problem reappeared with new and frightening immediacy.

There was another important obstacle after World War I to establishing international sanctions against atrocities: money. All of the powers agreed in principle that the perpetrators of war crimes should pay damages or reparations to those they had wronged. But in a war that had resulted in millions of deaths and crippling injuries, such damages would total tens of billions of dollars, particularly if the war itself was judged to be a criminal act. Soon it became clear to victors and vanquished alike that the definition of what would be classed as a war crime had sweeping implications for European trade and commerce in the decade ahead.

4

Bankers, Lawyers,
and Linkage Groups

GERMANY ALONE had instigated World War I, at least as far as the British, the French, and several of the smaller Associated Powers saw things in 1919. The war had been desperately destructive, and many believed that Germany should offer compensation for all damage left by the war, regardless of who had been the perpetrator. Others limited their claims to the costs of military pensions and medical treatment for wounded soldiers—though even this came to tens of billions of dollars worth of the currencies of the day.

The British delegation to the Paris Conference brought a demand for the equivalent of about $90 billion in reparation payments plus a share of German colonies abroad and German-owned industrial properties in Eastern Europe. The French demanded $200 billion.[1] The U.S. delegation's official point of view was that $25-$30 billion would be appropriate. Its confidential position, however, was that $25 billion was excessive, but a public claim for that amount was necessary to pacify political constituencies in both Europe and the United States. In any case, Germany must be permitted to retain "a requisite working capital," as U.S. negotiator Norman Davis put it, to rebuild a private-enterprise economy in the wake of the war.[2]

John Foster Dulles arrived at the Paris Peace Conference as a junior legal counsel to the U.S. delegates responsible for negotiating German reparations. By the time he left a few months later, he had emerged as an important negotiator in his own right, the drafter of much of the proposed treaty language concerning war reparations, and the principal U.S. legal expert in this lucrative new field.

The U.S. strategy on reparations reflected three interlocking concerns. The most frequently mentioned of these was to help rebuild the war-shattered lives of ordinary Europeans, to offer refugee relief, and to satisfy similar humanitarian concerns. German reparations could ameliorate suffering in other countries, the U.S. contended, but they must not be permitted to become so high as to delay German economic recovery, which was said to provide a longer-term solution to many of the same problems.

In confidential discussions, Dulles and the U.S. delegation placed greater stress on a second concern: the possibility of revolution or civil war in Europe. Secretary of State Lansing's comments quoted earlier concerning the "terrible . . . possibility of a proletarian despotism over Central Europe" directly argued that reparations must be kept low in order to avoid revolution.[3] The Berlin and Budapest rebellions—both eventually suppressed with considerable bloodshed—seemed to provide vivid evidence to ruling circles that there was substance to Lansing's fears.

Third, and perhaps most fundamentally, Dulles and the U.S. delegation were anxious to restart the engine of commerce that had been disrupted by the war. Without a German economic recovery, Norman Davis wrote, "it is impossible for the rest of Europe to get to work and be prosperous. It is most essential for the future stability of Europe that [business] confidence and credit be restored at the earliest possible moment, and these can never be restored as long as any large nation in Europe is struggling under a financial burden which the investors of the world think she cannot carry."[4] Davis was not speaking simply of stability in some abstract sense but, rather, of a particular type of order, one seen as sustainable by "the investors of the world." The issue was how to bring

Central and Eastern Europe from nineteenth-century monarchism to modern capitalism without bringing about a revolution like the one in Russia.

John Foster Dulles seemed driven to create and sustain this new structure. At Paris, he helped hammer out a compromise on reparations that, while not all that he had hoped for, was nonetheless less damaging to his vision for a prosperous Europe than the French and British alternatives. Dulles favored restricting the definition of war crimes to the greatest degree possible, then limiting the defeated powers' obligation to pay reparations to those few cases that had been successfully prosecuted.[5] While his efforts may have seemed at the time to be largely based on economics, and even to have a humanitarian tilt in their seeming compassion for defeated powers, his approach carried with it a de facto legalization of those wartime atrocities that fell outside the terms of his definitions.

The complex formula for German reparations that finally emerged from the Paris negotiations added up to the equivalent of roughly $25–$30 billion to be paid over thirty years.[6] Economists such as John Maynard Keynes established their early reputations in large part by attacking this reparations plan, contending that it would debilitate the German economy and thus damage France and Britain as well. Better for all, Keynes contended, to encourage a rapid and stable recovery of private enterprise in general, and to put the wartime animosities aside.

Although the German government bitterly resented the reparations, it agreed to pay them. This it did in part by what amounted to little more than printing new currency—and the infamous German inflation crisis of the early 1920s was the result. The Germans then cut off further payments as their economy staggered toward complete collapse. That in turn prompted the French and the Belgians to occupy the Ruhr Valley, the heart of the German coal and steel industries, in an attempt to enforce Germany's treaty obligations. By 1923, the prospect of renewed war or rebellion in Central Europe was again on the horizon.

John Foster Dulles had meanwhile returned to the law firm of Sullivan & Cromwell, where he became a full partner specializing in the legal aspects of German reparations and in international finance generally. In 1923–24, banker J. P. Morgan recommended Dulles to be special counsel to the Dawes Committee, which U.S.

and British banks had helped establish in the hopes of finding a way out of the reparations morass. Dulles helped engineer a scheme under which U.S. and foreign banks made new loans to the Reichsbank (the German state bank), which used the funds to pay reparations to Britain, France, and other European powers, who in turn paid off their own war loans from the U.S.[7] This financial merry-go-round generated millions of dollars in interest payments for international lenders and kept billions of dollars worth of loans current just a bit longer. How long the borrowed money could continue to revolve remained an open question, but as long as it worked, John Foster Dulles was hailed as a master of international finance.

Meanwhile Dulles's law firm and his major clients pioneered a roughly similar system for private U.S. investment in German finance and industry. This new network of trade relations proved to be the most important single push forward in elite U.S.-German relations prior to World War II, though of course some ties between U.S. and German businessmen can be traced back to the nineteenth and even the eighteenth century.

The United States had emerged from World War I with its currency and industry stronger than ever before, at least as long as Britain and other debtors continued to pay their bills. The 1920s boom, driven by imperialism, cheap oil, and the emerging automobile economy in the U.S., created enormous pools of investment funds in the banks of New York and Boston.[8] This led to an international financial situation that was similar, in some respects, to the Middle East oil crisis of the 1970s.

During the 1970s crisis, the central problem from the standpoint of international finance was to recycle the massive pools of funds that had shifted to the Middle East back through the international banking network in order to stave off a string of bankruptcies that would otherwise have resulted from illiquidity in the system.[9] During the 1970s, most of this "recycling" was carried out through the Eurodollar market.

During the second half of the 1920s, the most important international market for recycling the new private U.S. wealth was Germany. This investment was carried out mainly through loans to German industry, direct U.S. investment in German companies, development loans to German cities, and millions of dollars worth of Dawes Plan credits that indirectly financed German war reparations.[10] The scope of U.S.-German capital flows during the 1920s has never been fully documented, but the fraction of it that can be traced totals close to $1.5 billion, not including Dawes Plan credits. In today's currency this sum would be measured in the tens of billions of dollars.[11]

There was considerable direct U.S. investment in German companies as U.S. companies sought to buy into European markets at bargain prices. ITT purchased a half-dozen German telecommunications equipment manufacturers during the late 1920s and early 1930s,[12] while General Motors bought control of the Adam Opel corporation (and with it about 40 percent of the German automotive market) in 1929. Fritz Opel joined GM's board of directors as part of the deal.[13] Ford Motor Company built a vast factory at Cologne, then used it to manufacture cars for all of Central and Eastern Europe.[14] There were also joint ventures, such as IG Farben's pacts with Standard Oil of New Jersey, some of which were subsequently found to be violations of U.S. law.[15] General Electric purchased substantial shares of the German electronics giants AEG and Siemens, and entered joint ventures with both companies.*[16]

Specialized banks, law firms, and trading companies that focused on opening the German market to U.S. capital sprang up on both sides of the Atlantic. Practically without exception, the giant U.S.-German capital flows were administered by a small group of specialists at the very top of the social structure of both countries. A number of institutions and individuals who were prominent in this trade went on to play powerful roles in U.S.-German affairs over the next five decades.[17]

Dillon, Read & Co., private U.S. investment bankers, specialized in loans to Deutsche Bank, Siemens, and Flick interests. Between 1925 and the stock market crash in 1929, these loans amounted to

---

* U.S. corporate investment in Germany during the 1920s and 1930s was concentrated in the hands of fewer than two dozen major companies, reports economic historian Mira Wilkins. According to her data, U.S. industrial leaders in Germany included oil and chemical companies such as du Pont, Standard Oil of New Jersey, and Texaco; food and consumer products companies such as Corn Products Refining Co. (today CPC International) and United Fruit; and mining companies such as American Metal (today AMAX), Anaconda, International Nickel (based in Canada, but American owned) and the large Guggenheim mining interests. The most active category of U.S. industrial investors appears to have been automotive and light industrial manufacturing companies, including Ford, GE, GM, Goodrich, IBM, International Harvester, ITT, National Cash Register (joint venture with Krupp), Singer, and several smaller companies.

more than a quarter of a billion dollars. Friedrich Flick built his fortune during the 1920s using bonds sold by Dillon, Read to finance what today might be called leveraged buyouts of German and Polish coal and steel companies. Most of Dillon, Read's own capital was oil money, including substantial sums from the Rockefeller, Draper, and Dillon families. The bulk of the money lent to Germany, however, was raised via limited partnership bond syndications in U.S. markets. This meant that when Germany defaulted on a series of loans in the early 1930s, Dillon, Read and its major partners had already taken their share of the spoils, while the smaller investors who had bought these bonds lost tens of millions of dollars.[18]

Key Dillon, Read executives during this period included the company's president, James Forrestal (later U.S. secretary of defense), William Draper (later economics chief of the U.S. Military Government during the U.S. occupation of Germany and Japan), Paul Nitze (prominent U.S. diplomat and national security advisor), Ferdinand Eberstadt (later vice chair of the War Production Board and a central figure in the creation of the CIA), and C. Douglas Dillon (U.S. diplomat and later secretary of the treasury).[19]

Another Wall Street firm that specialized in U.S.-German trade was Brown Brothers, Harriman, a private investment bank dominated by W. Averell Harriman, whose family fortune rivaled that of the Rockefellers. Harriman went on to become one of the most influential figures in U.S. foreign affairs over the next fifty years. His key political allies who also served as senior executives of the bank included Robert Lovett (later U.S. secretary of defense) and Prescott Bush (prominent legislator and father of the U.S. president).[20]

And, of course, Sullivan & Cromwell acted as agent for U.S. companies investing in Europe. The law firm represented U.S. corporate interests involved in international cartels—the Allied Chemical Company (a participant in an illegal chemical cartel organized by IG Farben) and International Nickel Company (leader of a nickel cartel). It simultaneously represented German clients, such as the international shipping combine HAPAG and the IG Farben division General Aniline & Film Corporation (today known as GAF).[21]

Most of the records concerning John Foster Dulles's legal work during the 1920s have been destroyed or remain confidential. A few interesting fragments have survived, however, and have been assembled by biographer Ronald Pruessen, who used Dulles's appointments book to reconstruct a list of his personal clients. The list includes virtually all of the important U.S. banks involved in international trade: J. P. Morgan & Co.; Kuhn, Loeb & Co.; Lee, Higginson & Co.; Brown Brothers, Harriman and the closely related W. A. Harriman & Co.; Dillon, Read & Co.; Guaranty Trust Company of New York; First National Corporation of Boston; and others of similar stature.[22]

In most instances, his legal work for investors consisted of complex three- and four-sided financial projects whose success depended on Dulles's skills as a negotiator and his contacts inside U.S. and foreign governments. Typically, private banks and brokerage houses sought out leading German or other foreign companies, banks, and local governments with offers to loan U.S. dollars for the construction of new factories, municipal electrification, or similar projects. If the foreign party was interested, it would issue millions of dollars worth of bonds and sell them to Dulles's clients for somewhat less than the market price—at a wholesale rate, so to speak. The clients would then turn around and sell the bonds to other U.S. banks and individual investors at "retail" rates, usually paying Dulles and Sullivan & Cromwell two or three percentage points of the overall value of the bond offering for their services.

The foreign borrowers included not only dozens of companies but also governments as varied as Argentina, Czechoslovakia, and Denmark. However, Dulles clearly emphasized projects for Germany, for the military junta in Poland, and for Mussolini's fascist state in Italy. U.S. State Department documents assembled by Pruessen provide some indication of the nature and scope of the business in which Dulles played a personal role as a fixer, advisor, or middleman:

- The 1924 German External Loan of $100 million (Dawes Plan loan); managed in the U.S. by J. P. Morgan & Co., National City Co., Lee, Higginson & Co., and Kuhn, Loeb & Co.
- Bond sales underwritten by Harris Forbes & Co. for the city of Munich ($8.7 million), Electrowerke AG ($5.5 million), and Deutsche Raiffeisenbank AG ($10 million)
- A sale of $10 million worth of bonds for the First Mortgage Bank of Saxony managed by Brown Brothers, Harriman & Co.

- A 1925 loan by Lehman Brothers of $3 million to Leonhard Tietz Aktiengesellschaft
- A $5 million bond offering in 1926 for the city of Nuremberg underwritten by the Equitable Trust Co., Lee, Higginson, and one other partner
- Bonds sold by Brown Brothers, Harriman on behalf of the German Union of Mortgage Banks ($10 million), the Manfeld coal and iron syndicate ($3 million), the Hamburg railway ($8 million), the City of Berlin ($15 million), and the City of Hannover ($3.5 million)
- A 1927, $20 million bond sale for the North German Lloyd Steamship Company by Kuhn, Loeb & Co., Guaranty Trust Co., and Lee, Higginson
- A 1927 loan of at least $10 million to the Terni Societa per l'Industria e l'Electtricita of Italy by W. A. Harriman and Co., and a large purchase by W. A. Harriman of General Electric Company of Sicily bonds undertaken the same year
- Goldman, Sachs purchase of 400,000 shares of the Creditanstalt bank of Vienna
- A 1927 Bankers Trust Company (and associates) offering of $70 million of government of Poland bonds for industrial expansion

All told, these and more than a dozen similar transactions had a combined value in excess of a billion dollars.[23]

For John Foster Dulles, international banking seemed to be a distinctly noble and humanitarian profession. "It is the highest function of finance to move goods from the place where they constitute a surplus to the place where they will fill a deficit," he told a sympathetic audience at the Foreign Policy Association as the economic boom of the 1920s showed the first signs of unraveling. "[A]nd in performing this service during the past nine years our bankers have given an extraordinary demonstration of the beneficent use of financial power," principally by opening European markets to U.S. goods through the extension of loans to European customers. International banking, he said, "is a simple story . . . the story of how Europe has been saved from starving and we from choking."[24]

Banker and latter-day diplomat Paul Nitze describes a 1929 incident in his autobiography that captures much of the financial community's sense of its role. Nitze was in those years a protégé of Dillon, Read chairman Clarence Dillon. As Nitze tells the story, the elder executive explained to him that over the previous fifty years "the New York banking community had wielded more influence than politicians in Washington." Throughout history, Dillon continued, "societies have been dominated by one element of society or another—by priests, by royalty, by the military, by politicians either from the common folk or from the aristocracy, and from time to time by wealthy financiers. This last element had found its way to the top of the hierarchy for a while in ancient Greece, in Rome in the days of Lucullus, in the city-states of Italy during the days of the Medici, for a while in France, and . . . in the United States." At this time, Dillon believed that a major economic depression was on the way and that the ensuing political crisis would signal the "end of an era."[25]

The U.S. financial elite had great influence on U.S. foreign affairs, often manifested most directly in the Foreign Service, the career staff of the Department of State. As Nitze's own career was to demonstrate, there was a revolving door between international service for major banks and law firms and positions in the U.S. State Department. There were many family ties, too, as when Allen Dulles remained in the Foreign Service and his brother returned to Sullivan & Cromwell.

The top Foreign Service officers and investment bankers had often trained at the same prep schools and Ivy League universities; they belonged to the same social clubs and often shared similar preconceptions on issues ranging from social class and geopolitics to men's fashions. "Style, grace, poise, and above all, birth were the key to success" in the Foreign Service, writes historian Martin Weil. "The standards were similar to those of a fashionable Washington club: 'Is he our kind of person?' No one who clearly was not would pass.

"If a black slipped through the net, he was sent to Liberia until he resigned. Women were sent to the jungles of South America. Jews could not be handled as crassly, but they were made to feel unwelcome and shut out of the better assignments. Those who had the proper background, however, had a great time."[26] Not everyone in the Foreign Service actually trained at Groton and Harvard, of course, noted Supreme Court Justice Felix Frankfurter in his diary. But like some people "who have not had the advantages of the so-called well-born, but wish they had them, [they become] more 'Grotty' than the men who actually went to Groton in the State Department."[27]

Robert Murphy, Loy Henderson, Joseph Grew, Hugh Gibson, George Kennan, James Clement Dunn, Elbridge Durbrow, Ray Atherton, Arthur Bliss Lane, and a handful of others became the backbone of the Foreign Service, particularly in all aspects of U.S.-European and (later) U.S.-Soviet relations. These self-perceived "realists" believed that the USSR was the most dangerous long-term rival to the U.S. and that Germany and Central Europe should be integrated into some form of *cordon sanitaire* against the Bolsheviks. Their analysis was rooted in what Daniel Yergin has dubbed the "Riga Axioms," a collection of strongly anti-Soviet political postulates that crystallized among U.S. Foreign Service personnel during the 1920s at consulates in Riga (Latvia), Berlin, and Warsaw.[28] The Riga group's analysis was to have an enduring impact in escalating hostilities between the U.S. and USSR, as Yergin, Frederic Propas,[29] Martin Weil,[30] and others have documented.

The Riga faction drew much of its most important support from the foreign policy elite outside the government. John Foster Dulles was among Riga's most articulate spokesmen, and men like James Forrestal and Paul Nitze of Dillon, Read, Charles Edward Wilson and Philip Reed of General Electric, and much of the leadership of the integrated Du Pont–General Motors–U.S. Rubber empire of that era, among others, were early supporters of the Riga postulates.[31]

More to the point here, however, is the Riga group's impact on U.S.-German relations, particularly after Hitler came to power. Perhaps the most influential proponent of the Riga Axioms inside the government during the Roosevelt years was FDR's first ambassador to Moscow, William Bullitt. He had arrived in the USSR full of enthusiasm for normalized U.S.-Soviet relations, but he left soon after, convinced "that only Nazi Germany could stay the advance of Soviet Bolshevism into Europe."[32] As will be seen in a later chapter, many of the career State Department officials who were to specialize in U.S.-German relations, war crimes policy, and so-called Jewish issues such as rescue of refugees during World War II shared Bullitt's cynical enthusiasm for Hitler's talents.

Meanwhile there were roughly parallel developments among the German bankers and law firms that specialized in international trade and commerce. For example, at the Berlin law firm of Albert & Westrick, Heinrich Albert was one of the most important German boosters of U.S. loans to Germany during the 1920s. He advanced to director of Ford Motor's German subsidiary and other U.S. companies in Germany during the Hitler period, and after 1945 he became a custodian of U.S. and British corporate properties in Berlin. Albert had a close relationship with John Foster Dulles, working with him in a variety of projects for at least thirty years. In the immediate postwar period, Albert also played a pivotal role in the establishment of West Germany's postwar ruling party, the Christian Democratic Union. Albert's law partner Gerhardt Westrick served as chairman or board member of a half-dozen German subsidiaries of ITT and Kodak, in addition to representing Texaco interests in Central Europe and German industrial companies in the U.S.[33] Gerhardt Westrick's brother Ludger became a prominent banker and a director of several of the most powerful nonferrous metals companies in the world.[34]

Another example, Karl Lindemann, was director of the Dresdner Bank and the HAPAG shipping combine and simultaneously chairman of HAPAG's ostensible competitor, the North German Lloyd steamship company (Norddeutscher Lloyd) of Hamburg. Lindemann also directed German-American Petroleum AG, a wholly owned subsidiary of Standard Oil of New Jersey and the principal source of the fuel for Lindemann's shipping companies. During the 1930s, Lindemann emerged as a leading supporter of the Nazi SS[35] in German industrial circles.

The industrial and financial sectors of the German economy during the 1920s and 1930s were tightly interlocked and controlled by a handful of powerful interests. Antimonopoly and antitrust laws such as those used in the United States to encourage competition were unknown. German economic tradition had long encouraged industrial cartels, trusts, and similar organizations designed to dictate prices, exclude competitors from established markets, and coordinate bids for political power.[36] This resulted in a closely interwoven network of fewer than 300 men who made up the senior managers and the boards of directors of virtually every large-scale enterprise in the country. Within this group, power was further concentrated in the very largest banks, insurance companies, and manufacturing concerns.[37]

The general contours of this elite can be illustrated through the interlocking directorships and financial ties among Germany's two principal banks and their associated industrial concerns, which served as a central meeting ground and policy-coordination point for much of German industry. Deutsche Bank and Dresdner Bank exercised an "influence and control over [German] industry to a degree unparallelled in modern American banking," as a later U.S. government study put it.[38] They exerted power through interlocking directorships, control of voting rights to large blocks of company stock, authority over the financing and credits necessary for day-to-day business, and the banks' service as a go-between among the German state and private enterprises.

The U.S. government calculated shortly after World War II that the Deutsche Bank's board of directors and senior management sat on the boards of some 525 other major German companies, and that this pattern had been true since the 1920s.[39] Deutsche Bank had no fewer than three joint directors with the Allianz Insurance group (the largest insurance company in the world)[40]; six joint directors with Daimler Benz; four with Daimler's ostensible competitor, BMW; five with the Mannesmann steel combine; four with the electrical giant AEG; three with coal and steel specialists Hoesch AG; six with one of Germany's largest armament manufacturers, DEMAG[41]; and no fewer than eight with the Siemens group of companies, which has dominated German electrical engineering and communications equipment markets for generations.[42] Indeed, Deutsche Bank, Mannesmann, and Siemens can fairly be said to have grown up as a single economic unit.

Germany's second largest bank, the Dresdner Bank, was also allied with key businesses during the 1920s and 1930s, including the Krupp empire and steel magnate Friedrich Flick's. In later years, Dresdner bankrolled the SS concentration camp system and the government-sponsored Hermann Göring Werke, which served as a vast holding company for dozens of mining, steel, and armaments companies seized by the Nazis. The Krupps had used the Dresdner as a virtual in-house bank since the end of the nineteenth century, in much the same manner that the Siemens interests had dominated Deutsche Bank.[43]

These two major German financial institutions had long competed for business and political influence. At the same time, they often cooperated in dealing with business trusts that were simply too big to fit under any one bank's umbrella, such as the chemical combine IG Farben and Vereinigte Stahlwerke, or United Steelworks.[44]

Obviously, there were other prominent German and American financial leaders in addition to those mentioned here, but this brief list is characteristic. They were, first of all, a relatively small group, even within the closed world of U.S. and German law and banking. They specialized in foreign affairs and have had a substantial influence on U.S.-German relations and on both countries' conduct of foreign affairs, emerging at the core of a foreign policy establishment active in groups such as the Council on Foreign Relations. They built strong relationships over a period of ten, twenty and even thirty years. They often shared similar convictions on issues such as class, business, and the importance of U.S.-German economic ties. In many cases, they shared business partnerships and investments as well.

This does not mean that they had a single point of view concerning Hitler, either before or after the Nazis' climb to power in 1930–33. Contrary to the popular myths concerning the Dulles brothers, for example, Allen Dulles was a relatively early advocate of U.S. backing for the British in their showdown with Germany, while John Foster Dulles remained considerably more tolerant of Nazism. Others were prominent Jews who were destined to be dispossessed by the Nazis. Banker Eric Warburg was forced to sell off most of his German properties in the early 1930s, but he returned for the reconstruction after 1945.[45] Some members of the elite did become creatures of Hitler, however, such as Dresdner Bank's Karl Lindemann, who was characterized as a "rabid Nazi" by one of the bank's senior executives, Hans Schippel.[46]

The cement that bound these groups together was trade, not politics—or at least not politics in the narrow sense of the term. U.S. business magazines became regular critics of Hitler's politics during the 1930s, for example. But a review of the internal records of U.S. companies made public during wartime "trading with the enemy" scandals shows that, despite pious comments to the press, a dozen major corporations proved to be enthusiastic partners in trade and technology cartels exploited by the Nazis.[47]

Even Allen Dulles, who was among the more vocal on Wall Street in warning that German military adventures would come to no good, found himself caught up in this contradiction. Captured German records show that the United Fruit Company, where Dulles maintained a long and active directorship, became an international pacesetter in devising ways to expand trade with Germany despite obstacles from the U.S. and U.K. governments.[48] Similarly, while publicly advocating U.S. economic backing for the British on the eve of the war, Dulles was privately representing German corporate clients in their efforts to buy out the American Potash and Chemical Corporation, an important potential source of strategic chemicals and foreign currency.*[49]

Despite their differences, these U.S.-German "reference groups" or "linkage groups," as they became known to sociologists,[50] shared common convictions that were to them far more fundamental: the central importance of maintaining the viability of capitalism as a national and world economic system, and the key role of U.S. and German productive capacity and markets within that effort. Measured against these more basic values, the Nazis and their whole brutal apparatus were seen by much of the elite as transitory, at least during the 1920s and 1930s. From the standpoint of corporate ideology, this elite saw itself as a new generation

---

* Sullivan & Cromwell maintained strong ties to German corporate interests at the outbreak of World War II, notwithstanding Allen Dulles's public comments. As far back as the 1920s, John Foster Dulles and Sullivan & Cromwell had represented Metallgesellschaft AG of Frankfurt, the largest nonferrous metals company in the world. Dulles's task at that time was to reestablish the Frankfurt company's control of the American Metal Company, a U.S. subsidiary of Metallgesellschaft that had been seized as enemy property during the war. He succeeded.

Almost two decades later, in 1938, IG Farben director Hermann Schmitz, who had played a major role in the Metallgesellschaft affair, hired Sullivan & Cromwell to deal with the World War II version of U.S. Alien property regulations. According to U.S. Justice Department and Securities and Exchange Commission (SEC) investigators, IG Farben's photographic film subsidiary GAF was at that time engaged in complex financial maneuvers designed to conceal its relationship to the IG. GAF wished to avoid the Treasury Department's strict regulations on control of foreign funds, and to head off the possibility that it, too, might be seized as enemy property if war broke out.

According to Chester T. Lane, the general counsel of the SEC in the 1930s, "The German government, acting through its representatives here, its financial counselors and attorneys, who, as I remember, were Sullivan & Cromwell, filed a registration statement with us looking towards refunding of many of its securities held in the United States," Lane recalled. "It was obviously designed as a public relations gesture." Lane and the SEC responded with a demand that the Nazi state "give us a complete blueprint of [its] economy, including all its indirect assessments through party dues, its indirect taxes, and its whole financial structure." Frustrated, the Germans eventually abandoned the effort.

of the so-called managerial revolution; they considered themselves to be "forward thinking" and unencumbered by the stuffy formalism of earlier times.

The Nazis' advent to power presented both opportunities and risks for this informal network. Hitler delivered on his promises of large-scale government backing for rearmament, roadbuilding, and industrial-development projects like IG Farben's massive synthetic gasoline refineries. Hitler also guaranteed "stability" of sorts for business in the face of the gathering resistance of German Communists and labor unions. On the other hand, the big banks and cartels (including IG Farben) had been the target of Nazi propaganda and agitation, as Hitler advocated a major role for the National Socialist state in coordinating the German economy. Much of the industrial and financial elite supported Hitler's economic strategy—but only up to a point. They welcomed public-works projects, particularly during the lean years of the Great Depression, but they saw Hitler's more utopian vision of a German "socialism" under Nazi leadership as a challenge to their own interests.

The role of the German business community during the rise of Hitler has been argued at length elsewhere and need not be detailed here.[51] More important to this discussion are the activities of the U.S. and German business elites during the Hitler years and particularly during the Holocaust.

As will be seen, the Nazis often persecuted Jews during the 1930s through economic measures. They relied heavily on German banks and businesses for the success of anti-Semitic, anti-Communist, and antiunion programs crucial to the stabilization of the Hitler state. For the most part, the Nazis were not disappointed. Gestapo terror was always a key aspect of Nazi activities, of course, and police measures took on a terrible importance as the extermination phase of the Holocaust grew near, but the Gestapo could not be everywhere. Particularly during the early years of Hitler's rule, Germany's private sector served as the main instrument of persecution through economic boycotts, dismissal of Jews from the professions, Aryanization of Jewish property, and discrimination against Jews in wages, prices, and access to goods. Later, German industry often led the way in exploitation of concentration camp labor and systematic rape of occupied countries. By the end of the war, virtually all of America's most important German trading partners from the 1920s and 1930s were to have blood under their fingernails.

5

The Profits of Persecution

HITLER BECAME German chancellor on January 30, 1933, and in less than three months his government promulgated decrees restricting Jews from work as doctors, dentists, lawyers, teachers, and civil servants. In October a decree barred non-Aryans (or persons married to non-Aryans) from work as editors. Nazi officials denounced "Jewish culture" in literature and the cinema; storm troopers burned books.[1]

The Nazi party and the SS, not the industrial and financial elite, initiated the Holocaust. But they succeeded in their program of genocide only by enlisting a broad collection of collaborators. They gave financial incentives to the German business community to participate in, first, persecution and dispossession of Jews, later in outright murder. The business community's enthusiastic response to these initiatives at times actually outstripped the Nazi state's own anti-Semitic persecution, particularly during the first half of Hitler's rule.

The Nazis' genocide of Jews was not driven solely by economic factors. Noted Holocaust historian Raul Hilberg and others have presented convincing evidence that the Nazi party and the SS pursued the destruction of Jewry in the final stages of the Holocaust even in circumstances when it was economically or militarily disadvantageous to the Germans to do so.[2] But Hitler's government did make it possible for businesses to reap rewards from persecution of Jews as well as from exploitation of POWs and forced laborers from the East. German finance and industry made the most of the opportunity.

Private enterprise first fed on the German government's program to "Aryanize" Jewish property—that is, to force the sale of Jewish-owned property at a fraction of its value to ethnic German entrepreneurs. The first phase was the so-called "voluntary" Aryanizations, when Jews hoping to flee Germany sold off property at the best price they could find. These transfers took place mainly between 1933 and 1938 in Germany, and they continued as late as 1941 in some of the Nazi-occupied territories.[3]

Later came the compulsory Aryanizations, which began in November 1938.[4] The government seized Jewish property without compensation and sold the plunder to German companies or individuals. The Nazis also consolidated some formerly Jewish- or Polish-owned companies useful in war production into large manufacturing conglomerates run by the German state or the SS.

The forced sales of the 1930s usually maintained the trappings of ordinary commerce, complete with negotiations, attorneys, and formal bills of sale. German businesses were thus able to maintain a facade of legitimacy in the eyes of foreign affiliates and trade partners, so that international markets remained open and foreign exchange continued to flow. For some Jews there was still some room to play German off against German in an effort to reduce the damage inherent in any forced sale.[5]

The "voluntary" Aryanizations provided strong incentives for tens of thousands of Germans to profit from this supposedly minor form of persecution. Aryanization thus built support for Nazi rule, particularly among German merchants and the business elite, who relied on continued Nazi rule to ensure the legitimacy of their new acquisitions. Most of these expropriations continue to be recognized by German courts to this day.[6]

The earliest Aryanizations can be traced to the national boycott of Jewish businesses initiated by the Nazi party shortly after Hitler came to power. "For local Nazi leaders persecution of Jews [during the boycott] meant a show of power," historian Anne Bloch has written. "For Aryan businessmen, the boycott was a convenient means of ridding themselves of Jewish competitors, and of acquiring new enterprises cheaply. . . . It also served to fulfill the material promises made to prominent Party members."[7]

Large-scale theft through Aryanization soon became a fact of German business life. Early in Hitler's rule for example, Dr. Ignatz Nacher, a prosperous Berlin Jew, decided to sell Germany's second largest brewery, the Engelhardt Brauerei A.G., following repeated harassment and a Nazi-organized boycott of his brands. This was well before Hitler had consolidated his power, and Nacher hoped to flee the country with his fortune intact. The sale was to be finalized in May 1934.

But the Dresdner Bank caught wind of the arrangement. According to an affidavit filed in a Munich court, "the Dresdner Bank . . . due to the fact that they had an interest in acquiring the business, had seen to it that Nacher was arrested under some pretext. . . . He was put under such pressure that he had to give his lawyer unlimited power of attorney for the disposal of his possessions. He was informed that he would not be set free if he did not sign this power of attorney."[8] The attorney then sold the brewery to the Dresdner Bank for a fraction of its value, and Dresdner sold the largest share in the business to one of the bank's own directors, Karl Rasche, who installed himself as the chairman of the brewery's management board.

Nacher's partners sued Dresdner for breach of contract and damages, and for a time the dispute worked its way through Munich courts. Then the Gestapo summoned the partners to Berlin and threatened them with arrest. They dropped the case.[9]

Under Karl Rasche, the brewery became a center of Nazi power and patronage. Dresdner Bank handed out positions on the brewery's board of directors to a half-dozen major industrial figures, including steel magnate Paul Plieger. Nazi satraps took over local distribution rights, and many old Nazis remember the Engelhardt brew as the drink of choice at party gatherings. (Rasche was convicted at Nuremberg of crimes against humanity in connection with the organized plunder of entire countries. By then, the brewery extortion had been almost forgotten.)[10]

Legal expropriation soon became a gold rush. In June 1936, the mainstream business newspaper *Frankfurter Zeitung* published a glowing article praising German economic progress since the Nazis had come to power, appending a long table listing the biggest Aryanizations over the previous three years.[11] The entry for 1933 recorded six major deals, two of which were acquisitions financed by the Dresdner Bank on behalf of the Flick group. In another contract, German shoe manufacturer Richard Freudenberg purchased his major competitor, the Jewish-owned Conrad Tack & Co. This was the first of a number of such Aryanizations for Freudenberg, the U.S. government was later to report,[12] and helped build his business into the worldwide shoe and leather empire that it remains today.

The *Frankfurter Zeitung* table listed twenty-one very large transfers and consolidations in 1934; most were forced buyouts of multi-million-dollar Jewish firms by their German competitors. In 1935, thirty-two such large contracts were reported, including two major acquisitions of Jewish firms by the Siemens group,* one by the Robert Bosch concern, one by the Link-Hoffman Werke, and another by Flick. The pace accelerated during 1936 with twenty-two major acquisitions in the first five months alone, including two more by Flick and one by the German subsidiary of the Ford Motor Company.[13]

Ford's attempted Aryanization of Jewish property was symptomatic of the role U.S. business played in Germany throughout the first decade of Hitler's rule. At Ford headquarters in the U.S., executives indicated that they wished to acquire the former Stoewer-Werke AG, a "bankrupt German company," for use as an auto-body production plant building Fords for sale throughout

---

* One of these was the acquisition by the Deutsche Bank and Siemens of the Aronwerke Elektrizitäts AG of Berlin, a manufacturer of electric meters and radios. According to a later U.S. government study, Aronwerke's owner Manfred Aron had until 1935 been determined to hold on to his firm and to wait out the years of Nazi rule. But after the Gestapo arrested him several times and threatened his family, Aron decided to sell his company for a fraction of its value in the late summer of that year. The Deutsche Bank financed the deal on behalf of a Siemens holding company. The Siemens group dismissed the Aron family directors, installed its own men, and changed the company name to Heliowatt AG. Once under Siemens control, Heliowatt became a holding company for a number of other new Siemens acquisitions. The Siemens companies eventually emerged as one of the largest contractors for concentration camp labor in Germany.

Central and Eastern Europe. Although the company declined to disclose the terms of the deal, it did acknowledge that Ford's German subsidiary had become one of the U.S. company's most important overseas units.[14]

In Germany, *Frankfurter Zeitung* reported that Ford's purchase indicated a "realization of the world view of race as the basis of the [German] economy"—in a word, an Aryanization.[15] Ford's German director Heinrich Albert wrote to headquarters in Dearborn, Michigan, that taking over Stoewer was the best means to secure new German military contracts and to create the "psychological basis . . . [to win] the support of the dominating circles, especially the National Socialist Party," by assisting in the expulsion of Jews from the German economy.[16] Ford's German subsidiary—whose directors included Ford's U.S. president Edsel Ford, its overseas chief Percival L. D. Perry, Berlin attorney Heinrich Albert, and German automotive leader Carl Bosch—adopted race as a criterion for employment at the company as early as 1935. The next year Ford dismissed its general manager, Erich Diestel (who had carried out many of the dismissals), when it was discovered that he had a Jewish ancestor.[17]

In a revealing development, however, Ford abandoned the Stoewer-Werke acquisition, when the company discovered it would cost too much to introduce new technology and mass-production methods into the body works. Thus, Ford was willing enough to participate in Nazi anti-Semitism if it turned a profit.[18] This opportunistic pattern became typical of relations between large enterprises and Hitler's government for the remainder of the Nazi regime.

Other U.S. banks, companies, and investors participated in and profited from Aryanizations. In the early 1930s, Germany imposed tight currency restrictions on foreign companies, forcing U.S. corporations to choose between investing their profits from German sales exclusively in the Third Reich or abandoning the German market to the competition. Virtually all U.S. companies chose to stay.[19] This reinvestment requirement created pressure on foreign companies to find profitable new investments inside the Reich. Two areas seemed especially promising: Aryanizations and the semiclandestine German rearmament program.

New German conglomerates built mainly on the seizure of Jewish-owned companies sold bonds on the international market to raise capital to Aryanize still more companies at fire-sale prices.[20] Bankers traded German corporate securities that were de facto Aryanization bonds—though not called by that name—in New York, London, Zurich, and other financial centers. Dillon, Read vice president William Draper emerged as one of the most prosperous traders in these markets. As director of the German Credit and Investment Corporation of New Jersey, he specialized in U.S. investments in Hitler-era Germany. After the war, Draper was to become U.S. economics chief in occupied Germany.[21]

Many U.S. companies bought substantial interests in established German companies, which in turn plowed that new money into Aryanizations or into arms production banned under the Versailles Treaty. According to a 1936 report from Ambassador William Dodd to President Roosevelt, a half-dozen key U.S. companies—International Harvester, Ford, General Motors, Standard Oil of New Jersey, and du Pont—had become deeply involved in German weapons production, in part because of difficulties in repatriating profits from more conventional business. "Our airplanes people," Dodd continued, also "have secret arrangements with the Krupps."[22]

U.S. investment in Germany accelerated rapidly after Hitler came to power, despite the Depression and Germany's default on virtually all of its government and commercial loans. Commerce Department reports show that U.S. investment in Germany increased some 48.5 percent between 1929 and 1940, while declining sharply everywhere else in continental Europe. U.S. investment in Great Britain, while larger than that in Germany, barely held steady over the decade, increasing only 2.6 percent.[23]

The pace of Aryanization in Germany intensified to the point that some German bankers began contending that any failure to participate in the legalized looting of Jews would open them up to charges of being poor managers of depositors' funds. Dresdner Bank managers, for example, complained in 1935 to senior management that the rival Deutsche Bank had a five-million-mark Aryanization fund that could be exploited by lending officers without the usual time-consuming procedures for approving large investments. This gave Deutsche Bank a leg up when a particularly choice "object" came up for liquidation, Dresdner's managers said.[24] They got their own contingency fund.

By 1938, the shoe was on the other foot, at least as Deutsche Bank saw things. "Letters regarding Aryanizations were sent by the *Vorstand* [comparable to the chief executive officer's office in a U.S. corporation] of the Deutsche Bank to the individual main branches around the end of 1938," the bank's Berlin senior manager, Erhardt Schmidt, told interrogators after the war. "They stated first of all that Aryanizations were now quite common and then pointed out that the Dresdner Bank was deriving appreciable profits from such transactions. For [that] reason, the Deutsche Bank in its own interest would have to take advantage of all opportunities along these lines."[25]

The competitive dynamics are important here. These institutions saw Aryanization as a legitimate business opportunity that they could not afford to pass up. Further, their drive to take advantage of Aryanization continued regardless of whether individual bankers considered themselves to be anti-Semitic.

At first, the Nazis played only a limited role in the Aryanization markets. The state created the legal framework within which Jews could be exploited with impunity, but the profits from this form of looting flowed almost exclusively to private German interests. By late 1935, however, Economic Minister Hjalmar Schacht sensed the profits that the government could derive by imposing itself as a middleman in Aryanization deals. Under Schacht's plan, much of the capital gain would go to the German state, which would also collect a variety of taxes and transfer charges.

Schacht's comments and actions during the months leading up to the promulgation of the notorious anti-Semitic Nuremberg race laws in 1935 tacitly confirm that the German private sector had often been a driving force in the economic persecution of Jews. Schacht was not opposed to afflicting Jews, as even his self-flattering postwar memoirs make clear.*[26] But he was convinced that the Nazi state should play a greater role in regulating Aryanizations in order to maintain German economic stability and to avoid reigniting inflation.

Schacht agitated for faster liquidation of Jewish businesses in his speeches to manufacturers' groups and financial forums. But he insisted that Hitler's state should control the process and be-

---

* Here is Schacht speaking in his own defense in his memoirs, explaining why he did not consider himself to be an anti-Semite: "As I see it there is one single factor which gives rise to the widespread unpopularity of the Jews. It is not the religious antithesis; rather it is the fact that owing to his ability, and whenever he resides in

come its principal beneficiary. "The Jew must realize that their influence is gone for all times," Schacht proclaimed in August 1935. "We desire to keep our people and our culture pure and distinctive. . . . But the solution of these problems must be brought about under state leadership, and cannot be left to unregulated individual actions, which mean a disturbing influence on the national economy . . ."[27]

Overall, Aryanization appears to have been second only to the vast economic trauma of the Depression in its contribution to increasing the concentration of wealth and economic power in the hands of a few German combines during the 1930s, according to a 1939 study by Guenter Keiser. According to Keiser, virtually every major German company had adopted the practice.[28]

> The mining and armament industries, long before 1936, had been dominated by four mammoth concerns: the Stahlverein, Krupp, Kloeckner and Gutehoffnungshuette. [After 1936,] Mannesmann, Friedrich Flick, Otto Wolff and Reichswerke Hermann Goering gained influence in these fields. All four of the newcomers had directly benefitted from Aryanizations. . . .
>
> In the chemical industry, Jewish plants manufacturing soaps and cleansers, paints and varnishes were taken over by middle-sized Aryan concerns. [In] the paper and cellulose in-

---

a non-Jewish community, the Jew endeavors to insinuate himself into the intellectual and cultural leadership of that community . . . No one grudged the Jews a free hand in commerce and industry. But when the legal and medical professions showed an unusually high percentage of Jews; when most of the theaters, the press, the concerts, were under Jewish management, then this constitutes the incursion of a foreign element into the hostess nation . . . A nation whose civilization is rooted in Christianity will therefore always be at pains to preserve Christianity as the basis of its civilization and to discourage foreign elements in its cultural life. So long as the Jews fail to appreciate this fact they will come up against difficulties. . . ."

Thus it is *the Jew's fault* that there is anti-Semitism, as Schacht saw things. Further, he continued, it was entirely appropriate for a "Christian" nation such as Nazi Germany to take measures to attack the Jewish "foreign elements" in its midst, despite the fact that most German Jews had been resident in Germany for generations, and even for centuries.

Schacht's self-defense then goes on to claim that it was "almost painful [for Schacht] to have to recount all that I had done for the Jews—painful because to champion such persecuted people is, at bottom, no more than the duty of any decent man."

dustries . . . the large Hartmann holdings went into Aryan hands.

In the textile and clothing industries, the wave of concentration in the years of 1936–1939 coincided with the process of Aryanization. Many Jewish enterprises changed owners, many others were merged with existing Aryan concerns. Still others were totally liquidated, which meant an automatic increase in business for the remaining Aryan establishments. . . . In 1938 alone, 900 out of 6500 existing firms in the clothing industry were liquidated. The situation in the shoe and leather industries was similar. . . .

In the food industry, Jewish and foreign (especially French) enterprises, particularly mills, were put at the disposal of medium and small Aryan concerns. In the tobacco industry, the great majority of Jewish cigar firms in southern Germany were acquired by Aryans. Former employees [e.g., Germans] often took over Jewish firms in the wholesale and retail trade.

In the field of private banking, the process of shrinking which had its origin in the inflation of 1921–23 assumed an almost stormy tempo with Aryanization. The smaller Jewish firms were liquidated almost without exception. Some of the medium-sized private banks met with the same fate.[29]

The systematic expropriation of Jewish property was well advanced by the time the German government instituted compulsory Aryanization in late 1938. The new economics minister, Walther Funk, reported in November that of seven billion marks' worth of stocks, bonds, real estate, and business assets registered in Germany as Jewish-owned, some two billion had already been taken by German nationals through Aryanizations.[30] That month, the state announced a new tax, the Suhneleistung, or "atonement payment," designed to tax Jews for the damages of the Kristallnacht pogroms that the Nazis had themselves instigated. The collection of this new payment was reported to have been administered by the Deutsche Bank.[31] The amount stated at first was one billion marks, purportedly as recompense for the "abominable crimes" of Jews, but within a week, Reichsminister Goering increased the levy. Hitler's government collected still another 900 million marks through the Reich flight tax, which seized at least a quarter (and often more) of the assets of every person who emigrated from Germany.[32]

By mid-1940, Aryanizations and punitive taxes had seized roughly four billion marks from German and Austrian Jews. This was equal to more than 75 percent of Germany's annual investment in armament plants and military facilities on the eve of the war.[33] It was about equal to the total assets of the Deutsche Bank[34] and more than twelve times the assets of Nazi Germany's giant industrial holding company, the VIAG.[35]

Hermann Goering, the senior official in charge of war mobilization, was later to claim that Germany's preparations for war had been bankrolled by two main sources: Aryanization of Jewish property and the looting of the Austrian state treasury following the 1938 *Anschluss*.[36] Goering was exaggerating; German state borrowing under a variety of pretexts probably played a larger role than either of these factors in financing the military buildup. But his comment illustrates that the Nazi leaders saw the forced liquidation of Jewish assets as essential to the economic viability of the Third Reich.

The Aryanizations were probably crucial to the Nazis' political survival as well, at least during the first decade of their rule. The collaboration of German big business, shopkeepers, and professionals that was crucial to Hitler's power in the 1930s would likely not have occurred without widespread Aryanizations, according to economic historian Arthur Schweitzer. Each of these sectors prospered in part by preying upon Jews; without Aryanizations, their competing economic interests would likely have created political divisions that the Nazis could not control. "Violent anti-Semitism became accepted by various segments of the middle class as a policy of economic reform," Schweitzer wrote.[37]

Most members of the German economic elite were not Nazi ideologues or fanatical anti-Semites, at least not as individuals.[38] They were, however, willing to sacrifice the lives of innocent people in order to achieve or maintain a privileged position in German society. Many became "institutional" as distinct from "individual" anti-Semites, so to speak. They compensated for their complicity in mass murder through grumbling and doubts, acts of self-interest that in some instances ran counter to the wishes of the Nazi state, and in rare cases, acts of charity toward persecuted people. After the war, German executives (or military officers, religious leaders, etc.) often put forward some individual deed as proof of "resistance" to the Nazis. In reality though, during the Hitler years most of them had developed and maintained institutions essential to the system of destruction. This split between individual and institutional behaviors became central to the elite's largely successful effort to escape culpability for the Holocaust once the war was over.

A case in point is Deutsche Bank director Hermann Abs, who became probably the single most influential German economic leader after 1945. He has been remembered warmly in recent years by many senior German-Jewish bankers. Eric Warburg, of the powerful Hamburg and New York banking family, has termed Abs "my close friend" and praised his "extraordinary knowledge of the banking business and the economy."[39] William Petschek, whose family's extensive coal and steel holdings were Aryanized by the Nazis on the eve of the war, publicly expressed his confidence in Abs. Writing in 1970, Petschek remembered a September 1939 meeting in which Abs and the Deutsche Bank "agreed to do everything to help protect our capital for the future." More or less similar testimony on Abs's behalf has been offered by Rudolf Loeb, whose banking house, Mendelssohn & Co., was liquidated with Abs's assistance in 1938, and by other prominent Jews.[40]

There is no reason to doubt their accounts. Abs and a number of other members of the international banking and legal networks described in earlier chapters were quite open to assisting wealthy Jews flee Germany with as much of their family fortunes as possible. Providing welcome assistance to a colleague in distress had an obvious moral appeal—and so much the better if the one who is helped is a millionaire many times over. These rescues could also be a lucrative business, even when carried out without taking predatory advantage of the situation that the Nazis had created.

Thus, Abs reemerged in some circles after the war as the archetype of a decent German whose reputation had been unfairly blackened by public preconceptions—at least until the Simon Wiesenthal Center and Nazi-hunter Charles Higham stepped forward with a blistering exposé of Abs's institutional role during the

Third Reich.[41] For those more critical observers, Hermann Abs was not only the director of Germany's most powerful war industries, he was also the financier of slavery and Aryanization.

Abs's career during the Nazi takeover of Austria is a good example of the complex role played by the German financial elite in the Holocaust. Hitler's government, the Deutsche Bank, and most of Germany's large corporations regarded the absorption of Austria into the Reich as a test case for managing the emerging German empire in Eastern Europe. The theft of Jewish assets that had taken years in Germany was carried out in Austria in months. The persecution measures used in this new Reich proved to be faster and more sophisticated than those used in Germany itself.[42]

Hitler's Ministry of Economics tipped off the Deutsche Bank to Germany's plan to march into Austria in early 1938, well before the *Anschluss*. Deutsche Bank director Abs quickly assembled a team of the bank's foreign trade specialists to identify Austria's choicest Jewish-owned businesses and real estate for acquisition. At the top of Abs's list was the Rothschild-owned bank Creditanstalt-Bankverein AG, which the Deutsche Bank had been attempting to take over for almost a decade. Deutsche Bank held a small interest in the Creditanstalt, but it had been largely shut out of the Vienna bank's operations. Abs's team began a campaign to use the *Anschluss* and Aryanization to take total control of the Rothschild bank.[43]

The Deutsche Bank's chief rival in this effort was the German state-owned VIAG industrial combine, which owned a major Berlin bank, the Reichskredit Gesellschaft (RKG).

About a week before the Germans marched into Austria, Abs met with the Creditanstalt board to offer a deal that the Deutsche Bank team had hammered out over the previous three months: Cooperate with the Deutsche Bank and become its leading agency for further German corporate penetration into southeastern Europe, or face a takeover and probable liquidation at the hands of the VIAG when the storm troopers moved in. The Creditanstalt board considered Abs's ultimatum overnight, then appointed him to its board the following morning. The bank's directors did not reveal their knowledge of the coming Nazi invasion to the Austrian public, nor so far as can be determined, did they inform Austria's government. Two weeks after the Nazis' invasion, Creditanstalt formally became a subsidiary of Deutsche Bank.[44]

The transaction did not go smoothly thereafter. VIAG, its subsidiary RKG, and the Dresdner Bank objected vehemently and blocked the deal. VIAG used its status as a German state-owned syndicate to establish itself as a trustee for a large block of Creditanstalt stock on behalf of the Reich government.[45]

Different factions within the Reich offered competing strategies for empire-building in Europe. Nazi state agencies and government-owned companies such as the VIAG favored direct government control over most of the large enterprises in the countries coveted by Germany. They wanted production in these territories to be organized along a relatively centralized, planned-economy model, with maximum emphasis placed on satisfying the needs of a self-sufficient Third Reich. Private enterprises should be strictly subordinate to the needs of the Reich and to the racial ideology of Nazism. The "de-judification" of subject economies would be carried out as radically as possible, with little concern for its impact on private German businesses or for how Germany's behavior might be perceived outside of its borders. All these would be steps toward true National Socialism, they contended.

In contrast, much of the banking and industrial elite of Germany favored a more traditional, imperial approach to acquiring a new empire in Europe. Among their principal spokesmen were Economics Minister Hjalmar Schacht, Hermann Abs, and a young Reichsbank director, Karl Blessing. Their strategy favored integrating businesses in countries occupied by the Germans into private industrial syndicates coordinated through German-based cartels and through private institutions such as Deutsche Bank. The private companies in turn pledged their loyalty to Hitler's government. German military conquest should be used to create conditions through which German corporations could buy up the key enterprises in newly subjugated countries at very favorable prices, this faction contended, but only in rare instances should the state take direct command of industry. Much of the senior leadership of the Deutsche Bank, IG Farben, the Siemens group of companies, and other German-based cartels maintained that Germany should reenter the world marketplace rather than attempt to build up the orthodox Nazi dream of a self-sufficient German empire in Central and Eastern Europe. This faction's attitude toward Aryanization was often more complex than that of the Nazi ideologues. It was fine to absorb Jewish properties, but might the

National Socialists' radical economic measures one day be turned on the bankers themselves?[46]

The *Anschluss* with Austria and Germany's reemergence as a major military power crystallized the debate over German strategy. Abs's rivalry with the state-owned RKG over control of the Creditanstalt and other Vienna banks soon became a focal point of the struggle.

SS *Brigadeführer* Hans Kehrl confronted Abs shortly after the *Anschluss* and told him that the Reich "could not consent to the acquisition by the Deutsche Bank of the [Creditanstalt] share capital" because with it would inevitably come "control over the entire structure of Austrian industry."[47] SS banking specialist Wilhelm Keppler was more blunt: The Deutsche Bank wants to "rob" the Third Reich by acquisition of Creditanstalt, he wrote. "It came to Vienna with twenty men to take over."[48] The SS men were comfortable with Deutsche Bank's playing a subordinate role in Creditanstalt, but no more.

Hermann Abs replied in kind. He argued in policy meetings that "Deutsche Bank would be in a better position to exploit [Creditanstalt] for the Reich" if VIAG and the RKG were "not permitted to interfere." Using his strategy, Abs contended, Creditanstalt "was in a position to reinforce German economic influence in southeastern Europe, provided that its friendship with the Deutsche Bank were further cemented." His bank alone, he concluded, should be given the authority to select staff and set policy for the Austrian institution.[49]

Abs won undisputed control of Creditanstalt through a series of stock swaps with RKG over the next three years. He became Creditanstalt's vice chairman, and two other Deutsche Bank directors joined the board.[50] Meanwhile, Deutsche Bank carried out the transformation of Creditanstalt into an "Aryan" institution so abruptly and thoroughly that it was recognized during and after the war as a "model" of Nazification. A postwar investigation indicated that within days after the *Anschluss* the bank purged its Jewish employees, brought in new German directors from Deutsche Bank and IG Farben, and re-staffed the bank's senior management largely with Nazi party members.[51]

Abs helped Aryanize scores of properties in Austria, depriving hundreds of Jewish families of their livelihoods and setting the stage for their deportation to concentration camps. Creditanstalt eventually became the single most active bank in the Aryanization of Austrian businesses, according to captured records of the Nazi agency for "de-judification" in Vienna. Typically, these transactions involved provision of Creditanstalt loans to Nazi activists and to German businessmen interested in purchasing Jewish businesses at a fraction of their value. In some particularly promising transactions, Creditanstalt bought up Jewish assets for the bank's own portfolio.[52] Hermann Abs was at that time vice chairman of the Creditanstalt board with direct responsibility for approval of all of the Vienna bank's larger transactions, a later U.S. investigation reported.*[53]

The Nazi takeover in Vienna linked the special anti-Semitic machinery of the Nazi state—the Agency for Capital Transfer, the SS's Central Agency for Jewish Emigration, and so on—to the powerful existing social institutions of commerce, contract law, exchange, and other day-to-day structures of conventional enterprise. The Germans stressed observance of purported legality, orderliness, and careful paperwork when carrying out expropriations. In this way, the Nazis succeeded for a time in harnessing the vast inertial movement of ordinary society to their project of wiping out Jews.

The speed and efficiency of this form of looting startled even the Germans. The SS in Vienna used an early type of computer known as a Hollerith machine acquired from IBM to register Jewish properties and keep track of their liquidation. The Vienna edition of the Nazi party newspaper crowed that, as a result of this modern registration system, "within six weeks we shall have laid hands on all Jewish fortunes over 5,000 marks; within three years, every single Jewish concern will have been Aryanized."[54] Private German banks and businesses used the SS registration data to take over about 5,000 of the most prosperous Jewish companies in less

---

* Jewish businesses taken over as their owners sought to flee the country included the Delka shoe factory (purchased by Creditanstalt at 40 percent of the owners' asking price); the Brunner Brothers' lamp and metalware factory (asking price not disclosed); Samuel Schallinger's Hotel Bristol and the Imperial Wine wholesalers (at 64 percent of the asking price); and the Toffler family's "Tiller" brand textile and uniform company (at less than 25 percent of the asking price). The Aryanization of the Brunner factory was jointly handled by Creditanstalt and by Deutsche Bank's Berlin office, captured records show. Meanwhile IG Farben, which was also represented on Creditanstalt's board, Aryanized and took control of one of Austria's largest pharmaceutical manufacturers, Serum Union AG.

than eighteen months, according to contemporary SS reports, and liquidated about 21,000 smaller Jewish businesses to make room for competing German enterprises. About 7,000 cases were still left to process in early 1940, according to the SS, though as a practical matter many of the Jews who nominally owned the remaining enterprises had already been deported to the forced labor center at Mauthausen.[55] Most did not survive.

6

"Who Still Talks of the Armenians?"

MENTAL PATIENTS and disabled people appear to have been the first ones the Nazis actually gassed; they killed at least 50,000 in an experimental euthanasia program code-named *Aktion T4* that began in the fall of 1939.[1] Reports from German-occupied Poland suggest that the SS gassed a number of Polish prostitutes at about the same time.[2]

The bulk of the Nazi killings prior to 1941 were what the Poles termed "cold pogroms": deportation of tens of thousands of people to barren wastelands or to desperately overcrowded Jewish ghettos where death came slowly through hunger, disease, or exposure to the elements. Nazi concentration camps during this period were prison camps, not extermination centers. True, German security troops and paramilitary gangs undertook thousands of massacres of Jews, Communists, Romanis (Gypsies), and others. But they carried out these killings on a local scale, generally taking the lives of between five and fifty persons at a time.[3]

The cold pogroms were kindred to Turkey's World War I exter-

75

mination of Armenians in several ways. Both were driven primarily
by a determination to achieve "security" through wiping out a race
of people, rather than by conventional economic or military actions.
The Germans used administrative methods similar to those of the
Turks, and both campaigns chose local pogroms, hunger, and exposure to the elements as their chief instruments of death. The Nazis
organized the extirpation of between 700,000 and one million Jews
and Poles between September 1939 and the summer of 1942[4]—a
casualty rate approaching that which the Turks had achieved in a
comparable time using nearly identical methods.

Hitler was well aware of Turkey's genocide of Armenians and of
the failure of the international community to respond adequately to
it. As early as June 1931, Hitler commented in an interview that the
"extermination of the Armenians" had led him to "the conclusion
that masses of men are mere biological plasticine" over which Aryans would eventually triumph.[5] He returned to this theme in a
formal talk to his commanding generals on the eve of their invasion
of Poland in 1939: "Our strength is in our quickness and our brutality," he exclaimed. "Genghis Khan had millions of women and
children killed by his own will and with a gay heart. History sees
only in him a great state builder. . . . Thus for the time being I have
sent to the East . . . my Death's Head Units with the order to kill
without pity or mercy all men, women, and children of the Polish
race or language. Only in such a way will we win the vital space that
we need. Who still talks nowadays of the extermination of the
Armenians?"[6] On at least three other occasions, Hitler pointed to
the brutality of Turkey's regime and its willingness to strike without
mercy as a worthy model for his own government.[7]

A new and more terrible wave of slaughter began when the
Germans invaded the USSR during June of 1941. Special SS troops
dedicated to mass murder now followed close behind the advancing German army. Within thirty-six months, these *Einsatzgruppen*
and their subunits, the *Einsatzkommandos* and *Sonderkom-
mandos*, shot about two million people, according to the Nuremberg Military Tribunal. The large majority of the dead were Jews,
although the *Einsatzgruppen's* net also caught hundreds of thousands of Communists, Slavs, Romanis, Poles, homosexuals, hospital patients, unarmed prisoners of war, and even orphan
children. These two million murders, moreover, do not include the
gassings at Auschwitz, Treblinka, and other death factories that
began in the wake of the invasion.[8]

A 1942 report on the fate of Jews in eastern Poland smuggled out of Warsaw by the Jewish Labor Bund provided remarkably detailed and accurate early documentation of the work of the *Einsatzkommandos*.

> From the day the Russo-German war broke out, the Germans embarked on the physical extermination of the Jewish population on Polish soil, using the Ukrainians and Lithuanian fascists for this job. It began in Eastern Galicia in the summer months of 1941. The following system was applied everywhere: men, fourteen to sixty years old, were driven to a single place— a square or a cemetery, where they were slaughtered, or shot by machine-guns, or killed by hand grenades. They had to dig their own graves. Children in orphanages, inmates in old-age homes, sick in hospitals were shot, women were killed on the streets. In many towns Jews were carried off to an "unknown destination" and killed in the adjacent woods. Thirty thousand Jews were killed in L'wow [Lvov], 15,000 in Stanislawow, 5,000 in Tarnopol, 2,000 in Zloczow, 4,000 in Brzezany (there were 18,000 Jews in this town, now only 1,700 are left). The same has happened in Zborow, Kolomyja, Sambor, Stryj, Drohobycz, Zbaraz, Przemyslany, Kuty, Sniatyn, Zaleszczyki, Brody, Przemysl, Rawa Ruska, and other places. . . . The number of the Jews murdered in a beastly fashion in the Wilno [Vilna] area and in Lithuania is put at 300,000.[9]

The extermination campaign gathered momentum by integrating itself with the day-to-day activities of Hitler's government and German society. In January 1942, fourteen senior German government bureaucrats met at SS offices at Lake Wannsee, in the suburbs of Berlin, to coordinate efforts to exterminate the Jews of Europe. Up to that point, the various German ministries had often worked at cross-purposes in their approach to the "Jewish Question." Officials in charge of the economic exploitation of the Nazi-occupied territories in the East had sometimes advocated retention of able-bodied Jews as slave laborers, while Reinhard Heydrich of the SS had pushed for mass execution by the *Einsatzgruppen*. Still other ministries had favored a variety of deportation and resettlement schemes, though they were unable to agree on exactly where to relocate the refugees and the extent of terror to wreak upon them.

The Wannsee meeting changed all that. There, SS security chief

Reinhard Heydrich enlisted the support of each of the major government ministries and Nazi party organizations in a concerted effort to "clear . . . the German *Lebensraum* ["living space"] of Jews *in a legal way*," [emphasis added]. The tactics were relatively simple. "Europe will be cleaned up from the West to the East," Heydrich commented. "Able-bodied Jews will be taken in large labor columns to these districts [i.e.: Nazi-occupied territories on the Eastern Front] for work on roads . . . in the course of which action a great part will undoubtedly be eliminated by natural causes. The possible final remnant will, as it must undoubtedly consist of the toughest, have to be treated accordingly, as it . . . would, if liberated, act as a bud cell of a Jewish reconstruction." All German government agencies were to cooperate with the SS in this plan; it was to be the "final solution of the Jewish problem in Europe."[10]

Heydrich's assistant, Adolf Eichmann, estimated that there were approximately 11 million Jews to be "cleaned up" in this fashion; he provided a country-by-country breakdown of Jewish populations to help plan tactics. There were 5 million Jews to murder in the Nazi-occupied USSR, according to his list, and 2.3 million more in the former territories of Poland. Long-range plans called for the SS to eliminate all 4,000 Jews in Ireland once the German troops arrived.[11]

Heydrich's emphasis on "legality" was crucial to the social psychology of the extermination program and to its functioning on a practical level. For Adolf Eichmann, the Wannsee decisions dispelled his lingering doubts about the propriety of mass murder. "Here now, during this conference, the most prominent people had spoken, the Popes of the Third Reich," Eichmann said. "Not only Hitler, not only Heydrich, or [Gestapo chief] Müller, or the SS, or the Party, but the elite of the Civil Service had registered their support. . . . At that moment, I sensed a kind of Pontius Pilate feeling, for I was free of all guilt," Eichmann testified at his later trial for crimes against humanity. "Who was I to judge? Who was I to have my own thoughts in this matter?' "[12]

On an operational level, each German government ministry took responsibility for only part of the overall program—the registration of Jews, the seizure of their property, physical transportation across Europe, and so on—and each part had an easy appearance of legality, of sanction by the state and even of a certain sort of normality. Each act of the extermination program, except for the actual gassing, came complete with a more or less reasonable explanation available to the perpetrators and to the world at large. The government was deporting Jews as a security measure and to put them to work, the story went. This would benefit German society and perhaps even benefit the Jewish deportees (as in the case of aged Jews who were to be sent to a special ghetto at Theresienstadt).

By dividing up responsibility for extermination into explicable, functional parts, the Nazi party and SS enlisted and united the German state and most of German society in the countless little tasks necessary to conduct mass murder. They openly promoted the slogan "Final Solution to the Jewish Question" as a rallying cry in the Nazi-controlled press.[13] Knowledge of the true meaning of the phrase seeped slowly through the informal networks of the governmental, business, and police elites.

Note that even at Wannsee the truth that millions of Jews were to be gassed and shot rather than worked to death was not openly discussed. Almost all of the Jews were said to be "eliminated by natural causes," as Heydrich put it, rather than simply killed.[14] This simple deceit can be traced to the police security surrounding the gassing installations and to the psychological need of most people to evade open complicity in murder.

The SS did not fool German bureaucrats into cooperation. Rather, the Wannsee conference illustrates how Nazi-dominated society created a social consciousness that both facilitated the extermination program and denied its existence. The "legalization" established at Wannsee (and in related laws and decrees) achieved a relatively smooth linkage between the surface world of wartime life and the officially denied world of mass extermination. Many more people knew of (or suspected) the extermination program than could directly acknowledge it, in part because this was a classified government program during wartime. Yet, widespread possession of unofficial or "denied" knowledge became crucial to the success of the extermination effort; without it, the Third Reich would have failed to coordinate its constantly squabbling ministries well enough to carry out the massive effort.

Preparations for a blitzkrieg-style attack on Jews in the occupied areas of Western Europe had been under way for some months by the time of the Wannsee gathering. The SS had begun tests of

Zyklon-B poison gas for mass killings of Soviet prisoners of war and Jews at Auschwitz at least as early as September 1941, and the following month there were similar experimental executions at the Sachsenhausen camp. This new technique was extraordinarily effective, from the Nazis' point of view, and they immediately built centers devoted exclusively to murder by gassing at Belzec (near the Lublin Jewish reservation) and at Chelmno (near the Lodz ghetto). They gassed about 5,000 Romanis at Chelmno at just about the same time that Heydrich was meeting with the leaders of the civil service at Wannsee in mid-January.[15]

The previous October, Hitler had ordered that virtually all Jews remaining in Germany were to be deported to the East, supposedly as a security measure. The Nazi occupation governments in France, Belgium, Holland, Slovakia, and Greece soon issued similar decrees. They hit the so-called stateless, or refugee, Jews first; most of those people were deported to Auschwitz and killed there. In mid-July, French collaborationist police captured almost 13,000 stateless Jews in Paris and deported 9,000 of them—including about 4,000 children—to a transit camp at Drancy, from which they went on to Auschwitz. Vichy France then began rounding up French Jews, deporting at least 7,000 of them during August. The collaborationist governments in Belgium and the Netherlands co-operated in similar deportations. Mass deportations from the Warsaw ghetto to the Treblinka death camp began on July 22. Surviving SS records show that the Nazis murdered more than 200,000 people during the last two weeks of August 1942 alone at the death camps at Treblinka, Belzec, and Chelmno. Comparable killings were then under way at Auschwitz and Sobibor.[16]

Business channels—the information pathways of day-to-day commerce in German society—proved to be one of the most important sources of information about the extermination campaign. Officially, the gassings and mass murders were a German state secret of the highest order. But this information could not be fully concealed from the corporate community because many enterprises were closely intertwined with the murder effort. At Auschwitz, "The great extent of industrial activity in this camp resulted in a constant stream of incoming and outgoing corporation officials, engineers, construction men and other temporary personnel, all excellent carriers of gossip to the farthest corners of the Reich," Raul Hilberg reports. He recounts a revealing incident that took place in January 1942—only weeks after the initiation of mass gassings of prisoners at the camp—involving an IG Farben official, Ernst A. Struss. Returning by train to Breslau after a short visit to IG Farben's factory at the camp, Struss "overheard a [German] worker remarking in a loud voice that in Auschwitz large numbers of people were being burnt, that the cremations were being carried out in crematories and on stakes, and that the air in the IG Farben factory in Auschwitz was putrid with the smell of corpses.

"Struss jumped up and shouted, 'These are lies; you should not spread such lies!'

"The man answered, 'No, these are not lies; in Auschwitz there are 10,000 workers and all know it.' " Similarly, executives in the central insurance department at IG Farben were uncertain over how to process the reports of mass deaths among laborers at Auschwitz and other IG Farben facilities.[17]

The evidence shows that, despite later denials, much of the corporate elite of Germany was well aware of the Nazis' extermination programs. Thousands of German corporate directors and senior managers knowingly contributed to murders carried out by their institutions, in many cases even after they had become disenchanted with Hitler and knew that the war was lost. The SS and the Nazi party could at least point to their ideology as an explanation of sorts for their participation in crime. But the business elite could not make even that claim. For them, cooperation in years of genocide became simply a matter of doing business.

One clear indicator that corporate executives did often have detailed knowledge of the Nazi genocide campaigns is the record of a handful of businessmen who became spies for the Allies during the conflict. Significantly, these agents were not members of the Nazi inner circle; they were simply prosperous businessmen who broke with their government out of political or moral disgust. These spies were relatively isolated within German society, and their sources of information concerning the exterminations were limited to the usual business and social contacts typical of persons of their class. Nevertheless, within weeks after the gassings began, these men were able to report accurately on the existence and on many operational details of the supposedly highly secret mass murder programs.

Industrialist Eduard Schulte, for example, owned strategically important zinc mines and other real estate near what had once been the German-Polish border. He was a conservative Christian Democrat and a committed anti-Nazi who repeatedly risked his life and fortune to spy on the Nazis on behalf of the Polish, Swiss, and eventually U.S. intelligence services.[18]

Schulte picked up most of his information by listening to the political gossip of German industrialists, through family ties (his cousin was an Abwehr officer), and through talking with the local Nazi district leader, with whom he met because of his mining operations. Such sources consistently knew more of Germany's most secret affairs than they were officially supposed to know, and with a little prodding from Schulte, they showed off their knowledge in casual conversation. The results of this simple espionage were impressive: Schulte provided early warning to the Allies of the German invasion of Poland in 1939, of the USSR in 1941, and perhaps—though the evidence is less certain on this point—of Belgium, Holland, Norway, and Denmark as well. He passed on dozens of bits of information concerning German military campaigns, petroleum stocks, and resource shortages.[19] Though his information was sometimes incorrect, the Allied agents who handled him from Zurich had little doubt that Schulte was on the whole a reliable and effective secret agent.

As early as July 1942—less than six months after the Wannsee conference—Schulte reported the essential facts of the Final Solution in an urgent message to a representative of the World Jewish Congress in Zurich. The details were sketchy, but Schulte accurately reported that Hitler had decided to kill all Jewish deportees as quickly as was practical; that "3½ to 4 million" people in the territories then in German hands were already scheduled for extermination; and that the killings were to be carried out through gassings involving prussic acid.[20]

There was, of course, much more to the story than Schulte knew, and Polish intelligence had already pieced together a grim, horrifying study of Nazi crimes in Poland that was more detailed than Schulte's account*.[21] The point here, however, is that this rela-

---

* Schulte's information concerning mass executions of Jews through the use of prussic acid—*Zyklon-B* gas—was the capstone of a mountain of evidence concerning the Nazis' intentions that had been building over the previous twelve months. The Czech and Polish governments-in-exile in London had repeatedly brought forth detailed news of the "cold pogroms" and related terror. On July 2, 1942, BBC broadcasts featured Polish-Jewish spokesman Szmul Zygielbojm, who

tively minor industrialist, working on his own and without access to secret SS or Nazi party messages, had succeeded in piecing together the essential fact that an intentional campaign of genocide was under way.

Hans Deichmann, a junior executive at IG Farben during the early 1940s, reports a similar experience. In March 1942, Deichmann's work as a manager of Italian contract labor took him to the IG Farben plant at Auschwitz, where many of the Italian workers he had enlisted were working. Even at that early date, Deichmann says, "no one could have approached the IG Farben works without becoming horribly, fearfully aware of what was happening nearby." The stink of burning flesh hung in the air, and work columns from "the world of the dead" could be seen on the roads leading from the nearby concentration camp to the IG Farben factory. "I went to Auschwitz ten times between March 1942 and November 1944, each time for one day, and everyone I met spoke of almost nothing but the concentration camp and the systematic extermination," Deichmann recalls. " 'My' Italians, who in theory couldn't understand the people around them, quickly managed to learn even more of the ghastly details than the others knew."[22]

The fact that anti-Nazi "outsiders" such as Schulte and Deichmann learned of the extermination programs within weeks after they began does not prove that every other industrialist also knew, of course. But it does establish that such information was readily available through business channels for those individuals with the

---

stated bluntly that the Nazis' strategy in Poland consisted of the "planned extermination of a whole nation by means of shot, shell, starvation and poison gas. It will really be a shame to live on, a shame to belong to the human race," he continued, "if means are not found at once to put an end to the greatest crime in human history." Zygielbojm and the Polish National Council simultaneously presented a detailed report on Nazi atrocities in Poland to all members of both houses of the British Parliament. Even before the arrival of Schulte's news concerning poison gas, the British government was prepared to concede on the basis of the Polish evidence that some 700,000 Jews "had been murdered or starved to death [in Poland alone] since the outbreak of the war."

It was in this context that Schulte's message became a political rallying symbol, at least among those who had been paying attention to events in Europe. Here at last was "proof," said to be direct from the Führer's headquarters, that in a few taut sentences summarized the thousands of earlier fragmentary reports. The Schulte telegram was not new information: It was a conclusion, and a symbol that was capable of crystallizing substantial new action in defense of Hitler's victims.

moral conscience necessary to confront it. Schulte and Deich-mann's experiences strongly suggest that the postwar denials by many industrialists that their decisions during 1943, 1944, and early 1945 were made in ignorance of the ongoing extermination campaigns cannot be taken seriously.

IG Farben appears to have been the first company to fully inte-grate concentration camp labor into modern industrial production, and it eventually became known in Germany as a model enterprise for this new technique. Farben executives even provided advice and training on the large-scale use of forced labor for executives from Volkswagen, Messerschmitt, Heinkel, and other major com-panies.[23]

Hans Deichmann recalls a lunch he attended for senior IG Farben managers in the autumn of 1940, shortly after the fall of France and before the mass gassings of concentration camp prisoners had begun. "The Four Year Plan's administrators had given IG Farben the job of building a giant synthetic rubber factory in Upper Si-lesia, but a site had not yet been chosen," Deichmann recalled recently in an interview with journalist Harvey Sachs. "It would have to be near an area with an abundance either of essential natural resources—coal, for instance—or of manpower. The IG's commercial and technical directors, Georg von Schnitzler and Fritz ter Meer, assumed that the other people present at the lunch knew that Hitler's largest camp for enemies of the regime was at Auschwitz, and they referred to it as the only sure source of manpower.

"The sole inconvenient aspect [they said] was the probable ne-cessity of occasionally but suddenly having to replace carefully trained 'personnel' with people who were not yet ready for the task," Deichmann continued. "Although this was over a year before the implementation of the Final Solution—before the gas cham-bers and cremetoriums were put into action—Auschwitz was al-ready known to these industrialists as a place where thousands of the regime's opponents were being murdered. Yet they made their decision [to build the plant at Auschwitz] without a hint of criti-cism or displeasure or remorse, while sipping their soup."[24]

In the beginning, the SS intended to create its own factories for manufacturing war material right inside the concentration camps. This was strongly opposed by most of the German industrial elite, however, and by Albert Speer's Ministry for Armaments and War

Production. Industrialists complained bitterly that the SS had ambitions of competing with private industry and eventually supplanting it altogether in some National Socialist millennium to come. Furthermore, the critics continued, building new factories inside the concentration camps would only aggravate the acute shortages of labor and materials at existing production centers.

If the factories would not come to the camps, German industrial leaders contended, then let the camps come to the factories. The SS could supply forced laborers to industry for their mutual profit— and with relatively little reorganization of either the camps or the companies. "Concentration camp prisoners could be of valuable assistance in the factories already existing in the industrial sector," Albert Speer wrote. "These factories would merely have to be expanded by means of more buildings and additional machines. An experienced stock of specialists and engineers was already available. . . . This argument for private business instantly won Hitler over," Speer remembered.[25]

From mid-1942 on, the SS became a major provider of slave labor to industry. German corporate leaders assiduously courted the SS to obtain labor, contracts, and influence. Auschwitz commandant Rudolf Hoess confirms this; his affidavit during his trial for crimes against humanity states that "[t]he concentration camps have at no time offered labor to the industry. On the contrary, prisoners were sent to enterprises only after the enterprises had made a request for concentration camp prisoners. In their letters of request the enterprises had to state in detail which measures had been taken by them, even before the arrival of the prisoners, to guard them, quarter them, etc. I visited officially many such establishments to verify such statements. . . . During my official trips I was constantly told by executives of the enterprises that they want more prisoners."[26] Similarly, Oswald Pohl, the SS's chief of the entire slave labor program, testified that "nearly all arms producers came to my department to get labor from the concentration camps. Those who already employed such labor forces usually asked for an increase in their amount of prisoners."[27]

Members of the boards of directors at IG Farben, Siemens, Krupp, Volkswagen, and other major companies that desired large numbers of forced laborers personally took on the task of high-level liaison with the SS on labor matters. According to Pohl, senior corporate leaders with whom he personally negotiated for distribution of prisoners included IG Farben directors Otto Ambros and Fritz ter Meer, Siemens director Rudolf Bingel, and Volkswagen's Ferdinand Porsche.[28] Pohl's assistant, Karl Sommer, who was responsible for many of the day-to-day details of SS negotiations with corporate customers, left a similar affidavit. Sommer recalled SS agreements for provision of concentration camp inmates negotiated with Porsche of Volkswagen, director Paul Plieger of the giant Salzgitter steelworks and Reichswerke Hermann Göring, Fritz Kranefuss of the Dresdner Bank and the BRABAG energy syndicate, Siemens officer Friedrich Lueschen, and others.[29]

By the middle of the war, Germany had become dependent on forced labor in almost every important sector of its economy. Some 19.7 percent of the entire workforce in Germany was made up of forced laborers, later studies found. Most of them were concentrated in industry, where they made up almost a third of the workforce. Almost 40 percent of IG Farben's workers were forced laborers, including tens of thousands of inmates from Auschwitz and other concentration camps. At the Reich's vast holding company for aircraft and arms production, the Reichswerke Hermann Goering, no less than 58 percent of the employees were forced laborers.[*30]

These numbers reveal German industry's pervasive participation in human suffering on a massive scale. German business fed on forced labor throughout the war, exploiting the SS extermination-through-work programs to fulfill military production contracts. Contrary to postwar claims, the initiative for these programs came from industry, not from the Nazi state.

Private industry's quotas for steel production, aircraft, weapons,

---

* The true number of these workers will probably never be known, because postwar German industry has had a strong incentive to destroy all evidence of this aspect of its history. The estimate of the number of forced laborers most often cited is drawn from a 1944 end-of-year report to Hitler from Labor Minister Fritz Sauckel, where the minister proudly claims to have "recruited" 5.3 million foreign laborers, POWs, and concentration camp inmates for the Reich since his appointment as minister in 1942. The overwhelming majority of these "recruits" were in fact brought to Germany at gunpoint, as even Sauckel admitted. The 5.3 million figure was accepted by the prosecution at Nuremberg, in part because Sauckel could not deny having made it, and the enormous scale of the forced labor program eventually became an important factor in the court's decision to convict and hang Sauckel for crimes against humanity.

But 5.3 million forced laborers is clearly an underestimate. The Ministry for and other war materiel—and the labor requisitions necessary to produce these items—were determined through government/ industry consultation—not by Nazi fiat.[31] There were frictions, of course, and there was no shortage of Nazi bluster about the war emergency as the joint government/industry committees hammered out production schedules. In mid-1942, Hitler gave Albert Speer the task of coordinating German war production. "Realizing that he was no expert in industrial management, [Speer] personally went about selecting persons in industry who were considered experts by their peers," writes Edward Zilbert, author of the RAND Corporation's analysis of Speer's military production techniques. "The men were not made civil servants, but instead were recognized as honorary members of the Ministry, in a fashion analogous to the drafting of prominent industrial leaders in the United States for war production and attaching them to the government as 'dollar-a-year' men. . . . At the same time, [Speer] permitted these experts the greatest possible latitude in the operation of their particular specialities. This policy was given the name of self-regulation or self-administration of industry. That is, the responsibility for production programs rested on the individuals concerned with the actual production . . ." and not with the SS, the armaments ministry, or other German government agencies.[32]

German industry's unprecedented exploitation of slave labor became a crucial element of the Holocaust. But it is often overlooked in the popular imagination and in media portrayals of Nazi crimes, which tend to stress the role of the political police or the grotesque and horrifying extermination camps.

Forced labor in Germany can be divided into three overlapping

Armaments and War Production (the Speer ministry), for example, calculated at about the same time that 8.1 million foreign laborers had been compelled to work in German industry between 1942 and 1944. Sauckel's figures, as it turned out, concerned only the total number of work "slots" for forced laborers at the time of his report. He did not record statistics on those who had been worked to death or otherwise murdered, those who had escaped, or those who had been replaced for other reasons. Further, Nazi Germany had conscripted another five million laborers, most of them Poles and Jews, before 1942. These persons did not appear as statistics in either Sauckel's or Speer's report.

"This meant that a total of at least ten million foreigners were recruited" for labor, according to Edward Homze, a specialist in modern German labor history. "The [ten million] figure, however, must be considered a conservative estimate. . . . by the end of 1944, at the peak of employment of foreign workers, one out of every five workers employed in the Reich was a foreigner."

categories: press-ganged foreign workers, POWs, and concentration camp inmates. Each group is frequently described as slaves or even, as Ben Ferencz has eloquently described Jewish forced laborers, as less than slaves.[33] Still, there were important differences among these categories as far as the laborers themselves were concerned.

The foreign workers became what amounted to chattel slaves. Most were Poles, Ukrainians, French, and Russians, though virtually every European nationality was represented. The Nazi government effectively owned these workers and leased them out to private industry for war production or agricultural labor. "All of the men must be fed, sheltered and treated in such a way that they produce to the highest possible extent at the lowest conceivable degree of expenditure," Labor Minister Sauckel ordered.[34] (Sauckel refers here only to men, but in fact about 25 percent of these workers were female.) As ominous as Sauckel's phrase was, it nevertheless suggested that industry and the German state would make some minimal effort to keep most of these workers alive, if only to use them a bit longer. The workers were often euphemistically referred to as "foreign workers" or even as *gastarbeiters*—"guest workers."

In contrast, Jewish concentration camp inmates and many Soviet POWs were set to work in order to extract some labor from them during the process of destroying them. This procedure typically required between one and six months.[35] The SS, which ran the concentration camps, teetered uneasily between contradictory policies of deriving valuable labor from camp inmates or of simply murdering Jews and other targeted groups as quickly as possible, regardless of the economic consequences. In practice, the police agency pursued both ends simultaneously, selecting some inmates for death-through-labor while immediately killing others wholesale.[36] The prisoners worked to death were primarily Jews, though they were in time joined by groups of Polish and Russian POWs, homosexuals, "guest workers" who had attempted to escape from corporate work gangs, and others.

The Germans created a hierarchy among those they declared to be subhuman, and this structure—combined with heavy doses of police terror—contributed to keeping the system of forced labor and mass murder viable for several years. Typically, the Germans sent those at the bottom of the pyramid to be gassed: Jews who were old, weak, or very young; handicapped persons; and injured prisoners. They murdered millions of healthy Jews as well, as part of their Final Solution.

On the next step up, the SS in some cases preserved the stronger or more economically useful Jews, at least for a time. They worked these men and women to death in vast construction or mining projects; some were even used in less deadly skilled production tasks. On this same step could also be found many unskilled workers from the East, Soviet and French POWs, and others destined to be worked to death. Then came another group, which included laborers from Vichy France, Italy, Belgium, and Western Europe, who were ostensibly "volunteers" but who were in reality often captives of the German companies they served. There were still further variations of status and treatment among the foreign workers, depending upon the nationality and gender of the worker and the industry to which he or she was assigned.[37]

This system employed both coercion and reward within its cramped boundaries. Foreign laborers could gain improved rations or other benefits as a reward for increased production, for example. On the other hand, corporate managers could and often did push slackers and troublemakers down among the Jews and those marked for death.

As the war turned against Germany, the Labor Ministry turned to simple press-ganging of foreign workers. Sauckel told Albert Speer in early 1944 that "out of five million foreign workers who [recently] arrived in Germany, not even 200,000 came voluntarily."[38] Sauckel's ministry began manhunts and roundups in the Nazi-occupied areas that hit consumer-goods factories, workers' homes, theaters, and churches. In many instances, captives were shipped to Germany before they could bid good-bye to families or gather boots and winter clothes. Sauckel's men treated Ukrainian and Russian women with special cruelty; females surprised in their beds were in some cases loaded into boxcars and shipped across Europe wearing only their underwear or a nightdress, much to the amusement of the guards.

In Ukraine, the violence accompanying labor recruitment grew so severe that even the Nazis' own quislings complained to Berlin. One protest in 1943 from a German-sponsored local administration lists sixteen instances of violence during the supposedly voluntary labor enlistment campaigns; in one Ukrainian village that failed to meet its labor quota, the Germans murdered forty-five people, eighteen of them children between the ages of three and fifteen.*[39]

Industrial barracks for foreign laborers became de facto concentration camps, complete with barbed wire, searchlights, and armed guards hired by the companies. Corporate managers from Krupp, IG Farben, Daimler Benz, and similar companies enforced regulations under which laborers who "sabotaged production" or left their posts without permission were punished by beatings, hangings, or deportation to death camps. As the war ground down to its desperate conclusion, the rations for workers in some factories fell to fewer than 800 calories a day, guaranteeing epidemics, physical collapse, and a lingering death.

In the end, German industry worked several million of these men and women to death, and permanently injured millions more. One indication of the scale of the carnage can be gleaned from the difference between the number of job slots filled by foreign laborers and the number of workers actually shipped to fill those slots. If the German government reports are correct, German industry destroyed at least three million foreign workers between 1942 and 1944 alone. That, moreover, was before the winter of 1944-45, when mass starvation set in.[40]

The conditions in the SS concentration camps were still worse. In some, the starvation-killings began at least as early as 1939 and continued without respite for the rest of the war. There was no medical care to speak of, little clean water, no toilets, and no rest. Inmates who collapsed or failed to turn out for the morning roll call faced beatings or execution. There was no Red Cross, no correspondence with families, no redress for grievances, no holidays, no pay.

By the end of the war, the SS had created a network of twenty-three main concentration camps that served as the hubs of a submerged nation of prison laborers.[41] These camps included

* The Nazis' forced labor program actually contributed significantly to the growth of anti-Nazi resistance in the occupied areas, contrary to the Germans' intentions. That at least was the opinion of a committee of Wehrmacht generals, who petitioned Berlin during the war for a suspension of the labor program because it was sparking powerful opposition almost everywhere it was attempted. Similarly, the U.S. Army guerrilla warfare specialist Edgar Howell, who studied Nazi counterinsurgency tactics in the Ukraine during the development of the United States' own counterinsurgency doctrine, concluded after the war that "the German labor program . . . probably contributed more to the ultimate frustration of the German war effort in the rear areas than any one other policy."

Buchenwald in central Germany, Dachau near Munich, Mauthausen in Austria, Sachsenhausen just north of Berlin, and Auschwitz in Nazi-occupied Poland. These labor camps were usually separate from the extermination centers such as Sobibor, Treblinka, and Belzec. The sprawling complex at Auschwitz, however, combined slave labor and mass extermination, and the inmate population there was at times larger than that of a small city—at least until the gas chambers could catch up.

The main SS labor camps were surrounded by at least 1,000 *nebelgänger*, "side camps," established by German companies or by the SS.[42] These facilities came under the administrative umbrella of the main SS camps, but as a practical matter they were maintained and run by the corporation or SS unit sponsoring the side camp. The Krupp steelworks, for example, controlled fifty-five of these camps in the Essen area alone. The guards at each were Krupp company employees, not SS.[43] At some Krupp camps, inmates slept in barracks; at others, they slept in tents, in bombed-out buildings, or in piles of construction materials. The company kept 1,100 French prisoners of war in dog kennels at Noeggerathstrasse in Essen, where each six-foot-wide, three-foot-high enclosure provided sleeping space for five inmates. There was no water at the Noeggerathstrasse center.[44]

Health conditions were appalling. Many Krupp inmates had spotted fever, company doctor Wilhelm Jaeger reported to Krupp headquarters in 1942. "Lice, the carrier of this disease, together with countless fleas, bugs and other vermin, tortured the inhabitants of these camps." Nearly all of the inmates became infected with skin diseases as a result of the filthy conditions, Jaeger said. The shortages of food also caused many cases of hunger edema (the starvation affliction first seen in World War I camps), nephritis (kidney disease), and Shiga-Kruse disease (dysentery).[45] Most Krupp doctors refused even to enter the prisoners' camps, fearing that they, too, might become infected by the typhus and other plagues prevalent there.

Despite this widespread and often public brutality, industrial exploitation of concentration camp labor paradoxically provided an important element in the SS's cover story for the mass murders that it had begun at Auschwitz, Treblinka, and other killing centers. The relatively visible forced labor of camp inmates provided some answer, however unsatisfactory, to the nagging questions concerning what had become of the hundreds of thousands of German Jews who had been quite publicly deported to the East.

Meanwhile, the Allies' carpet bombing of Berlin and other cities accelerated German exploitation of forced labor. The Allied bombing—itself a war crime, some observers contend—tended to reinforce Nazi efforts to mobilize German society to carry out anti-Semitic measures, particularly the deportation of German Jews during the first years of the war. Clearly, Allied bombings did not *cause* the Holocaust. For Hitler, Himmler, Goebbels, and other committed Nazis, the elimination of Jews was desirable in itself, requiring no justification. But for millions of ordinary Germans—for the "bystanders," to use psychologist Ervin Staub's term—whose active and tacit cooperation was necessary to implement Hitler's genocidal designs, Allied bombing seemed to be a war crime against Germans that justified harsh retaliation against the supposed enemies in their midst, the Jews.[46]

The British bombing strategy was calculated to kill or maim as many German civilians as possible, to spread terror and demoralization, and to disrupt industrial production by burning the working-class quarters of cities to the ground. This was not pinpoint bombing of military-industrial targets, as Allied spokesmen frequently claimed at the time, but rather "a new offensive of which the primary target would now be the homes of the German people," according to strategic analyst George Quester. "No longer would a city in Germany be spared because of its remoteness from clearly military targets, [and] no longer would specific targets in large cities be aimed at, rather than the city as a whole. . . . The ferocity of the area assault was really now to be restrained only by technical or meteorological obstacles."[47] The U.S. in time adopted many aspects of the British air strategy, as demonstrated in the firebombing of Dresden and Tokyo and, later, in the atomic attacks on Hiroshima and Nagasaki.

In the opening years of the war, when the U.S. was still officially neutral, President Franklin Roosevelt had forcefully condemned as a war crime any airborne bombing of undefended cities and towns. Great Britain and the U.S. were signatories to the 1907 Hague convention, Roosevelt said, which had banned "attack or bombardment by any means whatever of towns, villages, habitations or buildings which are not defended." The phrase "by any means whatever" had been inserted specifically to deal with bombardments of undefended civilian targets from airplanes or—as had seemed more likely in 1907—from balloons.[48]

U.S. acknowledgment that bombing civilians constituted a war crime disappeared from Allied war propaganda after 1940. Great Britain and Germany began an escalating series of air strikes against one another in which each described its actions as legally sanctioned reprisals intended to deter attacks from the enemy. By the time the U.S. entered the war, the Allies had already concluded that British and U.S. air raids against German cities would remain among their most important tactics. Before World War II was over, both sides had killed hundreds of thousands of civilians in this fashion, each blaming the other for initiating the carnage. As the Allies gained control of the skies over Europe, they stopped claiming that these acts of bombing were crimes, while the Germans stepped up their argument that the raids on cities were serious violations of the rules of war. The Nazis used Allied airborne "crimes against Germans" as a compelling and seemingly convincing reply for German audiences to the Allied charges of Nazi crimes in the occupied territories.[49]

Thus, contrary to Allied intent, bombing raids tended to mobilize the German population (at least early in the war), reduce passive resistance to Hitler's policies among the German military and industrial elite, and facilitate a more dramatic shift toward total war mobilization than had previously been possible.[50] The U.S. Strategic Bombing Survey, for example, found that Allied bombing had little negative impact on German war production up to the fall of 1944, and that the earlier Allied raids were actually accompanied by increases in the level and efficiency of German war production.[51] (U.S. targeting of German oil and railroad centers in the last months of the war, in contrast, does seem to have had considerable military impact, though that conclusion remains in dispute among some senior bombing survey analysts.)[52]

Inside Nazi Germany, the Allied bombing fed directly into Hitler's war against Jews as well as into more conventional patriotic and civil-defense activities. Propaganda Minister Goebbels repeatedly linked the Nazis' genocide of Jews to Allied bombing in his broadcast speeches and in front-page editorials in the mass circulation weekly *Das Reich*. In May and June 1942, for example, shortly after the first 1,000-bomber Allied raids on Cologne and Essen, Goebbels declared that Germany would repay England "blow for blow" for the attacks on German cities. He went on to blame the purportedly "Jewish press" of London and New York for instigating Britain's "bloodthirsty malice" against Germany. These Jews, Goebbels continued, "will pay for it [the bombings] with the extermination of their race in all Europe and perhaps even beyond Europe."[53]

Goebbels was a master propagandist with a keen sense of Germany's mood and national culture. He clearly believed that the bombings fueled German mobilization for genocide, giving ordinary Germans a justification for the deportation of Jews, or at least a further reason to remain silent as government officials and Nazi activists did the dirty work. Further, the bombings provided an opening for Goebbels to publicly endorse race murder as a partial solution to Germany's problems—while at the same time maintaining the ability to deny that this was government policy when it was opportune to do so.

Otto Ohlendorf, a leading SS intellectual and ideologue, offered similar reflections during his postwar trial for the murder of 90,000 civilians by an *Einsatzgruppe* under his command. As Ohlendorf saw it, the Nazis' mass execution of Jewish children by gas and gunfire was directly comparable to Allied killings of German children by bombing. The murder of Jewish children, he claimed, was a "security measure," because otherwise "the children would grow up, and surely, being the children of parents who had been killed, they would constitute a danger no smaller than that of their parents." He continued: "I have seen very many children killed in this war through air attacks, for the security of other nations."[54]

The general public in Germany closely associated Jews with Allied bombing operations. At first, this took the form of popular hostility toward Jews as supposed foreign spies and manipulators behind Allied governments, a view that was systematically encouraged by the Nazi party and Goebbels's ministry. Indeed, diehard Nazis and their sympathizers to this day present Auschwitz and other concentration camps as "security measures" created in response to Allied initiatives.[55]

Later in the war, however, the reverse idea seems to have taken hold among the German public, much to Goebbels's distress. Beginning at least as early as the summer of 1943, confidential police reports indicate a widespread popular belief that Allied bombing was retribution for Nazi mistreatment of Jews. Many Germans believed that cities and religious bishoprics that had supposedly been less hostile to Jews would be immune to Allied air attacks.[56]

Similarly, many Germans throughout the war regarded Jews as useful hostages who could be employed to deter Allied bombers. In Schweinfurt, the elite Nazi intelligence service *Sicherheitsdienst* (SD) reported that "Many national comrades [i.e., Nazi party members] are of the opinion that the Jewish Question has been solved by us in the most clumsy way possible. They say quite openly that . . . our cities would still be intact if we had only brought the Jews together in ghettos [without deporting them]. In that way we would have today a very effective means of threat and counter-measure at our disposal."[57] These sentiments can also be found in letters sent by ordinary Germans to the Goebbels ministry, historian Ian Kershaw has reported. Such notes frequently included suggestions that Jews "should not be allowed in air-raid shelters but should [instead] be herded together in the cities threatened by bombing and the numbers of their dead published immediately after each air-raid," or that the "Americans and the British should be told that ten Jews would be shot for each civilian killed in a bomb-attack."[58]

None of these popular German myths had any basis in fact. There is no indication in available intelligence records that the Allies avoided bombing Jews in German cities, nor did the treatment of Jews in any German locality play a role in Allied targeting decisions.[59] In fact, Allied bombing may have taken a disproportionately high toll of Jewish lives, because the air raids often targeted factories and docks where the Reich had concentrated thousands of forced laborers. British raids in March 1943, for example, wiped out 100 prisoners at one Krupp works in Essen, killed 820 and wounded 643 at another Krupp plant, then killed 230 prisoners at the Heinkel aircraft works north of Berlin. A Krupp management report filed late in the war indicated that three company prison camps had been "partially destroyed," thirty-two camps had been "destroyed," and twenty-two had been "twice destroyed" by Allied bombing. All of the Krupp camps in Essen had been damaged, compounding the existing health and shelter problems.[60]

Allied bombing spurred German industry's demands for concentration camp labor and often encouraged public acceptance of mass slave labor as a legitimate war measure. For example, Hamburg was the center of German submarine production and a likely target for Allied bombers. The city prepared for the worst and undertook extensive civil defense measures, requiring millions of tons of cement, bricks, and other construction material.[61] The SS established a major concentration camp, brickworks, and stone quarry at Neuengamme, in Hamburg's suburbs, in part to meet this demand. In time, the Neuengamme forced-labor center became the flagship of the SS's commercial subsidiary, the Deutsche Erd- und Steinwerke AG (German Earth- and Stoneworks Company, or DESAG), which provided considerable income to the police agency. When the air raids came to Hamburg in 1943, the SS marched their tattered wretches out of the camp for new tasks in the center of town. There, tens of thousands of Germans saw forced laborers at work, excavating unexploded bombs, clearing rubble, and pouring new cement at docks and factories throughout the city.[62]

By the end of that year, the Hamburg city government and a score of private German military contractors acquired squads of prison laborers from the SS for use in heavy construction, clearing bomb damage, and similar tasks. Within a year, hundreds of large companies in northern Germany had their own forced laborers, and several factories maintained full-scale, company-owned concentration camps for these workers. By the end of the war, the Neuengamme camp alone had distributed more than 100,000 inmates to factories throughout northern Germany.[63]

City governments and private enterprises throughout Germany and the German-occupied territories followed roughly the same pattern of exploitation of concentration camp inmates for civil defense and bomb-clearing duties established by Hamburg. The Sachsenhausen camp fed much of Berlin's demand for forced labor, Dachau provided for Munich, and Buchenwald sent thousands of inmates to toil in central Germany.[64]

German subsidiaries of U.S. companies, including General Motors, Ford, and several oil companies, made extensive use of forced labor as well. Buchenwald concentration camp supplied labor to GM's giant Russelsheim plant (which the Germans converted to aircraft engine production for Junkers during the war) and to the Ford truck plant at Cologne.[65] International Red Cross records suggest that Sachsenhausen and Ravensbrück provided prisoners for the Ford and GM plants at Berlin and Brandenburg, but the evidence on that point remains fragmentary owing to the complexity of the German system for allocating forced laborers. It is clear, however, that camp inmates were used for bomb-clearing, clean-up, reconstruction, and other services essential to these factories, particularly during the later war years. Ford's German management also extensively exploited Russian POWs for war production work, which is generally considered a war crime under the Geneva conventions.*[66]

The prisoners' civil defense work became an important pillar of the system of mass forced labor in Germany. By bringing the violence of war home to German cities, the Allied bombings contributed substantially to the atmosphere where mass slave labor could be accepted as an "ordinary" fact of life by Germany's civilian population, at least for the duration of the war. If participation in genocide is in fact a learned behavior, as psychologist Staub contends, it was German industry's Aryanizations, forced labor, and and response to Allied bombing that helped infect ordinary Germans with this disorder. A somewhat similar pattern of "learning by doing" emerged among SS men and German soldiers on the Eastern Front, reports historian Christian Streit.[67]

Importantly, the framework of international law constructed by Robert Lansing, John Foster Dulles, and others in the wake of World War I obstructed efforts to confront Nazi crimes. Much of the expertise in international law in both the United States and the United Kingdom was centered in their foreign ministries, which dealt with international legal affairs daily. By the beginning of the Holocaust, these offices played a dominant and at times exclusive role in formulating international legal precepts and in defending the Lansing-Dulles status quo. The principal U.S. government experts on international law were usually staunch advocates of a cramped conception of legality that supported the Hitler government's claims that it could treat its civilians as it wished.

The international law experts at the U.S. Department of State

---

* These subsidiary companies were not run from Detroit during the war, as has sometimes been alleged, nor did the German subsidiaries repatriate profits to the U.S. or report their activities to the parent companies. It is nonetheless true that the German directors and trustees who did manage those factories during the war—who competed for political influence, war-production contracts, and supplies of forced laborers—were to a large degree the same German bankers, lawyers, and corporate leaders who had been appointed by the parent companies in the U.S. to run these facilities prior to the war, and who often continued in their posts after the conflict ended. In Ford's case, the ambitious Berlin attorney Heinrich Albert served as company director, tireless promoter of military production, and leader of Ford's effort to "de-judify" the company before and during the war.

considered German forced labor to be legal—or, perhaps more precisely, not illegal—under international law and custom as it then stood. They regarded it as inappropriate for outside governments to meddle in almost any form of exploitation that had been authorized by the German state, as long as it took place within the Reich itself. Further, Jewish (and other) activists in the West who sought to extend international legal authority to protect rights of slave laborers inside Germany were considered indirect threats to U.S. interests, because their proposals would require official U.S. recognition of the rights of laborers far beyond what the State Department regarded as prudent. Observers such as George Kennan, Joseph Grew, and other stalwarts of the "Riga" faction within the Foreign Service regarded almost any German depravity against the USSR to be legal, because they regarded the Soviet government to be an illegitimate regime that had refused to commit itself fully to civilized conventions.[68]

Most of these Western experts had difficulty coming to grips with the growing evidence of Nazi criminality. "It cannot be said that German policy is motivated by any sadistic desire to see other people suffer under German rule," wrote George Kennan in April 1941, when he was chief administrative officer of the U.S. consulate in Berlin. (He wrote this after almost two years of well-publicized pogroms in Poland and mass deportations of German, French, and Dutch Jews to concentration camps.) "Germans are most anxious that their new subjects should be happy in their care; they are willing to make what seems to them important compromises to achieve this result, and they are unable to understand why these measures should not be successful."[69] Kennan was out of step with President Franklin Roosevelt's hard-line policies toward the Nazis, but he was not alone.

The public pattern of Nazi crimes fell outside the realm of what these men considered criminal. For them, Germany's forced labor seemed little more than a particularly harsh solution to problems that were common to U.S. and German elites. They ignored the reports of the Holocaust that had begun to come out of Nazi-occupied Europe, and some even went out of their way to discredit accurate information about what the Nazis were up to.

7

No Action Required

BOTH BEFORE and during World War II, the U.S. State Department's European Division and legal advisor's office were dominated by specialists in U.S.-German and U.S.-Soviet relations who contended that American interests would be best served by staying out of the deepening European conflict. Until late 1941, they favored retaining cool but proper diplomatic relations with the Axis states. Like George F. Kennan, State's specialists discounted reports of Nazi atrocities, attributing those massacres that could not be ignored to the random violence of war. The "special measures" that the Nazis had publicly initiated against Jews were regrettable, they said, but were not a matter in which the U.S. government wished to interfere. The leaders of this informal grouping at the State Department included the chief administrative officer, Assistant Secretary Breckinridge Long;[1] the chief advisor on political affairs, James Clement Dunn;[2] wartime ambassador and political advisor Robert Murphy;[3] Undersecretary of State Joseph Grew;[4] legal affairs chief, Green Hackworth;[5] the chief for

Soviet and Eastern European affairs, Loy Henderson;[6] European expert H. Freeman Matthews;[7] European Division assistant chief John Hickerson;[8] Jewish affairs specialist R. Borden Reams;[9] and other senior staffers such as Elbridge Durbrow.[10] Each made his own interpretation of wartime events, of course, but taken together, these men became the core of a faction within the U.S. government whose conception of national security led them to deny the Holocaust, obstruct efforts to rescue Hitler's victims, and, later, to oppose trials of Nazi Germany's leaders.

The situation in the British Foreign Office was disturbingly similar. There the tone was set by Foreign Minister Anthony Eden, who was once described by his personal secretary Oliver Harvey as "hopelessly prejudiced" against Jews. "This is largely due to the blind pro-Arabism of the FO [Foreign Office] which A.E. [Eden] has never resisted," Harvey noted in his diary. "Indeed, he is a blind pro-Arab himself."[11] Harvey's comments were not entirely accurate: Eden's central concern was the maintenance of the increasingly rickety British Empire, and he was pro-Arab only to the extent that it served that end. Even so, there was an undertone of anti-Semitism in the British Foreign Office that frequently played a part in wartime policy concerning investigation of Nazi criminals and the rescue of Jewish refugees.

By the fall of 1941, reports of German atrocities were becoming harder to dismiss, on the one hand, and more useful as a theme in Allied propaganda, on the other. On October 25, 1941, just prior to the U.S. entry into the war, the Nazis' mass execution of prisoners in France led President Roosevelt and British Prime Minister Churchill to make an unusual joint public condemnation of German atrocities.[12] Within three months, nine European governments-in-exile in London established the Inter-Allied Conference on the Punishment of War Crimes and issued the first policy statement on the prosecution of Nazi criminals of the war. This Declaration of St. James, as it became known, accused Germany of creating in the occupied countries a regime of terror that was characterized by "imprisonments, mass expulsions, the execution of hostages and murder." Henceforth, they declared, one of the principal aims of the war should be "the punishment, through the channel of organized justice, of those guilty of . . . these crimes." The Nazis should be "sought out, handed over to justice and judged."[13]

Despite the tough language, the declaration was silent concerning those who were the central target of Nazi persecution: Jews. The earlier protests from Roosevelt and Churchill had also side-stepped mention of Nazi anti-Semitism, as had similar declarations from the Poles, Czechs, and the USSR. This "very delicate matter," as it was termed in a later official history of the United Nations War Crimes Commission, was temporarily finessed in the St. James Declaration by a claim by the signatory governments that "if no particular mention had been made of the suffering of the Jews, it was because it had been considered that such a mention would have been a recognition of German racial theories."[14]

The British Foreign Office meanwhile saw the Declaration of St. James—and, indeed, any public promise to punish war criminals—as a disturbing development. "This is getting pretty near the 'Hang the Kaiser' thing," a Foreign Office aide, Orme Sargent, told Eden. The declaration "throws the net very wide" in its definition of war crimes, commented another aide, Roger Makin, "and takes us into paths where we are very reluctant to tread."[15]

What Makin was getting at behind his garbled metaphor was a series of interlocking concerns over the implications for British foreign policy of Hitler's war crimes. First of all, Makin reasoned, too much attention to this issue by the Allies would surely increase pressure on Britain to loosen its immigration policies for Jews in Palestine—in fact, the pressure was already building from Jewish organizations at home and abroad. The Foreign Office had traditionally pursued a hard line against Jewish immigration to Palestine and was "terrifically worried," as Franklin Roosevelt put it,[16] about an Arab uprising against the British if it were permitted to increase. This concern was heightened by the situation in North Africa, where British troops were seeking a breakthrough against Rommel's forces and the Germans were trying to coax Arab leaders over to their side.

Second, and equally important, there was the controversial matter of how to go about ending the war. There was no doubt at the British Foreign Office that Germany must be defeated. But it was considerably less clear in 1942 exactly what the terms of an armistice might be. Foreign Office and War Office documents of this period reflect the assumption that there probably would not be an unconditional German surrender, but rather that Germany would likely retain control of a substantial portion of its occupied territories at the time of any negotiated peace agreement. That assumption, in turn, was tied up with what was probably the single most explosive strategic issue of the war: the possibility of a separate peace agreement between any one of the major Allies and Nazi Germany, perhaps on terms that would permit the Germans to continue their war against the USSR. A hard line on war crimes, particularly one that insisted on international trials for senior members of the German government, would inevitably undermine any British efforts to negotiate an armistice, the Foreign Office reasoned from its experience in World War I.[17]

Finally, a tough British declaration on this issue might lead to German war crimes trials of English POWs. The Germans had announced that they considered the British bombing of German civilians in undefended cities to be a war crime under the Hague convention, and even some Western legal experts were prepared to concede that they might be right. Hitler's government threatened to prosecute and hang captured British aviators if the bombings continued.[18] The Foreign Office and War Office agreed that this threat had to be taken seriously, notwithstanding Germany's own practice of bombing cities.

Consequently, the FO was determined to bottle up any public statements about putting Nazi war criminals on trial. They adopted a strictly "legalist" approach to the issue that narrowed the definition of war crimes as much as possible. As the British diplomats saw it, the legal concept of war crimes should be limited to a handful of specific acts that might typically be perpetrated by individual soldiers acting outside of orders, such as the torture or summary execution of POWs. The Allies' public promises to track down Nazis and bring them to justice might make good propaganda for the moment, in Eden's opinion, but in the end it would undermine his ability to negotiate with the Germans. It might also lead to a humiliation for the Allies like that which had followed World War I, where German war crimes suspects had evaded virtually all punishments. The Foreign Office contended that any wider definition of war crimes—such as including the persecution of civilians inside Germany—would enlarge the scope of international law to a degree that the British government might find itself in the dock after the war for its treatment of its colonies.

Much better, Eden thought, to avoid making inflammatory promises of justice that England was unlikely to keep. Eden's comments
at the St. James ceremony carefully separated British policy from
that of the rest of the Allies. While "welcoming" the declaration,
the foreign minister was at pains to point out that the promises of
punishment were an Allied, not a British, policy.[19]

In Washington, State Department officials responsible for monitoring conditions inside Nazi-occupied Europe sweated through the
summer of 1942 at their ponderous, ornate headquarters just down
the street from the White House. Offices there had once been large
and airy, but in wartime Washington much of the building had
been cut up into breathless cubicles without windows or ventila-
tion. Stale cigarette smoke sat for days, insinuating itself into
clothing, paperwork, and skin, as the temperature hung above 90
degrees for weeks at a time.

In late July, only six months after the Wannsee conference, the
State Department again received word of the systematic gassings of
Jews in Poland. German industrialist Eduard Schulte had smug-
gled new information concerning the murders into Switzerland
and arranged for intermediaries to pass his information to U.S. and
British authorities.[20]

The State Department's European Division was the first office in
the U.S. to receive this news. It made little impact. Elbridge Durbrow and R. Borden Reams were convinced that Hitler's mistreatment of Jews was limited to forced labor and petty persecution.
Schulte's message was a "wild rumor inspired by Jewish fears,"
they said, and refused to transmit his intelligence to President
Roosevelt or to Secretary of State Cordell Hull. Durbrow cited the
"fantastic nature of the allegation and the impossibility of our
being of any assistance" as reason enough to refuse to make the
message public.[21]

R. Borden Reams was at that moment engaged in burying a
second document, a letter from the U.S. embassy in London concerning a British proposal to create a joint Allied commission for
the investigation and prosecution of Nazi war crimes. British parliamentary leaders had been pushing for open debate on their
government's apparent failure to respond to the tide of Nazi atrocities, and there was some sentiment—though not a parliamentary

majority—that Great Britain should open Palestine to Jewish refugees. Anthony Eden was intent on heading off consideration of such radical measures, and he concluded that a war crimes commission would be an opportune way to avoid taking more concrete action. He told U.S. Ambassador John Winant of his dilemma, explaining that he would not be able to hold off a public debate much longer. He needed a quick U.S. approval of a paper war crimes commission to give him some ammunition to use once parliamentary talks began. Winant's wire to Washington asking for prompt White House approval ended up on R. Borden Reams's desk. Reams strongly opposed drawing any further attention to the Jewish refugee issue, however, and an international commission would do just that. He tucked the telegram away in the files without responding to it or sending word to the White House.[22]

The initiative for the joint Allied commission on atrocities, which would eventually become the United Nations War Crimes Commission, can be traced to a campaign backed by influential journalist Walter Lippmann and organized in large part by former League of Nations executive Arthur Sweetser. In late June 1942, Lippmann and Sweetser approached U.S. Assistant Secretary of State Adolf Berle with a series of suggestions on how to respond to the Nazi massacres earlier that month at Lidice, Czechoslovakia, where the SS had murdered 199 Czech men and boys in retaliation for the assassination of SS chief Reinhard Heydrich.

Lippmann and Sweetser proposed to attack Nazi terror by exposing Lidice and similar incidents to the intense glare of publicity, by military reprisals against Germany for crimes against civilians, by a public promise to try Germans for these crimes once the war was over, and by creation of a "central depository of the United Nations" to collect evidence concerning Nazi crimes. Allied intelligence services and underground movements throughout the Nazi-occupied territories should systematically send evidence to the depository, Lippmann and Sweetser contended, where "a thoroughly competent juridical committee" would examine each case and prepare it for trial after the war ended.[23]

The proposal was in a certain sense a continuation of the debate over crimes against humanity that had begun over twenty years earlier at the Paris Conference. Both Lippmann and Sweetser had participated in the Paris negotiations, Lippmann as a leading member of the embryonic U.S. intelligence organization known as "The Inquiry," and Sweetser as a member of the U.S. government's press bureau in Paris. At the time, both had specialized in the use of propaganda and psychological warfare in international affairs, and now both were convinced that tough, consistent psychological operations focusing on Nazi atrocities would undermine the Nazis' public support, contribute to Hitler's eventual downfall, and save lives in the meantime.

Berle liked the proposal. He did not think that the new commission and the associated publicity would end Nazi terror altogether, but he did think that it could temper German behavior and save innocent people. Berle made sure that the proposal immediately found its way to President Roosevelt.

The Lippmann-Sweetser forces appear to have made a nearly identical approach to Churchill. When the prime minister met with Roosevelt in Washington during late June, he proposed a United Nations Commission on Atrocities in language almost identical to what Berle had seen. FDR agreed with the thrust of Churchill's remarks, and the prime minister returned to London with an agreement in principle to move ahead quickly with the United Nations plan.*[24]

Although Eden was suspicious of the commission plan from the beginning, he sought to use it to derail more substantive action. In a War Cabinet meeting on July 6, 1942, Eden referred to recent papers by legal experts at the Foreign Office and War Office stating that however dreadful the Nazis' actions might be, they were "not recognized as crimes under international law to be dealt with and punished by a court," as the War Office put it. Further, the punishment of senior German leaders would be better determined at the end of the conflict, when it could be a bargaining chip during the negotiation of an armistice.[25]

Despite Eden's opposition, the Cabinet agreed in principle to back the "Commission on Atrocities" that had been outlined in the Churchill-Roosevelt meeting. The details of the new organization's responsibilities and of its role in Allied psychological warfare were to be hammered out at a special subcommittee meeting later

---

* The term "United Nations" as it was used during World War II referred only to the Allied countries fighting the Axis. The modern international organization called the United Nations was formed after the conflict was over.

that month. It was Eden, however, who dominated that subcommittee, and by the time the proposal had made it through his wringer, it had become ensnarled in bureaucratic contradictions and red tape that would take years to untangle.[26]

The subcommittee first dropped the recommendation that Allied intelligence agencies report evidence of war crimes to a central commission. Instead, fewer than a dozen commission clerks would be assigned to collect evidence of Nazi crimes throughout Europe and to report to each Allied country's courts and national war crimes investigators. The new group was "perhaps" to make recommendations on how to deal with captured war criminals, Eden's charter read, but at the same time, any "suggestion of some sort of international court for the trials of war criminals should be deprecated." The new charter stressed that it was neither "necessary nor desirable to create a new body of law, for war crimes are already sufficiently well defined."[27] Eden's narrow definition of war crimes and of Nazi culpability for them remained Britain's official policy.

Back in Washington, the State Department's legal advisor, Green Hackworth, lobbied to limit any international action on war crimes to the creation of a fact-finding body. Hackworth preferred that nothing be done to bring public attention to the question of whether most Nazi atrocities could actually be prosecuted as war crimes. He advocated a new name for the proposed commission, the United Nations Commission for the Investigation of War Crimes, to underline the strictly information-gathering role that the group was to play. The text of the formal U.S. endorsement of the commission (which was necessary to complete the earlier, informal Churchill-Roosevelt agreement) was at last relayed to London on the afternoon prior to Britain's parliamentary debate. There was no time at that point either for further discussion of the character of the new organization or for any but the most cursory briefings of the Dutch, Czech, Belgian, and Polish governments-in-exile, who had provided much of the initiative for the creation of the commission. The Soviet government was not informed at all.[28]

On October 7, 1942, British War Cabinet Minister Lord Simon announced the first formal initiative against Nazi crimes by the major Western Allies: the formation of the United Nations Commission for the Investigation of War Crimes (soon to be renamed the United Nations War Crimes Commission, or UNWCC). Its re-

sponsibilities, he said, would center on "naming and identifying
... the persons responsible for Nazi atrocities, and in particular
[for] organized atrocities." Conspicuously absent from Lord Simon's announcement (and from a similar declaration made by
President Roosevelt later that same day) was any indication of how
the commission's fact-finding task was to be carried out.[29] The new
UNWCC thus existed in a limbo without officers, structure, funding, staff, or any but the most vaguely defined mission.

The commission sidestepped the explosive question of whether
Nazi crimes against civilians inside Axis countries were considered war crimes within the scope of the UNWCC's responsibilities.
Instead, Lord Simon issued a tough denunciation of the Nazis
generally, leaving it to the public to assume that the UNWCC would
investigate the mass murder of German Jews.

In fact, however, these killings were not covered by the UNWCC
mandate, at least not as far as the British Foreign Office was concerned. Only two days after the October 7 announcement, the
secretary of the Jewish Aid Committee for Emigration in Zurich,
Leon Rosengarten, wrote to the Foreign Office seeking clarification
of Lord Simon's statement. "Is it to be understood," Rosengarten
asked, "that cruelties and massacres of stateless persons who formerly were German, Austrian and Romanian Jews are included" in
the new commission's inquiries? The British reply was vague and
noncommittal. The truth was that Eden's Foreign Office staff regarded the UNWCC as a means of erecting procedural roadblocks
to the actual prosecution of Nazis. Roger Allen of the Foreign
Office staff commented in the internal correspondence spurred by
the Rosengarten letter that this question was "surely too big for the
Commission: it is nothing less than a question of indicting Nazi
internal policy during the whole period of the regime. This is a
political, not a legal issue, and should be dealt with as such." It was
"difficult to envisage an appropriate tribunal" for bringing Nazis to
trial for crimes against German Jews, he continued. Further, because Jews did not represent a "separate nationality of their own,"
as he put it, it would be inappropriate for Jews as such to be
represented directly on the commission.[30]

By coincidence, it was at that moment that Adolf Hitler chose to
again discuss the treatment of German Jews during a radio address.
He was explicit: "In my Reichstag speech of September 1, 1939
[announcing the German invasion of Poland], I have spoken of two

things: First, that now that the war has been forced upon us, no array of weapons and no passage of time will bring us to defeat, and second, that if Jewry should plot another world war to exterminate the Aryan peoples of Europe, it would not be the Aryan peoples which would be exterminated, but Jewry. . . .

"At one time the Jews of Germany laughed at my prophecies," Hitler continued. "I do not know whether they are still laughing or whether they have lost all desire to laugh. But right now I can only repeat: They will stop laughing everywhere, and I shall be right also in that prophecy."[31]

Berlin radio boasted about Germany's "progress" in dealing with the Jewish Question, although the cover story remained that Jews were being deported for forced labor, not for extermination. The radio announced that western Poland would be "Jew free" by December 1942. The occupation government in Holland pledged to deport all Jews by June of the following year. The Germans had given Romania until December 1943 to remove all of its Jews, although, as a U.S. diplomatic report from London put it, "if the transportations go on at the present rate, the Romanian Government will have fulfilled its orders before then."

"In all parts of Europe the Germans are calling meetings, or issuing orders, to bring about what they call 'the final solution of the Jewish problem'," Ambassador Winant cabled to Washington.[32]

Meanwhile, Polish intelligence operatives working out of Switzerland provided a remarkably detailed accounting of the extermination and slave-labor program based on their penetration of the Nazi *Arbeitsampt* (Labor Office) in Warsaw. "The most convincing proof" of the liquidation of the Warsaw ghetto, they stated, "lies in the fact that for September [1942], 130,000 ration cards were printed; for October, the number issued was only 40,000." Polish sources in London also made public an accurate account of the deportations that specifically identified the death camps at Treblinka, Sobibor, and Belzek—the very existence of which were supposedly among the most closely guarded secrets of the Reich.[33]

As London and Washington manuevered, teams of Allied lawyers pieced together two activist committees that redefined the war crimes issue to cope with the unprecedented scope of Nazi atrocities. These were unofficial, semiprivate organizations, and their recommendations were not binding on Allied governments. Yet their work was crucial because it clarified the complex issues surrounding war crimes and established that as early as the summer of 1942, a number of influential jurists in Europe and the U.S. had concluded that the conventional interpretation of international law was not only ineffective against Nazi crimes, but actually provided an atmosphere in which they could prosper.

At Cambridge University, the long-standing, relatively conservative International Commission for Penal Reconstruction and Development established a committee to deal with the legal questions involved in putting Nazi officials and their collaborators on trial. Ten prominent European jurists volunteered for the task (seven of them would later represent their respective countries on the United Nations War Crimes Commission).[34] The Cambridge group recognized that although an ordinary person could readily understand the importance of prosecuting a particular Nazi responsible for, say, the murder-by-starvation of a thousand Polish Jews, it was quite another matter actually to bring that German to trial in an organized system of justice. In addition to the challenges of collecting evidence and establishing culpability that are part of any criminal proceeding, there were at least two more basic problems in any such case. First, there is the question of whether these acts violated any existing law; second, which court (if any) has jurisdiction to judge the alleged crime? These problems were particularly knotty in situations where the Nazis had "legalized" their acts of persecution by announcing laws and decrees that ordered deportations, compulsory labor, or seizure of property. Further, some mass murders of civilians appeared to be technically legal under existing international law, if the Germans could claim the killings came in response to guerrilla activities that had been specifically banned by the earlier Hague conventions.

The Cambridge Commission soon discovered that there was no clear authority for any court to try Nazis for many of the atrocities against civilians that had become the hallmark of German rule in the occupied countries. For example, after the war civil courts in the Netherlands could presumably try Nazis and their collaborators for conventional crimes such as murder, rape, or robbery that had taken place in the Netherlands. But the Cambridge group was not certain whether the Nazis' deportation of Dutch Jews and Resistance fighters to concentration camps was actually against

Dutch law, particularly since the Nazis had "legalized" such deportations as an emergency war measure. Dutch courts also might not have the necessary jurisdiction over acts that Nazis perpetrated against Dutch civilians outside of the Netherlands—such as those at slave labor centers or extermination camps in Poland. Even if the Dutch courts did have jurisdiction, it was unlikely that they could force German authorities to turn over suspects for trial.

Many types of Nazi abuses were almost certainly out of reach of civilian courts, the Cambridge group concluded. None of the Allied countries considered it proper to extend their national laws to offer protection to civilians *inside* Germany or the other Axis countries. As for international law, the prevailing conception of national sovereignty gave the governments of Nazi Germany and other Axis states virtually unlimited authority over their own populations. Jews and so-called stateless refugees in Germany, Austria, Hungary, Italy, and Romania enjoyed no real protection, under international law, from persecution by the governments of those countries. The same was probably true for civilians in Nazi puppet states such as Vichy France, Slovakia, and Croatia, though in those cases there was at least some grounds for legal debate.

Thus, Germans and German companies involved in forced labor inside of Germany seemed to be immune from prosecution, regardless of their depravity. True, German courts did have jurisdiction over crimes that took place inside Germany and over some types of crimes committed abroad by German nationals. But there was little hope at Cambridge that German courts would be capable of meting out justice in such instances.[35]

The possibility of using Allied military courts to try Nazi criminals presented other problems. The military courts of several of the occupied countries apparently lacked authority to try civilians at all, and in other countries they could try only those crimes that had a direct relationship to the military. Suspects who had abused Allied prisoners of war could be tried by a military court, but those who had abused civilian prisoners in the same prison camps might be out of reach.

Thus, the Nazis' systematic persecution of Jews and others trapped inside Axis countries appeared to be "legal." International law, as it then stood, seemed powerless to do anything. As a practical matter, almost any Nazis with the resources to hire competent legal counsel might be able to escape prosecution once the war was over, assuming they were captured and indicted in the first place.

Meanwhile, a second private committee attempted to articulate solutions to the problems that the Cambridge group had identified. This was the London International Assembly, a twenty-nine-member offshoot of the old League of Nations. Little is remembered of the London Assembly today, but in about a year's time during 1942 and 1943, the group sketched out much of the legal and theoretical foundation for the work of the United Nations War Crimes Commission and for the international trials at Nuremberg. Many of the innovations in international law—and even in international affairs—that were formalized at Nuremberg were first fully articulated by the London group.

A number of its more prominent members were also members of the Cambridge group, including Justice Marcel de Baer of the Belgian Court of Appeals, the legal advisor to the French provisional government, René Cassin, and Minister of Justice Victor Bodson of Luxembourg. The U.S. member was one of the most distinguished criminologists of his generation: Harvard University's Dr. Sheldon Glueck.[36]

The London International Assembly met in strict secrecy. Its purpose was to determine whether the activities of the Nazis that were then widely known—launching war in Europe, deporting civilians, and systematic persecution of people on the basis of race and religion—should be prosecuted as violations of international law rather than of the national laws of the various European countries. There were many related questions: Does international law apply *inside* of Nazi Germany and other Axis states? Should Nazis be acquitted if they had been acting under orders when they committed a crime? And what if particular actions—the summary execution of civilians who resisted German orders to evacuate their homes, for example—had been authorized by German law at the time they were committed? Was that, too, an "international" crime? For many people, the debates over these points might seem to be absurd technicalities when measured against the carnage that was then unfolding in Europe. But without answers to these questions, there was little hope that most Nazi criminals would ever be brought to trial.

In time, the London International Assembly put together a substantial legal argument. First, the group contended that the

Axis decision to launch a war in Europe was an international crime—specifically, a violation of the Kellogg-Briand Pact of 1928, by which Germany and most of the Allies (though not the United States) had pledged not to wage war on one another. Next, the London Assembly came out firmly in favor of the creation of a new international criminal court to try not only those cases that were outside the jurisdiction of the national courts of Allied nations, but also cases involving crimes that had been "legalized" by the Nazis inside Germany. The new court's proposed jurisdiction specifically included crimes committed against Jews and stateless persons. "[M]ere terminology or technicalities should not obscure the main issue," the London Assembly argued. "Covering their crimes under a cloak of apparent legality should not help the Nazis escape justice." The Assembly also helped pioneer the legal definition of what came to be called "crimes against humanity" by advancing the controversial concept that the men at the top of the German government who had "conceived and framed the plans of aggression, racial extermination, systematic terrorism, mass murder, deportations, economic looting . . . and the establishment of concentration camps" had violated such fundamental precepts of humanity that they could be put on trial on that basis alone.[37]

Next came the issue of the responsibility of heads of state for the actions of the countries they led. The prevailing legal doctrine, of which the United States had been the leading exponent, was that a head of state could not be put on trial in any international forum for the activities of his government, even if its actions had—as in the case of Hitler's Germany—"disregard[ed] the fundamental laws of mankind." Many experts contended that this de facto immunity for a head of state should be broadly interpreted: As some lawyers saw things, the field marshal of an army where war crimes had become routine practice could not be put on trial unless he personally ordered soldiers to commit them.[38] The London Assembly unanimously rejected this mainstream interpretation. In another important departure from the conventional wisdom, the group found that leaders were indeed responsible for the acts of their subordinates.

Finally, there was the problem of transferring captured war criminals from one jurisdiction to another, commonly (but inaccurately) called extradition. The Assembly agreed that it was possible for war criminals to exploit "technical imperfection[s] in legislation" of the various Allied countries in order to find refuge, and that the formal extradition process was so slow and cumbersome that it could not handle the thousands of cases that an effort to prosecute Nazi criminals would inevitably involve. Therefore, the Assembly suggested, ordinary extradition should be reserved for ordinary criminal cases, while new procedures should be adopted to handle suspected war criminals. The Allied countries should formally agree to "transfer" accused war criminals to one another without the usual extradition hearings, while any peace treaty with the Axis powers should force them to turn over suspects to any Allied country.[39]

The Assembly's conclusions were based in large measure on Sheldon Glueck's writings and arguments. Glueck contended that international law should not be regarded as fixed and unchanging, nor should it be reduced to simply those measures that countries had previously agreed to by treaty. For one thing, technological advances in war-making had made obsolete many of the specific protections for civilians and soldiers written into earlier international treaties. Similarly, a criminal regime was unlikely to agree to treaties that made its own activities illegal. If the international community waited for criminal regimes to declare their own actions improper, there would be no international law at all.

Glueck contended that international law could be better understood as a body of commonly recognized practices that had evolved slowly over centuries and that was continuing to evolve. In this sense, international law could be compared with some aspects of English common law, which does not specifically prohibit murder, yet regularly does justice in murder cases on the basis of legal precedent and custom. The basis for international law is not simply treaties, Glueck argued, but rather "moral law, the conscience of mankind and custom."[40] He stressed that technicalities should not be permitted to obstruct articulation of fundamental principles of justice, particularly in the case of Nazi war criminals. Yet, one problem was already evident: If action against state-sponsored atrocities was to be based on the conscience of mankind, who was to judge what that conscience might be, and on what basis?

Back at the State Department in Washington, Durbrow and Reams believed that they had put the lid not only on the new intelligence from Europe about Hitler's genocide, but also on the British proposal for a joint Allied war crimes commission. The two men apparently believed that they could continue more or less indefinitely to respond to news of Nazi atrocities by filing it away. Durbrow tried to shut down reports of the Holocaust that were now beginning to arrive with disturbing regularity from American embassies in Europe. He targeted Switzerland first, where the information from the German industrialist Schulte had originated. He attempted to bar the U.S. legation there from using State's telegraph network to send further messages concerning Nazi atrocities "unless, after thorough investigation, there is reason to believe that such a fantastic report has in the opinion of the Legation some foundation or unless the report involves definite American interests," as Durbrow put it.[41]

But in late November 1942, Assistant Secretary of State Sumner Welles returned from a journey to Europe and confirmed to American Jewish leader Rabbi Stephen Wise that the evidence of systematic extermination of Jews was inescapable. It "confirms and justif[ies] your deepest fears," Wise recalled Welles as saying; "there is no exaggeration."[42]

That same evening, Rabbi Wise called a press conference in Washington. He reported that a presidential envoy had confirmed reports concerning the Nazis' systematic execution of the Jews of Warsaw and their efforts to wipe out all Jews in Europe. Wise also stated that the Nazis were paying bounties for Jewish corpses to be "processed into such war-vital commodities as soap, fats and fertilizer."[43]

R. Borden Reams at the State Department seized upon Wise's chilling claims concerning human soap and fertilizer in an attempt to undermine the rabbi's credibility. Within hours after Wise's appearance before the press, the State Department issued a statement distancing itself from Wise and refusing to back up his contention that Hitler had begun to exterminate the Jews of Europe.[44]

Reams, Durbrow, and their counterparts in the British Foreign Office discredited and undermined each new report of Nazi atrocities. Shortly after the Wise press conference hit the news, the Foreign Office sent a note to the British news media acknowledging that the government was "soft-pedaling the whole thing as much as possible for the minute," though they denied the media's suspicion that the Foreign Office was trying to kill the story altogether. A corresponding series of later notes can be found in U.S. files, and they use remarkably similar language. There, State Department political officer A. E. Clattenburg confirms that the department's press chief, Michael McDermott, made "suggestions and recommendations" to the United Press news service in New York "that atrocity stories be 'soft-pedaled.' "[45]

But the story was out. In the wake of Wise's press conference, there was a rush of public attention to Nazi atrocities, but there was little agreement about what should be done about them. The most obvious response—the rescue of European Jews, Romanis, Communists, and other Nazi victims—was also the least palatable politically, owing to fears in Washington and London of an anti-Semitic and anti-Communist backlash if Jewish immigration to the West increased.

Soon the British Foreign Office hit upon a plan of offering a tough verbal protest that would for the first time stress Nazi persecution of Jews. Like earlier measures, the intent here was to present the image of taking action against atrocities in order to avoid taking more substantial steps. The early drafts of the new protest were quite hard-hitting: The U.S., Britain, and the USSR each acknowledged that the reports from Europe "leave no room for doubt" that the Nazis were "now carrying into effect Hitler's oft repeated intention to exterminate the Jewish people of Europe." Poland, it was said, had become a "slaughter house [where] the ghettoes are being systematically emptied of all Jews . . . none of those that are taken away are ever heard of again." The strongest among the deportees were worked to death, the draft declaration continued, while the weak were deliberately massacred or left to die of exposure.[46]

Reams again sought to block any official statement on the issue. "I have grave doubts in regard to the desirability of issuing a statement of this nature," he argued in internal discussions. The atrocity reports were "unconfirmed" and based largely on the information from Schulte, he said. Publication of the protest as it stood would "support Rabbi Wise's contention of official confirmation from State Department sources. The way will then be open for further pressure from interested groups for action which might affect the war effort"—an obvious reference to the growing demands for immigration relief. "A statement of this kind can have no good effect and may in fact induce even harsher measures toward the Jewish population. . . ."[47]

Reams intervened with the British Foreign Office as well. "No one questions that the Jewish peoples of Europe were being terribly oppressed and undoubtedly great numbers of them were being killed in one way or another," he told his counterpart in London. But issuing a protest would be a mistake, because the U.S. and British would thereby "expose themselves to increased pressure from all sides to do something more specific to aid those people."[48] Better to say nothing at all, Reams contended, and if the British had no choice but to speak out, then better to say as little as possible.

The maintenance of official doubt concerning the reality of Nazi genocide seems to have been crucial to Reams in order to accomplish the European Division's professional tasks, which consisted in important part of denying visas to Jewish refugees. He insisted that the phrase noting that there was "no room for doubt" concerning the Nazi extermination campaign had to be deleted. The problem, as he expressed it in memos, was that Jews (and others) would believe the reports of the genocide in Europe if this protest was issued, and would pressure their governments to do something about it. For Reams, the main problem was public protest in the West, not Hitler's Holocaust in Europe. His comments on Schulte's information are particularly revealing. For the State Department's Jewish affairs expert, Schulte was the cause of most of the trouble, not the death camps. Reams made his point, and the U.S. version of the protest dropped the assertion that there was "no room for doubt" concerning extermination.[49]

The three major Allied powers finally issued their first formal protest against Nazi crimes against Jews on December 17, 1942. The three governments "reaffirm[ed] their solemn declaration to ensure . . . that those responsible for these crimes shall not escape retribution," and that each state would "press on with the necessary practical measures" to track down and try Nazis.[50]

Despite this assertion, however, virtually all practical measures by the U.S. and the United Kingdom to end Nazi crimes or rescue refugees ground to a halt with the publication of the December 17 protest. The State Department's Theodore Achilles was almost blasé about it: "In due course our Government will no doubt be asked to appoint representatives to sit on the [war crimes] Commission," he told staffers in mid-December. But in the meantime, "no action is required."[51]

8

Katyn

NAZI ATROCITIES helped shape the alliance against Germany, and did so in ways that Allied governments on both sides of the cold war have often preferred to forget. For the Soviets, war crimes policy became one of several "barometers" of Western commitment to the alliance with the USSR. Because Nazi atrocities had seriously compromised much of the top strata of German society and many technocrats and notables of a half-dozen other traditionally anti-Communist European states, Allied plans to purge Nazi criminals and collaborators from positions of influence in the wake of the war opened the door to fundamental changes in European society. The USSR's relentless drive to destroy Nazism root and branch reflected a desire for justice, to be sure, but it was also a national security strategy that exploited the weaknesses of its opponents. Thus, the Soviets saw a hard Western line on Nazi crimes as an indication that the alliance with the USSR was solid. They interpreted Western waffling on this issue, on the other hand, as a warning that some new intrigue against the USSR might be afoot.[1]

There was more to this than Machiavellian politics. By early 1942, the Nazis had wreaked destruction in the USSR that went well beyond the understanding of most people in the West. They killed millions of Soviets, looted everything from machines in factories to the gold from the mouths of the dead, and destroyed all that they could not cart away. The Soviet public's demand for harsh punishment of Nazis was deeply felt and would last for generations.

Premier Josef Stalin's primary concern at the time was with the war, and he vitally needed the U.S. and Britain to fight it. But Stalin believed that a powerful, submerged faction of Western politicians and businessmen was manuevering behind the scenes to keep the U.S. out of the war or to reach a separate peace with the Nazis that would turn Germany's full force to the struggle on the Eastern Front. Stalin was well aware of the utility of such separate peace tactics: His own 1939 pact with Hitler was an attempt to reach a similar deal with the Germans at the expense of the Poles and the British. Stalin saw that those in the West who favored a separate peace might be able to change the course of the war practically overnight. A separate peace early in the conflict could lead to the military defeat of the USSR; later in the war, it would almost certainly leave a bloody stalemate and a permanent crisis on Moscow's western borders. Not surprisingly, then, the Soviets consistently pushed the U.S. and the U.K. toward tough public covenants requiring unconditional surrender from Germany and punishment for every senior Nazi. These Allied stands would almost certainly restrict Eden's (and others') ability to make deals with the Germans.

Thus, there was a deadly chasm between the Allies' public condemnation of Nazi crimes—words that they saw as strengthening the Alliance—and their frequent failure to rescue Jews from Hitler, the deeds that seemingly would be a logical consequence of their declarations. It was the fate of the perpetrators of genocide, not of the victims, that held the attention of policymakers in both the East and the West. Often the true force behind the Allies' responses to Nazi crimes was their geopolitical strategy and desire to retain legitimacy in the eyes of domestic constituencies. Concern for the prisoners of the Reich was considerably farther down the list.

During the months of the 1939–41 Hitler-Stalin pact, the USSR had said nothing about the Nazi persecution of Jews and, indeed, very little about the Nazis' brutal anti-Communist actions. But Soviet radio broadcasts accusing the Nazis of atrocities against Jews and Soviet citizens began almost immediately after the Germans invaded the USSR in the summer of 1941 and remained a major Soviet theme for the remainder of the war.

The Germans replied with a radio and propaganda campaign of their own. The SS and local Ukrainian collaborators discovered a series of mass graves of Ukrainian rebels that the Soviet secret police, the NKVD, had murdered in Lvov, Vinitsia, and Dubno, near what is today the Ukrainian-Polish border. The Germans aggressively publicized the NKVD killings to divert attention from the new executions undertaken by their own *Einsatzkommando* squads.[2] The Soviets vehemently denied the German claims, but the Germans turned out to be telling the truth about the NKVD murders, even as they lied about their own.

Isolationists in the U.S. seized upon the news of Soviet atrocities as a means of discrediting information about Nazi pogroms against Jews and as further proof of their long-standing contention that the U.S. should stay out of Europe's war. The *Wall Street Journal* editorialized that it would fly in the face of morals if the U.S. offered any aid to the Soviets in fighting the Germans. Harry S Truman, then a senator from Missouri, went a step further: The U.S. should extend aid to Europe, he contended shortly after the Nazi invasion of the USSR, but give it to "whatever side seemed to be losing. If we see that Germany is winning we ought to help Russia, and if Russia is winning we ought to help Germany and in that way let them kill as many as possible."[3] Truman's rhetoric changed after the U.S. entered the war, but the inter-Allied mistrust continued to run deep.

The offer of a separate peace to the British from Hitler's heir-apparent Rudolf Hess became the focus of one of the first inter-Allied controversies over response to Nazi crimes. Hess, long one of Hitler's most senior lieutenants, had flown to Scotland in 1941 in an ill-fated attempt to initiate clandestine peace negotiations. The British government claimed that Hess was clinically insane, and Hitler disavowed Hess and his mission. To the Soviets, though, Britain's refusal to hang Hess forthwith suggested that he might someday be used as a bargaining chip in negotiations with Hitler. In the fall of 1942, *Pravda* ran a series of bitterly worded editorials calling on the British to try Hess as a war criminal. How could British promises concerning tough punishment of Nazi criminals be taken seriously, *Pravda* asked, when Britain had already become "a place of refuge for gangsters"?[4]

The British ambassador to Moscow, Archibald Clark Kerr, soon confronted Stalin on the Hess issue. "Stalin felt extremely bitter toward Hess and during the conversation gave the impression that he was still suspicious that the British might use Hess to make some kind of deal with Germany at Russia's expense," Kerr told the U.S. chargé d'affaires in Moscow, Loy Henderson. But Kerr insisted that public accusations in *Pravda* were no way to deal with an ally, and he eventually succeeded in extracting an unusual admission from Stalin that perhaps the party newspaper had made a mistake in publicizing the Hess situation.[5]

Soviet Foreign Minister Viacheslav Molotov brought up the war crimes issue again in a mid-November meeting with Kerr. Molotov bridled at Kerr's suggestions that the fate of Axis leaders be settled through political negotiations and that any discussion of war crimes trials should wait until after the war was over. Molotov instead favored what Henderson described as "full dress political trials apparently similar to the Soviet purge trials of 1936-37 [except] on an international scale."[6]

Molotov particularly pressed Kerr for a statement clarifying British and U.S. relations with the French navy commander, Admiral Jean Darlan, whom the Soviets regarded as a harbinger of another Western deal with the Axis. Darlan was a key figure in Vichy France, even leading the collaborationist government's negotiations with Hitler. During the late-1942 Allied landing in French North Africa, however, he ordered French forces not to oppose the invasion. In exchange, he was named military governor of North Africa and received U.S. assurances that he would be recognized as a senior leader in any postwar French government. As far as Molotov was concerned, the "political situation in North Africa . . . had been confused" by the Allies' deal with Darlan. The admiral may have double-crossed the Nazis, but he remained a hard-line anti-Communist, and Molotov objected to his role in North Africa. An American diplomatic report on the Kerr-Molotov encounter underlined the value the Soviets placed on U.S. relations with Darlan. Molotov "said the matter was of great significance. . . . The Soviet Government . . . took a deep interest in this subject." It would be "embarrassing," Henderson stressed, "if the situation with regard to Darlan should develop into another Hess issue."[7]

In the Western view, the handling of Hess and of Darlan were two entirely different matters. To the Soviets, though, both incidents looked distinctly like backstage intrigues with the enemy, most likely at Soviet expense. Either way, a few weeks later a French rightist conveniently assassinated Darlan, while the admiral was in U.S. custody, thus ending the conflict with the Soviets for the time being. (The controversy over who was truly behind this assassination remains unresolved to this day.)[8]

Darlan's mantle in the West was then taken up by General Henri Giraud, who had much the same politics as his predecessor but who was less compromised by cooperation with the Nazis. One of Giraud's principal political and financial sponsors in Western circles was Allen Dulles,[9] who had recently returned to his old haunts in Switzerland, this time as an intelligence specialist with the Office of Strategic Services (OSS) and as a personal representative of President Roosevelt.

Dulles plowed his energy into a series of political operations, many of them abortive, designed to exploit the cracks and fissures in Hitler's empire. Dulles believed that he understood the political pressures within Germany's ruling coalition particularly well. He rejected what he regarded as poorly informed anti-German stereotypes that indiscriminately lumped together Nazi ideologues with German bankers and industrialists, with the military leadership, and with the old German aristocracy. Dulles contended that each of these groups had its own interests that were not necessarily the same as those of Hitler's government, particularly if the war turned against Germany. He believed that the Allies should make maximum use of these splits in fighting the war against Germany and— more controversially—in advancing U.S. interests in postwar Europe.

In time, Allen Dulles and his brother John Foster Dulles became two of the more influential advocates of separate peace tactics in elite U.S. circles. The wartime hatred of Hitler and the political dynamics of the U.S. system ensured that when a separate peace was publicly discussed at all, it would be stated in terms of support for Polish nationalists fighting both Hitler and Stalin, rather than as a settlement with Germany as such. The message was much the same in geopolitical terms, though, assuming that Nazi

Germany could be convinced to join a *cordon sanitaire* against the Soviets, to step back from its announced intention of obliterating Poland, and limit the Reich to the German-speaking territories it had already captured. Thus John Foster Dulles—already a senior foreign policy expert for the Republican party—publicly declared in the spring of 1943 that Poland was the place to draw the line against the Soviet Union, and that the Soviet response to such measures was, as Gabriel Kolko has written, "the test of future relations with Russia throughout the world."[10] Allen Dulles meanwhile opposed FDR's agreement to seek an unconditional surrender of Germany, calling it a propaganda disaster that made most clandestine negotiations to split the Axis impossible.[11]

Allen Dulles put himself forward as the U.S. contact point in neutral Switzerland for disillusioned Axis officials interested in speaking confidentially with the West. Prior to Dulles's arrival in Switzerland, U.S. and British intelligence had seen Germany almost exclusively as a target for espionage, not for political operations of the sort Dulles favored. (This quite un-British hesitancy to undertake clandestine political maneuvers was in part due to London's concern over Stalin's suspicion of such activities, and in part the result of a notorious 1939 double-cross at Venlo in which the Germans had used a promise of secret contacts with an ostensibly anti-Nazi underground to capture two British agents.)

"Dulles was the first [Allied] intelligence officer who had the courage to extend his activities to the political aspects of the war," wrote Hans Gisevius, a former Gestapo officer who became a secret liaison between Dulles and a small group of anti-Hitler conservatives. "Everyone breathed easier; at last a man had been found with whom it was possible to discuss the contradictory complex of problems emerging from Hitler's war."[12]

During the winter of 1942, the SS sent German socialite and businessman Max Egon von Hohenlohe to meet Dulles in Bern and feel out the possibilities for a U.S.-German rapprochement. Dulles and von Hohenlohe had known one another for almost twenty years, and their reunion in Switzerland was congenial. Dulles went to considerable lengths to convince the SS that he favored a rapid settlement with Germany. He told von Hohenlohe that he was "fed up with listening all the time to outdated politicians, emigrés and prejudiced Jews," according to captured German reports on the meeting now in U.S. archives. Germany would inevitably become a "factor of order and progress" in Europe following a settlement of the present conflict, Dulles indicated, and should be permitted to keep Austria and several other territories that Hitler had already claimed. Dulles "did not seem to attach much importance to the Czech question," the meeting notes continued. "He favored enlargement of Poland eastwards [into the USSR] and the maintenance both of Romania and a strong Hungary as a *cordon sanitaire* against Bolshevism and Pan Slavism. . . . He regarded a greater Germany, federated on American lines and allied to a Danube confederation, as the best guarantee for the orderly reconstruction of Central and Eastern Europe."[13]

Dulles told the SS envoy that "due to the inflamed state of public opinion in the Anglo-Saxon countries," the U.S. government would not accept Hitler as a postwar chief of state. But it might be willing to negotiate with a National Socialist Germany led by another powerful Nazi, such as SS chief Himmler. In a second meeting, Dulles advised Hohenlohe that the SS should "act more skillfully on the Jewish Question" to avoid "causing a big stir." There would be no war crimes trials for Nazis, obviously, with Himmler as head of state.[14]

The interesting question is whether Dulles's comments were in fact an initiative toward a separate peace or a psychological ploy designed to sow discord in the German camp by setting Himmler against Hitler. One bit of evidence that supports the latter theory is that Dulles was accompanied in his talks by Edmond Taylor, one of the OSS's most prominent anti-Nazi psychological warfare specialists.[15] Taylor made aggressively pro-Nazi and anti-Semitic comments during the talks in an apparent bid to secure SS cooperation, according to the meeting notes, and these were quite out of tune with Taylor's other work of the period.

The most likely explanation for the contradictions surrounding the Hohenlohe affair is that each side was attempting to deceive the other while at the same time leaving the door open to substantive negotiations should an opportunity arise. That is, both envoys sought approval from their superiors for what would otherwise be treasonous contacts with the enemy by describing them as covert operations designed to foster discord in the enemy camp.[16] Meanwhile, however, each representative and perhaps both intelligence agencies had an overriding agenda as well: They wanted the negotiations for a separate peace to be carried through to completion, leading to German concessions in exchange for peace in the West and a free hand to continue war against the Soviets.

Recently opened OSS archives make clear that Dulles favorably reported to Washington on an offer from Hohenlohe at the same time Hohenlohe was reporting to the SS that the initiative came from Dulles. On the U.S. side, the OSS cables show that Dulles lobbied on Hohenlohe's behalf,[17] ensuring that the proposal would be considered directly by President Roosevelt,[18] and continued to pursue contacts with Hohenlohe and other SS representatives for the remainder of 1943.[19] While Dulles was not blind to the possibilities of using the negotiations simply as a means of sowing dissension in the SS,[20] all of the available telegrams indicate that he saw Hohenlohe's proposal as a realistic and desirable basis for U.S. strategy in Europe. On the German side, captured SS records and the memoirs of Walter Schellenberg (a Himmler protégé and the chief of the SS foreign intelligence service) each indicate that the proposal was seriously considered by Himmler himself.[21] Himmler was tempted, by all accounts, but in the end failed to muster the courage necessary to overthrow his Führer.

Exactly what Stalin knew of Dulles's talks with Hohenlohe will remain unknown until further Soviet archives concerning World War II are opened. It is now certain, however, that the USSR had its own high-level espionage networks inside the German, British, and French intelligence agencies, and had gained limited access to U.S. and Canadian political and intelligence circles.[22] There are hints that the Soviets may have cracked the relevant U.S. codes that would have permitted them to read Dulles's messages for themselves.[23] (Stalin's correspondence with Roosevelt during Dulles's later negotiations with the SS suggest that he could have been reading Dulles's dispatches to Washington before FDR himself did, for example.)[24] And the USSR had opened its own clandestine contacts with the Nazis at Stockholm.[25] Taken as a whole, it seems likely that the Soviets had an opportunity to pick up rumors and, perhaps, solid intelligence on Dulles's meetings with the German representatives.

The fact that Dulles and the OSS went to considerable lengths to keep the negotiations secret from Stalin also suggests that the agency wanted to keep the door open to serious negotiations with Nazi Germany for a separate peace, if only as a contingency for the future. If all that Dulles and the OSS had desired was a psychological ploy to disrupt Nazi unity, then why not inform the USSR of what was up, and in so doing avoid any risk of damaging the strategic U.S.-Soviet alliance? The OSS and the NKVD shared secrets concerning other highly sensitive intelligence operations, but there is no evidence in the available records that the OSS attempted to do so in this case. That it did not seems most consistent with the conclusion that OSS leaders believed that separate peace negotiations could not be completely ruled out.

Meanwhile, the publicly announced East-West agreements to punish Nazi criminals provided an important countercurrent to the separate peace intrigues in Bern and other European capitals. The Allies pointed to the new UNWCC as proof of their commitment to purge Nazis, while the Soviets had mounted a large, relatively sophisticated effort to investigate Nazi crimes at least as early as the spring of 1942. (The USSR lays claim to having been the first of the Allies to formally call for international trials—not just investigations—of Nazis.)[26] One week after the British announced the creation of the UNWCC in early October 1942, the Soviet Union convened its own war crimes panel, the ponderously titled Extraordinary State Commission for Establishing and Investigating the Crimes of the German Fascist Occupiers and Their Collaborators and the Damage Caused by Them to the Citizens, Kholkhozes, Social Organizations, State Enterprises and Institutions of the USSR—more simply, the Extraordinary State Commission (ESC).[27] There was no formal affiliation between the ESC and the UNWCC, but the timing of the announcement and subsequent events made it clear that the Soviets' intent was to establish their own national commission to participate in the United Nations' work.

Stalin suggested that the ESC contribute to the UNWCC intelligence information on Nazi crimes—a significant concession that went well beyond what either the U.S. or Britain was then prepared to do. But there was a catch: The Soviets wanted an agreement from the Western Allies that the fate of Nazi criminals would not be left to a "political decision" after the war, as Eden favored. Instead, Stalin insisted that senior Nazis (such as Hess) should be tried by an international tribunal as soon as they were captured. The British would not agree, but negotiations continued toward formal Soviet membership in the UNWCC.

For a few months during the winter of 1942–43, it seemed as though these negotiations might bear fruit. By the middle of

March, internal correspondence between the State Department's legal advisor's office and Secretary of State Hull noted that "the Soviet Government . . . has now agreed to the immediate establishment of the [War Crimes] Commission and the appointment of a representative."[28] The U.S. should set about picking its own representative for the organization, legal advisor Green Hackworth indicated, because a formal meeting of the commission would take place soon.

But three weeks later, the Nazis scored a major propaganda coup against the Allies that was to shake the alliance to its foundations and leave a lasting mark on the postwar politics of Europe. On April 13, the German press agency reported that German army reconnaissance units had discovered a mass grave of thousands of slain Polish army officers in the Katyn Forest, near what had once been the Soviet-Polish border. The Germans charged that during the 1939 division of Poland between Germany and the USSR, the NKVD had arrested about 15,000 Polish officers, held them in POW camps for six months, then systematically murdered most of them in the spring of 1940. The German announcement said that 10,000 Poles were buried at Katyn, though later reports indicated the number of dead at Katyn was closer to 4,400, with about 10,000 more Polish prisoners still unaccounted for.[29] Either way, it was a massacre.

The early Soviet replies to the story claimed that the Polish officers had never been in Soviet hands at all, that the graves discovered in the Katyn Forest were relics of a medieval monastery. When that story fell apart, the Soviets came up with a new explanation, which remained their official version for the next forty-seven years. The Soviets conceded that the Polish officers had been arrested by the NKVD in 1939 and that a number of them had been interned in a prison camp near Katyn. But they were not murdered by the NKVD, the Soviets insisted. Instead, the Nazis were said to have captured the Polish prisoners during the German invasion of the USSR in 1941, a year after the Germans said they had been killed. It was the Nazis who murdered the Polish officers, just as they murdered so many others. The Germans concocted the "Katyn hoax," as the Soviets called it, as a means of splitting the Allies.*[30]

* On April 12, 1990, Soviet Premier Mikhail Gorbachev told Polish President Wojciech Jaruzelski during his state visit to Moscow that the NKVD had in fact murdered the Polish prisoners at Katyn, and had also killed all but a handful of the 10,000 missing officers. A radio broadcast by Tass, the official Soviet news

There were several problems with the Soviet claims. Some of them were apparent at the time, and others were discovered later. First, there were the documents found on the corpses. The Nazis displayed hundreds of personal letters, diaries, Soviet prison ID papers, newspapers, and other bits of material that they found on the bodies, all of which offered mute testimony to the fact that the prisoners had been murdered in the late spring or early summer of 1940, a year before the German invasion of the USSR. The method of execution also pointed to the NKVD: The prisoners' hands had been tied behind their backs with cord manufactured in the USSR, then shot, usually with a single bullet in the back of the head. The significance of this modus operandi was brought home when the Germans discovered other corpses at the camp, these clearly dating from the mid-1930s when the camp was under NKVD control, where the identical method was employed. Other forensic techniques available at the time pointed to 1940 as the time of the murders, though that date could not be established with the degree of scientific certainty that would be possible today.[31]

The Nazis' propaganda minister, Joseph Goebbels, knew that a psychological weapon of unprecedented power had fallen into his hands, and he was determined to exploit it to the fullest. The NKVD crime had the potential not only to split the Polish resistance movement beyond repair, but also to split the Western Allies away from the Soviets.

Goebbels knew that the Poles had been bitterly factionalized since the beginning of the war. The bulk of the Polish armed forces were loyal to right-wing General Wladyslaw Sikorski, who had established a British-funded Polish government-in-exile in London. But Sikorski's government was divided over which country was the greater threat, Germany or the USSR. More than a few Polish military officers considered the Soviets to be the greater long-term danger to Poland, despite Germany's ongoing occupa-

---

agency, stated that "According to ... recently discovered documents, those [15,000] prisoners were handed over to several commands of the NKVD, the then-security service, in April-May 1940, and were never mentioned anymore in area reports or [POW] statistical data. The sum of evidence points to the responsibility for the crime resting on the then-leadership of the NKVD department. The Soviet side expresses deep regret over the tragedy, and assesses it as one of the worst Stalinist outrages." At last report, the USSR had located two other mass graves of the missing Poles, in addition to the one at Katyn, and had begun to exhume them.

tion and near-obliteration of their country. This faction was rooted in the military juntas that had ruled Poland for most of the 1930s, when Poland had promoted itself in world politics as the linchpin of a *cordon sanitaire* of hostile states that could contain and some-day destroy Bolshevism in the USSR. Meanwhile, at the opposite end of the political spectrum, there was a smaller, well-organized group of Polish Communists and left-wing nationalists who had found refuge in Moscow. Despite nominal support for Sikorski's London government, most of the Moscow-based Poles had little affection for the general and described his right-wing allies as fascists.[32]

The discovery of the Katyn atrocity proved to be the breaking point. The London Poles at first refrained from denouncing their nominal ally, the USSR, but pushed hard for a full-scale Red Cross investigation of the Nazis' claims concerning Katyn. Then a previously unknown Moscow-based group, the Union of Polish Patriots, announced that Sikorski had been compromised by fascists and that his government no longer commanded the support of free Poles. On April 19, a front-page editorial in *Pravda* denounced the London Poles as "Hitler's Polish collaborators." Laying responsibility for the Katyn slaughter at the feet of the Nazis, the editorial asserted that the Polish exile government's request for a Red Cross investigation was a "direct and obvious assistance to the Hitlerite provocateurs." The Soviet news agency Tass went further: The fact that both the Germans and the London Poles had requested a Red Cross investigation was "grounds for surmise that the said anti-Soviet campaign is conducted upon a preliminary accord between the German occupationists and the pro-Hitler elements in Sikorski's ministerial circles." Two days later, the Soviets severed diplomatic relations with the Sikorski government.[33]

These events rapidly affected Allied war crimes policy. The Soviets now placed new conditions on their participation in the UNWCC. They wanted more seats on the commission's governing committee to offset what they perceived as British (and Polish) domination of the organization, in part owing to fears that the UN commission could become a sounding board for anti-Soviet publicity—perhaps even investigations—focusing on NKVD massacres in Eastern Europe. The British had allocated seats on the commission to each of the British Commonwealth countries involved in fighting the Axis—Canada, Australia, India, and even

South Africa—thus obtaining a clear majority of UNWCC seats and a virtual veto over the organization's affairs. Meanwhile, the London-based (and British-backed) Sikorski government continued to represent Poland.

To offset this perceived imbalance, the Soviets now demanded that several of their constituent republics—the Ukrainian SSR, Byelorussian SSR, and the recently appointed Soviet governments in Latvia, Lithuania, and Estonia—should each be accorded a voting seat on the Commission. As the Soviets saw things, this arrangement would guarantee them treatment no different from what the British had ensured for themselves.[34]

It was a sophisticated political manuever and a good example of how Allied response to Nazi war crimes was often held hostage to political concerns. In 1939-40, under a secret codicil to the Hitler-Stalin Pact, the Soviets had regained control of Latvia, Lithuania, and Estonia, which they had lost in the 1917 revolution. The U.S. and the United Kingdom had refused to recognize this new arrangement, however, holding that these small states remained independent countries. By insisting that representatives of these Soviet Baltic republics be seated at the UNWCC, the USSR hoped to take a long, quiet step toward international recognition of Soviet rule of these territories. What Stalin was now saying, in effect, was that the British would have to pay a diplomatic price for their war crimes commission.

Negotiations broke down after months of maneuvering on the representation issue. The British refused to accept the Soviet plan, and the Soviets refused to participate in the UNWCC. This split had symbolic and political consequences that extended well beyond the immediate question of who would sit on the UNWCC. It became one of the first major splits in East-West attitudes toward the treatment of Nazi criminals and, equally important, toward the Allied management of Germany after the war.

The USSR brought this tragedy upon itself. The NKVD's mass murder of Polish officers had no doubt seemed necessary to some of the more bloodthirsty elements in Soviet security in 1940, when the Polish officer corps represented the most direct threat to continued Soviet control of eastern Poland. Like the Nazis, Stalin and his security forces may have also learned genocide by doing it, considering their record during the earlier purge trials and the famine in the Ukraine.[35] But the NKVD's crime at Katyn, and

Stalin's refusal to take responsibility for it, seriously undermined Allied unity against Nazi Germany at a time when the survival of the USSR itself was at stake. The atrocity helped lay the groundwork for the cold war, and in time became an enduring symbol of Soviet-Polish enmity.

For his own reasons, Stalin had insisted that unity against Nazi atrocities be an important test of inter-Allied relations. Now that he had it, the most serious blow to his strategy had come, not from the Germans, but from his own security service.

In early March 1943, just as the British deal with the Soviets for participation in the UNWCC was about to unravel, the former U.S. ambassador to Hungary, Herbert C. Pell, shared an informal lunch with President Roosevelt at the White House. Pell had been without an assignment since the U.S. broke diplomatic relations with Hungary in late 1941, and he inquired of Roosevelt when he might be put back to work.

Herbert Pell was an anti-Nazi hard-liner who had been a valuable FDR ally in prewar struggles inside the U.S. government over what to do about Germany. He was also FDR's personal friend and former Democratic party chairman in Roosevelt's home state, New York. Shortly after the lunch, Roosevelt sent a note to the State Department: "Do you think there is some place where we could use Herbert Pell? As you know, he is a very devoted friend to the Administration."[36]

Pell was not well liked at the State Department. He was an outspoken liberal, intolerant of State's ponderous bureaucracy, and inclined to go outside of channels to make his diplomatic reports directly to the President. When the President had inquired the previous December whether there might be an opening for Herbert Pell, Assistant Secretary of State Sumner Welles curtly noted in an internal memo that as far as he was concerned there was "absolutely no place" for Herbert Pell in the department.[37]

When the President's note arrived seeking a new appointment for Pell, the department's political advisor, James Clement Dunn, first attempted to shuffle him off into negotiating relief for Jewish refugees. This was a dead-end position, in Dunn's eyes, where administration loyalists could be safely dumped in order to leave the real business of international politics to the professionals in the department. But that failed to pan out.

Meanwhile, the legal advisor at State, Green Hackworth, had been seeking an American representative to the UNWCC. He wanted someone who could "weigh the political implications involved" in decisions concerning war crimes issues, but most of the reliable nominees were considered to be too old for a wartime assignment in London, and the younger men declined the appointment.[38] Dunn thought he was solving two problems with one appointment when he settled on Pell for the UNWCC post, despite Hackworth's objections.[39] On June 14, the President formally offered Herbert Pell the office of U.S. representative to the United Nations War Crimes Commission. He quickly accepted.

9

Silk Stocking Rebel

H ERBERT PELL cut an impressive figure. At six feet five inches and 250 pounds, rich and handsome, he stood out in any crowd. The Pell family fortune can be traced back to the seventeenth-century land grants that gave his ancestor, Sir John Pell, much of what is today the Bronx and Westchester counties, New York. Pell's mother, heiress to the Lorillard tobacco empire, was also a major investor in New York real estate and industry.[1] For Herbert Pell, Rockefellers and Morgans were nouveaux riches.

Pell had what some called a "difficult" personality: obstinate, more than a little egocentric, convinced of both the rightness of his cause and of his tactics for achieving success. Put more charitably, he was a leader, determined to shape events in accord with his vision of right and wrong. And he was, as it turned out, one of the handful of men in the U.S. government who were brave and bullheaded enough to risk their careers to bring Nazi criminals to justice at a time when such actions were unpopular with most of the policy elite. In the end, Herbert Pell was to sacrifice his diplomatic career rather than abandon his commitment to justice.

He had from an early age shown a rebellious streak. He had dropped out of Harvard to pursue a life of travel and study of the arts. By the 1920s, Pell had lost whatever faith he may have once had in the American business community. "The destinies of the world," he later wrote, "were handed them on a plate in 1920. Their piglike rush for immediate profits knocked over the whole feast in nine years. These are the people, with an ignorance equalled only by their impudence, who set themselves up as leaders of the country." Pell thought both aristocrats and big businessmen to be "totally selfish," as Arthur Schlesinger, jr., has put it, "but the aristocrat at least thought of his grandsons, while the bourgeois thought only of himself."[2]

Pell's family estate at Hopewell Junction, N.Y., was just down the Hudson River from the Roosevelt home at Hyde Park, and the two families had been friends and occasional business associates for generations. Franklin Roosevelt encountered "Bertie" Pell, as FDR called him, at Harvard, where Roosevelt had completed college in three years at about the time Pell dropped out. Later, Pell emerged as an important supporter of Roosevelt's progressive faction of New York Democrats and served briefly as a congressman from Manhattan's silk-stocking district. In 1936, Roosevelt named Pell vice chairman of the Democratic National Campaign Committee. After the victory, Roosevelt appointed Pell to sensitive ambassadorial posts in Portugal and later Hungary.[3]

FDR's conflicts with the Foreign Service dated back to the first days of his administration. The disputes had often centered on what to do about Nazi Germany, and sometimes Pell had been involved. Roosevelt had come to distrust the European Division of the State Department, which disagreed with FDR's politics and often pursued its own agenda regardless of directives from the White House. State's Eastern European specialists, including William Bullitt, Loy Henderson, and George Kennan, leaned toward a strategy of rapprochement with Hitler and an anti-Bolshevik *cordon sanitaire* with Germany against the Soviets. Roosevelt favored normalized relations with the Soviets—in late 1933, he sent the first U.S. ambassador to Moscow since the 1917 revolution—and as the decade wore on, he increasingly viewed the German-Japanese Axis as the world's most dangerous imperial force. Pell agreed, strongly backing the President in his controversies with the Foreign Service. FDR even went so far as to dissolve State's Division of Eastern European Affairs, believing that the group was disloyal to the administration and was undermining efforts to strengthen international cooperation against the Axis.[4]

Pell had clashed with State's bureaucracy during his ambassadorial appointments, and the conflict began anew following his selection for the UNWCC. Pell and Green Hackworth failed to get along almost immediately. The problem was partly one of style, partly one of jurisdiction. As Pell saw things, he was working directly for the President, regardless of the administrative technicalities of his appointment. As State's legal advisor, Hackworth may have had some sort of bureaucratic oversight of Pell's paperwork, but beyond that he was a hindrance to actually getting anything accomplished at the UNWCC. "Hackworth was well named," Pell remembered from his first encounter with the man. "He was a little, legal hack of no particular attainments. He was manifestly not born a gentleman and had acquired very few of the ideas of a gentleman on his way up in the world. His manners were bad, his fingers were dirty [and] he was clearly unused to good society."[5]

Hackworth saw things differently. It was he who was responsible for oversight of the U.S. government's interpretations of international law, including war crimes policy. Pell may have been FDR's friend, but he knew little about international law or U.S. foreign relations. For his part, Pell considered his lack of legal training to be a strength in the search for justice for the victims of the Nazis— a laughable proposition in Hackworth's book. The legal advisor had seen political appointees like Pell before. He didn't like them, and he had outlasted them all, at least so far.

Hackworth turned sixty the year that FDR appointed Pell. He was by then a puffy, fussy man, a confirmed bachelor with a monkish devotion to the law and, at least as far as the available record indicates, a complete absence of social life outside of his workplace.

By almost all accounts except Pell's, Hackworth was a highly competent lawyer. He had been a legal specialist at State for more than twenty years by the time of his encounter with Pell, and chief legal advisor, reporting directly to the secretary of state, since 1931. During those years, he had emerged as the government's preeminent specialist in international law, the drafter of numerous treaties and international agreements, and a frequent delegate to international legal conferences. From 1937 on, Hackworth had served simultaneously at his State Department post and as the U.S. judge at the Permanent Court of Arbitration at the Hague.[6]

The State Department had begun publishing Hackworth's masterwork, an eight-volume *Digest of International Law*, in 1940.[7] There, Hackworth sought to articulate all of the precepts of international law as he saw them, complete with thousands of case citations, excerpts from famous judgments, and an extended commentary. In 1943, just as the controversy over the legal response to Nazi crimes was coming into focus, the State Department published Hackworth's volume six, on war and war crimes.[8] In his text Hackworth presented the conservative consensus on international law. He embraced the legal status quo, reviewing dozens of complex arbitration cases concerning ownership of goods in occupied territories; the proper and improper uses of a flag of truce; the subtle differences between an armistice and a peace treaty insofar as they concern disputes over fishing rights; and hundreds of other technical aspects of international legal custom and precedent.

Hackworth focused on what had long been the most active aspect of international law, the impact of war on commercial relations. This included subjects such as licensing companies under the Trading With the Enemy Act and similar legislation—John Foster Dulles's specialty—and the complexities of determining whether a multinational corporation was a "foreign" company subject to government seizure. Throughout his presentation, Hackworth contended that as far as international law was concerned, modern war should be regarded as an interlude between periods of conventional commerce. The important thing was to maintain a predictable structure for commercial relations during a conflict (taking into account the inevitable military restrictions on trade, of course) and to establish an orderly procedure for picking up the pieces once the shooting had stopped.

The concepts of a "crime against humanity" or of human rights were absent from Hackworth's text. So was any substantial consideration of the possibility that the international community might justly hold a government responsible for atrocities against its own people. He saw heads of state as beyond the reach of international law. It is clear in hindsight that the Nazis' extermination camps had rendered key elements of Hackworth's work on war crimes obsolete at the time it was published. Nevertheless, *Hackworth's Digest* (as the work came to be known) was embraced at the time as the definitive U.S. interpretation of international law.

Herbert Pell had different ideas. He requested that a Hackworth rival, Sheldon Glueck of the London Assembly project, be appointed as his chief assistant and legal advisor for the UNWCC. Glueck was probably the most authoritative legal voice in the U.S. then arguing for tough measures against the Nazis. Hackworth rejected Glueck immediately, without explanation. Instead, he saddled Pell with Lawrence Preuss, a young university lecturer whose qualifications for the new post reportedly included a confidential agreement with Hackworth to channel derogatory information about Pell back to Washington.[9]

Pell prepared to leave for Europe immediately following his appointment. At the last minute, however, the British government requested a delay of several weeks. The agreement with the Soviets for joint action on war crimes had come unraveled in the wake of the discovery of the Katyn massacre, and both sides were still attempting to patch things up before formally convening the commission. Pell was left cooling his heels at the Knickerbocker Club in New York, where he took up residence while waiting to depart.

This delay stretched on for months, and Hackworth used the time to undermine and discredit FDR's nominee.*[10] More than a year had passed since Churchill and Roosevelt's 1942 agreement on a war crimes commission, but the organization was still without a clear charter and had yet to meet for the first time.

The Nazi offensive against the peoples of occupied Europe meanwhile continued to gather force. Himmler had decreed in the fall of 1942 that all Jews in concentration camps within Ger-

---

* Prior to Pell's selection, for example, the British and the Americans had agreed that the U.S. commissioner would chair the new UNWCC. But when Pell was named, Hackworth cabled to London that this arrangement was off: British representative Cecil Hurst should now be the chair. Ordinarily, protocol called for the announcement of two such decisions—Pell's appointment and the U.S. reversal on the chairmanship—to be transmitted to the British in two separate cables, to avoid embarrassment to the U.S. nominee. Instead Hackworth put out the news in a single statement; a diplomatic insult that was apparent to both Pell and the British.

many's borders were to be driven out, resulting in mass deportations to the concentration camp at Auschwitz and to the pestilent Lublin reservation. The SS began gassing at Majdanek and then at Auschwitz, Belzec, Treblinka, and Chelmno. The extermination centers killed tens and even hundreds of thousands of people each month.

The murder program accelerated in the spring of 1943. German troops entered the Warsaw ghetto and killed thousands of Jews in street fighting. In the south, the Nazis began deporting Greek Jews from Salonika to Auschwitz. In the north, they deported Dutch Jews to Sobibor, gassing about 34,000 people there as they arrived. The SS also arranged a special transport for 3,000 Jewish mothers and children from the Netherlands; they murdered all of them.[11]

In June, Himmler formally ordered the liquidation of all Jewish ghettos in Poland and in the Nazi-occupied regions of the USSR. With this act, the last possible cover story for the Nazi genocide crumbled. Before, all Jews within Germany and its occupied territories were to be deported east, supposedly for labor and resettlement. Now the eastern territories, too, were to be made *Judenrein*—"cleansed of Jews." There was simply no place left where the millions of deported people could be placed.

Herbert Pell was still in the U.S. awaiting instructions to depart, and the State Department continued to reject reports of genocide in Europe. Pell met with Secretary of State Hull in August, but Hull seemed unable to change the situation. Pell then protested directly to Roosevelt. It was "time to get to work at once, to show the enemy we mean business." An active war crimes commission would help "check at least some of the outrages." He was eager to leave for London as soon as possible.[12]

"Why can't we get Herbert Pell off for London?" FDR wrote to Hull a few days later. "Is there any reason for the continued delay?"[13]

Meanwhile, unbeknownst to Pell, the British had decided to go ahead with an organizational meeting of the war crimes commission without the Soviets. The Foreign Office cabled Washington twice in September asking that the meetings necessary for the actual formation of the commission begin by the end of the month. Both communiqués ended up on Hackworth's desk: he kept them secret from Pell until months later.

A new problem had arisen, as Hackworth saw things. Popular

anger against Nazi atrocities was pushing the Allies into a more sweeping grant of authority for the UNWCC than had been contemplated in Eden's narrowly worded declaration of the previous October. Hackworth's vision of the commission was like Eden's: It would conduct a study, hold a few hearings, prepare a report, and then fold up its tents without disturbing U.S. or British policy on war crimes issues. FDR's decision to appoint Herbert Pell only made Hackworth more determined to keep the commission toothless.

Even though the UNWCC had not yet met, the scope of plans for its operations gradually grew as Nazi crimes continued unabated. The British Foreign Office had from the beginning used the UNWCC as a shield to ward off criticism of its failure to pursue refugee relief, to open Palestine to Jewish immigration, or to take other measures to slow Nazi atrocities. As public protests became more desperate and pressing, the Foreign Office made increasingly inflated claims concerning the UNWCC's on-paper authority to confront Nazi crimes. Finally, the Foreign Office had to push for a series of quick UNWCC organizational meetings to head off parliamentary criticism that the government had done little to stem atrocities.

Hackworth's apprehensions about the organization increased as fast as the group's on-paper authority. "The plans now outlined by the British are quite different from those which the [State] Department apparently understood at the time that Mr. Pell was designated," Warren Kelchner of State's International Conferences Division warned Hackworth. Its potential impact on foreign affairs had increased well beyond the original expectations, he continued. What could be done about Pell?[14]

Hackworth played for time. He quietly arranged for the U.S. ambassador in London, John Winant, to attend the first UNWCC meetings in Pell's place. There were only two conditions: "Our representative [Pell] is not to become the chairman under any circumstances," Hackworth cabled to London, and Pell was not to be informed of the gathering until after it was over.[15]

The first UNWCC meeting took place on October 20, 1943, and consisted of formal introductions of representatives from the various countries and discussions of arrangements for future meetings. Ambassador Winant represented the U.S. There was no voice from the USSR. Herbert Pell remained in New York, unaware that the gathering was taking place.[16]

The central purpose of the group, the UNWCC agreed, was to "investigate and record the evidence of war crimes," identifying the individuals responsible for specific crimes whenever possible. The commission was then to report to the governments concerned the cases where there appeared to be "adequate evidence" for prosecutions—to serve as what amounted to an international grand jury for war crimes trials.[17]

Pell soon learned of the meeting and descended on Washington in a fury. Hackworth was out of the office that day, but Pell cornered a junior assistant and gave him an earful. He glowered down at the young man and said he now knew of the earlier telegrams from London. He demanded to know when he would be given permission to leave and when he would be formally briefed by the department on his mission. "He [Pell] stated that in the absence of instructions, he would, should the occasion arise, act on his own initiative, and would use 'a strong hand,' " the shaken assistant noted in his memo to the files about the confrontation.[18]

Pell dismissed the narrow, legalistic approach to war crimes that was then, and would remain, the State Department's official view of his mission. Instead, he linked his role on the commission to the broader issues of the war and to the unresolved question of what was to be done with Germany following the defeat of Hitler. Pell warned that German business cartels had been instrumental in Hitler's rise to power and in the execution of the war, and unless this seeming monolith was dismantled, it would provoke yet another war after Hitler was gone. For Pell, a sweeping program of war crimes prosecutions of Germany's economic elite was not simply a matter of justice, it was necessary to ensure the security of postwar Europe.

"I believe that the business of my Committee will be to take its part in the great effort to prevent a third war, rather than merely to act as an instrument of vengeance for past wrongs," he wrote to Secretary of State Hull in November 1943. "The first thing is to make it clear to every last German in the world that war is not a profitable business. Unless prompt and severe justice is done they will go back to their old ideas.

"Five years after the end of this war, Germany, unless tremendously restrained, will be relatively far stronger than it has ever been in its history. Every other country in Europe has been bled white and will take anywhere from thirty to fifty years to recover. It is almost impossible to believe that Germany will be reduced to anything like that extent.

"I hope that you want the War Guilt Commission [i.e.: the UNWCC] to go as far as it can and to be as tough as possible" in addressing this problem, he told the secretary of state.[19]

Pell's dispute with Hackworth was more than just a clash of personalities. Pell called into question a decade of Hackworth's study and writing, challenged his interpretation of judicial issues, and defied his status as the principal American arbiter of questions of international law. Worse, Pell's analysis had a certain compelling logic to it. That Pell's disrespect could come from a man whom Hackworth regarded as an overbearing political appointee and a diplomatic naif proved to be reason enough for Hackworth to seek to engineer the unruly ambassador's dismissal, regardless of what the President wanted.

The U.S. war crimes commissioner returned to his temporary roost at the Knickerbocker Club in New York and from there booked passage to London on the *Queen Mary*, in those days traveling in camouflage paint and under an assumed name. He finally arrived in London in mid-December 1943, some fourteen months after the announcement of the UNWCC and a year and a half after its creation had first been approved by Churchill and FDR. In the interim, the Nazis had murdered at least two million people.

As news of Nazi genocide accumulated in the West, the press, the Jewish community, and the emigré governments in London slowly pushed the British and U.S. governments toward an aggressive UNWCC capable of doing something—few were sure exactly what—about German atrocities. The UN commission was the only inter-Allied group that had specific responsibility for collecting evidence of Nazi crimes. Sophisticated observers knew that the commission was also the only logical place to resolve the unsettled legal questions concerning how to put Nazis on trial, particularly for crimes against refugees or against Jews in Germany.

There was hope in many quarters that a strong, active war crimes commission could become an anchor for psychological warfare campaigns aimed at saving at least a few of those the Germans had slated for destruction. Of course, no threat is likely to have deterred the Nazi hard core from destroying Jews. Such Nazis embraced their own martyrdom on behalf of the Führer and the *Volk*. "All of us assembled here want to remember that we are on Roosevelt's war crimes list," the German governor of Nazi-occupied Poland, Hans Frank, boasted to a gathering of SS men shortly after an early Allied declaration against Nazi atrocities. "I have the honor of being at the top of the list. We are all accomplices in a world historical sense."[20]

At the same time, though, many other Germans and officials of the Axis satellite states were less committed to genocide. Indeed, some had second thoughts. "We have some dispatches to the effect that German officers in the Lowlands [the Netherlands and Belgium] are attempting to get 'certificates of good behavior' from the local inhabitants," U.S. intelligence reported as early as the spring of 1943. "This is evidently inspired by the announced determination of the United Nations to punish those guilty of war crimes."[21] Apparently, these German officers were responding to Allied radio broadcasts denouncing Nazi atrocities, despite the weaknesses in the Allied effort and Germany's draconian punishments for listening to foreign broadcasts.

Equally important, strong public action by the UNWCC during the war would almost certainly arouse further demands from the citizens of Allied countries for substantial action against Nazi crimes. R. Borden Reams's fear of such a reaction, it will be recalled, had led him to attempt to suppress news of the Holocaust.[22]

Presidential advisor Adolf Berle and some members of the OSS became convinced that Allied psychological warfare stressing just and sure punishment for war criminals would slow the pace of Nazi crimes and undermine support for the Germans in Hungary, Romania, and other Axis states. But Green Hackworth used legal technicalities to spike the OSS effort—twice.[23]

The British War Cabinet again confronted the question of whether to go ahead with a tough campaign aimed at deterring Nazi atrocities in the fall of 1943, when British forces discovered a new mass murder on the Greek island of Kos. German forces had arrested and massacred about 100 Italian military officers whom they feared might soon defect to the Allies. Winston Churchill seized on this news and, at the next meeting of the British War Cabinet, proposed that the Big Three issue a declaration at the upcoming Allied conference in Moscow pledging to pursue Nazi war criminals to the "uttermost ends of the earth."[24]

By late 1943, the fact that the Germans had embarked on a campaign of mass murder and persecution of unprecedented scope had already become clear. The Jewish, Russian, and Polish dead each already numbered in the millions. Yet Churchill focused on these 100 Italian officers. Why?

Part of the reason can be traced to the war situation. The Allies had invaded Italy about one month previously. They had taken Naples, but much of the country was still in German hands. The massacre in Greece offered an opportunity to demonstrate the Nazis' treachery against Italians, their one-time friends. Churchill's firm response to the atrocity also sent a message that the Allies might be willing to treat former Axis soldiers with some lenience if they, too, abandoned Germany.

Churchill was sensitive to the Soviets' view of the war crimes issue, and he was eager to demonstrate a hard line for that reason as well. "I attach great importance to the principle that the criminals will be taken back to be judged in the countries or even the districts where their crimes have been committed," Churchill wrote to Eden. "I should have thought that this would appeal to U.J."— that is, to "Uncle Joe" Stalin.[25]

Here again, revelations of Nazi atrocities became an instrument of political warfare against Germany, and Churchill, at least, regarded it as an effective instrument. The proposed declaration, he said, would convince at least "some of these villains to be shy of being mixed up in butcheries now that they know they are going to be beat."[26] Churchill was an acute judge of German political culture: A threat from the *Western* Allies that suspected Nazi criminals would be sent back for judgment to the "countries . . . where their crimes had been committed"—which for many suspects meant to the Soviet Union—was a message that even the dullest SS man could not miss.

Foreign Minister Anthony Eden remained unconvinced, however. "I am far from happy about all this war crimes business," he wrote to his staff in October 1943. "I am most anxious not to get into the position of breathing fire and slaughter against war criminals and promising condign punishment, and a year or two hence having to find pretexts for doing nothing. . . . Our pledges," he noted, were already causing "difficulty."[27]

The central question for each of the Allies at the upcoming 1943 conference in Moscow was how the struggle with Germany was likely to affect European affairs once the conflict was over. The answer to that turned to a surprisingly large extent on the symbolic and practical questions of what was to be done with Nazi war criminals. In the Soviet capital during late October and early November 1943, the three Allies' foreign ministers reached new agreements on the terms of the U.S.-British-Soviet alliance against Germany and on joint Allied policy for postwar Europe.

The foreign ministers announced their joint resolution in the Moscow Declaration on war crimes on November 1.[28] Each major element of the Moscow covenants attempted to establish proofs that the Allies would not betray one another during the war. These included new commitments to jointly prosecute senior Nazi criminals, to inform one another of any Axis peace feelers, and to handle jointly any armistice discussions with the smaller Axis states such as Hungary, Romania, and Bulgaria. The United States and Britain renewed their commitment to open the long-delayed second front in Western Europe, and all three powers formally agreed to demand an unconditional surrender from Germany.[29]

The treatment of Nazi criminals again became an important test of Allied intentions concerning Germany in the wake of the war. The Moscow Declaration began by agreeing to require the complete disarmament of Germany, then expressed commitments to dissolve the Nazi party in all of its forms, to return Nazis to face judgment in the countries where they were accused of committing crimes, to create a three-power advisory commission in London to make further recommendations on joint policies for postwar Germany, and to reach a "joint decision" among the three Allies concerning the disposition of Nazi leaders.*[30]

Two points are worth underlining. First, the Western Allies' agreement that "any armistice" would include provisions to ship

* The Moscow Declaration is worth quoting in detail, because it became the foundation for later policy and the center of many disputes between East and West in the wake of the war.

"At the time of granting of any armistice to any Government which may be set up in Germany," the agreement read, "those German officers and men and members of the Nazi Party who have been responsible for or have taken a consenting part in . . . atrocities, massacres and executions will be sent back to the countries in which their abominable deeds were done in order that they may be judged and punished according to the laws of these liberated countries. . . . Lists will be compiled in all possible detail" of these criminals.

"Those Germans who take part in wholesale shootings of Italian officers or in

Nazi criminals back to the site of their crimes, if it was respected, amounted to a renewed guarantee that there would be no armistice with Germany without Soviet participation. Second, there was no direct mention that the murder of Jews, stateless people, and other Axis civilians was in any sense a crime, because the legal advisors at the State Department and the Foreign Office believed it was not. Jews as such were not mentioned even in the lists of atrocity victims in the declaration. This pivotal question of international law and justice remained unresolved.

A curious blunder occurred on the way to making the Moscow Declaration public. Owing to what was termed "an unfortunate mistake in ciphering," the British Foreign Office staff in Moscow referred to the "wholesale shooting of *Polish* officers" in the Declaration's list of victims of Nazi atrocities, rather than to "Italian" officers, as had been agreed by the three foreign ministers.[31] The "Polish" version was released to the press in London and in Washington, while Moscow published the correct "Italian" version.

At the Goebbels ministry in Berlin, the propagandists noticed the difference between the Russian-language and English-language declarations, and exploited the blunder to call the Katyn massacre of Polish officers back to the center of public attention. The Soviets demanded and eventually won a formal correction from the British and the Americans, much to the dismay of the Polish exile government in London. Despite the correction, however, the incident had again placed the Katyn killings on the table, and Soviet enthusiasm for cooperation with the West in war crimes matters again soured.[32]

The Western Allies gutted Churchill's plan to reduce Nazi violence through aggressive psychological warfare less than two months after the dramatic pronouncements in Moscow. During early November 1943, U.S. psychological warfare specialists began a major campaign to use the Moscow Declaration's statements

---

the execution of French, Dutch, Belgian or Norwegian hostages or of Cretan peasants, or who have shared in the slaughters inflicted on the people of Poland, or in the territories of the Soviet Union which are now being swept clear of the enemy, will know that they will be brought back to the scene of their crimes and judged on the spot by the peoples they have outraged.

"Let those who have hitherto not imbrued their hands with innocent blood beware lest they join the ranks of the guilty, for most assuredly the three Allied Powers will pursue them to the uttermost ends of the earth and will deliver them to the accusers in order that justice may be done."

about trials for Nazi criminals as a centerpiece for messages aimed
at Germans and other peoples living under Nazi rule. But on November 23, U.S. Army Air Forces (AAF) headquarters in Algiers
aborted a planned war crimes trial of Germans accused of a second
Italian massacre, then issued directives to shut down all publicity
concerning investigations of specific Nazi crimes and plans to try
war criminals.[33]

The AAF feared that if the U.S. tried German criminals during
the war—or even threatened to put them on trial—the Nazis would
retaliate by ordering war crimes trials for American fliers who had
been shot down during bombing raids over German cities. The
perceived interests of the Allied airmen won out.

Green Hackworth's office at the State Department, which had
typically required months to respond to any previous initiative
involving Nazi crimes, heartily endorsed the AAF's new policy
within hours after it was transmitted to the Pentagon. Hackworth
worked through the weekend to put together a memo of support for
the AAF action and push it through the secretary of state's office
before AAF headquarters in Washington could back away from the
stand taken by the Algiers outpost. The State Department "agrees
most emphatically with AFHQ's decision against publicity in connection with the capture, collection of evidence and trial of war
criminals," Hackworth cabled to Algiers. "[A]ny temporary propaganda advantage that might be gained from such publicity would be
completely over-balanced by the danger of reprisals against American prisoners of war."[34] From that point until the end of the war, the
claim that action against Nazi crimes might risk American prisoners' lives became a staple feature of virtually every State Department comment on the war crimes issue.

The conflict within the Allied camp over failure to respond to
Nazi atrocities was at last coming to a head. Shortly after the Air
Force incident, a half-dozen senior administration officials responsible for various aspects of Jewish refugee issues met in the office
of Secretary of the Treasury Henry Morgenthau, Jr., the son of the
World War I–era U.S. ambassador to Turkey who had protested the
Armenian Genocide. The subject of the meeting was eliminating
obstacles to the rescue of refugees from Europe. Members of Morgenthau's staff were at that moment tracing State Department policy
concerning Europe over the previous four years. The title of their
report told the story: *Report to the Secretary on the Acquiescence
of This Government in the Murder of Jews.*[35]

Secretary Morgenthau, a close political ally of Herbert Pell in the war crimes debate, squinted down through his pince-nez spectacles at Assistant Secretary of State Breckinridge Long. The two officials had frequently locked horns over what to do about Nazi Germany, and both knew that this confrontation could not be put off any longer. Long insisted he was doing everything possible to rescue refugees and that rumors questioning his commitment to fighting fascism were untrue.

"I looked him right in the eye," Morgenthau noted for his diary shortly after the incident. "Well, Breck, as long as you raise the question, we might be a little frank," the secretary remembered. "The impression is all around that you, particularly, are anti-Semitic!"[36]

Morgenthau knew that a handful of Long's aides at State had for years systematically denied available U.S. visas to refugee Jews, suppressed intelligence about Hitler's Holocaust, and undermined efforts to establish a commission to document Nazi atrocities. Recently he had learned that Long's group at State had sabotaged a deal that could have purchased survival for 70,000 Romanian Jews for a mere $170,000 in Romanian currency.[37]

Long choked and denied Morgenthau's charge of anti-Semitism. Breckinridge Long—a tiny, rawboned man whose indiscreet praise of Mussolini and Italian fascism during the 1930s had once made headlines[38]—was not about to permit himself to be pinned down on the wrong side of this issue. He attempted to blame an assistant for the paperwork delays that had buried the Romanian plan. But Morgenthau continued: The position of Long's group, it seemed to him, was identical to that of the British Foreign Office. At bottom, both institutions had resigned themselves to what the secretary had recently called, "diplomatic double-talk, cold and correct and adding up to a sentence of death" for Europe's Jews.[39]

10

"The Present
Ruling Class of Germany"

HENRY MORGENTHAU, JR., had long led the opposition within
the U.S. government to any reconciliation with Nazi Germany. He was secretary of the treasury, a New York Democrat (as
were Roosevelt and Pell), and a Jew. Morgenthau's views concerning Germany enjoyed relatively broad public support in the U.S.
and won him some political allies in the Justice Department and
the War Department. But the State Department's specialists viewed
him as a dangerous rival for control of U.S. foreign policy.

Much of Morgenthau's popular appeal stemmed from his arguments against clemency for Nazi war criminals. For much of the
U.S. public, German industrialists like Gustav Krupp, steel baron
Friedrich Flick, and the IG Farben executives were an integral part
of the Nazi power structure and shared direct responsibility for a
long list of atrocities. Further, there was widespread suspicion in
the U.S. that Germany was in some sense intrinsically evil and
would rise from the ashes of World War II to instigate new and still
more deadly conflicts unless it was stripped of the economic and

military capacity for conducting war. Limiting this German enemy, as Morgenthau's supporters saw things, required a high degree of postwar cooperation between the U.S. and the USSR.[1]

Morgenthau's legal advisors at the Treasury Department favored a tough line on Nazi crimes. It was unthinkable that Germany would be permitted to legalize mass murder and the looting of an entire continent, they argued. If previous international agreements on war crimes had failed to deal with Nazi-style genocide, then justice demanded that new legal precedents be set. Morgenthau's allies contended that substantially all of the economic, political, and military elite of wartime Germany was implicated in one way or another in the Nazis' crimes. This was not the same as advocating collective German responsibility for Nazi crimes, though there was at times a tendency in that direction. The Treasury's legal specialists often acknowledged that there were "good" Germans (including "good" German businessmen) and that ordinary Germans suffering under a dictatorship should not be held personally responsible for the criminal actions of their leaders. Even so, the very fact that the Nazis had so efficiently purged their opposition suggested that the economic and political leaders who had survived those purges and gone on to prosper under Hitler had materially aided the Nazis. There was also direct evidence of culpability of the German economic elite in some crimes, including the use of slave labor and the plunder of Jewish property.

The Treasury group's strategy for postwar Germany favored what amounted to a massive antitrust action to break up the entrenched monopolies and cartels that were a prominent feature of the German economy. They contended that German corporate leaders should be held personally responsible for the institutional crimes that had been committed by the companies they led.[2] For Morgenthau, as for Herbert Pell, the systematic removal of the economic and political elite of Germany was necessary to ensure postwar stability in Europe—to "prevent World War III," as the slogan went. The Germans had been responsible for two world wars within thirty years, they reasoned, and the only way to prevent the outbreak of a third war was once and for all to break apart the power structure of Germany, particularly its heavy industry.

In contrast, the men and women at State who favored the strictly legalist approach to war crimes usually backed a rapid reintegration of Germany into the postwar world. This meant a revitalization of German business and a postwar restoration of German finance and industry to a major place in the overall economy of Europe.

George F. Kennan was among the first State Department officials to grasp the connection between Allied policy on war crimes prosecutions and U.S. political and economic policy toward postwar Germany and the USSR. He began lobbying quite explicitly at least as early as 1943 for the Allies to abandon any efforts to try Nazi criminals after the war. Kennan was a junior diplomat at the time, but he laid claim to comment on such questions because, as second-in-command of the U.S. diplomatic staff in Berlin at the outbreak of war, Kennan had been interned by the Germans (in a luxury hotel) for several months.[3] He had also long been a student of German affairs, and had been one of the State Department's principal back-channel links to the German nobility and business elite.

Kennan's wartime writings show that he was unable, or unwilling, to separate even the activities at Sobibor and Auschwitz from the carnage created by a more or less conventional war. "The day we accepted the Russians as our allies in the struggle against Germany," he wrote in a 1944 memo, "we tacitly accepted as facts . . . the customs of warfare which have prevailed generally in Eastern Europe and Asia for centuries."[4] Kennan's moral and intellectual failure cannot be attributed to a lack of information about the Holocaust, for the main picture of what was taking place in the death camps and slave labor centers throughout Europe was already widely known in 1944. Indeed, he wrote the memo precisely because of the Allied discussions concerning what was to be done about such atrocities. Kennan continues in his memoirs (where he quotes the 1944 memo) that even after the war, when the record of Nazi atrocities was laid out in all its grotesque detail, the Allies' "punishment for war crimes" remained "a particular reason for the unhappiness I felt" over the postwar treatment of Germany.[5]

In a second wartime memo, Kennan explained his objections to purging Nazis from the German state and economic structure. First, the elimination of Nazi influence in Germany "is impracticable," he said. The Allies could never cooperate well enough to carry out the task, and it would require a massive investigation that would undoubtedly be unpopular with the Germans.

Second, and most pertinent here, Kennan argued that even if a purge of Nazis could theoretically be successful, "we would not find any other class of people competent to assume the burdens [of leading Germany]. Whether we like it or not, nine-tenths of what is strong, able and respected in Germany has been poured into those very categories which we have in mind" for removal from power, namely those persons who had been "more than nominal members of the Nazi party." Rather than remove the "present ruling class of Germany," as he put it, it would be better to "hold it [that class] strictly to its task and teach it the lessons we wish it to learn."[6]

The same faction at State that was most committed to a revival of the German economy was also highly influential in the execution of wartime U.S. policy concerning Jewish refugees. Both issues were seen as foreign affairs questions involving Germany, so both ended up on the desks of a handful of mid-level State Department officials. The results were tragic. Men like Elbridge Durbrow, R. Borden Reams, and John Hickerson prided themselves on their professed realism toward Germany in the midst of what they saw as a wartime hysteria that had produced exaggerated reports that Jews were being systematically murdered by the millions. Their most potent argument at the time was that the only effective way to end suffering in Europe was to defeat Hitler as quickly as possible. Policies that they opposed were said to divert resources from the war effort, hence were counterproductive in the long run.[7] Meanwhile, the State Department's key legal and political specialists, Green Hackworth and James Clement Dunn, operated on the assumption that the Nazi persecution of German Jews and of non-Jewish Germans was an internal German matter and thus outside the reach of international law.[8]

This was not a "conspiracy," in the banal sense of that word, but these men did share common convictions concerning strategies for dealing with Germany and the USSR. As Kennan's comments suggest, they reasoned that if the U.S. wished to avoid a post-Hitler social revolution in Germany, it would be necessary to have some "non-Nazi" Germans with whom to negotiate, and that such people had to already have a substantial measure of power within that country.[9]

They favored, in brief, that the U.S. make a sharp distinction between the ostensibly non-Nazi German economic and military elite, on the one hand, and Hitler's inner circle, on the other. They saw the former group as essential to postwar reconstruction. Hitler's inner circle, on the other hand, could be made publicly responsible for the war itself and for all Nazi atrocities, then disposed of as quickly as possible—except for Hitler himself, who as head of state involved certain legal difficulties. In this context, the wartime rescue of European Jews raised several problems: it would likely mean increased Jewish immigration to the U.S., for example, which many at State opposed for political and anti-Semitic reasons; it would heighten U.S. conflicts with Britain over Palestine; and it would tend to criminalize the German economic and military elite in the eyes of the U.S. public, thus undermining longer-term efforts to focus public hostility on the USSR rather than on Germany once the fighting was over.

This faction was not sympathetic to Nazism as such. Rather, it viewed Hitler, as Kennan put it, as "stamping out the last vestiges of particularism [sic] and class differences . . . [by] reducing everything to the lowest and most common denominator."[10] Many were strongly sympathetic to the German business and cultural elite, however, and charitable to the point of blindness to the compromises this stratum had made with Hitler.[11]

Interestingly, both poles of the debate over Germany within the U.S. government tacitly acknowledged that Germany's economic elite had been deeply implicated in the work of the Nazis, though the two sides drew nearly opposite conclusions from it. At the State Department, the complicity of much of the German elite was seen as one reason that war crimes trials should be restricted as much as possible, in order to ensure continuity of the core of German society after Hitler was gone. For Morgenthau at Treasury and for Pell at the UNWCC, the same complicity was seen as proof that German society should be fundamentally reorganized and that the political and economic elite of the Hitler period had to be completely removed from power.

Thus, the question of what to do with Germany after the war became tied up in complex questions of international economics, U.S.-Soviet relations, and war crimes enforcement. Political developments in one issue had immediate and often substantial implications for each of the other concerns. This was the context in which the controversies over the Morgenthau plan for postwar Germany and the establishment of the International Military Tribunal at Nuremberg were to be hammered out.

By 1943, important changes were also under way among the German economic elite, and these had an indirect but nonetheless important effect on political debate in the U.S. Up until the German defeat at Stalingrad in late 1942, Adolf Hitler remained the best thing that had ever happened to the German financial elite from a strictly business point of view—notwithstanding the Nazi party's occasional flourishes of anticapitalist rhetoric. The sophisticated conservatives that dominated German business made the most of National Socialism. Virtually all major German enterprises adopted elements of Nazi ideology in their day-to-day operations, including the purging of Jews, decimation of labor unions, and exploitation of forced labor. Along the way, they invented a variety of triumph-of-the-will rationalizations for corporate brutality and theft.

But in early 1943, the German financial and industrial elite began to split on the future of Hitler. Increasingly, the very forces that they had helped set in motion were now dragging the whole of Germany toward catastrophe. Hitler had irrevocably blundered and, it was rumored, might even be mentally unbalanced. The banker Hjalmar Schacht—long the quintessential German establishment banker who had backed the Nazis since before Hitler came to power—left Hitler's government. Even Oscar Henschel, whose weapons companies made extensive use of forced labor, claimed to have concluded as early as December 1942 that the military situation was hopeless.[12]

The economic elite turned their attention to self-preservation. But such planning, regarded by Hitler's government as defeatist or even treasonous, could be carried out only under a thick veil of secrecy. Intriguingly, the existing social networks used by the economic elite to coordinate their actions and to secure influence within Hitler's government provided some of the most effective "covers" for German corporate efforts to prepare for the postwar world.

The notorious Himmlerkreis, the Circle of Friends of Reichsführer SS Heinrich Himmler, is a good example of the dynamics of Germany's high-level business networks during the decline of the Third Reich. The Nazis and leading German businessmen had jointly created the Himmlerkreis in the early 1930s as an informal communication link between the financial and industrial elite and the SS. Himmler sought the political and economic support of the business elite, and the elite in turn sought influence outside of official channels with the increasingly powerful police leader. Senior business leaders active in the Himmlerkreis included Siemens' general director Rudolf Bingel, Unilever and Kontinentale Öl director Karl Blessing, steel industrialist Friedrich Flick, Dresdner Bank's Karl Rache and Emil Meyer, shipping and oil executive Karl Lindemann, and board members or senior managers from the Deutsche Bank, RKG, IG Farben, Krupp, and a dozen other companies central to the German economy.[13] As the SS grew as an economic power, the SS members of the Himmlerkreis often migrated to new positions on corporate boards, where they could secure government contracts and embody corporate loyalty to the regime. SS men and Nazi party activists who made this transition included Wilhelm Keppler (of the BRABAG brown coal combine and SS enterprises), Fritz Kranefuss (BRABAG, Dresdner Bank), and Ritter von Halt, who joined the Deutsche Bank board.[14]

Officially, the Himmlerkreis meetings were not for conducting business, because that would have suggested corruption in National Socialist circles. As a practical matter, however, the encounters served as an informal coordinating point for German industry's negotiations with the SS on policy matters. IG Farben appears to have used Himmlerkreis meetings to seek support for the company's vast forced-labor complex at Auschwitz, for example. The companies represented in Himmler's circle became pacesetters in Aryanization, exploitation of concentration camp labor, seizure of foreign companies in the occupied territories, and similar business ventures that depended on SS cooperation.[15]

But as the war turned against the Third Reich, a number of business leaders in the Himmlerkreis began to cooperate in clandestine and semiclandestine contingency planning for the postwar period. Two of the best known of these groups, the *Arbeitskreis für aussenwirtschaftliche Fragen* (Working Group for Foreign Economic Questions) and the *Kleine Arbeitskreis* (Small Working Group), were nominally sponsored by the Reichsgruppe Industrie association of major industrial and financial companies. They brought together Blessing, Rasche, Kurt von Schroeder, Lindemann, and others from the Himmlerkreis with other business people such as Hermann Abs (Deutsche Bank), Ludwig Erhard (then an economist with the Reichsgruppe Industrie and later Konrad Adenauer's most important economic advisor), Ludger Westrick (RKG, aluminum industry, nonferrous metals), and Philipp Reemtsma (tobacco, shipping, banking), and with Nazi business specialists such as Otto Ohlendorf (the former commander of the *Einsatzgruppe D* murder troops) and Hans Kehrl (SS business specialist).[16] A half-dozen similar business forums emerged during the last years of the Third Reich. Most of these overlapped in membership, and all of them favored some variation of the "corporatist" strategy for empire articulated by Hjalmar Schacht, Abs, and others during the showdown over Aryanization in Vienna discussed earlier.[17]

A number of top German corporate officials initiated attempts to reach Allied governments with offers to serve as intermediaries in negotiations of a separate peace between Germany and the Western Allies. Men such as Hermann Schmitz and Georg von Schnitzler of IG Farben, the international lawyer Gerhardt Westrick (of the Albert & Westrick law firm, and brother of Ludger Westrick), and others were prominent in these efforts, precisely because it was they who had the international ties to powerful U.S. and British circles.[18] OSS man Allen Dulles became the focal point of many of their efforts, as noted earlier.[19] They extended somewhat similar peace offers from time to time to the USSR as well.[20]

The German industrialists' roles in these efforts have frequently been raised in their defense since the end of the war. Such activities are sometimes described as a form of resistance to the Nazi state, and there is some merit to that argument. But these industrialists wanted the Allies to permit Germany to keep most of what it had looted from Germany's Jews and from Eastern Europe. They also usually insisted that there should be no punishment for Nazi atrocities, and in several variations of the separate-peace proposals, the SS would remain in power, but without Hitler. Finally, they usually insisted that the Western allies tacitly support Germany's ongoing war against the USSR.[21] These were not "peace" proposals in a fundamental sense, but rather efforts to rationalize the management of the war and to gain time to digest the billions of marks worth of personal and industrial property that had fallen into German hands.

Some U.S. factions clearly supported the general concept of a separate peace with Germany, though very few other than Allen

Dulles knew the precise terms that German emissaries had offered. John Foster Dulles advocated consideration of this strategy in early 1943, for example.[22] There was also an undercurrent of support for a separate peace among some of the more conservative Democrats who, like Harry Truman, had an open mind about the advantages of encouraging an ongoing German-Soviet slaughter by withdrawing U.S. troops from the conflict.[23] Nevertheless, President Roosevelt forcefully ruled out any possibility of a separate peace—in part to help stabilize U.S. relations with the USSR.[24] As the likelihood of total victory over Germany became increasingly clear, the murmurings for a separate peace died away.

German industry's efforts reveal the moral bankruptcy of this group during the later Hitler years. They proved to be willing to engage in risky conspiracies to protect their company positions and corporate assets, but not to save the lives of the concentration camp inmates who worked for them. According to their own accounts, they knew that Hitler's strategy had collapsed and that the war would be lost. Many knew of Hitler's extermination programs, and some of them—members of the IG Farben and Siemens boards, for example—had personally procured slave labor from concentration camps or directly participated in other atrocities.[25] Yet in most cases they failed to remove themselves from positions of authority, or to ameliorate conditions for forced laborers working for their companies, or to resist the Holocaust in any way. As the war lurched into its final months, conditions in the corporate concentration camps deteriorated dramatically. Food ran out, and new epidemics ripped through the camps. The pace of exterminations actually accelerated during 1944, despite the Red Army's encroachments on the death camps in eastern Poland. Tens of thousands of the Jews who were gassed that year were veterans of the corporate camps in the East, and their murders often required active or tacit cooperation from company leaders.[26]

Jewish blood became the currency, in effect, with which German companies bought legitimacy in the eyes of the Nazis during Hitler's last years. Legally speaking, of course, corporate leaders must be judged on their individual acts, not as members of a group. But from a sociologist's point of view, from the perspective of how groups of people behaved, it is evident that most members of Germany's corporate elite were willing to sacrifice the lives of innocent people in their determined pursuit of institutional survival.

11

The Trials Begin

THE SOVIETS placed captured Germans on trial for the first time in late 1943, less than a month after the U.S. Army Air Forces had determined that it would not try Nazis for war crimes as long as imprisoned U.S. airmen were still in German hands. This was actually the second known Soviet trial, but it was the first to prosecute Germans.

The USSR had opened the first recorded war crimes trial of the war the previous July in Krasnodar, near the Turkish border in the southern part of the country. There, they tried eleven Nazi collaborators accused of taking part in the murder of 7,000 Jewish civilians. The Krasnodar collaborators had executed the men by shooting them, the women and children by loading them on closed trucks that had been modified to channel exhaust fumes into the rear of the van. The vans—nicknamed *Dushequbka* ("Soul-killers") by the collaborators and known as "black ravens" among the Jews—had been painted with false Red Cross insignia to encourage cooperation from the victims. (Interestingly, the inspiration for the design of these wagons has been attributed to SS Colonel Walter Rauff, who will return later in these pages during secret negotiations with Allen Dulles in the last weeks of the war.)

During the murder campaign, the SS had enthusiastically reported to Berlin that the *Dushequbka* saved German ammunition. But there were problems for the Nazis. The killing took a long time and sometimes failed. *Einsatzgruppe D* leader Otto Ohlendorf, who was in charge of mass-murder operations in the southern USSR, testified later that his troops experienced "spiritual shock" upon emptying the vans, because the dead had covered themselves with vomit and excrement during their death agony. The Nazis eventually developed more efficient death camp technologies to replace the vans.

The Soviet court in Krasnodar handed down prison sentences to three of the Nazi collaborators, then condemned the rest to death. The government encouraged a public celebration of the punishment and filmed the hangings in gruesome detail. Trucks brought the prisoners to the hanging ground, where executioners placed a noose around each convict's neck. The trucks then slowly pulled away, leaving the men dangling and twitching until life was choked out of them. The camera caught every shudder.[1]

The war crimes trials that placed Germans in the dock for the first time were held in Kharkov, USSR, in December 1943. The Soviets prosecuted three captured German *Einsatzkommando* officers and a Soviet collaborator. All were convicted and hung.[2] The Soviet announcement of the verdicts made direct reference to the Moscow Declaration on Nazi crimes of a month earlier. This was clearly the type of quick justice that the Soviets had in mind when they had pledged with their allies to bring the Nazis back to be "judged on the spot by the peoples they have outraged."[3]

Henry Morgenthau was at that moment struggling with the State Department to win approval for a U.S. program to aid European refugees, particularly Jews facing Nazi gas chambers. He issued a statement congratulating the Soviets on the trials, noting that by executing the *Einsatzkommando* officers at Kharkov, "the Russians are wiping from the face of the earth one of its most repulsive stains. . . . In so doing they are giving the freedom loving peoples firm confidence in the future."[4]

But the State Department and the British Foreign Office were aghast at the Soviet trials and at Morgenthau's response. Their concerns were amplified a week later when the Nazi party newspaper *Völkischer Beobachter* published on its front page photos of a captured U.S. pilot whose bomber jacket was emblazoned with a notorious gang's name. "USA Air Gangsters Name Themselves 'Murder Incorporated,' " the headline read. The prisoner was said to illustrate the "underworld character of the air terrorists." Coverage in this and other German newspapers stressed the pilot's destruction of civilians, including German women and children. The State Department interpreted the publication as an implicit threat that the Germans would place the airman and other American pilots on trial.[5]

Secretary of State Cordell Hull quickly announced that as far as the United States was concerned, the "direct handling of war criminals" did not fall within the terms of the recently signed Moscow Declaration—an ambiguous statement that raised obvious questions concerning just what it was that the declaration did cover. Green Hackworth's office at the State Department dispatched a message to the Germans via a Swiss government intermediary, promising that the United States had no intention of trying captured German soldiers.[6] Western press reports claimed that the U.S. and Britain appealed to the Soviets to postpone further trials of Nazis until after an armistice with Germany, though this was denied when it became public.[7] Meanwhile, State's political advisor James Clement Dunn huddled with colleagues at State and the War Department in an effort to line up critics of Morgenthau.[8]

The War Department distributed internal directives to U.S. forces stating that suspected Axis war criminals then in captivity were not to be separated from the general POW population, nor was there to be any indication that they were under suspicion.[9] The practical effect of this order was to sharply restrict U.S. efforts to collect evidence concerning Nazi atrocities, including those that had been committed against American servicemen. There was no effective way to investigate Nazi crimes without systematically questioning prisoners on the subject—exactly the type of probe that the War Department ordered U.S. interrogators to avoid.

The Western concerns over POWs then in German hands carried little weight with the Soviets, however. The Nazis had systematically murdered about two million Soviet POWs through starvation, gassing, and torture since 1941. Holding off on trials of captured Nazis now would not improve the Germans' treatment of surviving Soviet POWs.* To the Russians, their ongoing "demands for the immediate trial of Hitler and his savages fulfill the lawful rights of nations [and] are in accordance with international law," a Moscow dispatch in the Communist party magazine *War and the Working Class* stated.[10]

Herbert Pell's arrival in the United Kingdom was inauspicious. He disembarked in late 1943 with a serious case of influenza that hospitalized him for days. The weather was damp and chilly in England; the hotels usually unheated; and the food terrible. "The cold in London that winter was beyond anything I have ever suf-

---

* The issue touched Stalin personally as well. The Germans had captured his eldest son, Yakov Dzhugashvilli, in the opening days of the war and interned him in a special barracks at the Sachsenhausen concentration camp for prisoners they regarded as politically useful. The SS and German military intelligence pressured the young man to collaborate, but they had little success. This did not deter them from using Yakov's photograph and (purported) comments in propaganda leaflets that they showered on Soviet troops in an effort to convince them to surrender.

Stalin refused to intervene with the Germans on behalf of his son. Yakov, he said, must be regarded as just a Soviet POW, one of more than three million Soviet prisoners in Nazi hands. Any concessions to the Germans would almost certainly have been exploited by the Nazis as "proof" of Stalin's betrayal of his own troops on behalf of his family.

Yakov grew deeply depressed as he languished in the Sachsenhausen camp. In April 1943, there was a bitter fight among the prisoners in the privileged barracks, and some English POWs denounced Yakov's fellow inmate, Vasily Kokosyn, as a Gestapo informer. (Kokosyn was the nephew of Soviet foreign minister Molotov.) The English smeared feces on Kokosyn and apparently on Yakov's bunk as well. That evening Yakov committed suicide by deliberately trying to scale the camp fence in front of an SS guard, who shot him once in the head. Yakov died instantly.

The SS chose to keep their prisoner's death a secret, in order to continue to exploit Yakov's image in German propaganda. Nazi emissaries are reported to have even attempted to approach Stalin with a renewed deal to "free" Yakov in exchange for Soviet concessions more than a year after the young man had been shot. Stalin refused the offer.

According to Stalin's daughter Svetlana, the Soviet leader was moved by his son's condition, despite Stalin's earlier psychological and physical cruelty toward the young man. "He spoke to me about Yakov again in the summer of 1945, when the war was already over," Svetlana remembered in *Twenty Letters to a Friend.* " 'The Germans shot Yasha,' [Stalin said]. 'I had a letter of condolence from a Belgian officer, Prince somebody or other. He was an eyewitness. The Americans,' " Stalin concluded, " 'set them all free.' " Svetlana indicates that her father "spoke with an effort and didn't want to say any more"—one of the few displays of personal emotion by the Soviet leader recorded by his daughter.

fered," he remembered after the war, "and yet, it hardly ever got below freezing. It was the rarest thing. While you didn't see any ice all that winter, as far as real suffering from cold was concerned, I have never been as badly off." By all accounts the best kitchen in London was at the American officers' club, where a dollar would fetch soup, some tough meat, and a nonsynthetic dessert. It was, Pell said, "about as good as a rather poor college commons in America, but immeasurably better than anything else in London."[11]

Worst of all for Herbert Pell, there was little to do. The UN commission had remained dormant after its first organizational meetings. Pell had no offices, no telephone, and no fixed address for a number of weeks. "The result was that with no work to do and no particular place to go I walked and walked and walked over London, hour after hour. I lost a lot of weight and got to feeling more and more miserable," Pell remembered. "When I say I had nothing to do, I mean exactly what I say. The commission existed, the members would meet once a week, and decide to put off the definite organization until later. Then we would go home. . . ."[12]

After two months of frustration, Pell turned his restless energy to the task of extracting substantive action from the bureaucracies he believed were stifling Allied initiatives on war crimes, not least of which was the UNWCC itself. His vision of the task ahead was more than a little bit bloody, as was reflected in an unpublished memoir he wrote shortly after the war.

> The only book I read in preparation for the War Crimes Commission was a life of Antoine Fouquier-Tinville and the course of the Committee of Public Safety during the French Revolution. When the French Revolution was well under way a great many of the government officials were holdovers from the old administration. . . . Royalist and anti-government plots were going on all over the country. The Committee of Public Safety was organized. Fouquier-Tinville was put in charge of it, and the Terror began. A considerable number of people were executed. Many of them should have been perhaps only put in jail, a good many should have been let go completely; many of them were innocent. . . . However, the net result of Fouquier-Tinville's activities was that royalism was suppressed.
>
> I felt that we were facing much the same situation in Germany. It was far more important to prevent a third [world] war

than anything else. We were not there to distribute divine justice. That is God's business, not ours. It's perfectly clear that
the execution of a thousand people couldn't revive one child,
couldn't console one widow, and could not remedy the hard-
ships a single individual was suffering as a result of the
treatment in the camps. Our business, however, was to see that
those things did not occur again. I believed, and I still believe,
that it would have been best to hang the entire Gestapo. It
would have meant hanging a great many men, some of whom
had not been mixed up in any of the atrocities. It would have
meant that many . . . in the regular [German] army who had
perpetrated crimes in the occupied countries would [also] be
hung.[13]

Pell's thinking was much in tune with public opinion of the day.
Nine out of ten British men and women favored harsh punishment
of Nazi leaders, the British Institute of Public Opinion reported in
late 1943; some 40 percent of Britons favored summary execution
of Nazis without trial, and 15 percent more called for torturing
Nazis to death.[14]

In late January 1944, Pell wrote to Roosevelt and to Breckinridge
Long (his nominal supervisor in the Foreign Service) seeking support for the first of several hard-line initiatives he wished to raise
with the commission. In the letter to Roosevelt, Pell pushed for an
international tribunal to try Nazis "who have committed crimes
against the citizens of more than one country, or who have directed
inhuman policies in Germany itself." Pell was referring to actions
that fell outside of previous definitions of war crimes, particularly
atrocities against Jews and German civilians. "Delay and legalism
will certainly make it impossible to execute the policies which you
have outlined in many statements," he continued. "I need your
support."[15]

The appeal to Long was similar, stressing the need for U.S.
support for an "international authority" competent to try Nazis for
crimes against "stateless people . . . [and] German citizens." Pell
knew Breckinridge Long well enough that it was pointless to appeal to him on behalf of German Jews. Instead, he argued that
Allied radio propaganda had led "quite a number" of Germans to
commit sabotage against the Reich; some of these rebels were said
to have been caught and persecuted by the Nazis. "It does not seem
to me proper to abandon these people merely because we cannot

find any German statute which has been violated in their punishment," Pell contended.[16]

FDR responded to Pell on February 12 in a personal but ambiguously worded letter that lent moral support to the diplomat without actually endorsing his proposals. "My dear Bertie," FDR's note began, then went on to support joint international action against those who had "directed inhuman policies in Germany." But FDR's letter favored military rather than civilian tribunals because "such people know or should know what the rules of warfare are and should be able readily to detect violations of those rules."[17] Pell chose to interpret Roosevelt's comments as a strong endorsement of his own position, and he readily used this claim of presidential sponsorship in his political battles over the next few years. Many historians and journalists have accepted this correspondence as proof that FDR favored Pell's strategy on war crimes over that of the State Department.[18]

In fact, however, the State Department's archives show that FDR's telegrams to Pell were actually written by Pell's archrival, Green Hackworth, the man most active in State's attempts to throttle Pell's authority. The declassified memos and carbons show that the White House passed Pell's letter back to State to draft a reply, where it ended up on Hackworth's desk.[19] All of the surviving FDR and Department of State letters to Pell during 1944 were actually drafted by Hackworth, regardless of whether the notes went out over the signature of the President, Secretary of State Cordell Hull, or Hackworth himself. The carbons of each note now in State's archives carry Hackworth's initials and those of his secretary in the lower-left-hand corner—a long-established custom used by the department for designating authorship.

A closer look at the "FDR" letters to Herbert Pell shows that while the language of these notes is sometimes ambiguous, it is nonetheless consistent with Hackworth's restrictive interpretation of international law. This does not mean that FDR agreed with each of Hackworth and State's attempts to obstruct the UNWCC. Clearly he did not, and in fact he complained to Secretary of State Hull about the delays in getting the UNWCC under way. It does suggest, however, that Roosevelt did not place a high priority on the discussions over war crimes, once the toughly worded condemnations of Nazi atrocities had been distributed. FDR was willing to leave the details to subordinates, and Hackworth understood how to make the most of that.[20]

The ambiguities in Hackworth's texts for FDR seem to have been intended to manipulate Roosevelt, or at least to avoid alarming him about the overall thrust of State's policies. This is clearly indicated by the contrasts between the FDR notes and those that Hackworth wrote directly to Pell. In the latter, Hackworth explicitly ordered Pell to avoid UNWCC consideration of atrocities against Axis civilians. In the FDR letters, on the other hand, Hackworth sidestepped this explosive issue. If Hackworth actually had FDR's full support, presumably he would have sought a clearer statement from the President on this issue as a means of more effectively controlling Pell. Hackworth's resort to subterfuge in this case, as well as in his secret agreement with Pell's assistant, Preuss, strongly suggest that Hackworth was pursuing his own agenda without clear backing from the White House.

Regardless of what Hackworth or Roosevelt may have intended, however, Pell interpreted the FDR note as support for his own hard-line policies. He succeeded in convincing most of the rest of the UNWCC that Roosevelt was behind him.

The work of the UNWCC gradually began to fall into place in the spring of 1944. Pell pushed hard for what he took to be FDR's suggestion of military tribunals to quickly try many Nazis after the war, and he eventually got a UNWCC consensus on that point. The commission's task of collecting evidence on specific atrocities was still not really under way, though, because British and American intelligence agencies refused to share information on events inside the Nazi-occupied territories. Pell eventually made some progress on this front when the UNWCC convinced Allied military authorities in late 1944 to adopt a standard form for use in questioning German POWs about war crimes. This approach permitted reasonably systematic collection of war crimes data from POWs for the first time, and it also succeeded in sidestepping the earlier War Department regulations against "singling out" war crimes suspects by asking all POWs the same battery of questions.[21]

Nevertheless, basic problems remained. In March 1944, Secretary of State Hull sent Pell explicit instructions to ignore crimes against Axis civilians, obviously including the systematic murder of Jews in Germany, Austria, Hungary, and Romania. (Again, this note was actually written by Hackworth.) "To assume to punish officials of enemy governments for actions taken against their own nationals pursuant to their own laws would constitute an assumption of jurisdiction probably unwarranted under international law," the Hackworth/Hull message read. The Moscow Declaration, it continued, should be interpreted to apply only to Nazi actions inside the Allied countries they had overrun. A similar note signed by Under Secretary Edward R. Stettinius told Pell that Nazi crimes prior to the outbreak of war in September 1939 were to be regarded as outside the UNWCC's purview, based on much the same reasoning.[22]

Hackworth's position on these questions was strongly backed by Lawrence Preuss, Pell's assistant. Preuss "evidently had secret orders from the State Department to undermine me in the Commission as much as he could," Pell complained. "He told various members of the Commission that I was a personal friend of the President who had to be given some job ... that I was of no importance in the country and that he, Preuss, really represented the State Department and its point of view. As a matter of fact," Pell concluded, "he proved to be right."[23]

Pell confronted Preuss shortly after the arrival of Hull's directive to suppress UNWCC inquiries into crimes within the Axis countries. Shouting and waving his arms, the giant Pell cornered Preuss and insisted that Hull's narrow legalisms would have to be swept aside. "New laws will have to be created if necessary," Pell insisted, "The failure to prosecute would be a mockery of justice." Preuss claimed in secret reports to Hackworth that Pell also met with representatives of major Jewish organizations in Britain and the United States and urged them to organize a press campaign that would "build a fire" under their respective governments.[24]

Preuss's assignment in London was nearing its end. He leaked word of Pell's actions to the British Foreign Office before he left, painting the U.S. representative and several other commission hard-liners as unstable eccentrics. Pell was making "dangerous mistakes," Preuss confided, while the Czech representative, Dr. Bohuslav Ecer, was said to be "wild, unbalanced and indiscreet." Pell sent a decidedly negative evaluation of his assistant's work back to Washington, stating that Preuss had defied orders and violated UNWCC confidentiality rules. But Hackworth ignored Pell's report and gave Preuss a promotion and a raise.[25]

Foreign Minister Anthony Eden had appointed Sir Cecil Hurst as British representative to the UNWCC and as commission chairman. The Foreign Office regarded Hurst as a model of experience and probity. He had been legal advisor to the Foreign Office for many years, a member of the Permanent Court of International Justice at The Hague, and a regular representative of British interests in a variety of commissions and international conferences. Hurst was also into his seventies and unlikely to make waves— seemingly a perfect choice.

But Eden seriously underestimated his appointee, for Cecil Hurst joined Herbert Pell in engineering a basic shift in international law. In early April 1944, Hurst submitted an official report on the first four months of real work at the UNWCC. He stated bluntly that the stirring wartime pledges from Allied leaders that justice would be done to Nazi criminals would come to naught unless the Foreign Office changed its approach to Nazi atrocities. The Allies had submitted only a few cases to the commission, he reported, and those involved relatively minor incidents. The United States had not contributed any information concerning war crimes at all. Unless "drastic changes" took place, Hurst continued, "it will not be possible for the Commission to accomplish with satisfaction . . . the task which it was set up to perform."[26] The basic problem, he said, was the Foreign Office's insistence on a narrow definition of "war crime" that excluded the bulk of Nazi atrocities from review and required that each registered complaint be accompanied by detailed evidence typical of conventional court cases.

Hurst also pointed to the magnitude of the task that confronted the tiny commission. By now, it was abundantly clear that Nazi atrocities had involved tens of thousands of perpetrators. As a strictly practical matter, how could criminality on this scale be documented, much less effectively prosecuted, by a dozen or so employees in London?

By starkly laying out the UNWCC's failings, Hurst was attempting to gain for the group new authority and vigor. No longer would it be possible for the Foreign Office (or the State Department) to use the existence of the UNWCC to claim that the Western Allies were taking substantive action against Nazi crimes. Hurst pointed up the sharp contradiction between the sweeping promises made by Churchill and Roosevelt and the cramped legal instructions that had been given to the commission. Hurst's report made it clear that the Foreign Office and the Department of State would carry the blame if efforts to bring Nazis to justice failed.

His demands gained new urgency on May 15, when the Nazis

struck in Budapest, the largest surviving center of Jewish population in Europe. Hungary, a full Axis partner since the beginning
of the war, had long since made preparations for killing Jews. Yet
its government had generally held back from mass murder, much
to the dismay of the Nazis. In March, the Germans deposed the
existing regime and installed a more compliant government,
whose principal task was to systematically destroy Hungarian
Jewry prior to the arrival of the Red Army. Hungarian Nazis
backed by the SS began roundups of Jews from the countryside
and smaller cities immediately. In mid-May, they started the deportations to Auschwitz.

The Nazis and their Hungarian collaborators carried out this
destruction with greater speed, efficiency, and thoroughness than
any comparable extermination in the Reich. Within ten days they
deported some 116,000 Jews to Auschwitz, many of them families
with children. They shipped 250,000 more people to extermination camps before the end of June.[27] The Nazis gassed as many
people as they could directly on arrival, but even Auschwitz's gas
chambers could not keep up with the thousands of new victims
who arrived each day. The German death machine became glutted
on its own carnage.

The Allies knew of this slaughter, but they failed to stop it.
Worse, they formally declared in secret decisions that the perpetrators of this crime were to remain immune from prosecution for
what they were doing. Lord Simon of the British War Cabinet
opposed even investigating the Hungarian deportations. It would
only be "confusing" from a legal standpoint if those who had
deported the Hungarian Jews were included in Allied war crimes
lists, he contended on June 2. The Foreign Office representative, Sir
Alexander Cadogan, strongly concurred.[28] Lord Simon secured an
official rejection of most of Hurst's proposals for the UNWCC and
went so far as to argue that even the murders of Americans, Poles,
and French civilians in Nazi concentration camps were legal under
German law and were therefore probably impossible to prosecute.
The British War Cabinet ruled in late June 1944, at the height of the
gassings of Hungarian Jews at Auschwitz, that the UNWCC should
be prohibited from even collecting information on the murder of
Axis nationals.[29]

Three weeks later, the Soviets seized Majdanek, the first true
death camp to fall into Allied hands more or less intact.[30] The

Nazis had gassed to death about one and a half million people at Majdanek in less than two years, murdering an average of well over 15,000 people per week, about half of whom were children. This made Majdanek one of the "smaller" extermination centers, at least compared to Auschwitz and Treblinka. The overwhelming majority of the dead were Polish Jews.

Pravda carried an extensive account of the Majdanek camp, complete with photographs of gas chambers, crematoria, and heaps of human bones. The tabloid *London Illustrated News* soon picked up the photos and ran them as well. But the "prestige" press, refusing to accept the Soviets' evidence, provided only sketchy and skeptical accounts. War correspondent Alexander Werth prepared an extensive story for the BBC during early August, but his superiors suspected that Majdanek might be a "Russian propaganda stunt" (as Werth put it) and refused to air it. The *New York Herald Tribune's* response was similar. "Maybe we should wait for further corroboration of [this] horror story," the editors told Werth. "Even on top of all we have been taught of the maniacal Nazi ruthlessness, this example sounds inconceivable. . . ."[31]

12

Morgenthau's Plan

THE BROAD, popular demands that the U.S. take harsh action against those who had committed atrocities collided with the legal professionals at the State Department in much the same way as they had in the wake of the Armenian Genocide of World War I. This time, though, Herbert Pell and Secretary of the Treasury Henry Morgenthau, Jr., insisted upon clarifying the calculated ambiguities on war crimes policy in which the State Department had taken refuge for several years. State's bureaucrats fought back and boldly pursued their own policies as President Roosevelt's health deteriorated in 1944 and 1945.

By the summer of 1944, there were three main centers within the U.S. government engaged in long-range thinking about Germany and the USSR, and two of the three were dominated by leading advocates of the "Riga" faction within the State Department. The first of these was the European Advisory Commission, which was ostensibly an inter-Allied consultative committee created to work out the details of decisions reached at the Big Three summit in Tehran in November 1943. Roosevelt, Churchill, and Stalin had agreed in principle on key aspects of military strategy in Europe, a plan for a postwar United Nations Organization, and the general outlines of policies on war crimes and denazification. Though many details remained to be resolved, the three Allies agreed that they would eventually separate Prussia from Germany, that there would be some form of isolation or international control of the German military-industrial complex, and that Nazis would be permanently barred from any position of responsibility in postwar Germany. Stalin and Churchill disagreed on the location of several borders and on the extent of Soviet claims for reparations from Germany. Those questions were referred to the new European Advisory Commission (EAC) for study.

All of the U.S. representatives to the new commission—George Kennan, Philip Mosely, and E. F. Penrose—were openly hostile to any accommodations with the Soviets on postwar policy toward Germany.[1] Instead, they used the EAC to promote a strategy calculated to rapidly establish a post-Hitler Germany as an economic, political, and eventually military bulwark against the USSR. The Soviets could see the drift at the EAC and soon decided to remain aloof from the postwar planning process that they had agreed at Tehran to support.

The second main planning committee was a politically similar group with overlapping personnel organized at State Department headquarters in Washington. This group and the U.S. delegation to the EAC each pushed for a "stern peace with reconciliation," as the slogan went.[2] They favored rapid elimination of Allied controls on the German economy, maintenance of German industrial production at something close to wartime levels (though without arms production), and sharp limits on prosecutions for war crimes.

This ran counter to what Roosevelt had personally promised Stalin and Churchill on these issues at Tehran and other international conferences. This division between White House promises and the State Department's implementation planning can be traced in part to Roosevelt himself. By 1944, FDR had grown so suspicious of the Foreign Service that he withheld even from his own secretary of state the details of his international commitments, including those reached at Tehran.[3]

The third center for postwar planning consisted of civil affairs specialists on the staffs of the War Department and of SHAEF (Supreme Headquarters, Allied Expeditionary Forces, Europe), commanded by General Dwight D. Eisenhower. SHAEF anticipated carrying much of the responsibility for the U.S. role in the occupation of Germany, so its civil affairs departments took up consideration of war crimes prosecutions and even aspects of U.S. economic policy toward Europe. During the spring and early summer of 1944, the SHAEF staff drafted a handbook of directives for use in the military administration of Germany that recommended that the occupation government import food and relief supplies into Germany and use German labor to operate coal mines, public utilities, and the transportation network. Overall, SHAEF ordered that the occupation forces should ensure that "the machine [of German society] works and works efficiently."[4]

This strategy had considerable impact on the day-to-day conduct of the war itself. Army Air Forces officers favored saturation bombing of the coal mines in the Ruhr Valley in 1944, for example, as a means of striking at Germany's most important energy supplies. But outside specialists (notably Frank Collbohm of Douglas Aircraft, who was later to found the RAND Corporation) successfully argued that these resources should not be destroyed because they would be useful for postwar reconstruction of Germany. The bombing was canceled.[5]

Morgenthau got hold of a copy of the SHAEF occupation policy handbook and of a collection of State Department planning papers on Germany. He contended that their approach failed to make good on the Allied promises to the victims of the war. They did not extirpate the roots of Nazism and would thus set the stage for renewed German aggression within the next decade, he contended. Morgenthau traveled to London in early August 1944, officially to review U.S. financial policy toward Britain, but in reality to investigate the whole scope of U.S. postwar policy.[6]

He met with Churchill, General Eisenhower and his staff, and with the U.S. staff at the European Advisory Commission. Anthony Eden provided Morgenthau with the confidential notes taken at Tehran concerning U.S., Soviet, and British grand strategy during the years ahead,[7] and Herbert Pell briefed him on the obstructions faced by the UNWCC.[8] Morgenthau aides Harry Dexter White and Bernard Bernstein provided him with detailed reports and copies of the State Department and War Department's most recent policy documents, which they had obtained through service on interagency planning committees.[9]

For the moment, at least, Henry Morgenthau emerged as by far the best-informed senior U.S. official about the various inchoate U.S. postwar strategies for Europe.

He didn't like what he saw. In Morgenthau's eyes, the same factional split within the U.S. government over policy toward Germany and the USSR that had characterized much of the 1930s, and which had obstructed U.S. responses to the Holocaust, was also making it difficult to develop postwar plans for Germany, particularly in the case of U.S. war crimes policy and postwar treatment of the German industrial elite. SHAEF's proposed handbook was the most immediate problem, as he saw it: if adopted, it would institutionalize policies that Morgenthau saw as appeasement of Germany.

To Morgenthau, Germany had been responsible for two world wars within his lifetime. He had seen German complicity in the brutal crimes of the Armenian Genocide during World War I and Germany's direct responsibility for the Holocaust. The Nazis had ruled Germany with wide popular support for more than a decade, creating an effective system of indoctrination calculated to foster race hatred. More than that, Germany remained an industrial power capable of dominating European business and strongly influencing world events. Morgenthau tended to disregard the political (and legal) significance of splits and rivalries within Germany, because virtually the entire German power structure had publicly supported Hitler and participated to a greater or lesser degree in the regime's crimes.

He saw German militarism and the country's industrial and banking cartels as the root causes of European wars, and he believed that German culture showed an almost instinctive tendency toward brutality and aggression. Even if Germany was defeated militarily, the country was, for Morgenthau, inherently flawed, perhaps inherently criminal, and would remain the most important threat to world peace in the postwar years.

Meeting the German threat, he reasoned, required continuation of the U.S.-British-Soviet alliance into the postwar era. Only in this way could peace be maintained in Europe, and this in turn required Western acceptance of the USSR as an equal among nations, stripping Germany of its industrial centers in the Saar and the Ruhr, and implementing a broad program of mass reeducation of the German people—all of which had been agreed to at the Tehran Conference. At times, Morgenthau even argued that an entire generation of German children should be taken from their parents and educated in Allied schools. This extreme step was necessary so that the ideology the Nazis seemed to have so effectively inculcated in the parents might be trained out of the children.[10]

Upon his return to the U.S., Morgenthau approached FDR with a detailed critique of the SHAEF handbook. A few days later, Roosevelt blasted the handbook and sketched out for the first time his own vision of U.S. postwar policy for Germany. "This so-called 'handbook' is pretty bad," Roosevelt wrote in a long memorandum to the secretary of war. "I should like to know how it came to be written and who approved it down the line. . . . It gives me the impression that Germany is to be restored just as much as the Netherlands or Belgium, and the people of Germany brought back as quickly as possible to their pre-war estate." (That, of course, was precisely the intention of State's planners.)

Roosevelt went on: "It is of the utmost importance that every person in Germany should realize that this time Germany is a defeated nation. I do not want them to starve to death but, as an example, if they need food to keep body and soul together beyond what they have, they should be fed three times a day with soup from Army soup kitchens. That will keep them perfectly healthy and they will remember that experience all their lives. The fact that they are a defeated nation, collectively and individually, must be so impressed upon them that they will hesitate to start any new war."[11]

FDR singled out pages of quotations from the proposed directives to emphasize his point. The conception that postwar Germany should be made to work "efficiently" was fundamentally wrong, as Roosevelt then saw it. "There exists a school of thought both in London and here which would, in effect, do for Germany what this Government did for its own citizens in 1933 when they were flat on their backs. I see no reason for starting a WPA, PWA or a CCC for Germany. . . .

"Too many people here and in England hold the view that the German people as a whole are not responsible for what has taken place—that only a few Nazi leaders are responsible. That unfortunately is not based on fact. The German people as a whole must have it driven home to them that the whole nation has been engaged in a lawless conspiracy against the decencies of modern civilization."[12]

By September 4, Morgenthau's team at the Treasury Department had drawn up a detailed counterproposal. Its "Suggested Post-Surrender Program for Germany" began by laying out the Tehran program for division of Germany and creation of non-German "international zones" in the Saar and Ruhr. It included bans on parades and marching bands—FDR was convinced that this was an important psychological measure—and provided an outline of permissible structures for local governments once the Nazis had been driven out.

The heart of the plan, however, was a series of harsh measures against German industry and against Nazi war criminals. The Ruhr—"the cauldron of wars," in the words of the document— was to be "stripped of all presently existing industries [and] so weakened that it can never become an industrial area." All plants and factories in the Ruhr were to be dismantled and moved or destroyed. The mines were to be sabotaged so as to "make it as difficult as possible ever to return the mines to operation."[13]

The proposed measures against war criminals were equally harsh. Under the plan, the United Nations would draw up a list of "arch criminals . . . whose obvious guilt has been generally recognized." They were to be summarily shot shortly after capture. A simple system of Allied military courts would be set up to deal with less well-known offenders. These courts could set death sentences for any German who had murdered hostages, who had killed persons because of their race, religion, or political conviction, or who had committed certain other crimes. All members of the Gestapo, SS, and Nazi party were to be arrested and detained "until the extent of guilt of each individual is determined."[14]

Morgenthau convinced Roosevelt and Churchill to back the plan at the Quebec Conference later that month. He argued that title to the best German factories and industrial equipment should pass to the Allied countries, including the USSR, as partial payment for Nazi war damages. But Britain should become first among equals and assume virtually all of Germany's highly lucrative export trade. This move would eventually end Britain's growing financial dependence on the U.S. Some German resources would be closed down altogether to punish the Germans and, not coincidentally, to head off economic competition for Britain before it began. Morgenthau's aides reassured Churchill that this strategy not only had the support of the U.S. president and his secretary of the treasury, but of England's most prominent economist, Lord Keynes, as well. (Keynes had been among the most articulate opponents of heavy reparations for Germany after World War I, which gave his early support of the Morgenthau plan all the more weight.)[15]

On the legal front, Morgenthau strongly backed Pell's insistence that Nazis must be punished for crimes against Axis civilians and that tough, immediate action be taken immediately to rescue Hungarian Jews bound for Auschwitz. Learning of Pell's ongoing troubles with the State Department, Morgenthau contacted his former aide, John Pehle, the recently appointed chief of the U.S. War Refugee Board. Pehle went directly to the acting secretary of state, Edward Stettinius, who had taken over for the ailing Cordell Hull. Pehle said that the War Refugee Board needed a public U.S. commitment to punish those who were persecuting Axis Jews if its own efforts at rescue and relief were to be successful. Failure to take action against these atrocities would be a "fearful miscarriage of justice," Pehle said, and would result directly in further loss of innocent lives in Europe.[16]

Stettinius sent Pehle a vague but courteous reply that basically ignored his plea.

Herbert Pell continued to pepper Washington with reports on UNWCC activities and requests for new "instructions," by which he meant a reversal of State's veto of prosecution of Nazis for crimes against the Jews of Germany, Austria, and Hungary. Green Hackworth ignored him. He considered his earlier letter to Pell (which had gone out over Secretary of State Hull's signature) to have been perfectly clear. Hackworth was not about to issue new "instructions," and he certainly did not intend to change his mind about the jurisdiction of the UNWCC.

But the situation was becoming increasingly embarrassing for the State Department. UNWCC chairman Cecil Hurst dropped a bombshell at a press conference in late August: No war crimes case had as yet been prepared against Adolf Hitler and other senior Axis leaders, Hurst said. There were only 350 names now on the UNWCC's list, most of whom were small fry who had committed crimes against British POWs. The *Washington Post*, the *Chicago Sun*, and other major papers carried on their front pages a syndicated report from London stating that Herbert Pell had been "fighting a losing battle for speedy justice, but others have retarded

everything." The 350 names on the list were compared to "semioffi-
cial estimates"—most likely leaked from Pell himself—that put the
number of Nazi "war criminals" at 6 million: 1.5 million Gestapo
and SS officers and 4.5 million SA *(Sturmabteilung)* brownshirt
militia troops. These men were simultaneously criminals and "the
greatest potential force and manpower reserve for a Nazi military
rebirth," the press report continued. "The legal basis of the commission's work now bars punishment of Nazis for maltreating and
slaughtering the Jews of Germany or of other Axis nationality, stateless persons or German-Jewish citizens of Polish, Czech, French or
other Allied origin, [because] the Hague convention defines a war
crime as an offense by one belligerent against the army or citizenry
of another belligerent."[17]

Pell offered his solution through the newspapers. The definition
of international crimes should be rearticulated, he contended, to
include "all offenses against persons because of race, religion or
political beliefs, irrespective of the victim's nationality or the territory on which the crimes were committed."[18]

The proposal was visionary, yet it was in tune with the earlier
legal conclusions of the London International Assembly and similar groups. It infuriated Hackworth. Lobbying in the press for
policy changes was strictly forbidden for U.S. representatives
abroad. Worse than that, the prevailing political climate suggested
that Pell might succeed in his effort.

Hackworth began a determined campaign to have Pell dismissed once and for all. He cultivated Acting Secretary of State
Edward R. Stettinius, who appears to have disliked Pell for his
independence and refusal to be a team player rather than for differences over policy. The hostility was evidently mutual, for Pell
remembered the acting secretary of state as "one of the stupidest
men I have ever known."[19]

The War Department meanwhile organized its own effort to
head off Morgenthau's initiative. Secretary of War Henry L.
Stimson saw Morgenthau's plan as a disaster for Germany and for
Europe generally, for much the same reason that John Foster Dulles
and others had opposed high German reparation payments in the
wake of World War I. Harsh Allied punishment of Germany would
lead to an unraveling of European business, he reasoned, and
perhaps to revolution.

The secretary passed FDR's tough marching orders to draw up a new handbook on Germany to his aide John J. McCloy, who in turn passed the problem of war crimes prosecutions to his specialist on the topic, attorney Murray Bernays. During two weeks in early September 1944, Bernays hammered out a six-page memorandum that in time became the legal foundation for much of the work of the International Military Tribunal at Nuremberg.

As Bernays saw his task, he was to defer action once again on the war crimes issue until the war was over, thereby avoiding reprisals against U.S. POWs. He did not intend to develop a plan to slow the pace of Nazi atrocities, as was favored by Morgenthau, Pell, and Pehle. Bernays's work at the War Department up to that time had consisted in important part in heading off attempts by the American Jewish community, and from the OSS and other U.S. agencies promoting psychological warfare, to open anti-Nazi war crimes trials while the conflict was still under way.

"Bernays had trouble keeping his eye on wartime atrocities," historian Bradley F. Smith has written. "By 1944 he must have seen reports of the exterminations, but they apparently did not penetrate his consciousness any more than they did that of most others in Washington. Ingrained doubts about atrocity stories, an inability to grasp the reality of the Holocaust, and the seeming futility of any effort to stop it, all played a part in this failure to comprehend reports of Auschwitz and other camps."[20] Bernays's professional concern was primarily with U.S. POWs then in German hands, not with European refugees.

Bernays and the War Department did not create a war crimes prosecution strategy under their own steam: They were pushed into it by the White House, by Morgenthau and Pell, and by public sentiment. There is every indication that without this outside pressure, the War Department would have continued to let the matter drift, just as it had for the previous three years. Regardless of what Murray Bernays may have intended, the War Department used his legal advice primarily as a device to avoid taking direct action against Auschwitz and other death camps.[21]

Bernays is today widely credited with formulating a plan to try Nazi criminals for *conspiracy* to commit crimes in addition to the more conventional charges such as murder and pillage. Charges that the Nazis had a "common plan" to commit war crimes, crimes against peace, and crimes against humanity eventually became a centerpiece of the prosecution strategy at Nuremberg.

In fact, though, the concept of Nazi organizations as criminal conspiracies had been discussed among legal scholars since the beginning of the war. It was developed in part by Harvard's Sheldon Glueck in articles in the *New Republic*, the *Harvard Law Review*, and in his 1944 book, *War Criminals: Their Prosecution and Punishment*. President Roosevelt even referred directly to the Nazis as a "lawless conspiracy" in his order to the War Department that provided the basis for Bernays's work.[22]

Be that as it may, it was Bernays who drafted the legal memo that eventually became War Department policy. Under U.S. criminal law, prosecutors have the option of bringing an additional charge of conspiracy any time two or more persons act "by concerted action to accomplish an unlawful purpose," that is, to work together to violate a law. In prosecuting bank robbers, for example, the state can seek a felony conspiracy conviction of the suspect who drove the getaway car, even if he never entered the bank.

Bernays suggested extending this principle to international law. If the Gestapo was found by an appropriate tribunal to have been a criminal conspiracy, he reasoned, any member of the organization could theoretically be prosecuted for each crime committed by its members, assuming that the accused Gestapo man was acting "in concert" with the rest of his organization. The same would be true for members of the Leadership Corps of the Nazi party, the SS, the German high command (though it was unclear exactly who that term might encompass), and for other allegedly criminal groups.

He proposed that shortly after Germany's surrender an Allied tribunal should try several key Nazi organizations as criminal conspiracies, in addition to judging a handful of the highest-ranking Nazi leaders. If the court upheld the conspiracy conviction, that precedent would provide a legal framework for trials of thousands of second- and third-level Nazis who had carried out the criminal policies of their leaders. The finding also would likely eliminate the defense raised by subordinates of acting under orders.

All of the acts of the accused organizations could be placed in the public record during prosecutors' efforts to prove that a criminal conspiracy existed. This sidestepped the thorny issue of whether or not Nazi actions prior to the outbreak of war in 1939 could be considered war crimes, because evidence going back to 1933 could be presented even though the prosecution was seeking convictions only on acts after 1939. It also permitted prosecutors to present evidence of Nazi atrocities against Axis nationals such as German and Hungarian Jews, at least as long as those deeds could be logically linked to more conventional war crimes.

On the other hand, Bernays's strategy rejected the effort led by Pell and Morgenthau to set new legal precedents on crimes against humanity and, in fact, opposed almost any development of international law beyond the cramped structure that had existed since the 1919 Paris Conference. His brief failed to recognize any inherent human rights for Axis civilians beyond those granted by Axis governments, nor did it facilitate Allied action to rescue Jews bound for extermination camps. Regardless of what Bernays may have intended, his proposals often became props for those at the State and the War departments who favored a go-slow response to Nazi atrocities.

A bruising bureaucratic war of leaks erupted in Washington during the weeks that followed Bernays's first draft, as members of each faction spread their version of the facts to the public through news reporters. Morgenthau's group appears to have cast the first stone. Pell told columnist Drew Pearson in mid-September about the sabotage of the UNWCC. The following week, Pearson followed up with revelations of FDR's stunning criticisms of SHAEF's handbook on Germany. He also laid out Morgenthau's version of the debate inside the U.S. government over the prosecution of war crimes. The *Wall Street Journal* published what amounted to the State Department's reply the next day, stressing the most extreme features of Morgenthau's plan and its potential to "deindustrialize" Germany. The *New York Times* and *Washington Evening Star* then weighed in with detailed reportage almost certainly leaked from the State Department that painted Morgenthau's initiative as a nearly fanatic example of war hysteria. The *Washington Post* editorialized that Morgenthau's economic strategy for Germany seemed to be the "product of a fevered mind."[23]

At this point, the 1944 presidential election was only a month away, and the opposition Republican party made the most of the scandal in the Democrats' camp. Republican candidate Thomas Dewey charged that Morgenthau had handed the Nazis a propaganda bonanza, and contended that German fears of Morgenthau had caused the Wehrmacht to dig in deeper and fight harder. The newspaper barrage dealt Morgenthau a serious political blow. FDR stepped away from Morgenthau's plan in the weeks that followed, publicly opposing "deindustrialization" of Germany and favoring a more moderate approach. After Roosevelt won reelection, Dewey retracted the charge that Morgenthau had contributed to Germany's will to fight, but by then the political damage had been done.

Herbert Pell was eager to clear the air with Roosevelt. In early December, he used the occasion of his son's marriage to return to the U.S., where he hoped to win the President's backing in the debate over atrocities against Jews in the Axis countries. At the State Department, Green Hackworth had other plans. That November, Congress had placed new restrictions on the President's Emergency Fund, the source of Pell's salary during the past eighteen months. The money as such was nearly meaningless to Herbert Pell, as he could easily afford to work without pay if necessary. But Hackworth knew that without a congressional appropriation for the post, Pell would be legally forced off the commission.

The legal advisor sent his aide Katherine Fite to Capitol Hill with a budget proposal that put the request for Pell's salary at the bottom of the list of State's priorities. Fite spoke in favor of the appropriation for Pell, but in terms that made it clear to Congress that there was little regard for Pell's work at State and not much support for the UNWCC. After several meetings, a congressional conference committee deleted Pell's salary during the markup of the appropriations bill, and the 1945 budget was passed without it.[24]

Herbert Pell met with Hackworth at least twice during Fite's trips to the Hill, and at neither time did the legal advisor let on that Pell's fate and that of the UNWCC were under discussion before a congressional budget committee. Instead, Hackworth used the meetings to quash Pell's requests to attend war crimes policy gatherings then under way at the War Department and to pour cold water on Pell's assertions that FDR was backing his plan to reclassify crimes against Axis Jews as war crimes. "I thought I made it clear . . . that nothing final and definite could be said at this time" concerning crimes against Axis civilians, Hackworth reproved Pell.[25] The U.S. representative should not act on any of his "impressions." Acting Secretary of State Stettinius also knew that Pell's ouster was imminent, but he too remained silent when the two men met.

Hackworth and Stettinius worked through the Christmas holidays to prepare the paperwork for FDR that they hoped would administer the coup de grace. They rehashed Preuss's allegations against Pell from the previous spring, criticized Pell's willingness to make public comments without instructions from Washington, blamed his dismissal on the congressional funding cuts, and falsely assured the President that Pell's concerns were now being addressed by a new legal committee made up of Hackworth, Bernays, and other government attorneys. The only real question left, they said, was whether Roosevelt should personally tell Pell that his job was over, or if he preferred to let State do the firing.

"O.K.," Roosevelt replied to Stettinius in a terse note in early January. "You do it. At last."[26]

Hackworth believed he was meanwhile making considerable progress in his meetings with Bernays at the War Department. To Bernays's face, Hackworth accepted the War Department proposal, but in working sessions he helped draft policy directives for U.S. commanders in the field that were as close as possible to the State Department's (and Hackworth's) strategy on war crimes. At the same time, Hackworth continued a behind-the-scenes effort to quash the compromise plan that he was drafting with Bernays. Despite lip service to the Bernays plan, Hackworth's now-declassified memos document that he continued to try to head off use of a conspiracy prosecution against the SS and the Nazi party for at least the next six months.[27] In part due to Hackworth's prompting, Attorney General Francis Biddle also opposed Pell's initiatives and the War Department's suggestions for conspiracy prosecution of Nazis, raising many of the same objections to war crimes enforcement that Robert Lansing had argued at the end of the previous world war.[28]

The British Foreign Office remained of one mind with Hackworth on these issues, and its legal attaché in Washington leaked to him the classified Combined Chiefs of Staff policy papers on war crimes for his "personal use" in convincing other Washington departments to toe the line.[29] These orders limited war crimes prosecutions to narrowly defined cases, made no mention of crimes against humanity, and specifically excluded any "acts committed by enemy authorities against their own nationals"—which is to say, most crimes against European Jews—from postwar prosecution. There was, of course, no discussion whatever of prosecuting Allied leaders for bombing civilians (or hospitals and similar installations) in the Axis countries.

Equally important, the Combined Chiefs of Staff contended that no war crimes suspect was to be handed over to any other Allied country "except by arrangements among the governments concerned."[30] In the world of diplomatic etiquette, this last statement was worded to undermine compliance with the obligations of the Moscow Declaration without openly defying that agreement. The importance of blocking delivery of suspects was to grow considerably in the months ahead, and eventually it emerged as one of the most important means by which war criminals escaped justice.

In early January 1945, Hackworth's effort to engineer Pell's dismissal unexpectedly blew up in the legal advisor's face. Shortly after FDR's confidential note authorizing State to dismiss Pell, the President met Pell for lunch at the White House. As Pell tells the story in his unpublished memoirs, FDR reassured him of continuing support and encouraged him to return to London to lead the UNWCC in taking a tough stand on Nazi crimes against Jews. Elated, Herbert Pell returned to the State Department for what he believed would be a routine meeting with Edward Stettinius. It did not work out that way. Stettinius abruptly fired Pell without warning and with minimal courtesy. The dismissed UNWCC commissioner immediately called the White House, but FDR did not return his old friend's telephone calls.[31]

Pell refused to give up and took his case to the newspapers, charging that the State Department leadership was quashing prosecution of Nazi atrocities. He used his dismissal to bring new attention and credibility to his earlier accusations that the State Department had sabotaged or obstructed a whole range of activities undertaken in response to the Holocaust. Newspaper editorial writers and columnists took up Pell's cause and, more important, focused public attention on the legal technicalities that Green Hackworth and other department officials had quietly used to justify their policy of inaction in the face of the Holocaust.

A *Washington Post* editorial condemned Pell's firing and attacked "certain legalistic-minded old-school individuals . . . [who] had failed to find any precedent in international law for the punishment of a country's murder of its own citizens . . . and therefore refused to approve [U.S.] participation" in the prosecution of Germans who had destroyed German Jews. The problem, the *Post* continued in a second editorial, was "certain well-entrenched functionaries in the State Department." The liberal New York daily *PM* published a series of investigative articles on the whole affair. "Who are the U.S. officials seeking to sabotage trial of Nazi killers?" the paper headlined. "Legally, Hitler is still safe" because of a State Department policy that was, in *PM's* words, making "punishment of the men who perpetrated this war upon the world ... impossible."[32]

The firestorm of publicity forced the State Department publicly to cave in on the issue of prosecuting Germans for crimes against German Jews, though State continued to resist Morgenthau and Pell's broader conception of breaking up the German corporate elite. The State Department issued a formal statement insisting— quite falsely—that it had supported the "aims" of Pell's program all along.[33] Pell became a martyr, in effect, for the hard-line approach to Nazi crimes that had been espoused by the activists surrounding Morgenthau at Treasury and by much of the general public. "By crudely dismissing him," historian Michael Blayney has written of this incident, the State Department "enabled Pell to arouse public wrath to such intensity that the Department was forced to yield. . . . Pell's abrupt dismissal helped make the [Nuremberg] Trials virtually inevitable."[34]

The factional conflicts in Washington over what to do with Germany also began to emerge among U.S. military commanders in Europe well before the shooting war ended. U.S. troops crossed into Germany at Aachen in the fall of 1944, and it was there that the U.S. made its first effort to establish a post-Nazi government. The opposing drives underlying U.S. policy—toward continuity of German elites as a means of attaining stability, on the one hand, or toward a purge of the system that had given birth to Hitler, on the other—collided almost immediately. The events in Aachen became a prototype of what was to unfold throughout the Western zones of Germany and, in fact, throughout much of Europe.

The city had suffered severe war damage from Allied and German forces. Yet, within days of the U.S. victory, there emerged in Aachen "an elite made up of technicians, lawyers, engineers, businessmen, manufacturers, and churchmen," according to military sociologist Saul Padover, who led a U.S.-sponsored research team in Aachen. "This elite is shrewd, strong-willed, and aggressive. It occupies every important job" in the new German administration that the U.S. permitted under the occupation.[35]

Padover's team conducted in-depth psychological and sociological interviews with dozens of people in Aachen, including most of the "notables" identified there. "Their strong point, especially in dealing with Americans, is that they are 'anti-Nazi' or 'non-Nazi,' " Padover wrote. During the war, most had held senior positions at the Veltrup works, Aachen's leading war production plant. "A striking fact about this new Aachen elite is its comparative youth. Their ages run from thirty-three to fifty. They all represent the upper middle class. . . . The leading men in this group had spent their working life and grew prosperous under the Nazi system and they knew little else. They had an anti-democratic conception of government and a 'leadership' [i.e., *Führerprinzip*] view of business."

Aachen's new leadership clique had a fairly clear-cut, long-range political-economic plan. The plan, "about which MG [U.S. Military Government] knew little and cared less, was a significant index of what one may expect from similar business groups in Germany," Padover contended. Their vision, he said, was "an authoritarian corporate state," somewhat similar to the Austrian model of the 1930s. Economically, they favored a tightly knit community of owners and managers of small enterprises supported by a limited "labor aristocracy" of foremen and artisans. The new leaders were said to be "violently opposed to popular elections, political parties, and trade unions.

"Under the nose of the MG," Padover concluded, the new administration was "setting up the framework of an authoritarian, hierarchical, bureaucratic, corporate fascism—a type of *Staendestaat* that even the Nazis had rejected."[36]

This group entrenched itself in the city administration by placing insiders in control of local ministries, Padover continued. The new administration's chief building contractor and leader of its "Industrial Bureau," for example, had been Aachen's largest contractor under the Nazis and had made extensive use of forced labor. The executive officer and personnel director, Opt de Hipt, had been the Gestapo's liaison inside the city's most important war production plant, with responsibility for enforcing loyalty among the factory's employees.[37]

In short, the postwar leaders who emerged at Aachen were not ideological Nazis from the mold of Himmler or Hitler. They were instead the political, economic, and social technocrats who had actually run Germany during Hitler's regime under the watchful eye of Nazi party activists.

There was an alternative for the administration of occupied German cities, though it could have been implemented only in the face of resistance of the existing elites. At Aachen the town and its surroundings had been in the hands of a coalition government made up of left-centrists, Social Democrats, and Communists for most of the decade prior to Hitler's assumption of power. One of the first public opinion surveys conducted by U.S. forces in Germany found that 70 percent of the women and 83 percent of the men interviewed at random said that they would vote for Social Democrat or Communist candidates if elections were held.[38] Theoretically, at least, the citizens of Aachen would have elected a more democratic and anti-Nazi administration had the military government permitted elections to be held.

The American response to the emerging leadership clique foreshadowed what was to unfold in the U.S. occupation zone over the next year. This was months before Germany's surrender, at a time when Roosevelt was still in the White House, U.S. unity with the Soviets was still ostensibly strong, and anti-Nazi sentiment among U.S. forces was at a high tide. "Behind the scenes in the MG offices a storm was raging. It revolved around the basic question of retention of Nazis and other undesirable characters in office," according to Padover. "MG itself was split into three wings, Right, Left, and Center. A majority of MG officers were on the extreme Right and supported the [new] administration; their business, they said coldly, was 'efficiency,' and not politics. A minority, consisting of the deputy [military governor] and two lieutenants, were more or less on the Left and urged the elimination of Nazis. In the Center was Major J., the Military Government Officer. Major J., an affable officer who knew little about Germany and nothing of the German language, was perfectly neutral on the subject of Nazis." There were fifty-five Nazis in middle- and high-level posts in the local administration at that point, Padover reports. "Major J. said that one must go slowly in getting rid of them, because they were indispensable. 'Where,' he asked, 'would you find competent people who are not Nazis?' "[39]

Padover's study concluded that the root of U.S. inertia in Germany involved politics, bureaucracy, and social attitudes based on class.

An MG team is judged on its efficiency and performance record. Thus when an MG group enters a city, its first
consideration is functional, not political. No political intelligence officer accompanied the MG team into Aachen. In fact,
no officer, outside of the medical officer, could speak German;
none had any first-hand German experience.

An MG team, therefore, will employ almost anybody it believes capable of putting a town on a functioning basis. Thus
Nazi sympathizers, Party members, or German nationalists,
are appointed by MG as the only available specialists. These
specialists, who look extremely presentable and have professional backgrounds similar to those of MG officers, then place
their like-minded friends in secondary positions. As a consequence, MG's initial indifference to the politics of the situation
leads in the end to a political mess. Then comes the complicated attempts by CIC [Army counterintelligence] to weed out
the undesirables, and the MG officers find themselves in the
unpleasant position of having either to defend Nazis or of
starting all over again.[40]

Padover's study led to a scandal and reforms at about the same
time the controversy over Pell's dismissal erupted. Congressional
and public pressure led the U.S. military governor to purge about
two dozen former Nazis from the Aachen government. Most of
these officials were in fact small fry, including the janitor at the
local school. Aacheners responding to the U.S. public opinion
survey asked openly, "Are you going to sit back now and let the big
Nazis rule," as an elderly woman put it, "now that you are satisfied
that you have thrown out the Nazi janitors?"[41]

13

"This Needs to Be Dragged Out Into the Open"

T HE DAY after Christmas 1944, just as the Pell controversy was coming to a head, Allen Dulles proposed a plan to Washington under which German industrialists and "technical men . . . with brilliant industrial records" who had worked for the Nazis were to be offered amnesty by the OSS in order to retain them as "valuable sources of information" for postwar reconstruction.[1] The first men Dulles sponsored illustrate the moral questions that inevitably arise in such programs. They were a pair of brothers said to be named Schmidt—Dulles wasn't certain of the details. One of them ran a munitions plant at Eisenach, and the other was a senior executive with Messerschmitt in charge of that company's construction of underground factories and of warplane plants near Vienna. Now that the war was clearly lost, Dulles said, the Schmidt brothers were looking for a safe way out.

The ethical dilemma was obvious. On one hand, the Schmidt brothers might in fact have information useful to the Allied war effort. On the other hand, there could be little doubt that if the

Schmidts held the positions that Dulles said they did, their careers had been made at least in part through the exploitation of forced labor, for that was undeniably the foundation of German arms production throughout the war. The Messerschmitt Schmidt would also be a suspect in Nazi extermination-through-labor efforts, as prisoners made up most of the workforce in German underground factory construction. Dulles was surely aware, at least in general terms, of the criminal character of much of German war production: The French guerrillas he was underwriting were made up mainly of men who had gone to the hills rather than face forced labor in German munitions factories.

If one concedes that in certain circumstances a greater evil could be avoided by giving amnesty to men like the Schmidts, then exactly how far and on what terms should such protection be extended? In this case, Dulles based his appeal for the Schmidts on particularly flimsy evidence. He told Washington that he had been "reliably informed" that the two brothers were "nonpolitical" with "brilliant industrial records," yet the OSS man was uncertain of their names and had no means of checking any information about their activities. And what of the "Schmidts" who contacted the OSS after the German surrender? Should they, too, receive the same amnesty so that they could become "valuable sources of information," as Dulles put it, "in the post-collapse period"?[2]

Allen Dulles understood that there were splits between the German economic elite and the diehard Nazis, and he favored dividing these groups to the greatest degree possible. He believed he could extract economic and military intelligence from the Nazis' partners, sow disorder in Axis ranks, and preserve business and political leaders favoring private enterprise for postwar reconstruction.

Dulles offered cooperative Axis leaders promises of protection from prosecution for their crimes and asylum from the advancing Red Army.[3] The collaborators often faced charges of treason—a capital crime under most nations' laws—as well as accusations of exploitation of slave labor, racial persecution, looting, and other offenses regarded as war crimes or crimes against humanity. Dulles also appealed to the class interests of former collaborators, to their desire to protect Western civilization against communism, and to similar less tangible factors. But protection from prosecution was the *sine qua non* for collaborators' cooperation with Dulles. His effectiveness as an intelligence-network builder and as a political broker for peace negotiations was based largely on the premise that the West's wartime cooperation with the Soviets would soon collapse. This offered a brief window of opportunity for compromised Germans and Axis executives quick-witted enough to switch sides now, he said. Time was already running out.

The Western response to Nazi collaborators emerged as an important political debate among the Allies, because collaborators usually had a two-sided political character. On one hand, they had actively helped the Nazis achieve their ends—that, after all, was why the Nazis had recruited collaborators in the first place. On the other hand, many collaborators laid claim to having taken some action in opposition to the Nazis, usually in the last days of Nazi power, which they asserted proved that they had been secret sympathizers with the Resistance all along, operating in the heart of the enemy camp.

Collaboration during the Nazi occupation in Europe had been most pronounced in the political and business elites and in the police forces of the countries under Berlin's hegemony. In Vichy France, for example, "There were in fact few genuinely 'new men' in office at Vichy, men who had held no major responsibilities under the [pre-war] Third Republic," Robert Paxton wrote in a classic study of Vichy. While French brownshirts "found places in the realms of order [i.e., police] and propaganda, especially later in the regime . . . they never gained influence in the vital fields of finance, defence, or diplomacy. On the contrary, some elements of Third Republic leadership passed directly into the Vichy regime almost without change of personnel. Senior civil servants and the mass of public officials went on with their jobs, with the exception of Jews, officials of Masonic orders, some prefects tied too closely to the [leftist] Popular Front, and a handful of top officials personally linked to Paul Reynaud. . . . The Third Republic's business elite went on virtually unchanged. Jewish businessmen, of course, were penalized, along with those who joined de Gaulle, but no leading businessman comes to mind in that category.

"Vichy was run to a large degree by a selection of what French political sociologists usefully call 'notables': people of already high attainment in the worlds of public administration, business, the professions, and local affairs." In Vichy, Paxton continued, "the real power of the unelected French elite was made manifest."[4]

The situation in other conquered countries varied, of course, and in each country (including Germany itself) the elite's enthusiasm for the Nazis ebbed as the tide of war turned. Nevertheless, except in Poland and the occupied territories of the USSR,* the Nazis consistently succeeded in enlisting the assistance of much of the established power structure, civil service personnel, and police.

Wartime collaboration with the Nazis frequently had a distinct class character, as Vichy showed. Complicity with the Nazis tended to follow the lines of the existing political, economic, and social power in the countries dominated by Hitler's government. The same was true to an important extent within Germany itself.

Put bluntly, almost any conventional postwar government on the Continent that seriously attempted to free itself from the influence of wartime collaborators would soon be cutting into its own bone and sinew, just as Turkey had discovered when it attempted to prosecute the genocidal *Ittihad* leaders after the First World War. The "integrating institutions" of society had often played a crucial role in the Holocaust and other crimes. But this could not be acknowledged in Europe, much less prosecuted, without damaging the legitimacy of postwar society itself. This the U.S. and its non-Soviet Allies were unwilling to do, for fear of the geopolitical and economic consequences of potential revolutions in Germany, Italy, France, Greece, and perhaps other countries as well.

The State Department's "Riga" faction, which had refused to intervene in European affairs on behalf of Jewish refugees during the war, led the way in insisting that the U.S. intervene on behalf of threatened European elites after the conflict was over. These two tactics, which might seem at first to be contradictory, were in fact based on what seemed to them to be the overriding importance of preserving a stable European political center, with relatively open markets, and a willingness to cooperate with U.S. geopolitical and economic strategies. This was the purported "vital national interest" of which Allen Dulles had spoken.

---

* The Nazis had pledged to wipe out the existing social structure in these countries in order to increase German *Lebensraum* ("living space"), and were thus much less willing to encourage collaboration from prewar elites in either state.

General Eisenhower's political advisor from the State Department, Robert Murphy, became one of the most influential advocates of close U.S. relations with Nazi collaborators, particularly those of the Vichy type. Murphy had risen through the ranks at the State Department after World War I because of his talent for diplomacy and his ability to find common cause between U.S. foreign interests and the old guard of the European establishment. Early in the war, Murphy had brokered the deal with the one-time Vichy collaborator Admiral Jean Darlan.

For Murphy and for Allen Dulles, George Kennan, and other "Riga" faction advocates, men such as Darlan were integral to the overall U.S. political strategy for the war. As Murphy and his allies saw things, Communists and left-wing Socialists were likely to make substantial political gains after the war because of their roles in the Resistance, notwithstanding the Communist parties' ambivalence during the 1939–41 Hitler-Stalin pact. If the U.S. wanted something other than revolutionary governments in Europe, Murphy contended, it would have to reach an understanding with the indigenous leaders who had worked for the Germans. Why should the U.S. forswear the cooperation of such men, he asked, particularly when they seemed to have already proved their capacity to rule?

Secretary of the Treasury Morgenthau and his allies regarded Murphy as a complacent appeaser of Nazism, a man whose inaction and deceit had contributed significantly to the U.S. government's failure to rescue innocent people from the Holocaust and a reactionary who was willing to throw away possibilities for a peaceful postwar world to satisfy the ideological demands of anti-communism. The collision between the two officials began early and grew more and more bitter. By 1945, Morgenthau was using almost every audience he had with Roosevelt to argue for Murphy's dismissal as chief U.S. political advisor in Europe.

In the last days of 1944, as Dulles in Bern drafted his brief for the Schmidt brothers, Morgenthau was in Washington drawing up what amounted to a manifesto on Germany for Roosevelt. Three points seemed basic to Morgenthau: Germany had the will to try once more to conquer the world; it would require many years for democracy and reeducation to achieve any real change in Germany's political culture; and the survival of its heavy industry would once again give Germany a warmaking capacity in the near future, perhaps within the next five years. Morgenthau concluded his analysis as follows:

> The more I think of this problem, the more I read and hear discussions of it, the clearer it seems to me that the real motive of those who oppose a weak Germany is not any actual disagreement on these three points. On the contrary, it is simply an expression of fear of Russia and communism. It is the twenty-year-old idea of a 'bulwark against Bolshevism'—which was one of the factors which brought this present war down on us. But people who hold this view are unwilling (for reasons which, no doubt, they regard as statesmanlike) to come out in the open and lay the real issue on the table, all sorts of smoke screens are thrown up to support the proposition that Germany must be rebuilt. . . .
>
> This thing needs to be dragged out into the open. I feel so deeply about it that I speak strongly. If we don't face it I am just as sure as I can be that we are going to let a lot of hollow and hypocritical propaganda lead us into recreating a strong Germany and making a foe of Russia. I shudder for the sake of our children to think of what will follow."[5]

Robert Murphy was central to the problem, the treasury secretary believed, and his campaign to remove him continued up to the moment of FDR's death. As winter slowly gave way to spring in 1945, FDR invited Morgenthau to visit him at Warm Springs, Georgia, where Roosevelt was convalescing. Morgenthau dictated a long note to his diary about the encounter: The President, he said, "had aged terrifically and looked very haggard. His hands shook so that he started to knock the glasses over. . . . I found his memory bad and he was constantly confusing names. . . . I have never seen him have so much difficulty."[6]

But FDR seemed a little better after cocktails and dinner, so the two men settled down to talk politics, as had been their custom for almost three decades. "I told the President that [General Lucius] Clay had called on me and I had asked him what he was going to do about Robert Murphy, and he said that he realized that was one of his headaches. The President said, "Well, what's the matter with Murphy?" And I said . . . 'Murphy was too anxious to collaborate [with Darlan and Vichy].'

"The President said, 'Well, what have you got on your mind?' I said, 'In order to break the State Department crowd . . . just the way you broke the crowd of Admirals when you were Assistant Secretary of the Navy, my suggestion is that you make Claude Bowers political advisor to Eisenhower.' " (Bowers was a liberal New Dealer who was at that time U.S. ambassador to Chile.) Morgenthau continued that the "President thought that it was a wonderful idea, and so that he wouldn't forget it, I made him write it down."[7] Morgenthau went on to appeal for Roosevelt's support in his battle with the State Department over U.S. strategy on Germany and the USSR, and reports in his diary entry that FDR indicated he was with him "100 percent."

Roosevelt died the next afternoon. Morgenthau remained as secretary of the treasury during the transition to the new president, Harry Truman, but without FDR's backing he quickly lost influence within the government. Robert Murphy remained as Eisenhower's political advisor, and the "State Department crowd," as Morgenthau had put it, consolidated its hold on U.S. foreign policy toward Germany and the USSR.

Paradoxically, though, their influence in war crimes policy slipped sharply, at least for the moment. The combination of Pell's dismissal, Padover's report from Germany, Morgenthau's activism, and, perhaps most fundamentally, the increasing public knowledge of the Allied failure to respond effectively to Nazi atrocities, each took its toll on the authority of the State Department. U.S. newspapers began to discuss many aspects of the Holocaust and of U.S. war crimes policy in detail for the first time. These factors significantly undermined the ability of the "well-entrenched functionaries," to use the *Washington Post's* phrase, to make basic policy decisions outside of the public eye.[8]

Morgenthau worked with Murray Bernays's boss, Assistant Secretary of War John J. McCloy, to draw up a blueprint for denazification in Germany. This was a new compromise plan that melded Morgenthau's earlier proposals with those of the War Department, and produced relatively hard-hitting policies concerning Nazi criminals and denazification of German industry. The U.S. military command eventually promulgated the order in late April 1945 under the designation "JCS 1067," meaning Joint Chiefs of Staff order no. 1067.[9]

"The principal Allied objective is to prevent Germany from ever again becoming a threat to the peace of the world," its provisions began. "Essential steps in the accomplishment of this objective are the elimination of Nazism and militarism in all their forms, the immediate apprehension of war criminals for punishment, the industrial disarmament and demilitarization of Germany, with continuing control over Germany's capacity to make war, and the preparation for eventual reconstruction of German political life on a democratic basis."[10]

JCS 1067 detailed an FDR-style antitrust policy as the centerpiece of U.S. strategy for the reorganization of the German economy. The approach was very similar to that which had been the legal backbone of the U.S. Department of Justice Antitrust Division's criminal indictments of major American companies during the 1930s, though with the added feature that former Nazi officials would be barred from any substantial business role in the future.

Each of the economic reforms was well within the framework of American-style capitalism, and (with the exception of the political review of business executives) sometimes imposed fewer restrictions on German business than many U.S. companies then faced under American law.[11] The order prohibited German economic cartels and other industrial combinations designed to divide up markets, set monopoly prices, and squeeze out competitors. It set a policy of "dispersion of ownership and control" of German industry by breaking up interlocking corporate directorates.[12]

JCS 1067's denazification requirements were quite tough-minded, however. The U.S. planned to question under oath each senior executive of the German economic ministries and major banks to determine his (or, in rare instances, her) activities during the Nazi regime. Persons who had denounced Jews or dissenters to the Nazis, who had authorized violence in connection with their corporate activities, disseminated Nazi propaganda, or joined any of several Nazi cult organizations (such as the "German Christian" and neo-pagan movements favored by the SS) were to be regarded as "ardent supporters of Nazism" and removed from all positions of authority.

The U.S. regulations declared that the corporate leaders of the Deutsche Bank, Dresdner Bank, and four other large banks had been central to Nazi rule, and ordered them removed from their positions not only at those institutions but also at hundreds of other major German companies interlocked with the banks. Lower-level banking officials—branch managers, vice presidents, department chiefs, etc.—were to be vetted as well, but removed from their posts only if they were found to be "ardent Nazis." The U.S. promulgated roughly similar denazification policies for officials of the major insurance companies, stock exchanges, private banks, and similar institutions.[13]

Taken as a whole, then, official U.S. policy in the spring of 1945 favored strict measures to remove ideologically committed Nazis and their diehard supporters from positions of influence; a limited economic reform similar to U.S. antitrust measures intended to break up German cartels; and preservation of a competitive, private-enterprise economy.

The remaining officials of the Roosevelt administration, and Morgenthau himself, abandoned Morgenthau's earlier proposals to destroy German mines and shoot senior Nazis on sight. Nevertheless, Washington remained committed to punishment of a broad spectrum of German leaders—not just the Nazi party's elite—and to thoroughgoing economic reform that would hold Germany's corporate leaders accountable for the actions of their companies.

But a written policy is one thing; its implementation is quite another. Robert Murphy took personal charge of the political oversight of U.S. denazification work in Germany almost immediately, and he made little secret of his inclinations. Meanwhile, the sensitive task of overseeing U.S. intelligence evaluations of German business and political leaders fell to an enterprising OSS man who was stationed in Berlin shortly after Hitler's suicide. It was Allen Dulles.

14

Sunrise

SHORTLY BEFORE he took up his OSS post in Berlin, Allen Dulles
guaranteed de facto asylum to SS *Obergruppenführer* Karl
Wolff—the highest-ranking SS officer to survive the war—and to a
collection of Wolff's most senior aides. The details of Dulles's deal
with this particular Nazi have remained buried in classified U.S.
government files for more than forty years.[1] But the record is clear.
Whether Dulles intended it or not, his strategy for exploiting former Nazi leaders to advance purported U.S. interests had sweeping implications for U.S.-Soviet relations, U.S.-German relations,
for war crimes prosecutions and the UN War Crimes Commission,
and even for world peace.

Allen Dulles's pivotal role in this hidden but crucial phase of
European politics is at the core of Operation Sunrise—the secret
negotiations in 1945 for a German surrender in northern Italy. This
stepping-stone for Dulles's postwar intelligence career was his
covert diplomacy bringing together Western intelligence agencies,
fugitive Nazis, and certain leading Vatican officials of the day.

In late 1944, Pope Pius XII and Ildefonso Cardinal Schuster of
Milan had contacted the SS, the German military command in
Italy, and OSS agent Dulles in Switzerland, offering to serve as
intermediaries in negotiations to ease the surrender of German
forces in northern Italy. In a confidential memo, Cardinal Schuster
stressed that the Italian Communist party would likely gain from
continued fighting between the U.S. and the Germans on the Italian peninsula. "The Catholic Church regards the systematic destruction of public utility installations [gas and electric works,
etc.] together with that of industrial plant [that would come from
fighting in northern Italy], as a prerequisite of Bolshevik infiltration into Italy. This threat to living conditions on the one hand and
industrial potential on the other is intended to create disorder and
unemployment. This is the basis upon which [the Italian Communists' hope] the masses are to be won, first for Communism and
then for Bolshevism," Schuster wrote. He stated that a negotiated
German withdrawal, on the other hand, would stabilize the economic situation, undermine the popularity of the Communist resistance, and reduce the possibility that German military leaders
would be tried for war crimes once the conflict was over.[2] Schuster
and his senior assistant, Monsignor Don Giuseppe Bicchierai,
stood ready to help negotiate a suitable agreement between the
Germans and the Americans, the note concluded.

There was more to the Vatican initiative, strategically speaking,
than simply the rescue of factories in northern Italy. The Vatican
proposal would give U.S. and British forces control of the important port city of Trieste on the border of Italy and Yugoslavia. This
position would permit them to rapidly enter Yugoslavia, Hungary,
and Austria in advance of the Red Army, which was then approaching from the east. These historically Catholic territories had
been Axis strongholds for much of the war, but anticipating Germany's defeat, many people in this heartland preferred to surrender to American or British troops rather than be overrun by the Red
Army.

Dulles viewed Schuster's proposals as a means to dramatically
outflank both Germany and the USSR in Central Europe, reduce
Western casualties in Italy, and begin what would later come to be
known as the "dual containment" of both Germany and the USSR.[3]
Meanwhile, Axis leaders willing to surrender despite Hitler's
standing war-to-the-death orders saw the Vatican initiative as a

means to head off a probable Soviet military occupation of Central Europe, reduce casualties among their own forces, dramatically split the U.S. and Britain from the USSR, and, not least, win asylum for themselves and their families.

Cardinal Schuster and Monsignor Bicchierai had long been among the most prominent clerical supporters of fascism in Italy, according to SS Colonel Eugen Dollmann, who handled negotiations with the Vatican for the SS during the last days of the war. "His Eminence [Schuster] had been very favorably inclined toward Fascism in general and Benito Mussolini in particular," Dollmann noted. "Like Pope Pius XI, another native of the Milan area, he too had looked upon the Duce as a man sent by providence."[4] Dollmann, who had made his career as a liaison between Hitler and Mussolini on a number of sensitive issues, including the recurrent SS campaigns to deport Italian Jews to Auschwitz, had by 1945 lost his enthusiasm for the Führer, and preferred a role as an "interpreter and social butterfly," as he put it, in the declining days of the Third Reich.[5]

The SS-Vatican initiative was joined by the prominent Milanese industrialist and playboy Baron Luigi Parrilli—a papal chamberlain, leading Knight of Malta, and a man with strong contacts in the banking and intelligence communities of Switzerland, just north of the Italian border, where Dulles made his headquarters.[6]

This unlikely foursome—the gaunt, severe cardinal in ceremonial robes and peaked hat; his aide, Bichierrai; the foppish SS man with a closet full of Italian suits of the latest cut; and the skirt-chasing industrialist with a charming smile and a manner "like a character in a late-nineteenth-century French novel," as Dollmann put it[7]—became the core of a group determined to deliver Central Europe to the Western Allies before the Soviet troops arrived.

Dollmann's superior, Karl Wolff—the highest-ranking SS officer in Italy—opened secret negotiations with Dulles during the early spring of 1945, talks that would have a destructive effect on sensitive U.S.-Soviet relations.[8] SS *Obergruppenführer* Wolff was a tall, bulky man with thinning blond hair and the erect bearing characteristic of a career SS officer. He had big hands, expensive tastes, and a weakness for heavy gold and diamond rings, which he brandished so expressively that they became a standing joke among his SS rivals. Loyal and ideologically committed, Wolff had joined the Nazi party well before Hitler's ascent to power. For more than a decade, he had served as SS chief Himmler's most senior executive officer, adjutant, and chief of staff. He managed Himmler's personal slush fund of gifts from German financiers; handled the sensitive contacts that arranged SS transfers of slave laborers to IG Farben, Kontinentale Öl, and other major companies; and became the chief sponsor and cheerleader within the Nazi bureaucracy for the mass extermination center at Treblinka.

It had been Wolff who lobbied the German transportation minister to ensure that the SS had an ample supply of railroad cars to ship Jews to the death camp at Treblinka, in spite of competing demands from the Wehrmacht, which wanted the freight cars to move military supplies to the front. Wolff was successful in that effort and wrote of his "special joy *(besondere Freude)* now that five thousand members of the Chosen People are going to Treblinka every day."[9]

When Dulles opened contacts with Wolff in early 1945, the British military command in Italy notified the Soviets that new peace negotiations had begun for a rapid German surrender of northern Italy. The Soviets replied that they were glad to hear this; all that was required under standing Allied agreements on negotiations with the enemy was for a handful of senior Soviet military representatives to monitor the progress of the talks.

The U.S. ambassador to Moscow, Averell Harriman, vetoed that. Inviting the Soviets to the negotiations would make the Germans nervous, he contended, and would only encourage the Soviets to insist on participation in other upcoming decisions about the former Axis territories already held by U.S. and British troops. His was one of the most important voices on U.S.-Soviet relations, and his opinion carried the day.[10]

Roosevelt and Stalin exchanged increasingly bitter notes as negotiations continued in Switzerland among Dulles, the SS representatives, and a crew of senior U.S. military officers that included Major General Lyman Lemnitzer and General Hoyt Vandenberg. A week after the talks began, Soviet Foreign Minister Molotov sent a note to Harriman in Moscow expressing "complete surprise" that Soviet representatives were still barred from the talks. He said that the situation was "inexplicable in terms of the relations of alliance" between the U.S. and the USSR.[11] If the U.S. refused to permit Soviet representatives to participate, Molotov contended, the talks had to be abandoned.

Roosevelt wrote directly to Stalin a few days later. The USSR misunderstood what was taking place, he insisted. The talks in Italy were basically a local matter, comparable to that in which the Baltic coast cities of Konigsberg and Danzig had earlier surrendered to the Soviets. Roosevelt seemed to approve Soviet participation in the talks ("I will be pleased to have at any discussion of the details of surrender . . . the benefit of the experience and advice of any of your officers who can be present . . ."), but he insisted that the talks in Switzerland were an "investigation" of a local German commander's surrender offer, not a "negotiation."[12] Time was of the essence, he continued, and the U.S. representatives could not be faulted for being eager to accept the surrender of the German troops they were facing on the battlefield.

Stalin escalated the argument. His foreign minister, Molotov, suddenly had new commitments in Moscow and would not attend the founding of Roosevelt's most cherished postwar project, the United Nations Organization. This was a calculated slight, and both sides knew it. In a new note to FDR, Stalin replied that he was "all for profiting from cases of disintegration in the German armies," but in this case, the Germans were using the talks to "maneuver" and to transfer troops from Italy to the Eastern Front.[13] Roosevelt replied that Soviet actions in Poland and Romania had not lived up to the commitments made at the Yalta Conference less than two months previously. U.S.-Soviet relations had moved rapidly to an "atmosphere of regrettable apprehension and mistrust" owing to the confrontation over Dulles's talks with the SS, Roosevelt commented, and again insisted to Stalin that the talks were for "the single purpose of arranging contact with competent German military officers and not for negotiations of any kind."[14] Meanwhile, FDR cabled Dulles in Switzerland and ordered him to present the SS representatives with a take-it-or-leave-it offer of an unconditional surrender. No further negotiation would be permitted, the President said.

Stalin seemed to know many of the details of the Dulles-SS talks even before Roosevelt did. When FDR tried to soothe Stalin with a declaration that the Swiss talks were without political significance, Stalin shot back that "apparently you are not fully informed." Stalin's military intelligence agents in Switzerland were "sure that negotiations did take place and that they ended in an agreement with the Germans, whereby the German commander on the Western Front, Marshal Kesselring, is to open the front to the Anglo-American troops and let them move east, while the British and Americans have promised, in exchange, to ease the armistice terms for the Germans. I think my colleagues are not very far from the truth," he continued. If this perception was wrong, he asked, why were his men still being excluded from the talks?[15]

Stalin may have overstated his case, but he was not far off. These were in fact exactly the terms that Cardinal Schuster had proposed and that Dulles had discussed with Wolff. No final deal had been struck, though, and by early April both sides in Switzerland were once again seeking guidance from their respective home offices.[16] By then, though, the German front had begun to collapse throughout Europe, the Red Army was at the gates of Berlin, and Dulles's grand plan to take Central Europe by way of Trieste had failed. "The Bern incident," as Roosevelt described it in a last letter to Stalin written only hours before his death, ". . . now appears [to have] faded into the past without having accomplished any useful purpose."[17]

The talks had not been successful from either Allen Dulles's or SS General Wolff's points of view, largely because Roosevelt had ruled out any formal agreement with the Germans other than unconditional surrender. But FDR's ban on a formal agreement did not preclude Dulles from making more limited "gentlemen's agreements" with his SS counterparts for concessions that he saw as advantageous to the OSS or to U.S. geopolitical strategy. The SS delegation, the Swiss intelligence envoys who were serving as go-betweens, and the Soviet agents secretly monitoring the talks each came away from the talks convinced that Dulles had agreed to provide protection and assistance to General Wolff and his SS entourage in exchange for a quick surrender of German troops in Italy, although Dulles would deny this later.[18]

Wolff's ultimately empty promises of a dramatic German surrender that would advance U.S. and British forces far to the east captivated Dulles and his OSS colleagues in Switzerland. Dulles intervened on a half-dozen occasions in an effort to keep the Operation Sunrise negotiations on track, even after the joint U.S.-British military command in Italy ordered him to desist. By the last week of April, senior U.S. and British military commanders in Italy concluded that the Sunrise project was little more than a desperate SS effort to fracture Allied unity, and told Dulles to cut off all contact with Wolff and his emissaries. Nevertheless, Dulles's top aide Gero von Gaevernitz kept the negotiations open and acted with Dulles's tacit cooperation to rescue Wolff from Italian partisans.[19] The U.S.-British Combined Chiefs of Staff are known to have opened an investigation into Dulles's alleged dereliction of duty and refusal to obey orders in connection with the Wolff rescue, but the records of this inquiry have disappeared from OSS and military files and have yet to be rediscovered.[20]

The unofficial truce in Italy that took hold as the negotiations went on probably saved lives, if only because ground combat is so brutal that even a few hours' respite can reduce casualties. But Roosevelt's conclusion that the negotiations failed to achieve a genuine German surrender in Italy is accurate. As a practical matter, Operation Sunrise contributed considerably more to souring U.S.-Soviet relations, and to enhancing Allen Dulles's carefully cultivated reputation as a spymaster, than it ever did to winning the war in Europe.

Making use of splits in the enemy camp is, of course, among the most basic military tactics, and fundamental to almost any effort to recruit spies. But Operation Sunrise was seriously counterproductive from strategic and political points of view. The U.S. and its allies had formally agreed to forgo use of separate peace negotiations with the Germans in order to more fully ensure the solidity of their coalition. That policy did not make relations with the Germans easier, obviously, but any other approach would likely have facilitated Hitler's central strategy and last hope in the final years of the war, which was to conquer the Allies by dividing them. Roosevelt's demand for an unconditional surrender had not sprung from naïveté or starry-eyed idealism, as some critics have argued, but rather from a tough-minded appraisal of just how much blood would be required to defeat the Axis. The unconditional-surrender policy did not "cost" U.S. lives; it saved them, perhaps by the hundreds of thousands, by guaranteeing that the Soviet Union would carry most of the weight in the war against Hitler.

While FDR was right about Sunrise, he was mistaken in his hope that a struggle for control of the strategically important city of Trieste would be defused. In May 1945, only days after FDR's death, U.S. and British forces sought to consolidate control of Trieste as a beachhead for south-central Europe. But Josip Tito's well-organized Yugoslav partisans regarded the city and its environs as part of liberated Yugoslavia, and they opposed the U.S.-British initiative. This inter-Allied clash over what might otherwise be an obscure seaport became one of the first, crystallizing conflicts in the cold war.

Stalin opposed Tito's claim to Trieste and criticized his "adventurism" in backing left-wing nationalist guerrillas in Trieste and in Greece.[21] But that was not how things appeared in Washington at the time. The chief U.S. political advisor on the scene, Alexander Kirk, had been U.S. chargé d'affaires in Moscow during the 1930s and an early and influential advocate of the "Riga" faction's hardline policy against the USSR. Kirk convinced himself and Washington that Tito's forces were acting as the cat's-paw of the Soviets, and that the Yugoslav claim to Trieste was an example of totalitarian aggression.

Winston Churchill and Joseph Grew, a Morgenthau opponent who was now acting U.S. secretary of state, strongly backed Kirk. Kirk's dire reports only confirmed their long-standing analysis of Soviet policy. Grew regarded the Trieste crisis as nothing less than the first military confrontation in an unfolding U.S. war against the Soviets. World War II had thus far resulted in "the transfer of totalitarian dictatorship and power from Germany and Japan to Soviet Russia, which will constitute in future as grave a danger to us as did the Axis," Grew wrote in a programmatic statement against the Soviets at the height of the crisis. The situation unfolding in Trieste illustrated "the future world pattern" that the USSR aimed to create throughout Europe and eventually throughout the world.[22]

A new war between the U.S. and the USSR "is as certain as anything in this world can be certain," the acting secretary of state told the newly installed President, Harry Truman. Writing on May 19, 1945, as ashes still smoldered in Berlin, Grew recommended that "our policy towards Soviet Russia should immediately stiffen, all along the line. It will be far better and safer to have the showdown before Russia can reconstruct herself and develop her tremendous potential military, economic and territorial power." Above all, it would be the "most fatal thing," Grew continued, "to place any confidence whatever in Russia's sincerity," because the USSR regards "our ethical behavior as a weakness to us and an asset to her."[23]

Truman had stepped into Roosevelt's shoes only a few weeks

earlier, and he remained cautious on the Trieste confrontation. But he had voiced suspicions of the Soviets comparable to Grew's on several occasions, and the new President clearly accepted the thrust of his acting secretary of state's analysis. Truman resolved to maintain U.S. and British control of Trieste. After a show of military force against Tito's partisans, he succeeded in doing so.

Three points are worth stressing. First, senior U.S. officials, including the acting secretary of state, had concluded as early as May 1945 that a U.S. war with the USSR "is as certain as anything in this world can be certain" and that placing any confidence in Soviet intentions would be a "fatal mistake." These were not offhand comments; they were the substance of the State Department's policy recommendations to the President of the United States.[24] Second, the ideologically driven U.S. conviction that Tito was simply a pawn of the USSR expanded what was in reality a local dispute with Tito into a more fundamental clash between the superpowers. The Soviets saw their actions during the Trieste crisis as a concession to the West and as an illustration of good faith; Churchill, Grew, and Truman read the situation in almost opposite terms. To them, the outcome at Trieste seemed to prove the value of getting tough with Moscow—despite the fact that the Soviets had conceded U.S. and British dominance of Trieste from the outset. U.S.-Soviet relations deteriorated across the board.

Third, and most relevant to the present discussion, the political crisis over Trieste had immediate and substantial impact on U.S. policy concerning war criminals, quislings, and suspected collaborators from Central and Eastern Europe. Allied war crimes policy remained for most decision-makers primarily a tactic in the deepening East-West political rivalry, and only secondarily an issue of justice in its own right. The showdown with Yugoslavia emerged as a disturbing example of how the intrinsic weakness of international law concerning crimes against humanity helped shape the cold war and was in turn shaped by it.

Tito's government made repeated, detailed requests to the Western Allies to turn over scores of Yugoslav Nazis and collaborators who had fallen into U.S. and British hands. Most of these requests were straightforward and not particularly controversial: They sought the cabinet officers of the genocidal Croatian puppet government that the Germans had installed during the war, for example; leaders of the primitive clerical-fascist Ustashi organization;

commanders and guards of the Jasenovac concentration camp; wartime security police officers; and similar suspects.[25]

But the defeated anti-Tito factions in Yugoslavia had powerful friends abroad, not the least of whom was Pope Pius XII. For the pope, the militantly Catholic Ustashis seemed to be a viable alternative to Tito's Communists, and the pope and leading Croatian clerics provided repeated political and diplomatic support to the Ustashi state in Croatia throughout its rule. True, the Vatican had sought to distance itself from the Ustashis' bloodier public atrocities, particularly during the final months of the regime. Nevertheless, by the time the Ustashi collapse came, the Croatian Catholic hierarchy had blood on its vestments from years of tacit cooperation with genocide in the Balkans.[26] Worse, the Vatican compounded its blunder by indiscriminately assisting thousands of Ustashi criminals to escape to Italy and South America; many of these men were, by any standard, among the most heinous criminals of the war.[27]

When Tito's government began seeking transfer of accused Croatian quislings and war criminals, the Vatican and Catholic prelates in the West repeatedly intervened to block Allied cooperation, notwithstanding the U.S. commitments in the Moscow Declaration, at Yalta, and in other international forums. Similarly, conservative-nationalist and monarchist Yugoslavs lobbied on behalf of the rightist Yugoslav leader Draja Mihailovich and his forces, who had vacillated during the war between an alliance with the West against Hitler and an alliance with the Nazis against Tito.*[28] Yugoslav minority leaders, notably Slovenes, pressured U.S. congressmen on behalf of old comrades whose records during the war had been at best mixed.

* For example, a fraternal organization, the Serbian National Federation in the U.S., split over the issue of war crimes trials for Serbian leader Draja Mihailovich, an anti-Communist Serbian nationalist leader who controlled parts of Yugoslavia for most of the war. Mihailovich had attempted to maintain some ties to the Western Allies, but as a practical matter his troops had cooperated closely with German occupation troops and with the Gestapo in joint efforts to suppress Tito's partisans. By 1944, the Western Allies had disavowed Mihailovich as a Nazi collaborator. When the war ended, Tito tried and executed Mihailovich and much of his high command as traitors.

The ethnic Serbian communities in the West became bitterly split over Tito's revolution and over the Mihailovich trial. A substantial fraction of overseas Serbs embraced Tito's government, but many emigré religious leaders and businessmen opposed it.

The U.S. government's willingness to cooperate with Tito on war crimes matters broke down early in 1945 as these domestic pressures combined with the geopolitical confrontation with Tito over Trieste. The State Department suspended authorization for transfers of prisoners to the Yugoslavs on a bureaucratic pretext during the Trieste conflict, though State continued to publicly affirm U.S. commitments to the Moscow Declaration and other wartime agreements. By summer 1945, however, it had become "increasingly difficult to justify inaction on our part" in the face of Yugoslavian transfer requests, U.S. military commanders wired to the War Department in Washington. They requested permission from State to turn over "bona fide" criminal suspects.[29]

The U.S. State Department and British Foreign Office refused. They saw the Yugoslav transfer request as "so essentially political that it should continue to be dealt with through diplomatic channels" rather than through the procedures then used with all other Allied states, including the USSR. The prisoners sought by the Yugoslavs "are not war criminals in the proper sense" (that is, by a narrow definition), the British Foreign Office said. "Some of them are clearly collaborators of the blackest dye; but the Yugoslav request also covers others who may well be properly considered as political opponents of the present Yugoslav regime rather than as traitors to the Yugoslav state." For that reason, the British memo concluded, Yugoslavia would henceforth be a "special case," and Allied commanders were no longer authorized to hand over alleged traitors and renegades. Any Yugoslav requests for prisoners should instead be referred to the State Department and Foreign

---

Pro-Tito Yugoslavs protested the presence in the U.S. of Konstanin Fotich, Mihailovich's chief foreign policy advisor. Fotich and his comrades took control of the U.S. fraternal group Serbian National Federation's national leadership committee and of its newspaper, *American Srbobran*. When the Yugoslav trials convicted the Mihailovich government as traitors, pro-Tito Serbs saw it as their opportunity to expel Fotich from the U.S. and resume control of the federation and its newspaper. They sent their protest concerning Fotich's presence in the U.S. to the State Department, as protocol demanded.

The State Department's response was instructive: It took no action against Fotich, who had enjoyed friendly relations with the department throughout most of the war. Instead, it turned over the names of the protesters and copies of their letter to the FBI, the Office of Naval Intelligence, and other U.S. military intelligence agencies, with a suggestion that the security agencies take a new look into the affairs of the pro-Tito Yugoslavs in the U.S.

Office, where the matter had been "under active consideration . . . for some time."[30]

The obstruction of transfers to the Yugoslavs grew so blatant that even the U.S. ambassador in Belgrade, John Cabot, formally protested to Washington. "It is crystal clear even on the basis of material available in this embassy's files that we have flouted our own commitments and that by our attitude we are protecting not only Quislings but also [those who] have been guilty of terrible crimes committed in Yugoslavia," Cabot wrote in a top-secret telegram.

"I presume we must protect our agents even though it disgusts me to think that we may be using the same men we so strongly criticized Fascists for using," Cabot continued. "But so far as I can ascertain [the] record now is, despite our commitments and moral obligations: (1) we have failed to take effective action [to repatriate accused Yugoslav war criminals], (2) we have prevented [the] British from taking effective action, (3) we have not insisted that Italy take effective action, (4) we are apparently conniving with the Vatican and Argentina to get guilty people to haven in the latter country. I sincerely hope I am mistaken, particularly regarding [this] latter point. How can we defend this record? . . . ."[31]

The State Department legal advisor's office attached a note to Cabot's message stating that he was misinformed; that he had "not received all the telegrams on the subject" and "not estimated the situation correctly." The protest was buried in classified files, where it remained undisturbed for decades. Roughly similar treatment was accorded protests of U.S. unwillingness to transfer suspected war criminals to the Belgian, French, Polish, and Czechoslovak governments.[32]

In a related development, the Yugoslavs formally requested the transfer of Nikola Rusinovic, a leading Ustashi ideologue and quisling, whom the wartime Croatian regime had appointed consul general and minister plenipotentiary with special responsibilities for organizing Croat-Italian fascist counterinsurgency operations against Tito's rebels. Shortly after the request, the legal office of the U.S. Military Government in Europe denied the request without explanation.

The real reason for protecting Rusinovic has now come to light for the first time. "The basis of this decision which was not made known to the Yugoslav [War Crimes] Liaison Detachment was the fact that United States Military Intelligence authorities desired to exploit Rusinovic as a source of information," according to a classified note to State Department European chief James Riddleberger found attached to the Rusinovic file. "The [US] Political Advisor [Robert Murphy] is informed that there is a strong possibility that he will be taken to the United States for this purpose. Under these circumstances . . . the case for the present may be considered closed."[33]

By the spring of 1945, refugees from Eastern Europe found themselves mired in the deepening political rivalries among the Western Allies, the USSR, and the indigenous resistance movements in Yugoslavia, Greece, Italy, and other European countries. This problem became particularly acute for defectors from the USSR who had fought for the Germans during the war.

Hundreds of thousands of Red Army troops had surrendered to the Germans, particularly during the first weeks of the war. When service to the Germans became the only means of escape from starvation in German POW camps, many of these prisoners joined the German forces as laborers, soldiers, or concentration camp guards. Some became the executioners who carried out the horrifying day-to-day work of mass murder in the extermination camps. Tens of thousands of these defectors fell into Western hands as the Allies approached Berlin.

The Soviet government contended that under the Moscow Declaration of 1943, the West should immediately deliver any captured defectors to the USSR to face whatever justice was customary in Soviet society. No formal extradition was necessary, and there could be no review of individual prisoners' cases by Western governments. By the same token, the Soviets pledged to return to the U.S. and Britain some 50,000 to 100,000 Western POWs the Soviets had recovered from the Germans, including many rescued fliers and some captured defectors.[34]

During the war, U.S. psychological warfare strategists had favored offering amnesty to Soviet defectors still in German ranks as a means of encouraging rebellion behind German lines. Shortly before the D-Day invasion, for example, Great Britain's ambassador to Moscow suggested to Stalin that Western intelligence had discovered that a substantial number of Soviet defectors in German uniform had been deployed in northern France in work details and as soldiers. Why not offer these troops amnesty if they surrendered? Stalin refused. "The number of such persons in the German forces is very insignificant," Foreign Minister Molotov wrote back, "and a special appeal to them would not be of political interest."[35]

Before the month was out, however, the British captured about 2,500 Soviet nationals serving in the German army in France. Shipped as POWs to England, the new prisoners precipitated a series of East-West political crises over delivery of POWs and alleged war criminals that was to sour international relations in the wake of the war.

The British War Cabinet voted to return them to the Soviet Union. "They were captured while serving in German military or para-military formations, the behavior of which in France has often been revolting," Anthony Eden wrote during the debate. "We cannot afford to be sentimental about this." Soviet cooperation would be needed to recover thousands of U.S. and British POWs who had once been held by the Germans, Eden continued, and if Britain refused to turn over the new prisoners, Stalin would be immediately suspicious. "It is no concern of ours what measures any Allied government, including the Soviet government, takes as regards their own nationals," he said. In any case, "we surely do not wish to be permanently saddled with a number of these men."[36] The U.S. government reached a similar conclusion about two months later.

But things did not go smoothly. The British decision sidestepped most of the trickier questions concerning what was to be done with captured Soviet defectors. What was to be done with those who had *not* volunteered for the Germans, such as the millions of Soviet civilians whom the Nazis had forced to labor at gunpoint in German factories? And what of prisoners from Latvia, Lithuania, Estonia, and parts of the western Ukraine? Since 1939, the USSR had claimed these territories as its own, but the Western Allies did not recognize them as such. Were prisoners from these regions to be considered Soviets?

British and U.S. clandestine activities compounded these problems. In September 1944, the USSR filed a formal protest charging that British intelligence had begun recruiting camp inmates for anti-Communist paramilitary units whose most obvious target was the USSR itself. The Soviets said the British were also ship-

ping other Soviet POWs to new camps in the U.S. and Canada
without Soviet government permission. Anti-Communist religious
groups with special access to the British camps were bombarding
the prisoners with propaganda, the Soviet ambassador to Great
Britain, M. Gousev, complained, frightening the POWs from
returning to the USSR.[37]

The Western intelligence agencies' supposedly secret recruiting
among POWs and suspected war criminals emerged as a surprisingly potent issue in East-West relations almost a year before
the end of the war. To the Soviets, Western exploitation of these
prisoners seemed to be part of the same pattern they had seen in the
Darlan and Rudolf Hess affairs and in the West's failure to open a
second front early in the war. This time, the Soviets formally accused their allies of organizing an emigré army intended to fight the
USSR, an obvious violation of the joint declarations signed only
months earlier. This was well before Germany's defeat and almost
three years before the date at which most Western historians place
the emergence of the cold war. The timing of Gousev's complaint, its
formality, and the high-level attention it required is a practical
measure of the importance that Stalin attached to this issue.

By that autumn, tens of thousands of former Soviets had fallen
into U.S. or British hands. The Americans captured at least 28,000
former Soviet troops in German uniform in northern France. British POW totals, though less certain, were comparable.[38]

As the Western Allies' repatriation program moved ahead, some
prisoners bitterly protested, fearing they would be executed for
treason if they returned to the USSR. Others volunteered to go
back, believing that Moscow would view this demonstration of
renewed loyalty with favor. The various factions among the POWs
fought one another, and at least one such incident at a British POW
camp threatened to erupt into a general rebellion.

That November the British returned the first shipment of 10,000
prisoners—almost all of them former Red Army soldiers who had
defected to the Germans, been captured by the British, and then
volunteered to be repatriated—in an ocean convoy to Murmansk.
Only twelve of them clearly objected to repatriation; they were put
aboard by force. The first U.S. shipment of 1,179 Russian prisoners
left San Francisco on December 29 aboard the Soviet steamer SS
Ural. Seventy of those prisoners protested repatriation. Three attempted suicide.[39]

Little is known of the fate of those who returned to the USSR in these shipments. But rumors and intelligence reports drifted back to the West of execution of some prisoners minutes after they left the ships, of beatings, suicides, and forced marches to prison camps deep in the Soviet interior. The POWs still in Western hands became increasingly wary of returning, and some Western officials raised political and moral challenges to further cooperation with the prisoner transfers.

The Allied leaders discussed prisoner repatriations at least twice, once at Churchill's October 1944 conference with Stalin shortly before the first British shipments, and again at the February 1945 Yalta Conference.[40] They reached several simple agreements: Each of the powers retained authority to deal with its own nationals; the USSR would help repatriate 50,000 to 100,000 Western prisoners it had liberated from the Germans; and the West would return all Soviet nationals who had found their way into Western hands. Each of the powers stressed that compliance with these terms would be viewed as an important test of the commitment of the parties to Allied wartime agreements.

But the next three months brought Operation Sunrise, the Trieste crisis, and the breakdown of U.S.-Yugoslav cooperation in prosecuting alleged war criminals. By July 1945, Soviet suspicions that the Western Allies would not comply with agreements concerning POWs had reached center stage in East-West relations. Western powers had cooperated with the repatriations thus far, but they were now equivocating. The Soviets soon raised the issue in meetings with British officials and with U.S. Supreme Court Justice Robert Jackson, who was leading the U.S. negotiations toward establishment of the International Military Tribunal at Nuremberg.

The ongoing Nuremberg planning discussions had become "complicated by Russian insistence that we incorporate agreement concerning turnover of prisoners wanted in other countries for trial," Jackson reported back to Washington. "I have taken the position [that] all except the international cases are beyond the terms of my authority and, except to advise my own Govt whether we have objections in any case, the question of surrender[ing] prisoners is not before us."

Jackson was keenly aware of the political ramifications of the prisoner issue. "This is likely to become a very delicate problem as demands [are] probable for surrender [of] persons who are not war criminals but politically objectionable. You will need to decide what terms to impose and what showing will be required of criminality."[41] The Czechs had already demanded the surrender for trial of Hans Frank and other Nazi occupation officials, Jackson noted, and the U.S. needed a uniform policy on the issue.

Jackson—who was soon to be the chief U.S. prosecutor at the International Military Tribunal at Nuremberg—favored abandoning the international trials altogether if the Soviets insisted on U.S. conformity with the Moscow Declaration on prisoner transfers. The only alternative if the Soviets insisted on a public reaffirmation of existing agreements, Jackson wrote, would be for each of the Allies to "set up [its] own tribunal and try prisoners by its own system of procedure." That approach would be "easier for me and faster," he noted, "but [it would be] desirable [to] give [an] example of unity on the crime problem if possible."[42]

15

White Lists

I F OPERATION SUNRISE and the collision over Trieste demonstrated
the political factors that favored fugitive war criminals, Allen
Dulles's new assignment in Berlin was to exemplify some economic characteristics of the same problem. Dulles became one of
Robert Murphy's most strategically placed allies inside occupied
Germany. Beginning in early 1945, Dulles provided clearances for
senior German bankers and industrialists seeking permission to
remain active in Germany's postwar economy. As an OSS chief in
Allied-occupied Berlin, he personally oversaw compilation of
"white lists" of non-Nazi German executives believed to be useful
for German reconstruction. He thus exercised considerable influence during the first months after the war over the day-to-day
implementation of U.S. policy concerning German business
leaders.

Dulles usually favored amnesty for those whose class or economic status seemed to make them useful for postwar economic
revival, and for people who had assisted him in intelligence gath-

ering or covert operations. Culpability for Nazi crimes should be
limited in most cases to German leaders who remained diehard
Nazi enthusiasts, he concluded. In a striking memo to Washington in late 1944, Dulles erroneously reported that, with a "few no-
table exceptions, Berlin banking circles [are] secretly violently
anti-Nazi."[1] He said that Oswald Roessler of the Deutsche Bank,
Carl Goetz of the Dresdner Bank and the Krupp board, and key
Nazi industrialist Herbert Goering (Hermann Goering's brother)
had been arrested as anti-Nazi resistance leaders before Hitler's
fall.

Dulles was wrong on almost every count. It is true that by late
1944 many Berlin bankers were disillusioned with Hitler, but the
claim that they were "violently anti-Nazi" had no foundation whatsoever.*[2] Roessler, Goetz, and Goering were never in any sense
anti-Nazi resistance leaders; each had made their careers over the
previous fifteen years largely through services to the Nazi party
and the SS.

Dulles's recently declassified OSS telegrams show that his principal sources of information on the German financial and industrial elite were officials of the Bank for International Settlements
(BIS) in Basel, Switzerland, which had worked closely with Berlin banking circles since the first years of Hitler's regime. The
BIS provided sophisticated currency clearing services to a dozen

---

* The fact is that much of the intelligence Dulles provided to OSS headquarters
was poor, as were his evaluations of German bankers. True, Allen Dulles and the
Bern station provided more than their fair share of intelligence scoops during
the war, including the famous KAPPA documents that Fritz Kolbe smuggled out
of the German Foreign Ministry. But in January 1944, Washington cabled to
Dulles that "We think it is essential that you be informed at once that almost the
entire material [you] supplied disagrees with reports we have received originat-
ing with other sources, and parts of it were months old.... [There has been]
degeneration of your information which is now given a lower rating than any other
source. This seems to indicate a need for using the greatest care in checking all
your sources...." Or again: "The Bern estimate [of German military forces] is
most inaccurate and misleading. It contains grievous errors regarding locations
and also includes reports on non-existent divisions.... Only 30 of the divisions
reported located in the west are correctly identified [...] The remaining divisions are either incorrectly located or do not exist. In more than 50 instances, the
classification of divisions by type is wrong ..." Dulles's intelligence on the German war in the East was even worse, an internal OSS evaluation found. Even the
war diaries of the OSS, which tend to highlight every aspect of the organization's
achievements, found that much of the military intelligence the Bern station provided was "outdated" and of "minor interest."

industrial countries and served as a private policy council where representatives of central banks met to discuss monetary policy.[3]

The Dulles family had played an important role in the bank from its inception, so it was not surprising that Allen Dulles would turn to his contacts there. The institution had been founded to carry out the international clearing necessary for the reparations programs John Foster Dulles had helped pioneer after World War I, and the bank's first chronicler and most enthusiastic supporter was his sister, Eleanor Lansing Dulles.[4] Both Allen and John Foster Dulles sat on the boards of New York and London affiliates of European companies led by men on the BIS board of directors,[5] and an American with long social and business ties to the Dulleses, Thomas McKittrick, became president of the BIS in 1940.

At least two senior BIS officers, McKittrick and Roger Auboin, worked for Dulles as underground contract agents. McKittrick was agent No. 644 on Dulles's OSS payroll and regularly contributed information and services to the OSS station in Bern throughout the war.[6] Roger Auboin, the general manager of the BIS, appears as agent No. 651 (code-named "General Manager B") in Dulles's messages to OSS headquarters.[7]

Notwithstanding the fact that McKittrick was its president, the BIS was thoroughly dominated by Axis interests due to bank by-laws that allocated votes on bank policy according to financial contributions. Axis powers had controlled a plurality of BIS votes throughout the 1930s, and as the blitzkrieg progressed, control of more central banks fell into German hands. By the end of 1942, Germany and the Axis controlled more than 75 percent of the votes on the BIS board.[8]

The BIS remained officially neutral, but as a practical matter its allegiances shifted with the fortunes of war. During McKittrick's presidency, the BIS cooperated with the German Reichsbank's efforts to launder gold stolen from the mouths of death camp victims, in part because German Finance Minister Walther Funk was first among equals on the BIS's wartime board of directors. (After the war, McKittrick sold the concentration camp gold back to the Germans, stating, as the *New York Times* put it, that the BIS had purchased it "inadvertently."[9]) The institution also joined in a complex Nazi scheme to use currency manipulation and bank clearing procedures to loot the economies of entire countries. Both

programs led to charges of war crimes and crimes against humanity against the Germans involved in the scheme; McKittrick and
other BIS executives, however, were never charged.[10]

The bank clearing schemes deserve special notice because of
their significant but little-known role in looting the equivalent of
billions of dollars from Nazi-occupied territories. Importantly,
this form of looting was for the most part organized and managed
by ordinary German corporate executives and their foreign collaborators, not by the SS or diehard Nazis. Here again, the Nazis
succeeded in harnessing the in-place, more-or-less conventional
social machinery of trade to the tasks of the Hitler government. In
this way, billions of Reichsmarks worth of wealth in the countries
occupied by the Nazis shifted into German hands, often before the
victimized country even understood what was happening.

Germany had instituted basic monetary clearing procedures
during the 1930s as a means of controlling the flow of foreign
currencies in and out of the Reich. In its simplest form, a German
company interested in trade with, say, Belgium would pay for
Belgian goods in German currency to the German central bank, the
Reichsbank in Berlin. The Reichsbank would send what amounted
to an international IOU to the Belgian central bank for the amount
it had been paid by the German company. The Belgian central bank
would then pay the Belgian company the money for its goods in
Belgian currency. Hundreds of other companies in many countries
were involved in thousands of similar deals. Then, at regular
intervals, the central banks would meet at the BIS, total up the
credits and debits of all the business deals, and "clear" them by
making a settlement between central banks that balanced their
accounts.[11]

The creation of this central channel for foreign exchange permitted Hitler's government to monitor and license most transactions
between Germans and foreigners. These procedures contributed
significantly to the Aryanization of Jewish property, because they
closed off opportunities to transfer assets abroad for all but a
handful of the wealthiest and best-connected German Jews.

During Germany's wartime occupation of foreign countries,
Hitler's government took effective control of both sides of the
clearing equation and thus could manipulate each contract to its
advantage. German bankers took over most of the central banks in
the occupied countries, staffing those institutions with German
professionals and compliant foreigners.

In Belgium, for example, the Nazi occupation government declared the German currency, the Reichsmark, to be worth 12.5 Belgian francs. This rate overvalued the mark by as much as 50 percent, making everything in Belgium extraordinarily cheap for Germans. Next, the puppet Belgian government decreed that all trade with Germany or with the occupation government was required to use a special currency designed for German use in the occupied countries. In effect, Germany created a new type of money in Belgium and throughout Nazi-occupied Europe that it could print and spend at will.[12]

When it came time to settle up between the Reichsbank and the foreign central bank, the Reichsbank again enlisted the cooperation of the Bank for International Settlements in putting forward a variety of pretexts not to pay its debt. The occupied country was powerless to protest.

The Germans confiscated Jewish property in the occupied territories by using related techniques. In Belgium, the Nazi-appointed government forced Jews to sell most of their possessions for a price set by the government and paid the new currency into special bank accounts. Later, when most Belgian Jews were deported to be murdered, the occupation government simply seized the accounts that it had earlier insisted on establishing.

Soon, German banks and companies began buying up foreign companies, real estate, products, and raw materials all across Europe for a fraction of their value. Such transactions were usually completed "legally" with all of the contracts, deeds, and other documentation typical of conventional business. Meanwhile, those aspects of the economies in the occupied countries that were not dependent upon sales to Germany disintegrated. This was extremely profitable for the German companies, of course, and presented a major inducement for some businesspeople to collaborate with the occupation.

The postwar coalition government in Poland estimated that this type of theft had cost their country the equivalent of 20 billion marks between 1939 and 1945—equal to about 17 percent of Germany's total annual war budget at the height of the conflict in Europe.[13] While these numbers are an estimate, and the Polish government obviously had an interest in claiming a high level of damages, they nonetheless illustrate the effectiveness of this technique of draining wealth from occupied countries.

A study by the British Ministry of Economic Warfare reported

damages consistent with the Polish estimates and roughly propor-
tionate figures for eight other countries occupied by Germany. In
all, the British estimated that the Germans had extracted the equivalent of about $180 billion from occupied Europe as of 1943,
including both direct levies for occupation costs and a variety of
hidden techniques such as currency manipulation. These figures
were based on financial statistics published by the Germans themselves and do not include estimates for wealth seized from the
USSR and Greece. As such, even the $180 billion figure clearly
underestimates the true total.[14]

The BIS cooperated with and facilitated this scheme despite
protests from exiled Allied governments. The bank recognized the
Nazi-installed occupation governments, provided the clearing services essential to "legalizing" the operation, and even went so far
as to help Nazi leaders such as Walther Funk unload looted gold in
international markets.[15]

Once the war was over, Dulles and the OSS turned to McKittrick, Auboin, the BIS, and to Dulles's own prewar business contacts in Germany for advice on the political leanings of German
bankers. This was an obvious and even defensible move. Theoretically, the prejudices latent in McKittrick's recommendations to
Dulles should have in time been sorted out by Dulles himself or
by later OSS investigators. Each little bit of information is an im-
provement over having none at all, most intelligence agents will
contend. In reality, however, Dulles passed on McKittrick's evaluations of German bankers with only minimal checking in official
OSS white-list clearances for German corporate and government
personnel. The white list recommendations then tended to become institutionalized, only rarely to be critically reexamined
later.

In the summer of 1945, Dulles prepared a list of eight top German bankers, complete with biographies, whom he recommended
"on the basis of [their] ability and record" for senior corporate
posts in any German major enterprise.[16] Dulles drew heavily on
the protégés of Hjalmar Schacht—then already facing charges before the International Military Tribunal at Nuremberg—who had
been the gray eminence of German international banking since the
1920s. At the top of Dulles's list was Ernst Huelse, a former director
general of the BIS and a key Schacht aide at the Reichsbank. Next
came Karl Blessing—also a former Reichsbank director, BIS director, and Schacht protégé—and then a series of minor bankers, some

of whom had in fact been hostile to the Nazis. The men Dulles recommended usually ended up in senior positions in postwar Germany. Although they were not Nazi ideologues, most of them had made their peace with the Nazi party and served in trusted positions throughout the Hitler years.

A closer look at Karl Blessing's career illustrates not only the moral ambiguities of the German financial elite under Hitler, but also the role of U.S. intelligence in preserving that elite through the trauma of 1945–46. With Allen Dulles's help, Karl Blessing cultivated a reputation after the war as an anti-Nazi who had once resigned a seat on the board of the powerful multinational company Unilever rather than cooperate with SS efforts to take over the company. Following this purported act of bravery, Blessing later told the New York Times, he was reassigned by Hitler to be a "lowly functionary in the Ministry of Mineral Oil Industry" [sic], where he spent the war years hiding out from the Gestapo.[17]

This claim was remarkable, both in that Blessing should make it and in that the Times would swallow it. The truth is that Blessing served throughout the Hitler years as one of the most important liaisons between German big business and the Nazi party and SS. Karl Blessing represented Hjalmar Schacht and the Reichsbank at the meetings of the Himmlerkreis, the clandestine organization of bankers and industrialists who sought to curry favor with SS chief Himmler by secretly bankrolling some of his more exotic projects.[18] Blessing was among the most enthusiastic attendees at Himmlerkreis gatherings for more than a decade, according to Fritz Kranefuss, who became Himmler's adjutant and monitor for the meetings. During the war years, Blessing participated in thirty out of thirty-eight gatherings, a record of brown-nosing the SS leader comparable to Kranefuss's own.[19]

Blessing also joined various Nazi-sponsored businessmen's and German "patriotic" organizations at least as early as 1934, then joined the Nazi party in 1937. Schacht appointed him the youngest full director of the Reichsbank in that organization's history.[20]

When Schacht and Hitler had their falling out in 1938 over mechanisms for financing German war production, Schacht left the chairmanship of the Reichsbank to become Minister Without Portfolio in Hitler's government. He engineered Karl Blessing's appointment to several private banking posts and to a directorship of Margarine Union AG, the German branch of Unilever. Blessing served as Margarine Union's finance director in Berlin between

1939 and 1941, a post that was roughly equivalent to that of a German-government-appointed trustee for the company's property, given the wartime regulations that were then in effect.[21] From there, Blessing began participation in what many people would consider to be highly visible, criminal, corporate enterprises. He never was the "lowly clerk" that he told the *New York Times*. Instead, he helped organize Kontinentale Öl AG, and served on its board of directors and senior management team for the remainder of the war.[22]

Kontinentale Öl was for the strategically crucial petroleum industry what Hermann Goering's combine was to German weapons production: a government-licensed monopoly used by the Nazis to seize control of hundreds of companies in the territories overrun by German troops, particularly on the Eastern Front.[23] Under Blessing's leadership, Kontinentale Öl became an archetypical German corporation of the Hitler era, with all of the complexities and contradictions that entailed.

Throughout the 1930s, Germany's oil production had been coordinated through the state's oil ministry and through private cartel agreements, and the main German companies in the industry had remained privately owned. When war broke out, the first question for these companies was how to keep Eastern Europe's oilfields and production properties in private hands, rather than losing them to the SS (which had already begun building its own economic empire) or to Goering's Ministry for the Four Year Plan. Their second question was who among them was to enjoy the choicest spoils from the occupied countries.

Kontinentale Öl was the solution. The four largest German oil companies and IG Farben jointly created Konti as a new petroleum monopoly for Eastern Europe. The company enjoyed German government sponsorship, exclusive production contracts, and first claim on any petroleum-related properties in the Nazi-occupied territories, particularly those seized from Jews, Poles, or the USSR. The corporation paid 7.5 percent royalties on the petroleum to the Reich; all remaining profits from the operation were divided among the companies that had bankrolled Konti in the first place.[24]

Kontinentale Öl became one of the largest single exploiters of concentration camp labor, Jewish ghetto labor, and prison labor in history. According to International Red Cross records, Konti and its network of subsidiary companies maintained their own concentration camps for Jews at Boryslaw (1942–1944), Drohobycz (1942–1944), Iwonicz (1943–1944), Jaslo (1943), Lublin (1941–1943), Moderowka (1942–1944), Opary (1943), Stryj (1941–1944), Truskawiec (1943–1944), and Ugarsthal (1942–1944). It is quite likely that there were other such Konti operations as well in Nazi-occupied Poland and the Ukraine.[25] The prisoners did the crushing construction labor needed to reopen roads and oilfields sabotaged during the Soviet retreat, to lay pipelines to Wehrmacht supply centers, and to build—and then later destroy—new petroleum sites in areas under Nazi control.

Konti "leased" most of its personnel from the SS. The texts of several such SS-Konti agreements have survived, and one was entered into evidence at Nuremberg. "Jewish laborers will not receive any payment in cash," reads one 1942 SS-Konti note concerning exploitation of concentration camp inmates in the Ukraine. "The factory administrations will pay to the SS and the Pol. L. Galicia [German police administration in the Ukraine] for each Jewish laborer per calendar day and shift 5 Zloty a man, 4 Zloty a woman"—the equivalent of a few pennies per worker.[26] The system was orderly enough: Payments for inmates were to be delivered to the SS by the third day of each month; the punishment for prisoners damaging Konti property was death; and the SS quickly disposed of bodies.

No one knows how many inmates died working at Konti, though hard-labor camps of this type typically killed a third to a half of their inmates every six months through overwork, exposure, and disease.[27] Some sense of the death toll can be gleaned from the fact that SS spokesmen at the Wannsee conference contended that construction labor on the Eastern Front should become one of the main vehicles for wiping out every living Jew in Europe.[28]

Karl Blessing exercised special responsibilities for the company's financial affairs and its relations with German banks.[29] He could hardly have been ignorant of the character of the company he helped lead, considering his active participation in Konti's acquisition of looted properties in the East and his oversight of the company's payroll, which consisted in large part of payments to the SS for concentration camp labor. Even Konti's corporate offices in Berlin, where Blessing worked, were built with concentration camp labor.[30]

Much of this was known as early as the summer of 1945. Blessing's service as a director of Kontinentale Öl was widely noted in German biographical dictionaries, business magazines, and the like. Though many details of Konti's activities in the East remained to be filled in, the essential facts—that this oil monopoly had been created through looting and fed on forced labor—were readily available. Two of Blessing's colleagues from Konti's board—Walther Funk, of the Reichsbank and BIS, and Heinrich Butefisch, of IG Farben's Auschwitz complex—were even about to be put on trial for war crimes and crimes against humanity.

Nevertheless, with Allen Dulles's assistance, new respectability seemed to sparkle around Karl Blessing from the summer of 1945 on and cling to him as he climbed higher in corporate ranks. Dulles's de facto clearance became instrumental in Blessing's return to a variety of German government advisory commissions and corporate directorships, including the board of Unilever, where Blessing eventually served on the company's international board of directors and as chairman of its German subsidiary. (Blessing became one of the highest-paid business executives in the world, *Fortune* magazine gushed after the war, with an annual salary equivalent to $75,000.[31]) Blessing then stepped up to become chairman of West Germany's central bank, and by the early 1960s, he was by any measure among the most powerful men in Germany and, indeed, the world.[32]

By the time he retired to the Rhône Valley in 1970, Karl Blessing had emerged in his own stories and in the press as virtually an anti-Nazi Resistance hero.*[33] The prestige media in the U.S. and Europe seem to have convinced themselves that a man as sensible, respected, and well dressed as Blessing could not have committed serious crimes during the Nazi years. So far as can be determined, there were no substantial public discussions during Blessing's career about his membership in the Nazi party, his work for Konti, or Konti's activities in the East.

---

* For example, Blessing apparently told Allen Dulles that he had not joined the Nazi party—or at any rate that is what Dulles said of Blessing during Dulles's efforts to clear him for the white list. But in Blessing's *Fragebogen* (questionnaire) for the U.S. Military Government, where getting caught in a lie would result in a prison term, Blessing admitted that he had in fact been a longtime party member and a leader of Nazi-sponsored businessmen's organizations since the earliest days of the regime.

The heart of the matter is that Karl Blessing was willing to traffic in the lives of Jewish concentration camp inmates in order to maintain his corporate position and social status in Nazi Germany. He had three basic choices during Hitler's last years: He could resist Kontinentale Öl's role in the systematic murder of camp inmates; he could withdraw from his compromising activities without directly challenging them; or he could continue to advance his career by guiding Konti's fortunes in the East with the skill and administrative acumen for which he had come to be known. He chose the third path.

By any reasonable standard, this decision made Blessing as complicit in crimes against humanity as were, say, the members of the corporate board of IG Farben. (Indeed, the Farben representative on Konti's board, Heinrich Butefisch, was eventually tried and convicted for procuring slave labor for the construction of the IG's synthetic oil facilities at Auschwitz.)[34] Yet Blessing managed to escape the opprobrium heaped on the IG board during the first few years after the war, thanks mainly to Allen Dulles's intervention and to the fact that Kontinentale Öl had a somewhat lower public profile than did the internationally known IG Farben. Once the first round of war crimes prosecutions had passed, Blessing was home free. By the 1950s, his service to the Third Reich at Kontinentale Öl was widely perceived as an asset to his career.

The U.S. government's policy on the prosecution of war crimes, quislings, and collaborators was meanwhile developing out of the political battles among various factions spread through the bureaucracy—not through formal consensus on policy within any single committee or commission. The various centers within the government fought secretly among themselves, often going to considerable lengths to keep their disagreements out of the public eye. Rival bureaucratic centers that claimed loyalty to the same broadly worded general policies sometimes proceeded in day-to-day work with radically different agendas. This infighting became particularly pronounced in prosecutions of German industrialists and business leaders, since there were intense philosophical and ideological differences within the government concerning the culpability of these people.

While the U.S. team at the International Military Tribunal at

Nuremberg was prosecuting Blessing's longtime mentor Hjalmar
Schacht, for example, the legal advisor's office at the State Department was quietly helping in Schacht's defense. The heart of the
prosecution's argument was that Schacht had been instrumental in
bringing Hitler to power, in providing legitimacy and stability to
his regime during its first decade, in the clandestine rearmament of
Germany, and in early anti-Semitic initiatives. Schacht also served
the Nazi regime as Reichsbank director and minister of economics.
Prosecutors contended that these acts, taken together, showed that
Schacht participated in a Nazi conspiracy to initiate an aggressive
war. Schacht's later political split with Hitler might be a mitigating
factor, said prosecutors, but it did not change what he had done for
the regime when he had been a part of it.[35]

Meanwhile, though, the State Department helped drum up support for Schacht's defense by tracking down witnesses and inter-
viewing U.S. intelligence agents who might have evidence that
reflected favorably on the imprisoned banker. Of course, an argument can be made that the State Department had an obligation to
bring forward exculpatory evidence concerning Schacht or any
other defendant. But in this case, State's legal advisor Hackworth
went well beyond simply bringing forward evidence. Hackworth
sought out new defense witnesses, screened them, arranged transportation and scheduling on their behalf, and became a behind-
the-scenes advocate for Schacht.[36] These actions demonstrated
the depth of the split between U.S. war crimes prosecutors and
other sectors of the U.S. government, even at the height of the
government's public commitment to harsh punishment for German officials.

State dispatched messages seeking support for Schacht to the
U.S. consul in Zurich, Sam Woods—long one of the most important U.S. back-channel conduits to the German economic elite—
and to Hans Gisevius, a leader of the tiny nationalist-conservative
wing of the German Resistance, who had been an important member of Allen Dulles's intelligence network during the war.[37] Gisevius was still working full-time for U.S. intelligence in the
winter of 1945, and both he and Woods proved eager to work on
Schacht's behalf. The State Department engaged yet another of
Dulles's wartime agents, the former Axis Romanian ambassador
Gregoire Gafencu, to write memoirs that stressed that Germany
had been drawn into the war against its will, or at least against the

choice of men like Schacht and the German foreign service bureaucracy, who had opposed war with the Soviets.[38] This went
directly to the issue of whether there had been a "conspiracy" to
wage aggressive war.

Meanwhile, Robert Jackson's prosecutorial staff at Nuremberg
was split over the issue of whether to bring Schacht to trial at all.
The U.S. hardliners favored prosecution, as did Jackson himself.
But Jackson's most senior deputy, former OSS chief William Donovan, strongly opposed a trial. Donovan argued that Schacht had
been secretly sympathetic to the Western Allies early in the war,
and that a tough cross-examination of Schacht on the witness
stand would undermine pro-U.S. factions among Germany's business and financial elite.[39] Jackson, however, found himself
hemmed in by his commitments to French and Soviet prosecutors,
who strongly favored trying Schacht, and he went ahead with the
prosecution. Donovan then resigned over this and related disputes
with Jackson, but not before convincing the prosecutor to sharply
restrict his public cross-examination of Schacht. At the trial, Jackson's self-imposed limits on his interrogation of the banker cut the
heart out of his case. The International Military Tribunal eventually acquitted Schacht, but only after protracted debate in chambers, a close vote, and public protests by the Soviet judge.

In this case, as in others, the split within the U.S. government was
not over the facts of Schacht's career, which were mainly a matter of
public record. It was instead a political dispute, rooted in differing
appraisals of the extent of the German business elite's culpability
for the actions of Hitler's state and their responsibility for the actions of the institutions they led. Schacht's case became the focal
point for the ongoing debate over the role of private enterprises in
public society—a dispute that in one way or another has been at
center stage in American politics for most of this century.

When Western intellectuals looked east during the cold war, they
often found examples of Communist states employing ideology and
rhetoric to separate the Soviet government from its more odious
activities. Stalin never publicly discussed mass murder, Western
scholars pointed out. He spoke instead of class struggle and of
eliminating the kulaks as a class,[40] and in doing so diffused his
responsibility for their fate. The fact that the Western press

indulged in similar historical revisionism concerning Kontinentale Öl suggests that self-delusions about mass crimes sometimes take root in democratic societies as well. How would it be possible for the *New York Times* and *Fortune* to write about Konti's wartime business without considering that most of the company's assets had been looted from Nazi-occupied countries and that its laborers had worked at gunpoint? Discussion of Konti apart from such facts required either ignorance (which the Western media does not claim) or, more likely, the internalization of a powerful ideological framework that assumes that institutional leaders such as Blessing should be separated from responsibility for their companies' actions.

Karl Blessing's complicity in genocide was not as direct as that of the SS generals who led extermination squads. But he was an unusually talented man, and he had powerful friends, an enterprising personality, and an absolute commitment to the prosperity of German business. Those traits enabled him to prosper as a young executive under Hitler. They brought him to Schacht's attention and, in time, into contact with his counterparts at the Bank for International Settlements and in Western foreign policy and financial circles. After the war was over, the Allied leaders who were struggling with the day-to-day problems of managing Germany turned once again to Karl Blessing.

Just as with the Schmidt brothers, basic questions remained: Under what circumstances does offering amnesty to former Nazis such as Blessing avoid a greater evil? Who is to make those determinations, and on what grounds?

Robert Murphy and Allen Dulles believed they knew the answer. Such decisions should be left to competent governmental authorities, operating within a moral framework and motivated by a sincere sense of U.S. national security and national interest—themselves, for example. Murphy and Dulles repeatedly reached secret verdicts they believed necessary to construct a postwar order that fit their idea of progress, and they reached them with a clear conscience.

As early as the summer of 1945, Murphy was willing to defy U.S. treaty obligations concerning high-ranking Nazis and Axis collaborators when he regarded it in the U.S. interest to do so. Shortly after the German collapse, for example, Tito's government in Yugoslavia wished to try as a war criminal Miklós Horthy, who had been royal regent of Hungary and supreme commander of Hungary's armed forces during its years of alliance with Nazi Germany. Horthy also shared personal responsibility for establishing Hungary's anti-Semitic race laws and other persecutory measures. The Yugoslavs had suffered invasions and massacres at Hungary's hands during Horthy's regime, and they felt justified in bringing formal charges against him to the UNWCC.[41] According to their agreements with the U.S., they seemed to have legal authority to prosecute him in Yugoslav courts.[42]

The postwar (pre-Communist) Czech government of Jan Masaryk agreed. The "Czech cabinet on September 25 [1945] declared ex-Regent Horthy a war criminal. . . . [President] Masaryk took a serious view of Horthy's activities, characterizing them as aggression and invasion of Czech lands, persecution of Jews, responsibility for cruelties, ill treatment and executions of Czech citizens, destruction of property and forcing Czech citizens into the Hungarian Army," according to a U.S. diplomatic report.[43] The Czechs also brought charges against Horthy.

But Horthy, as will be seen, was not a typical war criminal.

16

Prisoner Transfers

MIKLÓS HORTHY had led the establishment of a Catholic, monarchist state in Hungary after suppression of the Communist rebellion in Budapest in 1919. U.S. aid to shore up the wobbly Horthy government, it will be recalled, had been the centerpiece of Allen Dulles's recommendations to President Woodrow Wilson during the young diplomat's days as the chief of U.S. political intelligence for Central Europe. Horthy had emerged as something like the grand old man of Hungary during the interwar years, at least in the eyes of his supporters. He was well liked in Washington, where many in the State Department had convinced themselves that Horthy had been "forced" to join the Axis.

Horthy had always been a conservative militarist, in the mold of Spain's Franco or Portugal's Salazar, rather than a Hitler-style Nazi. He preferred political and economic persecution of Jews and Romanis to outright murder, at least usually. Hitler had grown worried about Horthy's loyalty in the last year of the war, so the Germans deposed him, installed a more compliant regime, and swept away hundreds of thousands of Hungarian Jews to death camps within a few weeks.[1] Most experts agreed that the Horthy government's disenfranchisement and ghettoization of Jews had set the stage for their eventual destruction.

The U.S. Army captured Horthy during the summer of 1945 and interned him in Ashcan, the U.S. POW camp for high-ranking Axis prisoners. Within weeks after his arrival, U.S. political advisor Murphy sought Washington's approval for Horthy's release.[2] Legal advisor Green Hackworth agreed, provided the USSR did not formally object.[3] The Soviets said nothing.

Murphy wished to offer Horthy political asylum and protection from prosecution in exchange for his cooperation in establishing a postwar Hungarian regime sympathetic to the U.S.[4] The U.S. ambassador in Budapest, Rudolf Schoenfeld, believed that Hungary's postwar government of 1945 would secretly agree to this, providing it did not have to do so publicly.[5] The postwar coalition government of Hungary did not want to try Horthy for treason if it was possible to avoid doing so, according to U.S. embassy reports of the day, because many felt a trial would undermine the state.[6]

The chief U.S. prosecutor at Nuremberg, Robert Jackson, promised Horthy that if he cooperated with the U.S. political agenda, the United States would block any war crimes charges against him and refuse to transfer him to Yugoslavia or Czechoslovakia.[7] Horthy agreed. Jackson then met with Czech and Yugoslav war crimes officials, telling them it "would sit rather badly with the world" if their countries tried the regent, owing to Horthy's advanced age (he was then over seventy) and his "signs of senility."[8] (In fact, Jackson knew that U.S. doctors had examined Horthy and found him to be in excellent health; he lived for more than twenty years after the war.)[9] Jackson offered the Yugoslavs a confidential deal under which Horthy would be formally charged with war crimes but not actually turned over to Yugoslavia for trial or punishment. The Yugoslavs rejected the overture, however, insisting that Horthy must be transferred to Belgrade and put on trial.*

---

* In an interesting example of bureaucratic psychology, the State Department legal advisor's confidential memoranda on the Horthy case later began to contend that Jackson had said the Yugoslavs had accepted his proposal of a confidential deal in the Horthy affair, though this contradicts the rest of the written record in the case. As the legal advisor's office began to see things, Horthy's problems were mainly the Yugoslavs' fault, and their continued pursuit of him was further evidence of the perfidy of Communists.

At the UNWCC, the new U.S. representative, Colonel Joseph V. Hodgson, sought to derail the Horthy prosecution when consideration of the case came up a few weeks later. The UNWCC committee deadlocked over the case, split between the Yugoslavs and Czechs on one side and the U.S. and British delegations on the other. They eventually compromised by charging Horthy with crimes against humanity—the most morally compelling, but legally the weakest, offenses in his case—and adjourned the war crimes charges stemming from Hungary's invasions of its neighbors.[10] This action satisfied the Czechs, who refrained from further requests to place Horthy on trial. But the Yugoslavs would not give up.

U.S. military authorities in Germany meanwhile released Horthy from Ashcan, and he took up residence in Bavaria. Officially, the former regent was supposed to notify U.S. authorities if he planned to move, but other than that he was free—a remarkable status considering that he was facing formal charges of crimes against humanity in two Allied states. Despite Yugoslav protests, Robert Murphy and the U.S. ambassador to Hungary worked to clear Horthy's petition for permission to emigrate to Switzerland or Portugal, both of which were willing to provide him with asylum.[11] In the end, the U.S. State Department succeeded in protecting Horthy from trial on any charges, including crimes against humanity, even though the U.S. had itself supported such charges during the compromise at the UNWCC.

Some senior U.S. officials even made sure that Horthy was invited to U.S. diplomatic receptions in Germany. Less than two years after the fall of Berlin, the Yugoslav government formally protested to Washington after noticing a news dispatch from Munich describing the wedding of U.S. consul Sam Woods. The published invitation list included a dozen senior officials of the U.S. Military Government in Germany—and Miklós Horthy.

"The Yugoslav Ambassador has the honor to draw the attention of the Honorable [U.S.] Secretary of State to the fact that Admiral Horthy is a war criminal," the protest read. Horthy has been "registered as No. 2779 by the Yugoslav War Crimes Commission, and as No. 6 on page 26 of the International Commission for War Criminals in London. The Yugoslav Government requested the American Authorities at Wiesbaden for extradition of Admiral Horthy on March 6, 1946, and repeated this request on August 24, 1946, without result. . . ." The Yugoslavs wanted to know what disciplinary action was planned against Woods et al. for consorting with Horthy.[12] The U.S. responded stiffly that the wedding was of "a private nature ... [and] not a matter for representations on the part of the Yugoslav government." Secretary of State Marshall summarily rejected the protest.[13]

The more sophisticated Axis defendants soon learned how to make the most of the divisions among the Allies. The postwar careers of the SS men who had negotiated with Allen Dulles during Operation Sunrise provide an example of how symbiotic relationships evolved among the victors and the vanquished during the first years after the war. The Dulles case is interesting not only because it was typical of thousands of less prominent instances, but also because of the symmetry in Dulles's behavior in the wake of two different genocides—the Armenian Genocide and the Nazi Holocaust—more than two decades apart.

After the German surrender, SS General Karl Wolff proceeded on the assumption that Wolff's cooperation with Dulles had won him a place in a postwar German government. Wolff sought to pick up "the political threads" of his old command, an OSS report states, by "playing on the old discrepancy between Russia and America."[14] But by June 1945, when most of the concentration camps had been opened and public outrage was at a high tide, Allied troops arrested and interned Wolff and his senior aides.

Though Dulles was later to deny it, he extended de facto protection to Karl Wolff and at least two of his assistants, Eugen Dollmann and Eugen Wenner, both of whom were later indicted by Italian authorities for their roles in massacres of Italian partisans and deportation of Italian Jews to Auschwitz.[15] Circumstantial evidence links Dulles to the escape of another of Wolff's assistants, Walter Rauff, whose rise through SS ranks had been helped by his use of gas trucks to murder thousands of Jewish women and children on the Eastern Front.[16]

Allied war crimes investigators identified Wolff almost immediately as one of the most powerful members of the Nazi inner circle to survive the war. The French and Soviet governments favored prosecuting Wolff before the first international tribunal at Nuremberg—an "honor" of sorts, as this trial was reserved for the highest-ranking Nazi criminals in custody.[17] Had Wolff been tried there, he almost certainly would have been hung.

But the U.S. and British representatives on the Nuremberg planning committee demurred. There were too many high-ranking Nazis to try at the first tribunal, they contended. Only one SS officer should be prosecuted there; the others would surely get their turn later. The case against the Gestapo's chief, Ernst Kaltenbrunner, would be easier to make than that against Wolff, the U.S. contended, even though Wolff probably had more power in the SS as a whole. After much debate, the tribunal's planning committee decided to prosecute Kaltenbrunner first, in the autumn of 1945. They slated Wolff to be the chief SS defendant at a second international tribunal, scheduled to open sometime in 1946.[18]

But that was not to be. Within weeks of the opening of the first international trial at Nuremberg, Robert Jackson recommended to Washington that the U.S. should not cooperate in any further joint trials of Nazis, regardless of the commitments in the Moscow Declaration.[19] State-to-state relations between the U.S. and USSR had deteriorated sharply since Truman had come to office, notwithstanding generally good relations between American and Russian military commanders in the field. Jackson believed that the Soviet vision of justice in Europe required revolutionary reorganization of German society and a rapid expansion of Soviet geopolitical power beyond its old borders. Any new international trial of Nazi leaders would almost certainly provide the USSR with a forum where it could continue to make political gains. Jackson wanted no part in it.

Instead, Jackson convinced Truman, the U.S. should hold its own trials of Nazi defendants then in U.S. hands. These trials became known as the "later" Nuremberg trials or, more formally, as the "Subsequent Proceedings."[20] These later trials, prosecuted under the command of General Telford Taylor, proved to be one of the most comprehensive efforts ever attempted to prosecute the perpetrators of genocide. Taylor and his colleagues brought more than 180 individual German leaders to justice and simultaneously created a permanent record of tens of thousands of instances of Nazi criminality. The subsequent proceedings included three major prosecutions of SS defendants, one of German justice ministry officials, one of Nazi doctors active in the concentration camps, three of senior German military commanders, three of major German industrialists, and one trial of twenty-one leaders of the various ministries of the Hitler government.[21]

But Karl Wolff again succeeded in wriggling off the hook, despite the fact that he was personally implicated in one way or another in almost half of the cases brought to trial in the subsequent proceedings series. Meanwhile, Wolff's top SS aides who had been active in Sunrise—Walter Rauff, Eugen Dollmann, Eugen Wenner, and others—also escaped prosecution even though they were charged with crimes against humanity by postwar Italian authorities.

Allen Dulles and his colleagues in U.S. clandestine operations could not order Telford Taylor or the Italian government not to prosecute Wolff and the other SS men who had been active in Sunrise. He lacked authority to do so and, considering the strong personal commitment of Telford Taylor and his aides to the war crimes trials, any obvious attempt to derail a prosecution would likely have only strengthened their determination to proceed. But Dulles and the emerging CIA could nonetheless make their influence felt both directly and indirectly, even after Dulles had left his OSS post in Berlin and returned to civilian life.

In the fall of 1946, the Italian government issued arrest warrants for the former top SS and Gestapo officers in Italy, including at least three of Wolff's senior aides in the Sunrise affair. This in turn triggered inquiries from the State Department to the U.S. Central Intelligence Group (CIG) concerning what should be done with the SS men then in U.S. custody. (The CIG was the immediate predecessor of the CIA and had administrative responsibility for most aspects of U.S. intelligence affairs between the time the OSS officially ended operations in 1945 and the creation of the CIA in 1947.) The CIG's liaison officer with State, Robert Joyce, prepared a reply that in time became the standard language used to explain the U.S. commitment to the SS men who had participated in Sunrise.

> The records of the former OSS provide proof that Eugenio [sic] Dollmann, Aide to General Wolff and former SS Standartenfuehrer, as well as former SS Sturmbannfuehrer Eugen Wenner, also connected with Wolff and now being held captive in Italy, participated in the operation leading up to the German capitulation in Italy. Mr. Allen Dulles, formerly of OSS and later of SSU [Strategic Services Unit, a short-lived U.S. intelligence agency], who initiated the negotiations, has been

contacted here and confirms the foregoing. Major General [Lyman] Lemnitzer, who also participated in the negotiations is convinced, after an examination of the records and contact with Dulles, of Dollmann's participation. Present representations by the Italians would appear to be an endeavor to undermine, in Italy, the Allied position [two lines of text censored] . . . it would appear that Allied interests would be advanced if AFHQ [U.S. military headquarters] would confirm the fact of Dollmann's and Wenner's participation . . . and that these persons should receive such consideration as might be appropriate in the present circumstances.[22]

Italian authorities also tightened the screws on Walter Rauff, whom the Americans were then holding at a relatively high security prison at San Vittore. Rauff had been one of Wolff's most important links to Cardinal Schuster and Monsignor Bicchierai throughout the negotiations with Dulles, according to accounts by both Rauff and Dulles.[23] When the Italians sought to prosecute Rauff for his work as a Gestapo leader and SD chief in Milan, the U.S. authorities transferred him to a prison hospital in Milan, and from there to a low-security POW camp near Rimini that had seen a series of mass prison escapes during the previous summer. On December 29, less than a month after the CIG secretly declared its interest in protecting the Sunrise SS prisoners, Walter Rauff walked away from the Rimini camp and disappeared.[24]

"I went to Naples," Rauff told a Chilean immigration court almost two decades later. "There a Catholic priest helped me to go to Rome where I stayed more or less a year and a half, and always in convents of the Holy See. . . . With the help of the Catholic Church my family was able to come from the Russian zone in Germany to Rome. Reunited with my family, I [then] went to Damascus," and from there eventually on to refuge in South America.[25] The evidence points to Bichierrai and Schuster as the organizers of Rauff's escape, the Simon Wiesenthal Center has concluded.[26]

With Rauff hidden by the Vatican and Wolff in U.S. hands in Germany, Italian officials renewed their efforts to prosecute Dollmann, Wenner, and a handful of other senior SS officers whom they believed to be still in U.S. custody in Italy. An Italian military tribunal in Rome filed formal charges against Dollmann and three others on November 25, alleging that they had been instrumental in mass executions of civilian hostages. The U.S. then shuttled Dollmann from his internment center, where the Italian prosecutors knew he was being held, to a U.S. Army hospital. But that could only work temporarily, and by the following spring the U.S. military command in Italy was complaining to the State Department and to CIG of the necessity for a decision on what was to be done with Dollmann on a more permanent basis.[27]

After a flurry of discussions in Washington, the records of which are still classified today, the State Department determined that "both Dollmann and Wenner will be removed to Germany under security arrangements as soon as EUCOM [European Command, the U.S. military high command in Europe] confirms they will accept them." The U.S. shipped Dollmann immediately.[28]

Once Wolff, Dollmann, and Wenner were safely beyond the reach of Italian law, they renewed their appeals for a complete amnesty from war crimes prosecutions. "SS General Karl Wolff claims that in connection with Operation Sunrise leading to surrender of German forces in Italy certain oral promises were furnished him by von Gaevernitz of OSS, as well as Dulles, regarding personal immunity for Wolff and his assistants, in particular [Eugen] Dollmann and [Eugen] Wenner," Robert Murphy reported to Washington in the summer of 1947. "Wolff alleges Major Weibel of Swiss General Staff was witness and guarantor to these promises. Sworn interrogatory between Wolff and Swiss national Max Husmann on fifth July 1947 indicates this may have been the case.

"Some U.S. intelligence authorities in Germany are of definite opinion that military honor requires pardon and immunity for Wolff and his adjutants who are at present in automatic arrest category," Murphy continued. "Can you make discreet inquiries of Dulles and others concerning nature of possible promises and their opinion as to what extent moral obligation on part of U.S. may exist with respect to Wolff group. Early reply requested. . . ."[29]

Dulles, Major General Lyman Lemnitzer, and CIG Assistant Director Colonel Donald H. Galloway again intervened to assist the SS men, according to U.S. records. Galloway told the State Department's security chief Jack Neal that "the [Wolff] group rendered services to the Allies, therefore, the Allies were morally obligated to weigh the good along with the bad. Whatever they might be charged with should be weighed against the good which they did." Dulles again insisted that he had made no "promises of immunity, safe refuge or payment of money" to the SS.[30] But his claims on this point had begun to wear thin, considering that sworn testimony from four SS officers that he had made these promises had now been corroborated in affidavits by Max Husmann and Max Weibel, both of whom were widely reputed to be senior employees of the Swiss intelligence service who had worked extensively with Dulles throughout the war. Murphy's telegram to Washington indicates that "some U.S. intelligence authorities in Germany" had reached the same conclusion concerning obligations incurred by Dulles.

Jack Neal at State was a cautious man, and he could smell the potential for trouble in this increasingly messy affair. After talking to Galloway at CIG, Neal wrote a memo for the files pinning responsibility for his actions on Dulles and the CIG, then wired back to Murphy at the U.S. embassy in Berlin that the State Department had concluded the Allies owed an obligation to Wolff, Dollmann, and other SS men involved in Sunrise. "Therefore," he concluded in a top-secret cable on September 17, "definite consideration should be given to those favorable aspects when weighing any war crimes with which they are charged."[31]

Wolff's role in organizing the extermination camps and in administering forced labor had been so direct and extensive that almost any public trial would likely lead to a long prison sentence or a death penalty, regardless of the SS general's role in Sunrise. Dollmann and Wenner were more junior SS officers, but they faced many of the same problems as did Wolff, especially if the Italian authorities arrested them.

The U.S. government transferred Wolff from an internment camp to considerably more comfortable lodgings in a mental hospital, then later often claimed that a mental breakdown had rendered him incompetent to stand trial for war crimes and crimes against humanity.[32] Wolff nonetheless became a favored informant for the U.S. prosecution team at Nuremberg, contributing evidence to a number of cases against other SS men, including some of his own subordinates.[33]

British government prosecutors delivered the coup de grace to the efforts to bring Karl Wolff to justice. They formally requested that the U.S. turn over the SS general and several senior Wehrmacht generals for a full British war crimes trial. By then, Telford Taylor's prosecution group was running out of funds and

was under considerable pressure from the State Department and
White House to wrap up its activities as quickly as possible. Taylor
readily agreed to transfer Wolff to British custody for trial, and
promised full cooperation in any future proceedings.[34]

But the British did not try Wolff. Instead, they severed his prosecution from that of the Wehrmacht generals, despite the fact that
Wolff's case was considerably more clear-cut and easier to prosecute. They then kept Wolff in protective custody without bringing
him to trial until Taylor's war crimes unit had closed up shop and
returned to the U.S.

In late 1949, the British brought Karl Wolff before a denazification board (not an Allied court) in Hamburg—a move that might be
fairly compared to charging the SS leader with traffic violations.
Wolff's Sunrise colleagues turned out in force for the "denazification." Allen Dulles, Lyman Lemnitzer, and General Terrence Airey
each submitted an affidavit on Wolff's behalf to the German panel;
Dulles's senior aide, Gero von Gaevernitz, testified in person as a
defense witness. The board deliberated briefly, determined that the
Karl Wolff in the dock was in fact the well-known Nazi and SS
leader, then went on to conclude that the time Wolff had served in
Allied internment since the war had been punishment enough.
Karl Wolff was free to go.[35]

(Thirteen years later, the worldwide public attention to the
Eichmann trial spurred German prosecutors to reopen the case
against Karl Wolff for crimes against humanity. By that time, Allen
Dulles had retired from the CIA in the wake of the failed Bay of Pigs
invasion. The rest of the old Sunrise team seemed to prefer avoiding the highly public trial. German courts convicted Wolff of complicity in the murder of 300,000 Jews at Treblinka and sentenced
him to fifteen years in prison. He served seven years before he was
once again released.)[36]

The path that Wolff's aide Eugen Dollmann followed to freedom
remains murky, but new light was shed on his case recently when
some of the personal archives of military intelligence agent John
Valentine Grombach found their way into the public domain. In the
early 1950s, the CIA hired Grombach's private intelligence network at $1 million per year to perform a variety of espionage
services in Western and Eastern Europe. But Grombach's relationship with the CIA went sour, and he began compiling hostile
intelligence reports on CIA agents that he leaked to FBI Director

J. Edgar Hoover, Senator Joseph McCarthy, and other bureaucratic rivals of the agency.[37]

Dollmann "kept in touch with [the] American intelligence service" after the war, Grombach wrote in a confidential memo to the FBI in 1954. Dollmann "had his entry into Switzerland cleared by its influence, and began to work for CIA. His work became especially important during the period when General Walter Bedell Smith was Director and Allen W. Dulles was Deputy Director. Then, in November 1952, at a time when Mr. Dulles was in Germany, the whole thing blew up," Grombach noted. German press reports brought to light a series of scandals concerning former Nazi officials who favored a Soviet-backed proposal for a neutral Germany. Dollmann's role in the affair is not entirely clear to this day, but it was certain that he had some connection with the neutralists, who were enjoying clandestine support from both East German intelligence and nationalist German business interests in Argentina. That scandal in turn produced reports of Dollmann's association with both the CIA and British intelligence. Dulles was "somewhat abashed" by this latest imbroglio, Grombach wrote, and "left Germany in haste."[38]

In time, the Swiss deported Dollmann for abuse of his visitor's status. So far as can be determined, no court ever tried Eugen Dollmann for his role in the destruction of Italian Jews and the massacre of Italian hostages. Dollmann's autobiography eventually appeared in German and English editions,[39] and on the basis of his memoirs he today enjoys the reputation as something of a bon vivant. Dollmann's colleague and prisonmate, Eugen Wenner, who shared with Dollmann the benefits of the U.S. intelligence intervention, also appears to have avoided all war crimes charges.

There was a common pattern in the U.S. treatment of SS men involved in the Operation Sunrise negotiations. It began with early capture by U.S. forces, followed by transfer of the suspect to some form of privileged custody, such as a hospital or sanitorium, or into British custody. At least some of these transfers, such as Dollmann and Wenner's move to Germany, were arranged by U.S. military and State Department officials specifically to help the former SS men escape trial in an Allied country. The chain of documentary evidence concerning Dulles's role in the Wolff case is circumstantial but strong, and it indicates that Dulles joined with senior U.S. and British officials in securing an amnesty for the highest-ranking Nazi criminal to escape the war. As for Walter Rauff, he escaped from U.S. custody under mysterious circumstances, then made his way to safety, apparently with the assistance of a ranking Catholic prelate whose political operations in Italy were at that time bankrolled primarily by U.S. intelligence.[40]

Officially, the United States, Britain, and the USSR formally agreed at the Potsdam Conference during the summer of 1945 to a tough program of demilitarization, decentralization, and denazification of Germany in general and of the German economy in particular. They also specified that Germany would pay substantial war reparations to the countries it had damaged.[41] The Wolff and Horthy cases suggest that despite such public covenants, clandestine factions inside Western governments already enjoyed sufficient clout in the late 1940s to effectively derail prosecution of Nazi criminals, including those of very high rank, at least in certain circumstances. But this pattern of comfort extended to those who had once organized genocide was not simply some plot by insiders. It was, as will be seen, a *structural* problem, one that extended de facto amnesties to thousands of men and women who had promoted or profited from mass murder.

17

Double-Think on Denazification

THE UNITED STATES and other Allies agreed at the Potsdam Conference in August 1945 that Germany's industrial power had been integral to Nazi crimes and to Hitler's regime. Thus, the Allied occupation government in Germany would substantially reform the whole structure of the German economy, carry out denazification, break up the entrenched system of business cartels, and eliminate the Hitler era's version of a military-industrial complex. The threads with which Germany's economic elite and state had entwined one another during the Hitler years were to be broken forever.

The Allies publicly resolved jointly to ban all German production of weapons, ships, airplanes, and other "implements of war." German manufacturing of chemicals, steel, machine tools, "and other items directly necessary to a war economy" was to be rigidly controlled and limited to the nation's peacetime needs.[1] Germany was also to pay substantial war reparations to each of the countries it had damaged. The largest share of the reparations was to go to the USSR, which had paid the heaviest price at the hands of the

Germans, but each of the Allies—Britain, France, Belgium, and even colonial India—were to get a piece.

Detailed provisions specified the means for international cooperation in bringing accused war criminals to trial and purging Nazis from "public and semi-public office and from positions of responsibility in important private undertakings."[2] Written criteria distinguished major criminals from small fry. There were five basic categories of Nazi offenders, and the Potsdam agreements laid out a framework of procedures for handling each of them. The Allies publicly renewed their commitment to implement the Moscow Declaration of 1943 and to return accused Nazi criminals to the countries seeking them for trial.[3] Further, the Allies concurred that "major war criminals whose crimes . . . have no particular geographical localization"—the high command of the German state, Nazi party, and SS, for example—were to face joint international trials.[4] National courts of the Allied countries and Allied military courts in occupied Germany were to try the second echelon of accused war criminals.

Importantly, Nazis accused of "analogous offenses" to war crimes, such as extermination of Jews and atrocities against civilian populations, would be tried before Allied courts in occupied Germany. Each Ally promised to arrest and intern German "key men," including corporate leaders instrumental in Hitler's rule. Finally, all of the Nazi party's rank-and-file members were to be removed from offices of responsibility or influence, except in cases where party membership had been purely nominal.[5]

Despite the scope and specificity of this agreement, the conflict within the U.S. government over denazification of German industry intensified, rather than attenuated, in the wake of the Potsdam meeting. Before August 1945 was out, U.S. occupation officers sympathetic to rapid restoration of German industry organized an administrative attack on the stronghold of anti-Nazi hard-liners in the U.S. military government. That conflict soon spilled over into conflicts among the U.S., France, and the USSR.

The political issue was already explicit: "Major Scully denounced the denazification program as 'witch hunting,' and Lt. Col. Auffinger [chief of U.S. efforts to denazify German banks in Land Württemburg-Baden] declared that it would drive the German people into the hands of the Communists," reported a memo concerning one August confrontation. "Col. Auffinger explained further his opposition to the program: we did not fight this war to destroy one dictatorship and build up another; we must preserve a counter-balance or bulwark against Russia."[6]

Colonel Robert Storey, the U.S. executive trial counsel at the International Military Tribunal and a senior aide to Robert Jackson, had "passed the word down that the denazification directive was to be relaxed," Auffinger continued. Sympathetic U.S. officers promulgated this "relaxation" largely by word of mouth during the summer of 1945, but this rumor network had considerable effect. The hard-line U.S. officers targeted in Auffinger's attack resigned before the year was out, despite the fact that it was their position in the denazification debate, not Auffinger's, that the President of the United States had publicly endorsed at Potsdam.

The denazification that did take place in Germany was usually spearheaded by Germany's Socialists, Communists, and some religious leaders, who had resumed limited legal political activities inside their country for the first time in more than a decade. "Almost without exception as Allied troops captured the larger German cities they were met by delegations of left-wing anti-fascists, ready with programs, nominees for office in the local administration, and offers of aid in the process of denazification," remembered Gabriel Almond, a conservative sociologist who specialized in studying the European left. The anti-Nazi underground tended to be militantly left wing and based in the labor movement, Almond said, because few others had been willing to take the risks. Nevertheless, their "success . . . in preserving a corps of political leaders capable of giving German politics a new direction after the occupation cannot be doubted after study of the local leadership of the new [postwar] political parties," he continued, citing examples from Hamburg, Bremen, Lübeck, Frankfurt, and other cities. The groups made "rapid strides in recruiting members and supporters."[7]

The "Antifa" (antifascist) groups throughout Germany hastily organized local unions known as *Betriebsrats* (works councils) that took over management of hundreds of companies, particularly the larger factories. These committees then usually drove out the old boards of directors, Nazi-era personnel managers, Nazi Labor Front activists, and Gestapo informers.

This form of denazification proved to be considerably more effective than much of what was undertaken by the Allied military government, at least during the first year after the defeat of Hitler's regime. A later U.S. Military Government survey of sixty major German companies employing a total of more than 100,000 workers found that virtually all of the denazification activities at those plants had taken place *before* the beginning of Allied denazification efforts in the German economy.[8] Though the study did not say so directly, this could mean only one thing: The denazification work had been in the main carried out by the Antifa and *Betriebsrats* and by shop-floor purges of alleged Nazis.

But the radical politics of the Antifas disturbed Western military governments, which moved quickly to suppress the anti-Nazi groups under military regulations originally written to stamp out Nazi political activity. "Thus while the Antifa movement had some revolutionary potentialities, these were effectively restricted," Almond notes with approval. "Allied policy . . . was to break the elan of the Antifas and place them under considerable restraint" from the very first days of the occupation.[9] The U.S. and British occupation governments shut down the denazification work of the *Betriebsrats* by the summer of 1945, for the most part, and dispersed most of the more militant Antifa leaders by the end of the year.

Dillon, Read & Co. partner William Draper became pivotal to the semiclandestine shift in U.S. policy toward Germany that summer. By 1945, Secretary of War Stimson and Secretary of the Navy Forrestal (Dillon, Read's former president) engineered Draper's appointment as chief of the economic division of the joint Allied Control Council for Germany (the central occupation government at the time) and as director of economic policy for the German territories administered by the U.S. As such, Draper emerged as by far the most powerful U.S. industrial and finance official in occupied Germany, with overall authority for implementing JCS 1067 and other U.S. denazification programs aimed at German bankers and businessmen.

Draper was an imposing, broad-chested man with a bald pate and dark, bristling eyebrows that emphasized his high forehead. Prior to the war, he had been corporate treasurer at Dillon, Read and an officer of the German Credit and Investment Corporation of New Jersey, a Dillon, Read–sponsored holding company that specialized in international investments in Hitler-era Germany.[10] He prided himself on his willingness to make tough, even brutal decisions to protect his vision of the common good. The Draper family owned textile mills, patents on textile equipment, and a substantial share of the international trade in fibers. Their New England mill towns featured "model" workers' communities where the company enforced a Draper family formula of no unions, proper sanitation, and good behavior.[11] Draper's social philosophy, in short, shared many of the same roots as that of the new "non-Nazis" in Aachen described by Padover.

Draper's 1945 decision concerning rations for German coal miners illustrates the point. "The Ruhr mines had to be mined if we were going to get the factories started," Draper remembered during a later interview, "and we found that the miners couldn't mine coal on 1,560 calories [per day, the official ration in 1945], or even 1,800. So one of the first steps we took was to raise the calorie level for the miners to 4,000 calories, against great protest, obviously. Then the next step we had to take was to search the miners when they went home every night, because they were dividing their 4,000 calories with their families. Well, from the humanitarian point of view that's fine, but it couldn't work, and so we had to strip them of food and they had to eat it themselves. . . ."[12]

According to his own account, William Draper never had any intention of implementing JCS 1067, the Potsdam agreements, or Washington's other publicly announced policies on denazification and decartelization of German industry. Draper considered such programs to be naïve and counterproductive, and he obstructed them at every opportunity.[13] He surrounded himself with like-minded aides to the degree that he could, and together they often succeeded in undermining reform and denazification of the German economy before it began. Draper's factotum and electronic industries specialist was Frederick Devereux, a senior AT&T official specializing in that company's political operations. His steel industry chief was Rufus Wysor, the president of the Republic Steel Corporation, which itself had a long history of cartel agreements of questionable legality with the German steel companies he was now overseeing. Wysor was particularly aggressive: "What's wrong with cartels, anyhow?" he replied when confronted with his lack of progress in denazifying and breaking up German steel and coal combines. "Why shouldn't these German businessmen run things the way they are used to? . . . German business is flat on its back. Why bother them with all this new stuff?"[14] Other senior Draper aides shared roughly similar backgrounds and perspectives.

"It became evident to us very quickly that . . . the United States would have to support Germany for the rest of time, or as long as that policy [JCS 1067] stayed in effect," Draper contended in a later interview. "And so, we had to wiggle here and waggle there and do the best we could without openly breaking our directive to permit the German economy to begin to function. We argued with this one and argued with that one here in Washington and in Germany, wherever we had the chance, and bit by bit, we recouped or revised the situation so that it became possible.

"We didn't pay as much attention to it [JCS 1067] as perhaps we should from the point of view of military discipline. There were several efforts to pull me back [to Washington] and have me charged with not carrying out the directive. [But] General Clay always defended me. He knew perfectly well that such a policy couldn't last just as well as I did. We fought it out and finally persuaded Washington."[15]

Draper's critics pointed to the tough language in the JCS 1067 order and to U.S. public commitments at Potsdam, arguing that Draper failed to implement the letter and the spirit of official policy. But what the critics did not understand was that the hard-line declarations of JCS 1067 were not in fact U.S. policy at all, despite what was said on paper. Here is how General Lucius Clay, the U.S. military governor in Germany, explained it in an interview some years later:

"JCS 1067 would have been extremely difficult to operate under. . . . It was modified constantly; not officially, but by allowing this deviation, that deviation, et cetera. We began to slowly wipe out JCS 1067, [which] prohibited us from doing anything to improve the German economy. It was an unworkable policy and . . . [it was modified] by gradual changes in its provisions and changes of cablegrams, conferences, and so on." Clay was convinced that President Truman was on his side. "We had . . . a change of administration [after Roosevelt]. The people who had had the greatest influence and developed the occupation powers went out, and Mr. Truman's administration came in," Clay remembered. Truman never supported the hard-line approach, Clay continued. "He had nothing to do with its creation and I don't think he ever believed in it."[16]

What can be seen, then, was a tough policy on paper that was useful for pacifying public opinion in the West, for making promises to the Soviets, and for general public relations purposes. Meanwhile the upper echelons of the U.S. occupation government agreed as early as the summer of 1945 that a thorough denazification and decartelization of the German economy would never be attempted, regardless of what might be said for public consumption.

This institutionalized double-talk—even double-think, as George Orwell might have it—grew out of the splits inside the Roosevelt administration discussed earlier. Perhaps more fundamentally, it was a product of the division between mass public desire in the U.S. for harsh punishment of the whole structure of Nazism, on the one hand, and the U.S. economic and foreign policy elite's determination to revive German markets and producing capabilities as quickly as possible, on the other. The revivalist point of view was buttressed at least in part by consensus among specialists and Western elites that there had been splits between businessmen and the state in Nazi Germany. Such schisms presented opportunities for the West, they reasoned, and made it easier for German industry to downplay its role in Nazi crimes.

Draper's administrative techniques from the summer of 1945 on became a classic example of bureaucratic maneuver. He announced tough anti-Nazi measures in accordance with the official policy; then, shortly afterward he proclaimed success in carrying out those measures while at the same time undermining the very policies he publicly claimed to support.

That fall, for example, some Draper subordinates attempted to initiate a program to arrest and interrogate several hundred top German bankers and industrialists for the roles they had played during the war. This was not an indiscriminate program aimed at all German businessmen. It focused only on those who had thrived under National Socialism, or who had played some personal role in Nazi expropriation and looting. And the proposal did not call for criminal trials of these suspects: The aim was simply to investigate what they had actually done during the Third Reich while the evidence was fresh.

Draper blocked the measure as soon as it came to his attention. He refused to permit the investigation, contending that it would interfere with German economic recovery. When subordinates complained to sympathetic congressmen in Washington, Draper's allies Robert Murphy and Colonel Clarence Adcock (General Clay's most senior aide and longtime colleague) issued a series of reports

stating—in October 1945—that the main work of denazifying the
German economy had already been completed, so there was no
need to go ahead with any further studies. "What [the investiga-
tors] are doing here through denazification is nothing less than a
social revolution," Murphy's top aide Charles Reinhardt complained. "If the Russians want to bolshevize their side of the Elbe
that is their business, but it is not in conformity with American
standards to cut away the basis of private property."[17]

Draper's rebellious subordinates nonetheless managed to win
some congressional support in Washington, notably from a West
Virginia Democrat, Senator Harley Kilgore, and from FDR loyalists
in the Senate's liberal caucus. Kilgore delivered a broadside
against Draper's Economic Division, using ammunition provided
by dissident insiders. U.S. Military Government officials were
countenancing and even bolstering Nazism in the economic and
political life of Germany, Kilgore charged. They "take the position
that German businessmen are politically neutral and that no effort
should be made to penalize German industry or prevent it from
recapturing its prewar position in world markets. . . . They look
forward to resuming commercial relationships with a rehabilitated
German industry whose leading figures are well known to them,
rather than striking out on new paths of economic enterprise."
Kilgore named William Draper, Frederick Devereux, Rufus Wysor,
and others as particular problems. "Nazi industrial organization is
not repugnant to them," Kilgore charged, "and they have shown
every disposition to make peace with it."[18]

Over the next four months, Kilgore returned again and again to
the theme that the U.S. Military Government in Germany was
refusing to carry out the mandate of the Potsdam agreements and
the publicly professed U.S. policy on Germany. Much of his information was leaked to his staff by dissidents inside the U.S. Military
Government's decartelization branch, who believed—accurately,
as it turned out—that Draper and other higher-ups had systematically thwarted their initiatives against IG Farben and many
other German companies. Kilgore charged that top U.S. officials in
Berlin were "reluctant to carry out the policy of military and
economic disarmament of the Reich as agreed upon at the Potsdam
Conference," as the New York Times summarized it, and that
"some of our officials were connected with [U.S.] industrial and
financial firms that had close pre-war ties with the Nazis, would

like to resume commercial relationships with Germany, and were working for a strong Reich as a counterbalance to Soviet Russia."[19] But the *Times* report provided few specifics and declined to name names. Reportage on the issue, which had once been a front-page story, gradually drifted toward smaller articles buried deeper in the paper.

Kilgore, however, provided increasingly specific information, though it only rarely found its way into the prestige media. State Department and U.S. Military Government spokesmen bitterly denied his accusations. But the senator was in time proven to be substantially correct by an independent 1949 Federal Trade Commission investigation and—decades later—by the frank comments of Lucius Clay, William Draper, and others who had once aggressively rejected Kilgore's claims.[20]

18

"It Would Be Undesirable if This Became Publicly Known"

THE POLITICAL conflict among the Allies over how to deal with accused quislings and war criminals such as Miklós Horthy, SS General Wolff and his aides, and others with similar war records propelled the UNWCC into an important new role as what amounted to an international grand jury on war crimes. Because bringing most war criminals to justice was ostensibly an international, inter-Allied matter—as distinct from an issue on which the U.S. or Britain could rule without consultation—the UNWCC became the proper forum to make a prima facie determination whether any particular defendant was being charged with war crimes appropriately. As will be seen, this new authority spurred U.S. State Department and British Foreign Office efforts to shut down the commission and seal its records so that they might never be seen again.

The UNWCC's task since its beginning had been registration of the criminal complaints filed by a dozen Allied countries. The commission naturally made a determination when processing a registration whether the complaining government had made a prima facie case against the defendant. Though not particularly controversial at first, these determinations took on new significance as cooperation among the Allies over transfer of prisoners began to break down. After the UNWCC accepted the registration, the U.S. and Britain found it quite difficult to argue credibly that the defendant was a "political" rather than "criminal" suspect, as they had in some of the Yugoslav cases. That meant their efforts to bury cases or to refuse to turn over suspects became considerably more troublesome.[1] If the UNWCC did not find a prima facie case, of course, the country holding such prisoners was within its rights to refuse to turn them over or to release them.

The UNWCC's work thus became more urgent than ever. True, the Big Four Allied governments agreed to handle the crucial International Military Tribunal at Nuremberg through a new committee set up among themselves rather than through the UNWCC—an important blow to the authority of the commission. But the judgment of the two dozen prominent Nazi leaders at Nuremberg served to drive home with new force how manifold and complex Nazi crimes had been. Tens of thousands of criminals and collaborators remained scattered across Europe, some of them in positions of authority in postwar governments.

The UNWCC's work in this sensitive and symbolically potent area of East-West relations gave the commission a prospective power far beyond anything that the State Department or Foreign Office had ever envisioned. Worse yet, as Green Hackworth of the State Department saw things, the smaller Allied states were relatively strong in the UNWCC, and included aggressively anti-Nazi delegations from the Czechs, Yugoslavs, French, and the London Poles. Though the U.S. and United Kingdom dominated key UNWCC committees, their authority was by no means absolute.

The State Department and Foreign Office moved to shut down the UNWCC as quickly as they could, given the political realities of 1945. Their first step was to choke the commission by systematically denying it funds and personnel.[2]

The U.S. had replaced Pell early in 1945 with Colonel Joseph V. Hodgson and a legal assistant, Navy Captain John Wolff. That summer, working nearly alone, Hodgson and Wolff shared nominal responsibility for scores of demanding assignments, such as reviewing UNWCC war crimes case registrations, developing consolidated case lists of war crimes suspects and witnesses, facilitating

the international evidence-sharing necessary for successful prosecutions, doing legal research in a dozen different countries and
languages, attending endless meetings and making regular reports
to Washington, drafting international agreements on the transfer of
war crimes suspects, and keeping up with all the aspects of international liaison among the Allies on war crimes issues. Some of
these jobs were being simultaneously pursued by rival committees
in the U.S. War and State departments and by Justice Jackson's
prosecution staff at the International Military Tribunal. That left
Hodgson and Wolff with yet another assignment: attempting to
straighten out the bureaucratic infighting and confusion created by
the overlapping spheres of authority.

John Wolff collapsed from overwork shortly after the Nuremberg
tribunal convened that fall, according to State Department records.[3] Hodgson pleaded with State for at least two new assistants
to handle just the correspondence from U.S. war crimes staffs at
Nuremberg, Wiesbaden, and Washington, but there is no record
that help arrived.[4] A few weeks later, Hodgson resigned. Wolff,
then still convalescing, replaced his former chief and carried the
U.S. administrative burden at the UNWCC single-handedly.[5]

Hodgson's resignation precipitated a renewed effort at State to
dissolve the UNWCC altogether. Green Hackworth, still on the job,
approached H. Freeman Matthews, State's senior specialist on Europe who was at that time representing the department in interagency meetings with the War Department and the White House,
and convinced Matthews to move against the War Crimes Commission as soon as possible. Hackworth "wishes to have the Commission discontinued and desires to use the question of appointing a
successor to Col. Hodgson as the occasion to bring this about,"
Matthews noted during the first weeks of 1946.[6]

This strategy had evidently already been informally discussed
by key officers at State, for it received prompt support from the
department's leading European and legal affairs specialists. "In
view of the troublesome Yugoslav activity, [State] is inclined to
favor the prompt dissolution of the United Nations War Crimes
Commission," said James Riddleberger, the department's expert on
Germany. Unfortunately, "it would be very undesirable if it were to
become publicly known that this Government took the initiative in
bringing about the dissolution." Therefore, he continued, Hackworth proposed to "informally and discreetly approach the British
in order to ascertain their views. . . . Such approaches could be

made in such a way that any eventual publicity would not be likely to be damaging."[7]

Riddleberger, Hackworth, and Matthews set up an ad hoc committee to delicately close the doors of the UNWCC without being held accountable for having done so. Hackworth delegated his assistants for war crimes issues, Katharine Fite and Albert Garretson, both of whom had been active in the firing of Herbert Pell, to head the new group.

Fite was the State Department's chief liaison with the UNWCC, responsible for guiding the U.S. representative's votes on the commission. She meanwhile carried the burden of explaining the least popular aspects of State's legal policy to Congress, the media, and the public. Fite and Garretson also served as State's representatives on a half dozen other interagency committees dealing with war crimes policy issues, including those drafting policy for the War Department and for the U.S. occupation government in Germany. Fite and Garretson were responsible for drafting and implementing high policy, not for determining it, and were in that sense junior players. Nevertheless, their work on these coordinating committees illustrates the means by which Hackworth and his staff undermined the UNWCC and extended his influence into related issues such as the denazification and decartelization policies for Germany.

To outsiders, Washington seemed strongly committed to openhanded cooperation with the Allies in war crimes prosecutions and to a thoroughgoing reform of German society. In reality, though, opponents of these policies occupied many key posts at the State Department, the White House, in the U.S. occupation government in Germany, and in U.S. financial circles interested in foreign affairs and foreign trade. The influence of the advocates of rebuilding Germany as a bulwark against the USSR was well established, and on the rise.

Paradoxically, the challenge of prosecuting even major Nazi criminals grew more complex as evidence of the scope and character of Nazi crimes came to light. The International Tribunal at Nuremberg adopted the substance of a U.S. proposal for a joint prosecution of the SS, Nazi party leaders, and a handful of similar groups as "criminal conspiracies" responsible for crimes against humanity and crimes against peace.[8]

The occupation government's Control Council law No. 10 applied the conspiracy theory to hundreds of thousands of individual cases. This law specified that any person who "held a high political, civil or military position in Germany or one of its Allies, co-belligerents or satellites or held a high position in the financial, industrial or economic life of any such country" was deemed to have committed a crime against peace, namely, planning and executing an aggressive war in violation of treaties.[9] Membership in an organization such as the SS became sufficient cause for arrest. Law No. 10 did not require that all persons declared criminal be prosecuted; it simply gave the commanders of the occupation forces authority to investigate what individuals may have done during the war and, if appropriate, to bring charges against them.

But this solution raised almost as many questions as it answered. First, it was by now clear that thousands of suspects shared direct responsibility for some atrocities. Contemporary estimates concluded that there were about 250,000 to 300,000 members of the SS (this includes the militarized Waffen-SS units), 70,000 full-time Nazi party executives, 15,000 in the party intelligence service *Sicherheitsdienst* (SD), 15,000 in the Gestapo, and as many as 1.5 to 2 million in various brownshirt paramilitary and militia units. Even considering that these numbers might be inflated and the categories overlap with one another, it seemed in late 1945 as though "not less than 2 million persons in all of Germany (and probably not less than 500,000 persons in the U.S. Zone) will be war criminals under the Control Council Law."[10]

The U.S. apparatus for war crimes trials in Germany "obviously cannot prosecute anywhere near this number of cases," a U.S. Denazification Policy Board concluded in December 1945. "No matter how summary the proceedings, it will be necessary to determine the degree of culpability of the accused, the existence of mitigating circumstances, and other factors affecting the punishment to be imposed." The presumption of criminality in the cases of the Gestapo, SS, and SD was so strong that in many cases "relatively quick determinations" would be possible, the board said. But the role of other Nazis varied so widely that even summary justice would take time. And the complexities of the cases of collaborators from foreign countries, or of those who "held a high position in the financial, industrial or economic life" of Axis puppet states were more complicated still.[11] The main U.S. war crimes prosecution group would be able to handle at most "a few hundreds or thousands of cases," the board contended.

The joint occupation government in Germany temporarily interned about 1.1 million Nazi officials, major businessmen, and former government administrators under various provisions of JCS 1067 and the Potsdam agreements during the summer and fall of 1945, according to U.S. statistics. Some 78 percent of those cases—868,566 people—had been processed by Allied officials by December 1945. Of those, half had been acquitted, in effect, with findings that they had not substantially participated in Nazi activity. About 20 percent of the accused were found to have been so deeply implicated in Nazi crimes or in the maintenance of Nazi power that they were banned from the postwar German government and from prominent positions in the private sector. The remainder of the accused faced sanctions that varied with the circumstances of the individual's case.[12]

Most of the German civilians still interned during the winter of 1945 were persons against whom reasonable suspicion of serious criminal activity existed. There were 117,512 German internees that December; of these, more than 38,000 had been executive-level Nazi party officials; 9,222 had been members of the Gestapo, SD, or other German police and intelligence organizations; and about 5,000 more had been senior members of various Nazi paramilitary groups.[13]

The speed of the "official" denazification thus far had been achieved by identifying categories of suspects—Nazi party officials, government officials above a certain professional grade, Gestapo officers, and so on—whom the Allies regarded as prima facie threats to the occupation government. Contrary to the later myths about denazification, these categories were usually relatively clear and limited to elite sectors of the German population, who were assumed to have had most influence during Hitler's rule and, hence, the greatest responsibility for Nazi activities.[14] The paperwork for persons in each category was then processed through a string of administrative steps that were similar in most respects to the procedures used in almost any government office. The difference, of course, was that this time the bureaucratic product was not distribution of social security benefits or unemployment insurance. It was, instead, the first step in the allocation of legal and political responsibility for mass murder.

Critics could see that these techniques often captured small-fry while permitting major criminals to escape. Not surprisingly, those who had been most powerful in wartime Germany usually had the most resources to evade the system.

Business leaders seemed to be particularly immune. "The present procedure fails in practice to reach a substantial number of persons who supported or assisted the Nazis, both in their rise to power and in carrying out their programs," the confidential study of the Denazification Policy Board reported. "This is probably especially true of business leaders," who did not necessarily join the party but whose "influence may have been much greater than that of party members."[15] Owners of businesses that played a major role in the regime often escaped responsibility, the board concluded, because regulations in the U.S. zone made it quite complicated to seize a business from its ostensible owner.

Meanwhile, the U.S. occupation government's reliance on conventional bureaucratic techniques tended to catch many so-called "little Nazis," whom the board did not regard as "really active supporters of the Nazi regime." Such cases would in time be processed and often dismissed, but in the meantime these suspects required endless labor-hours to investigate and administer, and their internment fed German discontent with the occupation government.

"The net effect of these inadequacies is to bear more heavily on the 'small Nazi' and to leave loop-holes for influential supporters. As a result, our actions often seem arbitrary and capricious to the Germans and tend to alienate even those who favor denazification," the board concluded. "In large measure, these defects arise from our reliance on mandatory categories. Yet, as outsiders to the community, we can not arrive at sound judgments in individual cases, and need some rule of thumb as a substitute."[16]

Similarly, the U.S. occupation government's effort to block the bank accounts of Nazi-era political and business leaders bogged down by the autumn of 1945. The program was supposed to prevent Nazi officials or profiteers from laundering stolen money or smuggling it out of the country. In reality, however, "there has been a general breakdown in the effectiveness of Law 52 [which blocked the bank accounts] in the entire zone," the financial branch's field investigations chief, Louis Madison, reported. "The breakdown is characterized by a failure on the part of the responsible American and German agencies to block the accounts of Nazis, and by violations of the law by German individuals and banks." Madison's study reviewed 200 cases chosen at random in the U.S. zone of Germany; of those, only 32 (16 percent) had been handled successfully. Even when an account was blocked as required by law,

German banks simply ignored the order. Further, the shortage of U.S. investigations personnel and the labyrinthine bureaucracy that administered the program guaranteed that the little progress could be made without a thorough-going organizational reform.[17]

By December 1945, the publicly mandated denazification program sharply collided with the unofficial (but actual) political and economic objectives of the U.S. occupation government. That month, the U.S. Denazification Policy Board confidentially recommended that existing policies and practices be shifted to better fit the "longer term" goals of the occupation. Publicly, the orientation of the denazification program was to remain the same as it had been under JCS 1067. "Every person who exercised leadership and power in support of the Nazi regime should be deprived of influence or power," the board recommended, "whether or not he was formally affiliated with the Party or any other Nazi organization." At the same time, however, the board introduced a new consideration that would fundamentally alter the program in the U.S. zone of Germany: "Denazification . . . should not be carried so far as to prevent the building of a stable democratic society in Germany . . . we must avoid the creation of a huge mass of outcasts who will provide fertile soil for agitators and a source of social instability."[18]

This turned an important corner. Up to then, the continuation of Nazi influence within German social structures—business, education, the arts, etc.—had been seen as the most dangerous source of potential instability in Germany. But at least as early as December 1945, the opposite formulation came to the fore, even in official documents. Now, it was the *denazification* effort that was seen as the source of disaffection.

Opposition within the U.S. to denazification and decartelization in Germany was led almost exclusively by the corporate and foreign policy elite that had been most active in U.S.-German financial relations during the 1920s and 1930s. The disproportionate political leverage of this group, its ability to shape media coverage of foreign policy issues, to influence government policy, and eventually to shift public opinion was dramatically manifested in the realignment of U.S. policy concerning denazification and decartelization in the brief period between 1945 and 1947.

One of this group's most effective lobbying tactics was sponsorship of junkets to Europe by American politicians and businessmen, financed by U.S. multinationals, to "study the problem of

German recovery." Draper paid close attention to these visits, staging elaborate briefings intended to shape public opinion at home concerning the professed realities of business in Europe. These events were almost ceremonial: The attendees and the briefers had selected one another largely through their existing social networks based in powerful U.S. companies with investments in Europe. The men on both sides of Draper's briefing table were receptive to his message and usually knew pretty well what it would be.

A stream of U.S. experts visited the headquarters of the Economics Division during the first two years after the war, and Draper provided them with privileged access to the inside thinking on U.S. policy concerning German business. "The reports of these visitors echoed the conclusion that German recovery demanded greatly increased emphasis on heavy industries," decartelization chief James S. Martin (a Draper rival) remembered later. "In their reports the visitors frequently referred to the 'proven impossibility' of something that no one had yet tried to do [i.e., actually break up German banking and industrial oligopolies]. With equal frequency they reported the 'mounting chaos' that was supposed to have resulted from the ruthless 'Morgenthau Plan of deindustrialization.' " Similar problems were alleged to have been caused by drastic reforms that had not actually been carried out. "It became customary to refer to the urgent necessity for 'reversing the former policy of destroying German industries,' " Martin wrote, and of reversing a decartelization policy that in fact had not yet been implemented.[19]

A popular example of Martin's point can be found in Lewis H. Brown's *A Report on Germany*, a 1947 bestseller that had substantial influence in Washington at the time and remains quoted to this day.[20] Brown was chairman of the Johns-Manville Corporation, a major military contractor and international mining company that held a near-monopoly on the U.S. market for asbestos. The company has frequently been accused in U.S. courts of corporate crimes, including antitrust violations.[21]

Brown toured Germany during 1946 and 1947 and returned to the U.S. with detailed arguments against economic reform in Germany that had been prepared mainly by Draper's staff. Brown's preconceptions clearly shaped the conclusions he drew from the visits. He wrote quite frankly that he approached Germany "from the standpoint of an industrialist's attempt to analyze the problem of a bankrupt company [seeking] to determine the simple common-sense fundamentals necessary to get the wheels of production turning."[22]

His acknowledgments of the experts he consulted concerning Germany read like the guest list of a dinner sponsored by the Council on Foreign Relations: AT&T's Frederick Devereux, Sullivan & Cromwell's John Foster Dulles, former president Herbert Hoover (who had been enlisted by Truman to cement Republican party support for his administration's emerging policy on Germany), General Lucius Clay, William Draper, Sears, Roebuck president A. S. Barrows (who was then serving as U.S. Comptroller in Germany), British and Swiss banking and industry officials, and twenty-five unnamed German industrialists. In more than five pages of Brown's detailed acknowledgments of those he interviewed, there appears no speaker for German labor, no small businessman of any nationality, no female, none of the then-well-known public advocates of denazification and decartelization of German industry (including those still in government posts inside Germany), no Social Democrats, and no known veterans of European Resistance movements of any political persuasion.[23]

Brown's argument was simple and in some ways convincing. He said that the Morgenthau Plan had shaped JCS 1067—as was true enough—and that JCS 1067 was a disaster. The economic and denazification commitments that the U.S. made at Potsdam should be unilaterally disavowed as quickly as possible, Brown contended. The U.S. should block further German reparations to the USSR, because German uncertainty over which equipment might be shipped to the Soviets had "helped destroy the incentive to put plants in Germany back into operation." The postwar punishment of Nazis by France and the USSR had been indiscriminate and brutal, Brown said. The U.S. and British system of trying accused criminals before courts and administrative commissions was better, he argued, but "many of the industrial and technical leaders of the economic life of Germany, who had climbed on the Nazi bandwagon much as people climb on any new and apparently successful bandwagon, were permitted to do only common labor pending the years required to go through the denazification courts." The Potsdam agreements had "deprived the economic machine of Germany of the very leadership necessary for its revival . . . [and was now] fatally slowing down the rehabilitation and reconstruction of the industrial machine of Germany and Western Europe."[24]

Brown said he expected no support for his proposals from "the enemies of the American Way of Life." But "from our friends who abhor all forms of totalitarianism . . . I hope for tolerance and ultimate understanding of the imperative need for getting together on a plan of action under which we may minimize the [Soviet] threat to Western civilization . . ."[25]

Brown's lobbying trips to Germany were underwritten mainly by General Electric's chairman Philip D. Reed, who was one of the single most influential U.S. corporate leaders on postwar U.S.-German issues. In addition to his role in Brown's project, Reed and the business organizations he led organized a series of similar conferences in 1946 and 1947. Typical U.S. delegations included the chairman of the executive committee of the National Association of Manufacturers, the chairman of the (U.S.) National Foreign Trade Council, and senior executives of the National City Bank of New York and the Chase Bank, among others. On some occasions, Reed traveled as a representative of General Electric; on others, he came as head of the U.S. delegation to the International Chamber of Commerce; or as the personal envoy of Secretary of Commerce Averell Harriman.[26]

Like Brown's book, Reed's report to Harriman lambasted the denazification and decartelization policy the U.S. had approved at Potsdam as the work of FDR-era "extremists" (Reed's term) at the Department of Justice. The U.S. policy was harmful and unnecessary, he said, and was interfering with Germany's economic recovery.[27]

Reed's company was not an entirely disinterested party. General Electric was among the most important U.S. investors in Germany, owning about 25 percent of its German counterpart, the electrical giant AEG, plus factories and dozens of smaller interests.[28] At the time Reed was lobbying the U.S. government against antitrust policy in Germany, GE was facing no fewer than thirteen criminal antitrust prosecutions in U.S. courts for price fixing, gouging consumers and the U.S. government through its monopoly on electrical equipment manufacturing, conspiracy, Sherman Act violations, and similar corporate crimes. (GE settled most of these cases out of court in 1949, then went on to a series of remarkably similar abuses that in time led to still another round of criminal convictions for senior General Electric executives about a decade later.)[29]

As Morgenthau, Pell, James S. Martin, and other reformers saw things, the arguments of General Electric and Johns-Manville had become the dominant point of view in Western policy circles and in the media. They had become "standard fare" in U.S. newspapers within a year after the occupation began, Martin commented,[30] even though in reality only two steps had been undertaken to implement U.S. antitrust efforts in Germany by the time Brown's denunciation of the program appeared: the seizure of plants and assets of IG Farben; and the appointment of a trustee to administer coal wholesaling firms in the U.S. zone.

The Allies and the Germans both knew that German manufacturing, including war production, had survived the war surprisingly intact, despite the massive Allied bombing campaign. Senator Kilgore publicized a congressional study based mainly on U.S. Strategic Bombing Survey data that concluded that Germany's production of armored cars, fighter bombers, and several categories of strategic supplies had actually increased under U.S. and British bombing, in some cases expanding eightfold over 1942 production figures. True, the air attacks had crippled the German transportation network and oil production during the final months of the war—a telling blow. But that damage was repaired relatively easily once the fighting stopped. From the point of view of production, at least, Germany was already "better prepared for war than it was at the end of World War I," Kilgore contended.[31]

Kilgore stressed that a distinct drift toward postwar accommodation with German business had already set in. "There is a natural inclination on the part of many of our [U.S.] administrators to take over in order to get things running again, and there is a natural inclination on the part of many Germans to lie back and let them do it. . . . [In] the desire for efficiency our military administrators may keep in positions of power the Nazi plant managers," Kilgore said. "In Italy, I heard certain American Army officers deplore the fact that Italian partisans had killed many of the Fascist plant managers, which made more difficult the reorganization of Italian productive capacity. In Germany there has been no such [partisan] revolt. The Nazi industrial hierarchy remains intact."[32]

The reports of Brown and Reed were in reality briefs for the European Recovery Program—the Marshall Plan. They illustrate the extent to which that enormously popular and respected program became entangled with the revival of German businessmen who had participated in Nazi crimes. Particularly important in this effort was the "Committee for the Marshall Plan," founded in September 1947. It labeled itself a citizens' organization but was in reality funded and administered by the same economic and foreign policy elite that has been discussed thus far. Its initial sponsors included Averell Harriman and Robert Lovett (who will be remembered from the Brown Brothers, Harriman bank), Allen Dulles, Dean Acheson, Winthrop Aldrich (chairman of the Chase Bank), Philip Reed (of GE), and others of similar stature, most of whom had been active in U.S.-German finance since the 1920s. Labor was represented by hard-line anti-Communists active in the CIA-sponsored penetration of European trade unions, such as James Carey and David Dubinsky.[33]

This Marshall Plan lobby operated as a "distinguished propaganda committee," as AT&T executive Arthur Page described it.[34] Its goal was never described as the revitalization of the German business elite but, rather, as "saving Europe" and "providing American jobs" through implementation of the Marshall Plan. But whatever one may think of the plan, the restoration of much of the prewar German corporate elite was an integral part of the package.

General Clay used the case of Deutsche Bank director Hermann Abs to explain this concept. "We were never able to make Hermann Abs the financial minister [of Germany] as we would have," Clay remembered in the same interview quoted earlier, because of the German and American public's refusal to accept a man who had been so deeply compromised during the Hitler years. But not to worry, Clay continued. "We were able to finally put him in charge of the Reconstruction Finance Corporation, which was somewhat outside of government," and which was instrumental in distribution of Marshall Plan funds for Germany.[35]

Sponsors of the Committee for the Marshall Plan were simultaneously at the cutting edge of renewed efforts to invest in German industry. "If you have been trying unsuccessfully to get to Germany to reestablish prewar business contacts, don't be discouraged," *Business Week* told its readers early in 1947. "You can expect [a] program for reviving business in western Germany to be pushed by all U.S. factions . . . Republican backing was assured when John Foster Dulles, Republican spokesman, recently called for the revival of business in Germany and western Europe whatever the price. German goods are already trickling into the U.S. market. Anticipating some consumer resistance [in the U.S.], Military Government authorities have shrewdly met customs requirements by marking them: 'Made in Germany, U.S. Zone.' . . . Before large-scale arrivals of German goods begin, Washington is likely to release a press barrage explaining that German exports help pay [U.S.] occupation costs in Germany."[36]

Shortly after its founding, the Committee for the Marshall Plan placed full-page advertisements in the most influential U.S. newspapers; sent thousands of personally addressed telegrams signed by the former secretary of war, Henry L. Stimson, to businessmen asking for their donations and political support; and made a mass mailing to hundreds of thousands of U.S. "opinion leaders" in the upper strata of business, media, labor, and social organizations. The group chartered Marshall Plan clubs in a dozen cities, opened business offices in New York and Washington, and initiated a series of heavily publicized meetings between President Truman and business leaders designed to convey the impression of broad popular support for the Marshall Plan. As Congressman Charles Plumley (a Republican from Vermont) put it, "There has never been so much propaganda in the whole history of the nation as there has been for the Marshall Plan." The campaign created an "overwhelming conviction among the American people and among members of Congress that we must have the Marshall Plan right now," he continued.[37]

The claim of "overwhelming support" was, in fact, overblown. Public opinion polls of the period indicate that about 65 percent of the U.S. population either opposed the Marshall Plan or did not know what it was.[38] Even so, the Marshall Plan passed the Congress by a large margin. The plan's sponsors used the relatively broad, popular support for doing something constructive about Europe as a means of putting through the distinctly unpopular idea of reestablishing the German economic elite.

These factors—insiders' opposition to reform, the passive resistance of German business, Allied suppression of indigenous Antifa radicals, the sheer magnitude of the task of denazification, the self-mobilization of U.S. and international business elites, and an often paranoid geopolitical competition with the USSR—combined with other factors to stall denazification and reform of the German business structure by the summer of 1945. Within three years they had shut it down altogether.

19

The End of the War Crimes Commission

ORIGINALLY, a second international trial at Nuremberg was to focus primarily on the activities of German finance and industry during the Third Reich. The "industrialists trial," as it was called at the time, was widely regarded as of equal importance to the prosecution of the Nazi and SS high command. Hermann Abs and other major bankers were important targets, at least judging from the recommendations made by U.S. war crimes investigators at the time.[1]

But Justice Jackson vetoed this plan, declaring in the autumn of 1945 that the United States would refuse to participate in any further international trials of German defendants and would instead hold separate prosecutions on its own. These trials became the "Subsequent Proceedings" organized under the leadership of General Telford Taylor. His group brought twelve cases against a total of 182 defendants; these were the famous trials that judged *Einsatzgruppen* murder squads, concentration camp doctors, business executives from Krupp and IG Farben, Nazi judges, and similar defendants.[2] U.S. military commissions tried additional 950 war crimes defendants, though that figure includes cases in the Far East in addition to Europe. The majority of cases tried before U.S. military commissions involved German civilians who had murdered downed U.S. pilots.[3]

Yet these trials, as important as they were, were very much "symbolic measures," as Taylor commented in a recent interview, and were designed to teach Germany and the world a lesson about the crimes of the Hitler dictatorship.[4] They succeeded brilliantly in that mission. The record of Nazi crimes compiled by Taylor's team remains to this day the single most important source of information and documentation ever assembled.

But these proceedings were not, and were not intended to be, an effort to prosecute the power structure of Nazi Germany as such; nor were they an effort to remove the German "ruling class" (to use Kennan's phrase) that had operated during the Hitler years from its position in postwar society. The Subsequent Proceedings were in many respects a rear-guard action by the hard-line anti-Nazi wing of the U.S. government, which was already in retreat. Washington hobbled the prosecutions with budgetary restrictions, and some U.S. agencies in Berlin tacitly refused cooperation, particularly during trials of German industrialists. Taylor's three U.S. trials of industrialists lasted slightly more than a year altogether, resulting in nineteen convictions and fourteen acquittals. The U.S. judges tended to be hostile to the prosecution, particularly in the Friedrich Flick case. The court "was apparently unable to feel that offenses by industrialists fell into as severe a category as when committed by a common man," as noted legal historian John Alan Appleman put it.[5]

Flick's successful defense depended directly on the social dynamics of international law and of genocide. Flick beat all but one of the slave labor and plunder charges, because three prominent U.S. judges concluded that the director and owner of a corporation should not be held accountable for slavery and looting by his companies, unless the prosecution could prove that he personally ordered each particular crime to be carried out. Without proof of that type, every bit of ambiguous evidence had to be interpreted by the court in favor of the individual defendants, namely Flick and his circle of executives.

Worse, the Flick case established a legal precedent for a corporate defense of "necessity"—a close cousin to the defense of acting under orders—that went beyond even what Flick had argued on his own behalf and that contradicted many aspects of the earlier ruling on this issue by the International Military Tribunal.[6] Amazingly, the legal precedent left by this series of trials seems to be that a nineteen-year-old draftee accused of war crimes cannot successfully plead that he was acting under orders, but the owners and directors of multi-billion-dollar companies can.

The U.S. government cut off funding for the prosecution staff at Nuremberg in mid-1948, bringing the Subsequent Proceedings to an abrupt end. The staff abandoned pending investigations and potential prosecutions, sometimes with little more than a note to the files indicating the case had been closed. Less than two and a half years after that, the new U.S. high commissioner for Germany, John McCloy, granted clemency to every single industrialist who had been convicted at Nuremberg.[7]

In the end, neither the "Treasury" nor the "State" factions of the wartime U.S. government fully achieved the goals they had sought during the war. Many of the State Department's specialists in German affairs and international law went on to long careers at State, serving in influential posts involving U.S. policy toward Europe and the USSR until well into the 1960s. Herbert Pell's archrival Green Hackworth ended up as president of the International Court of Justice at The Hague.[8] As Secretary of Defense, Dillon, Read's James Forrestal oversaw much of the birth of the postwar military-industrial complex and the dramatic shift in U.S. relations with the USSR. He committed suicide in 1949 during a paranoid nervous breakdown during which, his biographers tell us, he believed he was pursued by a vast conspiracy of Communists and Jews.[9] William Draper went on from Germany to become assistant secretary of the army, where he dismantled the antitrust campaign against Japanese multinational companies that had been instituted in Tokyo by General MacArthur.[10]

Many lawyers and economists from Henry Morgenthau's team at Treasury went on to serve a year or two in the U.S. occupation government in Germany, some of them on Telford Taylor's war crimes prosecution staff. Some found themselves tarred by Senator Joseph McCarthy's brush when a dubious spy scandal erupted involving former Morgenthau aide Harry Dexter White. Secretary Morgenthau went on to serve as chairman of the United Jewish Appeal and as chairman of the board of the American Financial and Development Corporation for Israel.[11]

Herbert Pell attempted to reverse U.S. policy in Germany after he left the government, but after a few years, he returned to a life of travel and as a patron of the arts. He died in 1961. His son, Claiborne, whose wedding Herbert was attending at the time he was fired, went on to become a prominent U.S. senator and, eventually, chair of the Senate Foreign Relations Committee.[12]

The German economic elite and corporations that had been active under Hitler have continued, for the most part, though without the Nazi rhetoric and police state powers of the Nazi period. There were of course generational changes in the leadership of German companies in the years following the war, and other reforms took place in response to pressure from German unions and international competition.[13] But the fundamental pattern in German finance and industry has been continuity and stability. Regardless of how one views the U.S. decision to step back from prosecution of the German economic elite, it is evident that the U.S. policy necessarily entailed an amnesty for much of what German business had done during the Holocaust.

There are to this day unresolved war crimes charges against prominent German business leaders that were brought before the UNWCC and other international bodies by governments as varied as the Netherlands, France, Poland, and Yugoslavia.[14] Jewish efforts to extract even modest restitution payments for work performed by concentration camp inmates for prominent companies such as Messerschmitt, Ernst Heinkel, and others continue to be rejected by those corporations. The same is true of German construction companies such as Philipp Holzmann, which has repeatedly been identified by survivors as a major beneficiary of forced labor. Holzmann refuses to pay restitution and continues to enjoy contracts all over the world.[15] Even those companies that have made some form of welcome restitution—Daimler Benz being the most recent case—go to considerable lengths to deny any culpability whatsoever for the Holocaust, portraying their payments to their former slaves as a form of charity.[16]

On the U.S. side of the Atlantic, the Dulles brothers' tangled role in U.S.-German relations was bound to bob to the surface from time to time as liberal Democrats leveled charges against them during election campaigns. But after the political atmosphere in the U.S. shifted sharply to the right in 1945, the more respectable media declined to take such criticisms seriously.

The harsher assessments of the Dulles brothers' role that did find their way into print often carried ideological baggage or included just enough errors for the Dulleses to sidestep and discredit the charges. The Soviet-backed Cominform (the late-1940s successor to the Comintern) published a broadside against the Dulleses' financial and political role in Germany, as one element of the USSR's postwar publicity offensive against U.S. policy in Europe. The statement contended that the flood of capital into Germany during the 1920s had in the end helped build the industrial infrastructure of Hitler's state, and that Allen Dulles, John Foster Dulles, and the law firm of Sullivan & Cromwell had been instrumental in that process. All of that was true enough. The Cominform then went on to claim that Allen Dulles was "director of the J. Henry Schroeder [sic] interests in London, Cologne and Hamburg"; that the German steel trust played the "leading part" in Schroeder bank affairs; and that Sullivan & Cromwell was "closely connected" with Standard Oil, the Chase National Bank, and with Rockefeller interests in general.[17]

By the time these charges aired in 1948, almost any comment from a Communist source was easily discredited in the United States. In this particular case, the facts were that the J. Henry Schroder Bank of *London* did indeed join with the Rockefellers and Dillon, Read during the 1920s to invest millions of dollars in the German steel trust, which in turn used the capital to build new factories that were within a few years engaged mainly in military production. Allen Dulles had been a director between 1937 and 1943 of the New York subsidiary of the London Schroder bank. The London bank did have substantial familial, banking, and business ties with a Schroder-family-owned bank in Germany that had been a major financial backer of the SS. But the German Schröder Bank was incorporated and financed separately from that of the London and New York Schroders. The various Schroder banks often cooperated in international investments, but they were not exactly the same institution, Dulles's defenders pointed out. Meanwhile, although the Sullivan & Cromwell partners most certainly shared with the Rockefellers many investments, political causes, and social clubs, the law firm as such had not been attorneys of record for Standard Oil or for the Chase Bank during the 1920s investment binge.

The Dulles brothers used these discrepancies to denounce the Cominform criticism as "wholly without foundation,"[18] then succeeded in using the Soviets' denunciation as "proof," of sorts, that any such criticisms were by definition inaccurate and probably Communist-inspired. When the liberal *New York Post* raised questions about John Foster Dulles during a hard-fought senatorial campaign, he wrote in reply that the *Post* article was "totally misleading and merely paraphrases the smear line that has been adopted by the Soviet communist newspapers. See, for example, the Moscow *New Times* issue of February 28, 1947 . . ."[19]

And there the matter rested, despite occasional grumblings from the political left. A few years later, John Foster Dulles's nomination as U.S. secretary of state came before the Senate in what would prove to be the last opportunity for a public inquiry into the lingering questions concerning Dulles's relationship with the German financial elite during the Hitler years. The confirmation hearings took place just as the Korean War had opened a new and more dangerous phase, when Senator Joseph McCarthy was riding high, and when the Republican party had won the White House for the first time in twenty years. John Foster Dulles's confirmation hearings went smoothly. A month later, President Eisenhower appointed his brother Allen to be director of the CIA.

The United Nations War Crimes Commission staggered on for about another eighteen months after Hackworth and the State Department decided to shut it down. The British wanted to close it immediately,[20] but the U.S. preferred to let its budget peter out, thereby avoiding the embarrassing political questions that would inevitably accompany the abandonment of war crimes enforcement less than thirty-six months after the end of the war. General Lucius Clay, acting in coordination with secretary of war and State Department officials, announced in the summer of 1947 that all requests for U.S. assistance in the transfer or prosecution of alleged quislings and war criminals had to be filed by November 1 of that year, and that all evidence necessary to make a prima facie case against suspects must be submitted by December 31, unless there were "exceptional circumstances."[21] These deadlines brought bitter protests from Dutch, French, Belgian, and other national authorities,[22] and were adjusted slightly over the next few months in a series of contradictory announcements that left many European diplomats and war crimes specialists scratching their heads over just what U.S. international legal policy actually was.[23]

France, Poland, and Czechoslovakia responded by filing hundreds of requests for transfer of war criminals with the UNWCC and with the U.S. military government. Some of these cases raised basic questions of law and justice that had up to then been carefully sidestepped by U.S. and British prosecutors. Polish case No. 7593, for example, charged five German air force and army generals with "deliberate bombardment of undefended places," in connection with the September 1939 attack on Warsaw.[24] This attack had been formally condemned as a war crime by President Roosevelt prior to the U.S. entry into the war, it will be recalled, and the U.S. and the United Nations had nominally recognized such attacks as war crimes. A second Polish case laid out the complex scheme through which German banks and businesses looted the economies of a half-dozen European countries through the predatory currency-clearing arrangements operated in part via the Bank for International Settlements.[25]

The majority of the UNWCC voted to accept both new Polish charges. The U.S. and British delegations blocked this action, however, fearing that those prosecutions could set legal precedents that neither government was prepared to accept. Less than two months later, the UNWCC shut its doors for good without having reached a decision. Hundreds of other war crimes charges were processed in the last weeks of the commission's work. Some were rejected, but most were accepted as prima facie cases, which presumably would have obligated the U.S. and Britain to deliver these suspects and any available evidence. As a practical matter though, all of the case filings were packed away in cardboard boxes to await a decision from the United Nations as to what was to be done with the UNWCC records.

The U.N.'s assistant secretary general in charge of its legal department, Ivan Kerno, declared a few months later that there was "no precedent" for releasing the UNWCC records, even to government prosecutors, and that the material in the UN files "with the exception of a relatively few cases . . . had not yet been submitted to judicial process or otherwise subjected to legal evaluation." Kerno determined that the War Crimes Commission records— including some 25,000 case files on alleged Class A war criminals, most of whom had not yet been tried—were to be retired to a UN warehouse and to remain closed in all but the most extraordinary circumstances.[26] There the records remained for more than forty years, until the worldwide controversy surrounding Kurt Waldheim finally pried them open.[27]

Kerno's claim that the records had not been submitted to judicial process was actually "blatantly false," noted historian Alti Rodal, who was the first to bring Kerno's action to public attention. "In fact, this was the primary task and competence of the UNWCC's Committee I. . . . Throughout, the Committee insisted that only crimes of 'reasonable importance' be examined. Chairman Hurst, whose distinguished legal career included a period as judge on the International Court at The Hague and service as a legal advisor to the Foreign Office, took pains to insure that evidence and allegations presented by the exiled governments was judiciously tested before each individual name was listed [in UNWCC files]. This is in stark contrast" to Kerno's assertion, Rodal points out.[28]

It would be impossible today to fully reconstruct the motives behind Kerno's decision, of course. But the information that has come to light recently is enough to raise troubling questions concerning his impartiality, because Ivan Kerno was a clandestine U.S. agent during his years on the staff of the United Nations. He first encountered Allen Dulles at least as early as 1919, as it turns out, when both served on the Czechoslovak Boundary Commission that drew the borders of the new Czechoslovak state at the Paris conference.[29] Kerno spelled his name "Krno" in the traditional Slovak form in those days, and he became Dulles's entrée to Czechoslovak president Eduard Beneš, with whom Dulles forged a lasting relationship. Kerno went on to become Czech delegate to the Reparations Commission and to a reasonably accomplished career in the Czech diplomatic service. His activities during World War II remain murky, but heavily censored records released by the State Department and FBI suggest that he may have worked with the OSS or British intelligence on behalf of the Czech government-in-exile in London. Posted to the new United Nations after the war, Kerno became an informant and intelligence contact for the U.S. State Department and FBI at the time of his ruling blocking the

UNWCC records, according to U.S. files obtained under the Freedom of Information Act.[30] Many of Kerno's contemporaries who knew his position and background believe he spied for the CIA as well. Kerno eventually defected to the United States in 1952 and became active in the Committee for a Free Czechoslovakia, Radio Free Europe, and other organizations financed primarily by the CIA.[31]

20

Money, Law, and Genocide

T HE BREAKDOWN of East-West cooperation in the wake of World War II was rooted not only in economic and geopolitical disputes over Europe, Asia, and the Mideast, but also in mutual paranoia and in deep ideological and cultural divisions. Within that well-known context, however, it is clear that Western statesmen seriously underestimated the profound symbolic and practical importance to the USSR of the United States' abandonment of denazification of the German elite in 1945.

Allen Dulles's "March 1945 secret talks with Germany were connected in Moscow with everything," remembers Soviet scholar Sergo Mikoyan. Stalin saw it as of a piece "with the pre-war anti-Soviet diplomacy of England and France; [and with] the delay of the second front. It had a very great impact on the psychology of Stalin.

"For men such as Stalin, for whom betrayal was a normal way of life, he could not but understand those actions like this [i.e., as a betrayal]," Mikoyan continued in a recent forum at the Smithsonian Institution's Wilson Center in Washington. "He regarded it as an attempt to make a kind of Ardennes for our side"—that is to say, a last-ditch German effort to split the Allies.

"The main issue for us was American behavior toward Germany" once Truman came to power, Mikoyan stressed, particularly the end of denazification and of Western cooperation in reparations, the economic and military reconstruction of Germany, and the unification of the three Allied zones of occupation. U.S. policy in Germany "was seen in Moscow at the time as an effort to make Germany strong again, and strong enough to menace our country. Particularly important for us was ... the political support for Germany." Without understanding the Soviet state's near-obsessive concern with German power during that period, he concludes, it is impossible to understand Stalin's actions during these first, crystallizing months of the cold war. Mikoyan contended that the U.S. decision to halt denazification in Germany was of great political importance at the time, and in fact remains difficult for many Russians to understand or accept to this day.[1]

The U.S. abandonment of denazification and decartelization was not a product of the cold war—it was a cause of it, and a considerably more important cause than was recognized in the West at the time. Some people may say that, looked at in geopolitical terms, denazification was a largely "psychological" issue. But for the USSR, the U.S. decision to end denazification went to the heart of the mystery of what U.S. intentions in Europe might be, and that in turn was the pivot upon which turned Stalin's interpretation of all the "objective" data about U.S. troops, weapons, and diplomatic initiatives. From the very first days of the occupation, the U.S. practiced what appeared from the outside to be a duplicitous policy toward denazification and decartelization of Germany. This was not surprising, considering that the policy was a product of an unresolved factional conflict within the U.S. government that went back a decade or more. The USSR—and particularly Stalin, for it was he who almost single-handedly made key Soviet foreign policy decisions at that point—interpreted the contradictions in U.S. behavior as proof of the Americans' bad faith.

Stalin's own crimes and blunders are not justified, of course, nor can the past fifty years of Soviet publicity concerning Nazi crimes always be taken at face value. But whether the U.S. government intended it or not, its actions cast the die for the cold war not in 1946 or 1947 (as most Western observers would have it), but by the end of 1945 and arguably earlier.

The U.S. foreign policy and international law experts of the day—men like Murphy, Grew, Draper, Hackworth, the Dulles brothers, and others—significantly miscalculated the true political and military price of their decision to undermine denazification in 1945. The *Realpolitik* that to them seemed so useful in other circumstances proved to be a serious error for strictly practical reasons, even when its ethical and moral dimensions are put aside.

Morgenthau's dire prediction that Germany would return to a campaign of world conquest within five or ten years clearly proved to be mistaken. This can be traced to the traumatic lessons that millions of ordinary Germans learned from their experience with Hitler, war, and genocide, and to the fact that the onset of the Cold War resulted in four decades of division and military occupation for Germany.

But it does not follow from Morgenthau's error that the provocative U.S. and Soviet policies that precipitated the Cold War should therefore be regarded as having been wise after all. On the contrary, the Cold War has been dangerous and costly in its own right. It has bankrupted the USSR and very nearly the United States as well; led to a string of civil wars and "ethnic cleansing" campaigns in Eastern Europe; repeatedly threatened to spark a general nuclear war; and institutionalized a pattern of advanced weapons proliferation that has left most countries and peoples in a far more precarious position than they were when the conflict began. Morgenthau's 1945 insight that a thorough denazification and demilitarization of Germany would help avoid this perilous collision proved to be remarkably prescient.

Meanwhile, the events of the Armenian Genocide and of the Holocaust also reveal a basic dynamic in the relationship of great powers to mass crimes. The problem is fundamentally structural; it is built into the system and not simply a product of a particularly evil or inept group of men. The terms of international law concerning war crimes were articulated at the turn of the century primarily by the countries then dominating international affairs: the major European powers, czarist Russia, and the United States. The big powers crafted the Hague and Geneva conventions to help manage the expensive arms race of the day and to set new, ostensibly more rational rules for wars and occupation of disputed territories. The conferees limited "legal" wars to those fought among regular, uniformed armies—a provision that greatly favored the larger and established powers, for they had the clear advantage in such conflicts. They asserted the absolute sovereignty of nation-states over their subjects; declared most revolutions, most forms of civilian resistance to occupying armies, and colonial rebellions to be war crimes; and strengthened the claims of heads of state to legal immunity for acts in office. They set out detailed rules for commerce during wartime that tended to insulate business and trade from the disruptions of war to the greatest degree possible. Nevertheless, these treaties did lead to some important humanitarian advances, particularly in improving treatment of prisoners of war.

This structure for international law was put to the test during World War I, and failed. Despite some amelioration of the conditions for soldiers on the battlefield, the new framework of law did not confront or contain one of the signal crimes of the day: the Turkish *Ittihad* government's destruction of some one million Armenians. Nor did existing international law achieve justice for the Armenians when the killing was over, in part because Britain, France, and the United States saw greater advantage in cooperating with Turkey in a new division of Middle Eastern oil than they did in bringing *Ittihad* criminals to justice.

The failure to do justice in the Armenian Genocide can be traced in important part to the overlapping, interlocking dynamics of economics, international law, and mass murder. The more predatory aspects of international law dovetailed well with the destructive social patterns of the Turkish killing. The law proved to be incapable of prosecuting genocide without drawing more "conventional" aspects of colonialism, national development, and international trade into the dock as crimes as well.

The legal and economic precedents set in the wake of World War I had considerable impact on the course of the Holocaust during World War II, just as the more widely understood political precedents did. Hitler himself repeatedly raised the international community's failure to do justice in the wake of the Armenian Genocide to explain and justify his own racial theories, and the Germans' pattern of "learning through doing" genocide was similar in important respects to that of the Turks. While the two crimes were different in important respects, they both were led by ideologically driven, authoritarian political parties that had come to power in the midst of a deep social crisis. Both the *Ittihad* and the Nazis—each originally a marginal political party—managed to perpetrate genocide by enlisting the established institutions of conventional life—the national courts, commercial structures, scholarly community, and so on—in the tasks of mass persecution and eventually mass murder. In both cases, the ruling party achieved its genocidal aims in part by offering economic incentives for persecution, the most basic of which were the opportunity to share in the spoils of deported people and the ability to transfer the costs of economic crisis onto the shoulders of the despised group.

These dynamics of the Holocaust also had a powerful influence on the international *response* to the Holocaust. This book has focused mainly on the responses by the small community of international affairs specialists on Wall Street, in London, and in Washington, D.C.

This small group played a key role in molding U.S. policy on Jewish refugees in Europe, in the analysis and prosecution of Nazi crimes, and in the articulation of U.S. policy toward Germany and the USSR. Officially, of course, their work was subordinate to the broad policy outlines laid down by the White House and the secretary of state. As a practical matter, however, these men and women enjoyed considerable influence over policy implementation, and they used this influence to pursue their narrow vision of U.S. interests. Even during the war, they often acted on the assumption that preservation of the "integrating elements" in German society was a prerequisite to achieving U.S. postwar goals, particularly that of maintaining capitalist democracies in Europe.

The U.S. State Department and its allies orchestrated an effort to preserve and rebuild Germany's economy as quickly as possible as an economic, political, and eventually military bulwark against new revolutions in Europe, even though much of the corporate and administrative leadership of German finance and industry that they wished to preserve had been instrumental in Hitler's crimes. Many critics, not least of whom was the U.S. secretary of the treasury, accused this State Department faction of anti-Semitism, blocking rescue of refugee Jews, appeasement of Hitler, and protection of Nazi criminals in the wake of the war.

The final problem examined in this book is that this strategy for Germany entailed substantial economic costs for the United States, in addition to the tragic human cost of the Holocaust. One of these was the rapid build-up of an enormously expensive and dangerous military competition with the USSR that for almost half a century repeatedly threatened to lead to nuclear war.

The similarities between the Armenian Genocide and the Holocaust suggest that the "Nazi problem" in postwar Germany is only partially traceable to the pressures of the cold war. Throughout the twentieth century, regardless of the prevailing atmosphere in East-West relations, most powerful states have attended to genocide only insofar as it has affected their own stability and short-term interests. Almost without exception, they have dealt with the aftermath of genocide primarily as a means to increase their power and preserve their license to impose their version of order, regardless of the price to be paid in terms of elementary justice.

Several dozen new international treaties intended to defend human rights have been signed since the end of World War II, including conventions against slavery, torture, race and sex discrimination, apartheid, and genocide.[2] Each new agreement suggests that there is broad popular support for fundamental change in this aspect of state behavior and international relations. This sentiment is embodied, albeit imperfectly, in the United Nations, the European Commission on Human Rights, the Inter-American Commission on Human Rights, a similar intergovernmental organization in Africa, the private association Amnesty International, and many other groups that monitor human rights issues and publicize offenses. Today's popular resistance to crimes against humanity is more sophisticated, better equipped, and better informed than ever before in human history.

But the actual implementation of these treaties and the legal framework supporting human rights efforts remains notoriously weak. The horror of the Nazi gas chambers was unambiguously condemned in the wake of the Holocaust, for example, but both sides' practice of bombing civilians (and its tactical cousin, missile attacks on cities) has not only escaped criminal prosecution, it has become the centerpiece of the major powers' postwar national security strategies. Usually there is little effective protest on behalf of the people living under the bombs.[3] Similarly, after dragging its heels for four decades, the U.S. Senate in 1986 finally approved a simple international convention declaring genocide to be a crime. At the same time, however, the senators wrote a restriction into their endorsement that effectively barred any U.S. court from actually enforcing the measure until the Congress passed new implementing legislation—which it has yet to do.[4] Such loopholes are present in virtually all international agreements concerning crimes against humanity.

In each of these examples, the institutions purportedly regulated by international agreements have succeeded in creating a legal structure that permits abuses to thrive. For many senior policymakers in the U.S. and abroad, international law remains "a crock," as former Secretary of State Dean Acheson put it,[5] when it imposes any limit on one's own government.

The logical question, then, is, What should reasonable people make of the defects in international law on issues of war, peace, and mass murder? For some, there will be a temptation to conclude that humanity might be better off discarding the present body of international law altogether and somehow start again with a fresh slate.

But there is no such thing as a truly fresh slate, of course. The gutted and imperfect form of international law concerning war crimes and crimes against humanity that is presently embraced by the major powers is better than none at all, at least so long as those who seek the law's protection have no illusions about its scope. Compassion and good sense demand that the best features of international law be preserved and extended, even when existing treaties provide for little more than moral suasion in defense of human rights.

International law has often been a kind of pact between strong and weak nations. Not surprisingly, the powerful have stipulated most of the terms. But the weaker nations and peoples are not powerless, and for manifold reasons they are today gathering force. This means that they can at times obtain the rights and responsibilities written into international laws and legal precedents such as the Nuremberg Charter. The same is true, though to a much lesser degree, for individuals facing brutality at the hands of their governments. International law has to that extent become a tool for human progress; it has sometimes ameliorated the suffering of prisoners, helped contain those who would resort to aggression, and provided some platform, however fragile, for the assertion of basic rights by indigenous peoples.

Perhaps some additional hope for the future can be derived from the way in which the frustrated ideals of an earlier era are sometimes taken quite seriously by later generations. True, many aspects of the Nuremberg principles have yet to be implemented by national and international courts. But millions of people have nonetheless accepted some sense of these principles as a reasonable standard of justice that they have a right to expect. Thus, Nuremberg's impact has sometimes been felt in popular demands for human rights, justice, and humane treatment for the victims of war even in countries where the courts refuse to recognize the Nuremberg principles as legally binding.

For exactly that reason, some powerful nations today view international law and the Nuremberg precedents with greater suspicion than previously. The most powerful forces working against an evenhanded application of international law today are those that have up to now usually gained the most from its terms.

Major powers continue to cynically exploit international law to support propaganda claims against their rivals. They call for strict enforcement of international sanctions when it suits their purpose, but they ignore rulings by international courts when it is opportune to do so. In recent years U.S. administrations (and the media, "opinion leaders," and so on) have consistently invoked international law to justify actions against Libya, Iran, Iraq, Grenada, Panama, and other enemies *du jour.* U.S. leaders usually present themselves as the only real defenders of international order in a world that would otherwise be cast into anarchy. Yet, they maintain an icy silence when the law is less to their liking, as when the International Court of Arbitration at The Hague ruled that the U.S. mining of Nicaraguan harbors, shooting down of an Iranian civilian airliner, and a list of similar acts constituted serious international crimes.[6] The fact that such obvious deceits pass by largely without comment in most parliaments, newspapers, and journals vividly illustrates the extent to which double-think on genocide and human rights remains ingrained in the present world order.

Who then, or what, is the splendid blond beast? It is the destruction inherent in any system of order, the institutionalized brutality whose existence is denied by cheerleaders of the status quo at the very moment they feed its appetite for blood.

The present world order supplies stability and rationality of a sort for human society, while its day-to-day operations chew up the weak, the scapegoats, and almost anyone else in its way. This is not necessarily an evil conspiracy of insiders; it is a structural dilemma that generates itself more or less consistently from place to place and from generation to generation.

Much of modern society has been built upon genocide. This crime was integral to the emergence of the United States, of czarist

Russia and later the USSR, of European empires, and of many other states. Today, modern governments continue extermination of indigenous peoples throughout Asia, Africa, and Latin America, mainly as a means of stealing land and natural resources. Equally pernicious, though often less obvious, the present world order has institutionalized persecution and deprivation of hundreds of millions of children, particularly in the Third World, and in this way kills countless innocents each year.[7] These systemic atrocities are for the most part not even regarded as crimes, but instead are written off by most of the world's media and intellectual leadership as acts of God or of nature whose origin remains a mystery.

It is individual human beings who make the day-to-day decisions that create genocide, reward mass murder, and ease the escape of the guilty. But social systems usually protect these individuals from responsibility for "authorized" acts, in part by providing rationalizations that present systemic brutality as a necessary evil. Some observers may claim that men such as Allen Dulles, Robert Murphy, et al. were gripped by an ideal of a higher good when they preserved the power of the German business elite as a hedge against revolution in Europe. But in the long run, their intentions have little to do with the real issue, which is the character of social systems that permit decisions institutionalizing murder to take on the appearance of wisdom, reason, or even justice among the men and women who lead society.

Progress in the control of genocide depends in part on confronting those who would legitimize and legalize the act. The cycle of genocide can be broken through relatively simple—but politically difficult—reforms in the international legal system. It is essential to identify and condemn the deeds that contribute to genocide, particularly when such deeds have assumed a mantle of respectability, and to ensure just and evenhanded punishment for those responsible. But the temptation will be to accept the inducements and rationalizations society offers in exchange for keeping one's mouth shut. The choice is in our hands.

✣

Appendix

THE CHART THAT FOLLOWS summarizes publicly available reports of corporate use of concentration camp inmates. It is compiled from official records of the West German government, International Red Cross reports, captured SS records, International Military Tribunal affidavits, and studies by leading scholars.

Companies reported to have contracted with the SS for use of concentration camp prisoners, or which established their own in-house prison camps with SS approval, are displayed below in regular type. The name of the main SS concentration camp from which prisoners were drawn is in bold type. The source that states the company's relationship to the administration of the concentration camps is indicated in the brackets next to each entry and identified at the end of this Appendix (p. 310). The notes inside parentheses summarize the type of work performed by prisoners, when that data is available. Minor variations in the rendering of corporate names in the original reports have been corrected in this table for the sake of clarity.

This list is not complete. In hundreds of instances, available records identify the location of an SS labor camp but not its corporate customers. Conversely, there are hundreds of corporate forced labor centers known to have operated in cooperation with the SS whose link to a particular concentration camp has been lost because of the Germans' destruction of witnesses and records. That was the case with Kontinentale Öl's short-lived empire, for example, and with many other forced labor projects in the Nazi-occupied zones of Poland, the USSR, and Yugoslavia. The SS's own proprietary corporations, such as the German Earth and Stone Works (Deutsche Erd- und Steinwerke—DES), German Armament Works (Deutsche Ausrustungswerke—DAW), various labor commandos, and others, have also been passed over in this list, except in instances where the private sector customers for the SS services can be established.

The pattern is nonetheless clear. Germany's largest companies exploited forced labor on a massive scale, at hundreds of factories, and for central elements of their production. Even in instances when companies went out of their way to avoid documenting their use of slaves—and that often became standard operating procedure—Germany's private sector dependence upon the laborers became so great as to require large administrative staffs to account for the prisoners' work and to make economic projections concerning the availability of forced laborers for future production.

TABLE OF GERMAN COMPANIES AND MAIN SS CONCENTRATION CAMPS REPORTED TO BE ACTIVE IN EXPLOITATION OF FORCED LABOR DURING THE THIRD REICH

Auschwitz

AEG (electronics) [5]
Barthl (construction) [5]
Bata Schlesische Schuhwerke (leather, shoes, and factory construction) [10]
Benton-Monteur-Bau (construction) [10]
Berle Hoch- und Tiefbau (construction) [10]
Berliner Baugesellschaft (construction) [10]

BRABAG (mining, synthetic fuel) [3]

Breitenbach Montanbau [10]

Borsig-Koks-Werk (coal processing) [10]

Charlottengrube (Hermann-Göring-Werke) (tunnel construction) [10]

Concordia Kohlenbergwerk (coal processing) [10]

Deutsche Gasrusswerke, Gleiwitz [5] [8]

Dyckerhoff & Widman (construction materials) [5]

Egefeld (construction) [10]

Emmerich Machold (textiles) [10]

Energie-Versorgung-Oberschlesien AG (electrical construction for Elektrizitätswerk "Walter") [10]

Erdöl Raffinerie Trzebinia GmbH (oil refining) [10]

Fürstengrube GmbH (coal mining) [10]

Fürstlich Plessische Bergwerks AG (coal processing) [10]

Godula (factory construction) [10]

Grün und Bilfinger (construction) [10]

Gute Hoffnung Janinagrube (coal mining) [10]

Heinkel (aircraft components, munitions) [5] [10]

Hubertushütte (coal processing) [10]

IG Farben—Buna Werke (construction, synthetic fuel) [3] [4] [5] [8] [10]

Junkers (aircraft) [5]

Klotz und Co. (construction) [10]

Königshütte Metallwerke (metal works) [10]

Königs- und-Bismarckhütte AG (armored cars and tanks) [10]

Krupp (munitions) [4] [5]

Krupp—Laurahùtte (munitions) [8]

Lasota (tunnel & road construction) [10]

Oberschlesische Gerätebau GmbH [10]

Oberschlesische Hydrierwerke (construction of synthetic gasoline works) [5] [8] [10]

Ölschieferanlagen (oil refinery construction) [8]

Ost-Maschinenbau GmbH (OSMAG) (cannon) [2] [5] [8] [10]

Pfitzner und Kamper (munitions, loading) [10]

Philipp Holzmann (construction) [10]

Pluschke und Grosser (construction) [10]

Portland-Zement-Fabrik AG (construction materials) [10]

Riedel (tunnel and roadbuilding) [10]

Rheinmetall-Borsig (munitions) [3]

Schuchtermann und Kremer Bau AG (construction) [10]

Schweinitz (construction) [10]

S. Frankel—Schlesische Feinweberei AG (textiles) [10]

Siemens-Schuckert (electronics for aircraft) [2] [3] [10]

Union Metallindustrie (munitions) [4] [5]

Vacuum Öl (oil refinery) [5] [10]
Vereinigte Aluminiumwerke (aluminum) [5]
Wayss und Freytag (construction) [10]
Zieleniewski (munitions) [10]
Zwirnfabrik G. A. Buhl und Sohn (textiles) [10]

Bergen-Belsen

Rheinmetall-Borsig (munitions) [8]

Buchenwald*

AEG (electronics for V-2 project) [10]
AGO Oschersleben (production for Focke-Wulf) [2] [5] [10]
AGO (Arbeitsgemeinschaft Otto) Flugzeugwerke (Siebenberg GmbH)
    [10]
Allgemeine Transportanlagen GmbH, Leipzig (loading) [8] [10]
Amoniakwerke Merseburg GmbH [10]
Anhydrit (production for Junkers in Stollen) [2] [5]
Annaburger Gerätebau GmbH [10]
Anschütz & Co. [5]
Architekt Wilhelm Fricke (construction) [10]
Bauwens (construction) [10]
BMW (Eisenach plant, aircraft engines) [5] [8] [10]
BMW (Abteroda plant, aircraft engines) [5] [8] [10]
Bochumer Verein AG (Eisen und Huettenwerk Bochum AG, steel) [5]
    [8] [10]
Bode (construction) [10]
BRABAG (mining, synthetic fuel) [1] [3] [5] [8] [10]
Bruns Apparatebau (aircraft components for Heinkel) [5] [8] [10]
Büro Prinz (V-2 project) [10]
Christian Mansfeld AG (construction) [1] [5] [8] [10]
Dessau Waggonfabrik AG [8] [10]
Dietrich & Hermann (construction) [5]
Dora Mittelbau Projekt (construction and rocket assembly) [1] [5] [10]
Dortmund-Horder Hüttenverein AG (munitions) [10]

* In October 1944, the Dora Mittelbau project was administratively separated
from Buchenwald, its "parent" concentration camp, and became the separate KL
Mittelbau. This camp, also widely known as "Dora" and "Nordhausen," provided
the majority of forced laborers used in the German rocket program. For simplicity's sake, the table here uses the format adopted by the West German government in its *Bundesgesetzblatt* report on concentration camps, which presents the
Dora Mittelbau project as a side camp of Buchenwald.

Dynamit Nobel (explosives) [3] [5] [10]
Eisen- und Hüttenwerke AG [10]
Erla-Maschinenwerke (aircraft components) [2] [5] [8] [10]
Ford-Werke Köln (trucks) [1] [5] [8] [10]
Gebrüder Thiele (munitions) [10]
Gerätebau GmbH (aircraft components) [10]
Gelsenberg Benzin AG (munitions) [10]
Geyer und Sohn [10]
Gollnow und Sohn [10]
Grün und Bilfinger (construction) [10]
Gustloff-Werke (Krupp munitions) [5] [8] [9] [10]
Heerbrandt Werke AG [10]
Heinkel (aircraft components) [5] [10]
Heinrich Kalb (construction) [10]
Hermann Göring Werke (factory construction) [10]
Heyman, Darmstadt [8]
Hugo Schneider AG (HASAG) (munitions, panzers) [5] [8] [10]
Ingenieurbüro Prof. Dr. Rimpl [10]
Ingenieurbüro Schlempp [10]
IG Farben (construction of film factory) [5] [10]
Iser-Werke (aircraft components) [10]
Julius Schmidt (construction) [10]
Junkers Flug-und-Motorenwerke [1] [2] [3] [5] [8] [10]
Kabel-und Leitungswerke AG [10]
Kaliwerk Georgi (construction) [10]
Kranz und Co. (at Nordhausen) [5] [10]
Krupp (munitions) [3] [5] [6] [10]
Kühlhaus Weimer (refrigeration plant construction) [5] [8]
Kurt Heber Maschinenfabrik (munitions) [10]
Langenwerke AG (aircraft components) [5] [10]
Leichtmetallwerke Rautenbach [2]
Leichtmetallwerke Wernigerode (production for Junkers) [8]
Lippstädter Eisen und Metallwerke (metal working) [1] [10]
Lippstädter Metallindustrie (metal working; may be same as previous
    entry) [8]
Ludwig Renner (construction) [10]
Luftmunitionsanstalt (air munitions) [8]
Maschinenbau GmbH (aircraft parts) [10]
Maschinenfabrik Schmidt (at Nordhausen) [5] [10]
Maschinenfabrik Kurt Heber, Osterode (aircraft components) [8] [10]
Maibaum [10]
Maifisch (construction) [5] [8]
Malachit AG (also: Malachyt) (tunnel building) [5] [10]
Mauserwerke (munitions) [8]

Max Gerthwerke (aircraft components) [5] [10]
Mittelwerke GmbH (joint project for V-2 rocket construction) [10]
Moiski (construction) [10]
Mühlenwerke AG (production for Junkers) [10]
M. Wagner (construction) [10]
Nationale Radiatoren (V-2 electronics) [10]
Ohl und Vattrodt (construction) [10]
Ortelsbruch-Bauleitung (excavation) [10]
Polte-Werke (munitions) [10]
Rautal-Werke GmbH [10]
Reichsbahn Ausbesserungswerk Jena (construction) [1]
G. E. Reinhardt, Sonneberg [8] [10]
Reh, Strassfurt und Hecht (construction) [5] [8]
Rheinmetall-Borsig (munitions) [3] [5] [8] [10]
Roeder (munitions) [10]
Ruhrstahl AG [10]
Saupe und Mulke (paper factory) [10]
Siebel Flugzeugwerke (aircraft components) [5] [8] [10]
Siebenberg GmbH (aircraft components) [10]
Siemens Bau-Union GmbH (construction) [3]
Siemens-Schuckert Werke AG (underground factory construction) [10]
Solvay Werke [5] [10]
Starkstromanlagen AG (construction) [10]
Staupendahl (loading, transport) [5]
Stein (construction) [10]
Tanroda Papierfabrik (paper) (Mitteldeutsche Papierwerke)
    [5] [10]
Thyra-Werke (aircraft components for Junkers) [5] [8] [10]
Vereinigte Westdeutsche Waggon-Werke AG (Westwaggon AG) (motor
    vehicles) [5] [8] [10]
Walzer & Co. (panzers) [1] [8] [10]
Wernig-Werke, Hasserode [10]
Westfälisch-Anhaltische Sprengstoff AG (WASAG) (chemicals,
    explosives) [10]
Westfälische Metallindustrie (munitions) [8] [10]
WIFO Wirtschaftliche Forschungsgesellshaft mbH [10]
Wilhelm Bischoff (air raid shelter construction) [5]
Wintershall AG (fuel, energy) [5] [8] [10]

Dachau

AEG (electronics) [3]
AGFA-Kamerawerke [10]
Anorgana GmbH [10]

Arnold Fischer [10]
Bartholith-Werke [10]
Berliner Baugesellschaft (BBG) [10]
BMW (aircraft motors) [1] [2] [5] [8] [10]
Chemiegauer Vertriebsgesellschaft [10]
Chemische Werke GmbH Otto Barlocher [10]
Dachau Entommologisches Institut (construction) [1]
Dornier-Werke GmbH (aircraft components) [2] [10]
Dyckerhoff & Widmann (construction) [1] [5] [10]
Dynamit Nobel (munitions) [3] [5] [10]
Feller-Tuchfabrik [10]
Fleischkonservenfabrik Hans Wulfert (butchery, food processing) [5] [8]
    [10]
Formholz [10]
Franz Nutzl [10]
Gebrüder Helfman [10]
Giesing Kamerawerke (optics) [1]
Hebel [10]
Hess, Ilse [10]
Hochtief GmbH [10]
Philipp Holzmann (construction) [3]
I. Ehrenput [10]
IG Farben[10]
Dr. Jung [10]
Karl Bucklers [10]
Keller und Knappich [10]
Dr. Ing. Kimmel (generators) [2]
Kirsch [10]
Klockner-Humbolt-Deutz AG [10]
Kodel und Bohm [10]
Kuno (munitions for Messerschmitt) [10]
L. Bautz [10]
Loden-Frey, München [8] [10]
Luftfahrtforschungsanstalt München (airfield construction) [2]
Magnesit [10]
Messerschmitt AG (aircraft) [1] [2] [3] [5] [10]
Michel-Fabrik Augsburg [1]
München-Allach Porzellan Manufaktur (ceramics) [1]
Ölschieferanlagen (oil refinery construction) [8]
Praezifix (aircraft components) [2] [5] [8] [10]
Pumpel und Co. [10]
Reichsbahnausbesserungswerk München (construction) [1] [8]
Reichsstrassenbauamt Innsbruck (construction) [1]
Sager und Worner [10]

U. Sachse-Kempten KG (factory construction) [2] [8] [10]
Schuhhaus Meier [10]
Schurich [10]
Dr. Schweninger [10]
Unic [10]
Zeppelin Luftschiffbauu (dirigibles) [8] [10]

Flossenberg

AEG (electronics) [10]
Agaricola GmbH [10]
Alu-Werke Nürnberg (factory production) [5]
A. Schulze Jr. (textiles) [5] [10]
Astra-Werke AG (factory production) [5] [10]
Auto-Union (momtor vehicles) [5] [8] [10]
Bäckerei Hans Kraus (food processing) [10]
Bäckerei Paul Rotgen (food processing) [5] [10]
Ballauf [10]
Bayreuther Bekleidungsindustrie (textiles, uniforms) [5]
Bernsdorf & Co. (munitions) [1] [5] [8] [10]
Broer [10]
Danzer [10]
Deutsche Erd- und Steinwerke (DES) (construction for Messerschmitt)
    [2] [5]
Deutsche Kühl- und Kraftmaschinen GmbH [10]
Deutsche Schachtbau GmbH [10]
Elbtalwerk Elektrizitäts AG [10]
Elbabefertigung AG [10]
Erla-Maschinenwerke GmbH (aircraft components) [2] [5] [10]
E. Warsitz [10]
Fortuna GmbH (munitions) [5] [10]
Framo Werke (munitions, automotive) [5] [10]
Freia-Werk Freiberg (munitions) [5] [8] [10]
R. Füss [10]
Gemeinschaft Schuhe, Berlin (shoes and leather) [10]
Göhlewerk Dresden [8]
Hans Müller [10]
Helmbrechts [8]
Hermann Göring Werke (chemicals) [5]
Max Hildebrand [10]
Hochtief AG [10]
Hollein und Co. [10]
Hotel Glasstuben, Steinshönau (construction) [5] [10]

Hubscher undWanninger [10]
Industriewerke AG [10]
Institut für physikalische Forschung [10]
J. G. Müller und Co. [10]
Josef Witt Weberei (textiles) [10]
Junkers Leng-Werke AG [10]
Kabel- und Metallwerke Neumeyer AG [10]
Kabis [10]
Keramische Werke Bohemia (ceramic production for Messerschmitt)
    [2] [5]
Knorr GmbH (food processing) [5]
Lorenz AG (electronics) [5] [10]
Luftfahrtgerätewerke Zwodau (airfield construction) [2] [5]
Luftfahrtgerätewerke Graslitz (airfield construction) [10]
Mechanik GmbH [10]
Mechanische Baumwollspinnerei (uniforms, cotton textiles) [5]
Messerschmitt (aircraft components) [5] [8] [10]
Metallwerke Holleischen (munitions) [5] [8] [10]
Mineralölgesellschaft, Leitmeritz (petroleum) [5]
Mitteldeutsche Stahlwerke (steel) [5] [10]
Mühlen- und Industrie AG (MIAG) [10]
Neue Baumwollspinnerei (uniforms, cotton textiles) [5]
Opta Radio (radio production) [5] [10]
Plauner Baumwollspinnerei AG (uniforms, cotton textiles) [1] [8] [10]
Polensky und Zollner [10]
Pressewerke Münchberg (steel) [5]
Reichsbahn Dresden (railroad construction, loading) [1] [5]
Rudolf Chillingworth AG [10]
Rudolph Otto Meyer [10]
Sager und Worner [10]
Schlie [10]
Siemens-Bau-Union GmbH [10]
Siemens Schuckert (electronics) [3] [5] [8] [10]
Stahl [10]
Stohr [10]
Tauber [10]
Thormann und Steifel [10]
Dr. Th. Thorn GmbH (construction) [5] [10]
Universelle (munitions) [5] [8] [10]
Venuswerke (textiles for aircraft) [5] [8] [10]
Verwertchemie Hertine (munitions) [8]
Vogtländische Maschinenfabrik AG (VOMAG) [10]
Weberei Jos. Witt (textiles) [5]

Weidemann & Co. (machine parts) [5] [10]
Weser-Flugzeugbau GmbH (aircraft) [5] [10]
Zeiss-Ikon (optics) [1] [5] [10]

Gross Rosen

Ackermann (tunnel construction) [5] [10]
AEG (electronics) [3] [10]
Alois Haase (textiles) [10]
Anorgana GmbH (chemicals) [10]
Arado-Werke GmbH [10]
Argo-Waldenburg [10]
Askania-Werke [1] [5] [10]
Atur Becker, Tiefbau AG (construction) [10]
August Nitsche [10]
Becker und Zelle [10]
Beuchelt (machine work) [10]
Borsig-Werke (munitions) [5] [10]
Boswau und Knauer [10]
Buhl und Sohn (textiles) [10]
Busch [10]
Butzer und Holzmann (construction) [5] [10]
Christian Dierig AG [5] [10]
Christoph & Unmack AG [5] [10]
Christwerke (munitions) [10]
Concordia (textiles) [10]
Deutsche Aluminiumwerke (aluminum) [10]
Deutsche Emailwarenfabrik (DEF) [10]
Deutsche Hoch- und Tiefbau AG [10]
Deutsche Industriewerke AG (DIWAG) (munitions) [10]
Deutsche Wollwaren-Manufaktur (textiles) [1] [5] [10]
Deutscher Mess- und Apparatebau Gesellschaft (MESSAP) (munitions) [10]
Dorries-Fullner (munitions) [10]
Dubner (construction) [10]
Dybno (construction) [10]
Dynamit Nobel AG (munitions) [3] [5] [10]
Elektroakustik KG [10]
Erdmannsdorfer Leinenfabrik AG (textiles) [10]
Eule (construction) [10]
Falke [10]
FAMO Fahrzeug und Motorenwerke Bunzlau (aircraft maintenance for Focke-Wulf) [1] [2] [5] [10]

Ferdinand Haase (textiles) [5] [10]
F. G. Alter (textiles) [10]
Fichelkamp und Schmidt [10]
Focke-Wulf Flugzeugwerke (aircraft construction) [10]
Forster [10]
Fritz Schubert [10]
Gebrüder Hermecke (construction) [10]
Gebrüder C. C. Walzel (textiles) [10]
Geppardt (construction) [10]
Gesellschaft für technisch-wirtschaftliche Entwicklung mbH
    (GETEWENT) [10]
Getewent, Reichenau (electronics) [8]
G. F. Flechtner (textiles) [10]
Glasfabrik Weisswasser (electronics) [8]
Goldschmidt (production for Luftwaffe) [5] [10]
Gottwald [10]
G. P. Fletchner (textiles) [5]
Grolich [10]
Grün und Bilfinger (construction) [5] [10]
Gruschwitz Textilwerke AG [10]
Hagawerke (production for Luftwaffe) [5]
Hanseatische Apparatebau Gesellschaft [10]
Hansen und Neumann [10]
Hegerfeld [10]
Heinz Wendt (metalwork) [10]
Henkel und Sohn [10]
Hess [10]
Hoffmannswerke [10]
Hotze (tunnel construction) [5] [10]
Hubert Land (wood cutting) [5] [10]
Hubsch (construction) [10]
Hutto (tunnel construction) [5] [10]
IG Farben AG [10]
Ignaz Etrich (textiles) [10]
Ilase (textiles) [10]
Iser-Werke [10]
J. A. Kluge (textiles) [10]
Kraus (construction) [10]
Kuppers (munitions) [10]
Jank (tunnel construction) [5] [10]
Johann Etrich KG (textiles) [10]
Josef Fröhlich (textiles) [10]
Junkers (aircraft) [5]

Karl Barthel und Co. (textiles, factory construction) [5] [10]
Karl Diehl (foundry) [5] [10]
Kemna und Co. (construction) [5] [10]
Kerner (tunnel construction) [5]
Knopf (textiles) [10]
Koder (construction) [10]
Konrad (construction) [10]
Kramsta-Methner und Frahne AG (textiles) [10]
Krause (construction) [10]
Krupp—Berta Werke (munitions for Luftwaffe) [3] [5] [8] [9] [10]
Krupp—Fabrik Meyer Kauffmann [10]
Kunigals (construction) [10]
Kunnith (construction) [10]
Kurt Laske [10]
Lehmann [10]
Leistikoff (construction) [10]
Lenz Barackenbau (barracks construction) [5] [10]
Leonhard Moll (construction) [10]
Linke-Hoffman (locomotives, railroad cars) [5] [10]
Lorenz (radio electronics) [10]
Luranil Gesellschaft (munitions) [5]
Madebrun [10]
Mathies AG (construction) [5] [10]
Mertens [10]
Meschner & Frahne AG [5]
Messinger (construction) [10]
Milde [10]
Mischke (construction) [10]
Molke Werke (munitions) [10]
Mühlhausen (construction) [10]
Neufeldt und Kunke (electronics) [10]
Nordland GmbH [10]
Oskar Schindler [10]
Osram (electronics) [10]
Otto Trebitz [10]
Otto Weil (construction) [10]
Patin (aircraft industry) [10]
Paul Urbanski/Deutsche Lissa (construction) [1] [5] [10]
Peuke und Jeche (construction) [10]
Pischel (construction) [10]
Philipp Holzmann (construction) [3] [5] [10]
Phrix-Werke (cellulose) [1] [5] [8] [10]
Poikett [10]

Preschona Flugzeugfabrik (aircraft industry) [10]
Putzer und Holzmann [10]
Rebich [10]
Reckman [10]
Reiners [10]
Rheinmetall-Borsig AG [10]
Richter und Schadel (construction) [10]
Rosenberg (textiles) [10]
Sager & Woerner (construction) [5] [10]
Sanger und Laninger [10]
Schallhorn AG (construction) [5] [10]
Schroll und Sohn (gas masks, textiles) [10]
Schulz [10]
Seidenspinner (construction) [10]
Siemens Bau Union GmbH [3] [10]
Siemens Motorenwerke Jungbuch [10]
Singer und Müller [10]
Speer [10]
Spreewerke GmbH [10]
Stein und Teer (construction) [10]
Steinhage [10]
Sturchan [10]
Synthetische Benzin-Fabrik Mathildenhöhe (synthetic fuels) [10]
Tannenwald [10]
Tebe und Bucer (tunnel construction) [5] [10]
Teichgräber (textiles) [10]
Telefunken (electronics for Luftwaffe) [5] [10]
Tiessler [10]
Valvo-Röhrenwerke (electronics) [10]
Vereinigte Deutsche Metallwerke (V-2 production) [10]
Waggon- und Maschinenbau AG Görlitz (machine tools) [5] [8] [10]
Walker (construction) [5]
Walther-Werke (munitions) [10]
Wayss & Freytag (construction) [5] [10]
Weberei Jordan (textiles) [10]
Websky (machine tools) [10]
Weiden und Petersil (metal work) [10]
Weidermann (aircraft industry) [10]
Dr. Wiesner [10]
Wilhelm Fix (construction) [5] [10]
Zill und Knebich [10]
Zimke [10]
Zittwerke AG (production for Junkers) [10]

Herzogenbusch (occupied Netherlands)

Continental-Gummiwerke AG (gas masks) [10]
Philips (electronics) [8] [10]
Volkswagenwerke (autos) [7]

Mauthausen (Austria)

AFA-Werke [10]
Alpine Montanwerke (coal and steel) [5] [10]
Arnold Fischer, Forschungsinstitut München (construction) [10]
Auto-Hanzel [10]
Bayerischer Lloyd (loading) [10]
Beton und Montierbau [10]
Braun und Boveri [10]
Chrystof (construction) [10]
Deutscher Bergbau Hermann Göring (underground factory
   construction) [5] [9] [10]
Deutsche Bergwerks- und Hüttenbau GmbH [10]
Deutsche Erd- und Steinwerke (DES) (construction for Messerschmitt)
   [2]
Dyckerhoff und Widmann (construction for munitions factory) [10]
Eisenwerke Oberdonau (iron and steel) [8]
Esche II (aircraft production) [2]
Ennser Kraftwerkebau AG (construction) [8] [10]
Florians AG [5]
Flotte [10]
Flugmotorenwerke Ostmark GmbH (aircraft motors) [2] [5] [8] [10]
Fohmann [10]
Grossdeutscher Schachtbau (underground factory construction) [5] [10]
Gustloff-Werk (munitions) [10]
Heinkel Flugzeugwerke AG (aircraft) [2] [3] [5] [10]
Hermann-Göring-Werke (panzers, munitions) [10]
Hinteregger und Fischer (underground factory construction) [5] [10]
Hoffmann (cement work) [10]
Hofherr, Schrantz & Shuttleworth [1] [5] [10]
Hopferwieser [10]
Hummel und Baumen [10]
IG Farben (factory construction) [5]
Kirchmeyer & Söhne [5]
Klaus und Fuchs [10]
Lang und Manhoffer (construction) [10]
Lenzinger Zellwolle und Papierfabrik AG (rayon, parachutes) [5] [10]

Mayreder und Kraus [10]
Messerschmitt (aircraft) [3] [5] [10]
Negrelli (construction) [10]
Nibelungenwerk (tank factory) [5] [10]
Nibelungenwerk (underground factory construction) [5] [10]
Österreichische Saurerwerke AG [5] [8] [10]
Östmarkische Brau AG (brewery) [10]
Philipp Holzmann (underground factory construction) [5] [10]
Polensky (underground factory construction) [5] [10]
Quarz GmbH (mining) [5] [10]
Radebeul [10]
Raubl (construction) [10]
Rax-Werke GmbH [1] [10]
Rella (construction) [10]
Sägewerke Prachmanning (woodcutting) [5]
Siemens-Bauunion (underground factory construction) [3] [5] [10]
Siemens-Schuckert (electronics) [5] [10]
Solvay Kalksteinwerk (cement) [5] [10]
Steinveredelungswerk AG (stonework) [5]
Steinverwertung AG (stonework) [10]
Steyr-Daimler-Puch (munitions) [5] [8] [10]
Uberland AG [10]
Üniversale Hoch- und Tiefbau AG (construction) [10]
Waldwerke Passau-Ilzstadt (woodcutting) [10]
Wayss und Freytag (construction) [10]
Zistersdorfer-Maustrenk-Ölfelder [10]

Naatzweiler (Struthof, occupied France)

Acier (iron foundry) [10]
AEG (electronics) [3] [10]
Adlerwerke AG [1] [10]
Berger (mining at Heilbronn saltworks) [5] [10]
BMW, Neunkirchen [5] [8] [10]
Boley GmbH (construction) [10]
Bruckmann & Söhne [5]
Buttler [10]
C. Baresel AG (construction) [10]
Daimler Benz (underground "Vulcan" factory for aircraft engines)
    [5] [10]
Deutsche Bergwerks- und Hüttenbau Gesellschaft [10]
Deutsche Erd- und Steinwerke (DES) (construction for Junkers) [2]
Deutsche Ölschieferforschungsgesellschaft GmbH (construction) [10]

Diehl (construction) [10]
Dohrmann [10]
Eisenrieth [10]
Elsasser-Spezial-Grosskellerei [10]
Elsassische Maschinenbau GmbH (ELMAG) (construction) [10]
Eple (construction) [10]
Franz Kirschhoff (construction) [10]
Gerätewerk Pommern GmbH (munitions) [2]
Goldfisch (at Neckarelz) (underground factory construction) [5] [8]
Grün & Bilfinger (underground factory construction) [5]
Heilmann und Littmann AG (underground construction) [10]
Heinkel Flugzeugfabrik (aircraft) [5] [10]
Dr. Ing. H. Heyman (construction) [10]
H. Kirchhardt (construction) [10]
Hoch- und Tiefbau (underground factory construction) [5] [10]
Hüttenwerkverwaltung Westmark GmbH (Hermann-Göring-Werke) [10]
Johannisberg GmbH (munitions) [10]
Kali-Chemie (munitions) [5]
Kohle-Öl-Union von Busse KG [10]
Knorr AG (food processing) [5]
Koch & Meyer (underground factory construction) [5]
Kronibus [10]
Krupp (munitions) [10]
Lufah [8]
Maschinenfabrik Alfing Kessler KG [10]
Metallwerke GmbH [10]
Messerschmitt AG [10]
Minette AG (production for Volkswagen) [8] [10]
Munding (construction) [10]
Ölschieferanlangen Dormettingen (oil refinery construction) [8]
Presswerk Leonberg (production for Messerschmitt) [10]
Staud [10]
Suka [10]
Wayss & Freytag (construction) [10]
Württembergische Metallwarenfabrik (munitions) [8] [10]
Zublin und Cie AG (airport construction) [10]

Neuengamme

Ahlem (chemical industry construction) [5] [8]
Albrecht und Co. (oil and chemicals) [10]
AL Dragerwerke (gas masks, metalwork) [7] [5] [8] [10]
Akkumulatorenfabrik AG (Varta) (batteries) [1] [7] [10]

Anschütz und Co. [10]
Askania-Werke AG [8] [10]
August Prien (construction) [7]
Bedecker (construction) [10]
Blohn und Voss (dock- and shipbuilding) [1] [5] [7] [8] [10]
Borgward Werke [10]
Braunschweig Stahlwerke (steel) [1] [8]
Bremen Vegesack (munitions) [5]
Brinker Eisenwerke (iron and steel) [5] [8] [10]
Bussing NAG-Vereinigte Nutzkraftwagen GmbH (trucks) [3] [5] [7] [10]
Continental Gummi-Werke (gas masks, rubber) [1] [5] [7] [10]
Degesch (chemicals, Zyklon B) [7]
Deurag-Hannover-Misburg (oil refinery) [8]
Deutsche Schiff- und Maschinenbau AG (DESCHIMAG) (dock- and
   shipbuilding) [10]
Deutsche Werft (shipbuilding) [5] [10]
DIAGO-Werke [10]
Draht- und Metallwarenfabrik (metal cable) [5] [8]
Dresdner Bank (construction) [7]
Ebano-Oehler Teerfabrik (tar) [10]
Ebeling (construction) [10]
Ehlers (construction) [10]
Eurotank[10]
Focke-Wulf [10]
Friedrich Rodiek [10]
Gewehr- und Munitionsfabrik (munitions) [10]
Grün und Bilfinger (construction) [10]
Hamburg Eidelstedt (munitions) [5]
Hamburger Elektrizitätsgesellschaft (electric utility, construction)
   [7] [10]
Hannoverische Maschinenbau AG (HANOMAG) (metalworking,
   munitions) [5] [8] [10]
Hanseatische Kettenwerke (chains) [10]
Hermann Göring Werke (Salzgitter AG) (munitions) [1] [5] [7] [8] [10]
Hochtief AG (construction) [7]
Horneberg/Elbe Lederwerke (leatherwork) [5]
Hornisse (marine construction) [8]
Howaldtswerke—Deutsche Werft AG (HDW) (shipyard) [1] [5] [7]
Jastram (reconstruct diesel motor factory) [5] [7] [8]
Johannes Heitmann (construction) [10]
Junghans Messap GmbH (gun barrels) [2] [7]
Jung-Öl (petroleum) [5] [10]
Kirbitz und Breiter Hoch- und Tiefbau (construction) [10]

Kowal und Bruns (construction) [10]
Krupp (munitions) [1] [5] [7] [8] [10]
Luning und Sohn (construction) [10]
Malo (construction) [10]
Maschinenfabrik Niedersachsen (munitions) [10]
Möller (underground construction) [10]
Olschieferverwertungsgesellschaft (production for IG Farben) [8]
Philipp Holzmann AG (construction) [7] [10]
Philips-Valvo (electronics) [7] [10]
Phrix-Werke (cellulose) [5] [8] [10]
Polte-Werke (underground construction) [10]
Poppenbüttel-Sasel (petroleum) [5]
Rheinmetall-Borsig (munitions) [7]
Rhenania Ossag (Shell oil) [7] [10]
Rolf [10]
Rosseburg [10]
Salzgitter AG [5]
Schindler Erdöl Fabrik [10]
Siemens und Müller (underground construction) [10]
Stahlwerke Braunschweig (steel, construction) [8]
Steinol GmbH (coke and cement work) [10]
Stülckenwerft (construction) [5] [8] [10]
Thomsen und Co. (construction) [5] [8] [10]
Valentin Marine Oberbauleitung (marine construction) [8] [10]
Valvo Radioröhrenfabrik Hamburg (Valvo Röhrenwerke—electronics) [8] [10]
Vereinigte Metallwerke (munitions) [5]
Volkenreich (construction) [10]
Volkswagenwerke (munitions, armored cars) [5] [7] [8] [10]
Walther-Werke (firearms) [7] [8]
Wayss & Freytag AG (construction) [7] [10]
Wesseloh (construction) [10]
Zementfabrik Hamburg-Tiefstack (cement) [10]

Ravensbrück

AEG (electronics) [3] [5]
Ardelt Werke (munitions) [5] [10]
Chemische Fabrik Malchow [8]
Erprobungstelle d RLM [2]
Dornier-Flugzeugwerke (aircraft) [10]
Flugplatz Rechlin (airport) [8]
Gerätewerke Pommern (missile assembly) [2] [8] [10]

Havelschmelzwerk GmbH [5]
Heinkel-Werke AG (aircraft) [2] [3] [5] [10]
Hugo Schneider AG (HASAG) (munitions) [10]
IG Farben (film factory) [10]
Ikaria-Werke GmbH [10]
Kabel- und Metallwerke Neumeyer AG [10]
Luftfahrtgerätewerk [10]
Markgraf und Heger [10]
Mechanische Werkstätten GmbH (munitions) [2] [5] [10]
Metallwerke Holleischen GmbH (munitions) [10]
Munitionsfabrik Finower Industrie (munitions) [10]
Munitionsfabrik Silberwerke Treuenbrietzen Zweigwerk Röderhof
  (munitions) [10]
Polte-Gruneberger-Metall-Konzern (munitions) [10]
Polte-Werke (flak munitions) [10]
Siemens Bauabteilung (construction) [10]
Siemens und Halske (electronics) [2] [3] [5]
Silva-Metallwerke GmbH (munitions) [2] [8] [10]
Sprengstoff Chemie-Werke (munitions) [10]
Veltener-Maschinenbau GmbH (aircraft components) [2] [10]

Riga- Kaiserwald and Baltic KLs

AEG, Riga (electrical cable) [1] [3] [5] [10]
Baltische Ölgesellschaft (petroleum) [10]
Bazun (construction) [10]
Dallmann Hoch- und Tiefbau (construction) [10]
Dunawerke [10]
Fabrik Lenta [10]
Frankel (leatherwork) [10]
Hahn (construction) [10]
Hardt, Knittel und Welker [10]
Hebel-Schreder [10]
Hollaender [10]
Kopperschmidt und Söhne, Riga (antiaircraft munitions) [2]
Müller [10]
Licht und Kraft [10]
Ottlieb und Berger, Riga (railroad construction) [5] [10]
Philipp Holzmann (construction, synthetic benzine site) [3] [10]
Rippel, Riga (railroad construction) [5] [10]
Rubereit [10]
Sager und Worner (construction) [10]
Sägewerk Zunda (woodworking) [10]

Schichau (antiaircraft munitions, loading) [5] [10]
Vinzent Langelot (airport construction) [10]
Wolf und Dering (construction of bunkers) [10]

Sachsenhausen

AEG Kabelwerk Oberspree (electrical cables) [1] [3] [5] [8] [10]
ARADO Flugzeugwerke Rathenow (aircraft components)
    [8] [10]
Argus-Werke [1] [5] [10]
Auerwerke Orianberg (gas masks) [3] [5] [8] [10]
BMW [9]
Borsig-Werke [10]
Braunkohle-Benzin AG (BRABAG) (mining, synthetic fuel)
    [3] [10]
Daimler Benz, Genshagen [8] [10]
Deutsche Industriewerke AG (munitions) [10]
Deutsche Maschinenbau AG (DEMAG) (panzer manufacturing) [5] [8]
    [10]
Deutsches Rote Kreuz, Berlin [8] [10]
Dreilinden Maschinenbau GmbH (aircraft components) [10]
Dynamit Nobel AG (munitions) [10]
Heinemann und Busse [10]
Heinkel-Werke AG (aircraft components) [2] [3] [5] [8] [9] [10]
IG Farben [10]
Ikaria Werke GmbH [10]
Keltenborn und Stenvers [10]
Kreiselgeräte GmbH [10]
Krupp (munitions) [1] [5] [8] [10]
Luftfahrtgerätewerk [10]
Luranil-Bau GmbH [10]
Märkisches Walzwerk [10]
Metallwarenfabrik Treuenbrietzen GmbH [10]
Mitteldeutsche Stahl- und Walzwerke-Friederich-Flick KG [10]
Munitionsfabrik Gloewen (munitions) [8]
National-Krupp Registrier-Kassen GmbH [10]
Pertrix (Varta) (aircraft batteries) [1] [10]
Phrix-Werke (cellulose) [8] [10]
Rheinmetall-Borsig (locomotives) [1] [5]
Siemens-Schuckertwerke (electronics) [1] [3] [5] [8] [10]
Silva-Metallwerke GmbH (flak munitions) [10]
Spinnstoff-Fabrik Zehlendorf (textiles) [1]
Sprengstoff-Fabrik Meissner und Sohn AG (munitions) [10]

Steinwertz und Siefert [10]
Telefunken (electronics) [10]
UFA—Universum-Film-AG [10]
Veltner Maschinenbau GmbH [10]
Wagner und Csastek [10]
Zellwolle (textiles) [8]
Zeppelin Luftschiffbau GmbH (dirigibles) [2]

Stutthof

AEG Kabel, Thorn (electrical cable) [1] [3] [5] [10]
Bauer Dyck [10]
Behrend [10]
Carl Steppuhn [10]
Danziger Werft (shipyard) [10]
Deutsche Werke Gotenhafen (shipyard) [10]
Dirksen, Muggenhabl [1] [10]
Dridiger [10]
Dynamit Nobel AG (munitions) [10]
Epp, Stutthof [8]
Fast [10]
G.H.T.O. [10]
Hans Carstens, Danzig (food processing) [1] [10]
Heinrich Ott Penner, Danzig (construction) [1] [10]
Huth-Reitschule [10]
Hydrierwerk Poelitz [8]
Jost Fassfabrik (textiles) [1]
Kemna und Co. (concrete) [10]
Kieferling [10]
Marine Bauleitung (shipyard) [10]
Metzger und Co. (munitions) [10]
Milka Hoch- und Tiefbau AG (construction) [10]
Moll (construction) [10]
Müller und Co. (construction) [10]
Otto Jost (barrel makers) [10]
P. Borchardt, Danzig (construction) [1] [10]
Pinow (construction) [10]
Romer und Dehlert (mining) [10]
Schichau-Werft GmbH (submarine construction, loading) [5]
   [8] [10]
Thiel und Co. [10]
Thiersen (stone mining) [10]
Voss [10]

Waggonfabrik Koenigsberg [8]
Waggonfabrik Steinfurt AG [10]
Wagner [10]
Welko und Cohen (construction) [10]
Wilhelm Bötzel, Danzig [1] [10]
Zemke (construction) [10]

Sources

[1]. *Bundesgesetzblatt*, September 9, 1977.
[2]. Himmler report to Goering, February 18, 1944, (Nuremberg doc. PS-1584 (III)).
[3]. Benjamin Ferencz, *Less Than Slaves*. Cambridge, MA: Harvard Univ. Press, 1979.
[4]. Raul Hilberg, *The Destruction of the European Jews*. New York: Harper, 1961.
[5]. International Red Cross, International Tracing Service, *Catalogue of Camps and Prisons in Germany and German-Occupied Territories*, vol. 1 (1949), vol. 2 (1950), and supplement (1951), compiled and indexed in Martin Weinmann (ed.), *Das nationalsozialistische Lagersystem*. Frankfurt a/M: Zweitausendeins, 1990.
[6]. *Trial of the Major War Criminals*. International Military Tribunal, 1947.
[7]. Hamburger Stiftung zur Förderung von Wissenschaft und Kultur, *Industrie, Behörden und Konzentrationslager 1938–1945, Reaktionen 1988–1989*.
[8]. Karl Sommer affidavit, October 4, 1946, (Nuremberg doc. NI-1065).
[9]. Joseph Billig, *Les Camps de Concentration dans l'economie du Reich Hitlerien*. Paris: Presses Universitaires de France, 1973.
[10]. International Red Cross, International Tracing Service (Internationaler Suchdienst), *Verzeichnis der Haftstätten unter dem Reichsführer-SS, 1933–1945*. Arolsen: International Red Cross, 1979.

Notes and Sources

Chapter One

The Splendid Blond Beast

1. Nietzsche, Friedrich, *Zur Genealogie der Moral*, ch. 11, pp. 288–91, in Giorgio Colli and Mazzino Montinari (eds.), *Nietzsche Werke*. Berlin: Walter de Gruyter & Co., 1968, vol. 6, pt. 2. For a good popular introduction to Nietzsche, see Marc Sautet (with illustrations by Patrick Boussignac), *Nietzsche for Beginners*. New York: Writers and Readers Publishing, 1990; discussion of "Splendid Blond Beast" at p. 153. For an interpretation of Nietzsche from a leading German intellectual magazine of the Hitler era, see Kurt Liebmann, "Nietzsche und Das Reich," *Das Reich*, July 21, 1940. For a recent, penetrating critique of the malevolent aspects of Nietzsche's work, see Philippe Foot, "Nietzsche's Immoralism," *New York Review of Books*, June 13, 1991, p. 18.

2. Irving Louis Horowitz, *Genocide; State Power and Mass Murder*. New Brunswick, NJ: Transaction, p. 73.

3. Ervin Staub, *The Roots of Evil; The Origins of Genocide and Other Group Violence*. New York: Cambridge Univ. Press, 1989.

4. For an extensive defense of German industrial leaders, see Henry Ashby Turner, *German Big Business and the Rise of Hitler.* New York: Oxford Univ. Press, 1985; on anti-Semitism issue, see pp. 252, 336–39. For a more critical view of the role of German business in what has come to be called the "prehistory of fascism," see David Abraham, *The Collapse of the Weimar Republic,* 2nd edition. New York: Holmes & Meier, 1986, pp. 271–72.

5. Johannes Ludwig, *Boykott, Enteignung, Mord; Die 'Entjudung' der deutschen Wirtschaft.* Hamburg: Facta, 1989; Dieter Swatek, *Unternehmenskonzentration als Ergebnis und Mittel nationalsozialistischer Wirtschaftspolitik.* Berlin: Dunker & Humbolt, 1972, pp. 88–93ff.

6. Karl-Heinz Roth and Michael Schmid, *Die Daimler-Benz AG, 1916–1948. Schlusseldokumente zur Konzerngeschichte.* Nordlingen: Delphi (Greno), 1987; Hamburger Stiftung für Sozialgeschichte des 20. Jahrhunderts (ed.), *Das Daimler-Benz-Buch. Ein Rustungskonzern im "Tausendiahrigen Reich."* Nordlingen: Echo (Greno), 1988.

7. Max Stein, *Report on the Employment of Slave Work by the Siemens Concern During World War II,* 1961, ms. in Benjamin Ferencz papers. Copy in author's collection. I am grateful to Mr. Ferencz for permitting me access to this collection. For an excellent account of Jewish forced labor in Nazi Germany, see Benjamin Ferencz, *Less Than Slaves.* Cambridge, MA: Harvard Univ. Press, 1979; on AEG, Telefunken, and Siemens, see pp. 105–27.

8. Artem Ohandjanian, *Armenien. Der verschwiegene Volkermord.* Vienna: Bohlau, 1989, pp. 84–119 passim; Hovannisian, *Armenian Genocide,* op. cit., p. 30; Vahakn Dadrian, "The Documentation of the World War I Armenian Massacres in the Proceedings of the Turkish Military Tribunal," *International Journal of Middle East Studies,* November 1991, pp. 549–76; *Documentation of the Armenian Genocide in Turkish Sources.* Jerusalem, Israel: Institute on the Holocaust and Genocide, 1991. For an extensive collection of archival evidence concerning the Armenian Genocide, see Rouben Adalian (ed.), *The Armenian Genocide in the U.S. Archives, 1915–1918,* (microfiche collection). Alexandria, VA: Chadwyck-Healey, 1991–92.

9. For a summary and bibliography, see Frank Chalk and Kurt Jonassohn, *The History and Sociology of Genocide.* New Haven, CT: Yale Univ. Press, 1990, pp. 195–203, 443–46.

10. Telford Taylor, *Nuremberg and Vietnam. An American Tragedy.* Chicago: Quadrangle, 1970, pp. 19, 22.

11. Christian Streit, "The German Army and the Policies of Genocide," in Gerhard Hirschfeld (ed.), *The Policies of Genocide*. London: German Historical Institute and Allen & Unwin, 1986; Foreign Languages Publishing House, *Documents on Adolf Heusinger's Crimes Against Peace, War Crimes and Crimes Against Humanity*. Moscow: Foreign Languages Publishing House, 1962.

12. Roosevelt statement: Department of State *Bulletin*, vol. 1, 1939, p. 181, with British and German replies claiming cooperation at pp. 182–83. For German reply, see U.S. Department of State press release No. 369, September 2, 1939, 740 001 EW1939/252, box 2915, RG 59, National Archives, Washington, DC. By the following May, the ratcheting escalation of British and German bombing raids led the British to state formally to the U.S. that they had abandoned their previous policy of refraining from bombing strictly civilian targets and that they would "reserve to themselves the right to take any action they consider appropriate in the event of bombing by the enemy of civil populations." See Kennedy to Secretary of State, May 10, 1940, 740.00116 EW1939/216, box 2915, RG 59, National Archives, Washington, DC. A good summary of this issue drawn from original sources can be found in Frits Kalshoven, *Belligerent Reprisals*. Leyden: A. W. Sijthoff, 1971, pp. 161–78.

    For definition of war crimes found in footnote that follows, see Leon Friedman (ed.), *The Law of War. A Documentary History*, vol. 1. Westport, CT: Greenwood, 1972 (original publisher: Random House), pp. 908–909.

13. Staub, op. cit., pp. xii–xiii, 6; author's interview with Ervin Staub, March 20, 1991.

14. Yehuda Bauer, *The Holocaust in Historical Perspective*. Seattle, WA: Univ. of Washington Press, 1978. This brief characterization of Bauer's analysis is drawn from Helen Fein's valuable overview, "Genocide: A Sociological Perspective," *Current Sociology* (Sage, London), vol. 38, no. 1, Spring 1990, p. 54.

15. Fein, ibid., pp. 51–78.

16. Basic books on the sociology and social dynamics of genocide, in addition to the Chalk and Jonassohn, Fein, Hovannisian, Ohandjanian, and Staub texts mentioned above, include Raphael Lemkin, *Axis Rule in Occupied Europe*. Washington: Carnegie Endowment, 1944; Raul Hilberg, *The Destruction of the European Jews*. New York: Harper, 1961; Leo Kuper, *Genocide, Its Political Use in the Twentieth Century*. New Haven, CT: Yale Univ. Press, 1981, and *The Prevention of Genocide*, New Haven, CT: Yale Univ. Press, 1985; Vahakn Dadrian, "The Structural-Functional Components of Genocide," in Israel

Senderey and Emilio Viano (eds.), *Victimology.* Lexington, MA: Lexington Books, 1974, and "Genocide as a Problem of National and International Law: The World War I Armenian Case and Its Contemporary Legal Ramifications," *Yale Journal of International Law,* Summer 1989; Israel Charny (ed.), *Toward the Understanding and Prevention of Genocide.* Boulder, CO: Westview, 1982; Henry Friedlander and Sybil Milton, *The Holocaust: Ideology, Bureaucracy and Genocide.* New York: Kraus, 1980; Arno Mayer, *Why Did the Heavens Not Darken? The Final Solution in History.* New York: Pantheon, 1988. For bibliographies, see Israel Charney (ed.), *Genocide: A Critical Bibliographic Review,* 2 vols. New York: Facts on File, 1988, 1991.

17. Richard Breiting (Edouard Calic, ed.), *Secret Conversations With Hitler, The Two Newly Discovered 1931 Interviews.* New York: John Day, p. 81; U.S., Office of United States Chief of Counsel for Prosecution of Axis Criminality, *Nazi Conspiracy and Aggression,* vol. 3. Washington, DC: USGPO, 1946, p. 753; Adolph Hitler, *Hitler's Secret Conversations, 1941–1944.* New York: Farrar, Straus and Young, 1953, pp. 188, 317, 493.

18. U.S., Department of the Treasury, *Report to the Secretary on the Acquiescence of This Government in the Murder of the Jews,* January 13, 1944, unpublished staff study, now found at Henry Morgenthau, Jr., *Diaries,* vol. 693, pp. 212–29, Franklin D. Roosevelt Library, Hyde Park, NY.

19. Robert Lansing, *Diary,* entry for May 25, 1915, Library of Congress, Washington, DC; cited in Ronald Pruessen, *John Foster Dulles. The Road to Power.* New York. Free Press, 1982, p. 46.

20. Mira Wilkins, *The Maturing of Multinational Enterprise: American Business Abroad from 1914 to 1970.* Cambridge, MA: Harvard Univ. Press, 1974, p. 185; U.S., Department of Commerce, *American Direct Investment in Foreign Countries.* Washington, DC: USGPO, Trade Information Bulletin No. 731. Moody's Investors Service, *Moody's Manual of Investments, American and Foreign Industrial Securities.* New York & London: Moody's, 1939, pp. 1798, 1800, 1801, 1804, a113–a117: "Six-Year Price Range of Foreign Industrials" (blue section).

21. See, for example, Tom Bower, *Blind Eye to Murder.* London: Granada, 1983, pp. 47–51, or more detailed discussion below.

22. Marjorie Housepian Dobkin, "What Genocide? What Holocaust? News from Turkey 1915–1923, A Case Study," in Richard Hovannisian (ed.), *The Armenian Genocide in Perspective.* New Brunswick, NJ: Transaction, 1986, pp. 97–110; Bernard Baruch, *The Making of*

the Reparation and Economic Sections of the [*Versailles*] *Treaty.* New York: Harper, 1920; particularly speeches by John Foster Dulles and Australian Prime Minister W. M. Hughes at pp. 289–315; see also more detailed notes in the chapters below.

23. Murphy to Secretary of State, 740.00116EW/8-1147 (Top Secret, No Distribution), August 11, 1947; Robert Joyce (Central Intelligence Group) to Walter Dowling, "Subject: Former SS Colonel Dollmann" (Top Secret), December 1, 1946 (sanitized), 740.00116EW/12-146; Leghorn to Secretary of State, 740.00116EW/5-1547 (Top Secret), May 15, 1947; Jack Neal, "Memorandum for the Files" (Top Secret), September 16, 1947, found at 740.00116 EW/8-1147. These records, which had been previously withheld from the State Department files in the National Archives, were obtained by the author through the Freedom of Information Act and are now available at RG 59, National Archives, Washington, DC. See also "Interrogation Report on SS Standartenfuehrer *Rauff,* Walter," May 15, 1945 (Confidential), in U.S. Army Counter Intelligence Corps file No. D-216719, *Rauff, Walter,* obtained via Freedom of Information Act from U.S. Army IN-SCOM, Ft. Meade, MD; and "Summary Prepared by W. M. Chase on 'The Role of the Wolff Group in Operation Sunrise,'" March 10, 1947 (Top Secret), 740.00116EW/11-1047, box 3625, RG 59, National Archives, Washington, DC. For Dulles's account of his encounter with Rauff, see Allen Dulles, *The Secret Surrender.* New York: Harper, 1966, pp. 66, 83, 102, 107, 158, 188, 192–93.

24. See State Department records described in previous source note and Bradley F. Smith and Elena Agarossi, *Operation Sunrise.* New York: Basic Books, 1979, pp. 189–90.

25. FBI file No. 100-380802, *Ivan Kerno,* obtained via Freedom of Information Act; Department of State records on Kerno: Maney to Bender, Department of State July 20, 1954, in Department of State FOI Case No. 8901702. The Kerno affair was first brought to light by historian and author Alti Rodale in an unpublished paper, "Canadian and Allied Governments' Policies with Regard to Nazi War Crimes." I am grateful to Dr. Rodale for sharing a draft of this paper with me.

Chapter Two

"The Immediate Demands of Justice"

1. H. W. V. Temperley (ed.), *A History of the Peace Conference of Paris,* vol. 1. London: Oxford Univ. Press, 1969, pp. 137–38. Temperley and many others underestimate the number of U.S. dead; for a discussion, see Gary Putka, "Readers of Latest U.S. History Textbooks

Discover a Storehouse of Misinformation," *Wall Street Journal*, February 12, 1992, p. B-1.

2. Some scholarly estimates place the number of Armenian dead at 1.5 to 2 million. For discussion concerning the number of fatalities, see Leo Kuper, "The Turkish Genocide of Armenians, 1915–1917," in Richard Hovannisian (ed.), *The Armenian Genocide in Perspective*. New Brunswick, NJ: Transaction, 1986, pp. 43–59. The interior minister of the postwar Turkish government, citing Turkey's own records, admitted some 800,000 Armenian deaths in connection with the deportations as of 1919, though this total excluded several categories of fatalities; see Vahakn N. Dadrian, "The Naim-Andonian Documents on the World War I Destruction of Ottoman Armenians: The Anatomy of a Genocide," *International Journal of Middle East Studies*, August 1986, pp. 342 and 358–59, fn111.

3. Temperley, op. cit., p. 162.

4. William McNeill, *Plagues and Peoples*. Garden City, NY: Doubleday/Anchor, 1977, pp. 195, 252, 255.

5. Temperley, op. cit., p. 139. Estimate has been converted from pounds sterling to dollars at contemporary exchange rate. Later estimates were higher and probably more accurate; see Eugene Meyer testimony at U.S. Congress, War Policies Commission, *Hearings*, March 5–18, 1931. Washington, DC: USGPO, p. 222.

6. David Albert Foltz, *The War Crimes Issue at the Paris Peace Conference*. Washington, DC: American University, Ph.D. thesis, 1978, pp. 10–37; Arthur Ponsonby, *Falsehood in Wartime*. New York: Dutton, 1928; Harold Lasswell, *Propaganda Technique in the [First] World War*. Cambridge, MA: MIT Press, 1971. On "symbiotic relationship": George Bruntz, *Allied Propaganda and the Collapse of the German Empire*. New York: Arno, 1972, pp. 86–91, 194–201. On Lippmann's role as an intelligence specialist and propagandist, see Ronald Steel, *Walter Lippmann and the American Century*. New York: Vintage, 1981, pp. 128–70 passim.

7. James Willis, *Prologue to Nuremberg: The Politics and Diplomacy of Punishing War Criminals of the First World War*. Westport, CT: Greenwood, 1982, pp. 37–64; Foltz, loc. cit.

8. Perhaps the most complete explanation of how the Hague conventions were viewed in 1919 can be found in a series of handbooks prepared for the U.S. delegation at Paris concerning issues involved in establishing culpability for war crimes, reparation policy, and related matters. These have been republished as: U.S., American Commission to Negotiate Peace (The Inquiry), *The Inquiry Handbooks*. Wilmington: Scholarly Resources, 1974. See particularly vol.

2 (Laws of Land Warfare), vol. 3 (Selected Topics in the Laws of Warfare), vol. 7 (Neutrals' Person and Property Within Belligerent Territory), vol. 8 (Maritime Warfare, Land Warfare), and vol. 9 (Blockade). For note concerning British sponsorship of the formulation of the maritime provisions, see Alfred de Zayas, *The Wehrmacht War Crimes Bureau, 1939–1945.* Lincoln, NE: Univ. of Nebraska Press, 1989, p. 123.

9. The Hague, International Peace Conference, *The Proceedings of the Hague Peace Conferences,* vol. 2. New York: Oxford Univ. Press, 1920, pp. 329, 698–700. Of particular interest in this context are the brutal suppression of the Boxer Rebellion in China and of a Philippine nationalist insurrection during the course of the second Hague conference itself, see Calvin DeArmond Davis, *The United States and the Second Hague Peace Conference.* Durham, NC: Duke Univ. Press, 1975, p. 37; and Leon Friedman, *The Law of War. A Documentary History,* vol. 1. Westport, CT: Greenwood, 1972, pp. 799–841.

10. For contemporary disputes concerning Belgian "peoples war" (civilian resistance), see Jules Valery, *Les Crimes de la Population Belge; Réplique à un Plaidover pour le Gouvernement Allemand.* Paris: Fontemoing/Libraires des Écoles Françaises, 1916; Belgium, *Reports on the Violations of the Rights of Nations and of the Laws and Customs of War in Belgium* (2 vols.). London: HMSO, n.d. (1916?); Fernand Passelecq, *Deportation et Travail Force des Ouvriers et de la Population Civile de la Belgigue Occupée 1916–1918.* Paris: Les Presses Universitaires, n.d. (1927?). For general problem of "legalized" slaughter of rebels, insurgents, guerrillas, and other irregulars, see Keith Suter, *An International Law of Guerrilla Warfare.* New York: St. Martin's, 1984, pp. 1–19, 175–85; and Frits Kalshoven, *Belligerent Reprisals,* Leyden: A. W. Sijthoff, 1971, pp. 1–44.

For more recent reflections on the persistence of this structural problem in international law, see Noam Chomsky, "The Role of Force in International Affairs," in *For Reasons of State.* New York: Pantheon, 1973, pp. 212ff; Jean-Paul Sartre, "On Genocide," in John Duffett (ed.), *Against the Crime of Silence.* New York: O'Hare, 1969, pp. 612ff; Donald Wells, *War Crimes and Laws of War.* Lanham, MD: University Press of America, 1984; and Joseph Weiler, Antonio Cassese, and Marina Spinedi, *International Crimes of State. A Critical Analysis of the ILC's Draft Article 19 on State Responsibility.* Berlin & New York: Walter de Gruyter, 1989. Philip Thienel, Special Operations Research Office, *The Legal Status of Participants in Unconventional Warfare,* Washington, DC: American Univ. Press, 1961.

11. *The Proceedings of the Hague Peace Conferences,* vol. 2, op. cit., p. 5. For a profile of the delegations, see Davis, op. cit., pp. 178–85.

12. Bernard Baruch, *The Making of the Reparation and Economic Sections of the [Versailles] Treaty.* New York: Harper, 1920; see particularly speeches by John Foster Dulles and Australian Prime Minister W. M. Hughes at pp. 289–315.

13. Ronald Pruessen, *John Foster Dulles: The Road to Power.* New York: Free Press, 1982, pp. 1–13; see also Leonard Mosely, *Dulles.* New York: Dial, 1978, pp. 13–27.

14. Pruessen, ibid., pp. 16–17.

15. Nancy Lisagor and Frank Lipsius, *A Law Unto Itself: The Untold Story of the Law Firm Sullivan and Cromwell.* New York: William Morrow, 1988, pp. 39–57.

16. Ibid., pp. 61–64; Pruessen, op. cit., pp. 17–20.

17. Pruessen, op. cit., pp. 23–44.

18. Richard Harris Smith, *The OSS.* Berkeley, CA: Univ. of California Press, 1972, p. 204.

19. Charles Seymour (Harold Whiteman, ed.), *Letters from the Paris Peace Conference.* New Haven, CT: Yale Univ. Press, 1965, pp. 61–62, 174n, 176–77; see also Mosely, op. cit., pp. 44–45, 48. On Kerno: FBI file no. 100-380802, *Ivan Kerno,* obtained via the Freedom of Information Act; and Department of State FOI case no. 8901702.

20. Baruch, op. cit., p. 18, with transcripts of Dulles's speeches at pp. 289–97, 323–37. See also: Arthur Walworth, *Wilson and His Peacemakers: American Diplomacy at the Paris Peace Conference, 1919.* New York: Norton, 1986, p. 21fn; Pruessen, op. cit., pp. 30–31.

21. Seymour op. cit., pp. 65, 86, 92. See also: U.S., American Commission to Negotiate Peace, *Minutes* July 1–September 4, 1919, from collection of Carnegie Endowment for International Peace, now at George Washington University Gellman Library, Washington, DC.

22. Allen Dulles, "The Present Situation in Hungary: Action Recommended by A. W. Dulles," March 24, 1919, Woodrow Wilson papers, VIII A:27, cited in Arno Mayer, *Politics and Diplomacy of Peacemaking, Containment and Counterrevolution at Versailles, 1918–1919.* New York; Knopf, 1967, pp. 576–78.

23. Walworth, op. cit., p. 214.

24. Edward M. House, *Diary,* entry for July 24, 1915. Yale University Library, New Haven; Willis, op. cit., p. 41.

25. Willis, loc. cit.

26. Robert Lansing, *Diary,* entry for May 25, 1915, Library of Congress, Washington, DC, cited in Pruessen, op. cit., p. 46.

27. Willis, loc. cit.

28. United Nations War Crimes Commission, *History of the United Nations War Crimes Commission and the Laws of War.* London: HMSO, 1948, pp. 32–36, with quote concerning charges at pp. 33–34. This text is cited hereafter as *UNWCC and the Laws of War.*

29. Ibid., pp. 35–38.

30. Foltz, op. cit., pp. 165–71; Walworth, op. cit., pp. 214–15.

31. Foltz ibid., pp. 219–23; Willis, op. cit., p. 86.

32. *UNWCC and the Laws of War,* op. cit., pp. 36–41.

33. Walworth, op. cit., p. 215.

34. Willis, op. cit., p. 79.

35. Walworth, op. cit., p. 216.

Chapter Three
Young Turks

1. Vahakn Dadrian, "Genocide as a Problem of National and International Law," *Yale Journal of International Law,* Summer 1989, pp. 230–45.

2. For an overview, see Artem Ohandjanian, *Armenien. Der Verschwiegene Völkermord.* Vienna: Bohlar, 1969, pp. 84–124; Dadrian, "The Naim-Andonian Documents" and "Genocide as a Problem . . . ," op. cit.; and Richard Hovannisian (ed.), *The Armenian Genocide in Perspective.* New Brunswick, NJ: Transaction, 1986. For an extensive documentary collection, see Adalian, *The Armenian Genocide in U.S. Archives, 1915–18* (microficle collection). Alexandria, VA: Chadwyck-Healey, 1991–92. For a smaller collection of key U.S. government documentation concerning the genocide, see Armen Hairapetian, " 'Race Problems' and the Armenian Genocide: The State Department File," and Armen Hovannisian, "The United States Inquiry and the Armenian Question, 1917–1919 Archival Papers," both with accompanying selections of archival records, *Armenian Review,* Spring 1984, pp. 41–202. For a British collection of detailed contemporary reports, see Arnold Toynbee (ed.), *The Treatment of the Armenians in the Ottoman Empire 1915–1916.* London: HMSO, 1916. For a German collection, see Johannes Lepsius, *Deutschland und Armenien 1914–1918, Sammlung Diplomatischer Aktenstücke.* Potsdam: Tempelverlag, 1919. For a discussion of Turkish records, see Vahakn Dadrian, *Documentation of the Armenian Genocide in*

Turkish Sources. Jerusalem, Israel: Institute on the Holocaust and Genocide, 1991.

3. On seizure of Armenian property, see Dadrian, "Genocide as a Problem . . . ," op. cit., pp. 267–72.

4. Christopher Simpson, "Women and the Armenian Genocide," paper presented at the Seventh Berkshire Conference on the History of Women, Wellesley College, June 19, 1987. In some cases, Turks protected Armenian girls by announcing their religious conversion and taking them into their families; see Donald Miller and Lorna Miller "An Oral History Prespective on Responses to the Armenian Genocide," in Hovannisian, op. cit., p. 190.

5. See, for example, Deutsche Gesandtschaft Nr. 906 (Bern, October 19, 1915), in which the German ambassador reports to Berlin concerning confidential discussions with Turkish representatives. Turkish ambassador Salioh Bey Gourdji indicates that "If Turkey wishes to be a vital force, it must cut out, eliminate (auschalten) the Armenians in some way . . . the government has chosen the path marked by violence . . . even if we cannot find another way of moving the Armenians, the way that this is portrayed to the outside world must be different"; National Archives microfilm publication T-139, captured German records, reel 463, band 39.

6. For a useful summary of Morgenthau's role, see Henry Morgenthau, Sr., "Ambasssador Morgenthau's Story," *The World's Work*, November 1918.

7. Virtually all Western news coverage of the massacres included the theme of Muslims persecuting Christians. For examples, see Rev. Robert Labaree, "The Jihad Rampant in Persia," *Missionary Review of the World*, July 1915; "Several American Missionaries Dead," *New York Times*, September 18, 1915; "Spare Armenians, Pope Asks Sultan," *New York Times*, October 11, 1915; "The Greatest of the Religious Massacres," *The Independent*, October 18, 1915; "Assassination of Armenia," *Missionary Review of the World*, November 1915. For a content analysis of contemporary reporting, see Marjorie Housepian Dobkin, "What Genocide? What Holocaust? News from Turkey 1915–1923, A Case Study," in Hovannisian, op. cit., pp. 97–110. For a large collection of typical newspaper and magazine articles concerning the genocide, see Richard Kloian, *The Armenian Genocide: News Accounts from the American Press 1915–1922*. Richmond, CA: ACC Books, 1985.

8. *UNWCC and the Laws of War*, op. cit., p. 35.

9. David Fromkin, *A Peace to End All Peace*. New York: Avon, 1989, pp. 214–15; Firuz Kazemzadeh, *The Struggle for Transcaucasia, 1917–1921*. New York: Philosophical Library, 1950, pp. 27–30.

10. Dadrian, "The Naim-Andonian Documents" and "Genocide as a Problem . . . ," op. cit. A number of the *Takyimi Vekayi* documents are reproduced in English translation in Kloian, *The Armenian Genocide,* op. cit., pp. 309–32.

11. Dadrian, ibid., pp. 311ff.

12. Dobkin, op. cit., pp. 97–110; H. M. V. Temperley, (ed.), *A History of the Peace Conference of Paris,* vol. 6. London: Oxford Univ. Press, 1969, pp. 178–92.

13. Temperley, ibid.; "Chronology of Events Relating to Development of Oil in Iraq, Compiled by the Library of Congress," in U.S. Congress, Senate, Committee on Foreign Relations, Subcommittee on Multinational Corporations, *Multinational Corporations and United States Foreign Policy,* pt. 8. Washington, DC: USGPO, 1975, pp. 497–99.

14. Anthony Sampson, *The Seven Sisters.* New York: Bantam, 1975, p. 72.

15. On Treaty of Sèvres: *UNWCC and the Laws of War,* op. cit., p. 45; Temperley, op. cit., vol. 6, p. 184; Dadrian, "Genocide as a Problem . . . ," op. cit., pp. 288–91, 314; Hovannisian, op. cit., p. 36; Sampson, op. cit., p. 70–82; Leonard Mosley, *Powerplay: Oil in the Mideast.* New York: Random House, 1973, pp. 41–50.

16. Dobkin, op. cit., p. 105.

17. Loc. cit.

18. Ibid., p. 106; Allen Dulles to Mark Bristol, April 21, 1922, Bristol Papers, RG 45, National Archives, Washington, DC.

19. Henry Morgenthau, Sr., op. cit.; or Adalian, op. cit.

20. Dobkin, op. cit., pp. 97ff.

21. For a large collection of news accounts of this activity, see Kloian, *Armenian Genocide,* op. cit.

22. Dobkin, op. cit., p. 104.

23. Colby Chester, "Turkey Reinterpreted," *Current History,* September 1922, pp. 939–47.

24. Dobkin, op. cit., p. 105.

25. For selected U.S. documentation concerning U.S. representatives at Lausanne, including the roles of Joseph Grew, Allen Dulles, Green Hackworth, and others, see: U.S. Department of State, *Foreign Relations of the United States,* 1923, vol. 2, Washington, DC: USGPO, 1938, pp. 879–1258. See particularly pp. 879, 972, 974–80 (Dulles); pp. 889, 900ff (Grew); 901; 926–27, 949, 954, 958, 991, and passim (oil).

26. On war crimes aspects of Treaty of Lausanne: Willis, op. cit., pp. 162–63; Dadrian, "Genocide as a Problem . . . ," op. cit., p. 310. On oil aspects of same treaty: Temperley, op. cit., vol. 6, pp. 178–92; "Chronology of Events Relating to Development of Oil in Iraq," op. cit., pp.

497–99. For a collection of articles opposing the treaty, see American Committee Opposed to the Lausanne Treaty, *The Lausanne Treaty, Turkey and Armenia,* np: American Committee, 1928; and Eugene Borell, *Sentence Arbitrale, Repartition des Annuites de la Dette Publique Ottomane, Article 47 de Traite de Lausanne,* Geneva: Albert Kundig, 1925.

27. Dadrian, ibid., p. 310; Jacques Derogy, *Resistance and Revenge: The Armenian Assassination of Turkish Leaders Responsible for the 1915 Massacres and Deportations.* New Brunswick, NJ: Transaction, 1990.

28. For example, Embassy of Turkey, *Setting the Record Straight on Armenian Propaganda against Turkey.* Washington, DC: 1982.

29. James Willis, *Prologue to Nuremberg: The Politics and Diplomacy of Punishing War Criminals of the First World War.* Westport, CT: Greenwood, 1982. pp. 82–85.

30. Ibid., p. 83.

31. Ibid., p. 84; David Albert Foltz, *The War Crimes Issue at the Paris Peace Conference.* Washington, DC: American University, Ph.D. thesis, 1978, pp. 219–23.

32. Willis, ibid., p. 85.

33. *UNWCC and the Laws of War,* op. cit., pp. 46–49.

34. Ibid., pp. 46–47.

35. Loc. cit.

36. Ibid., p. 48.

37. Ibid., p. 44; Walworth, *Wilson and His Peacemakers. American Diplomacy at the Paris Peace Conference, 1919.* New York: Norton, p. 216. For an extended discussion of this issue, see Foltz, op. cit.

38. Willis, p. 86.

Chapter Four

Bankers, Lawyers, and Linkage Groups

1. Ronald Preussen, *John Foster Dulles: The Road to Power.* New York: Free Press, 1982, p. 33.

2. Ibid., p. 42.

3. Ibid., p. 46.

4. Ibid., p. 48. On stabilization politics in Continental Europe during this period, see Charles Maier, *Recasting Bourgeois Europe.* Princeton, NJ: Princeton Univ. Press, 1975, esp. pp. 579–94.

5. Bernard Baruch, *The Making of the Reparation and Economic Sec-*

tions of the [Versailles] Treaty. New York: Harper, 1920, pp. 294–95, with text of Dulles speeches at pp. 289–97, 323–37.

6. Karl Bergmann, *The History of Reparations.* Boston: Houghton Mifflin, 1927, pp. 69–77.

7. For a concise summary of the terms of Dawes Plan loans, see Moody's Investors Service, *Moody's Manual of Investments: Foreign and American Government Securities.* New York: Moody's, 1925, p. 422; see also Preussen, op. cit., pp. 87–88.

8. U.S. Congress, Senate, Committee on Finance. *Sale of Foreign Bonds and Securities in the United States.* Washington, DC: USGPO, 1931.

9. Martin Wolfson, *Financial Crisis: Understanding the Postwar US Experience.* Armonk, NY, and London: M. E. Sharp, 1986; Anthony Sampson, *The Money Lenders.* New York: Penguin, 1983, pp. 148–96; Martin Mayer, *The Bankers.* New York: Ballantine, 1974, pp. 449–503.

10. *Sale of Foreign Bonds . . .* op. cit. See also: Bernhard Menne, "How Germany Used Her Foreign Loans," *Prevent World War III,* No. 18, December 1946; Paul Einzig, *Germany's Default: The Economics of Hitlerism.* London: Macmillan, 1934. For details concerning German reparation loans, state debt, and municipal debt, see Moody's Investors Service, "Deutsches Reich," *Moody's Manual of Investments, Governments.* New York: Moody's, 1927, pp. 496–555.

11. *Sale of Foreign Bonds . . .* op. cit.

12. International Telephone and Telegraph Corporation, "Memorandum Concerning 'External Assets' of German Subsidiaries" (with December 1945 balance sheet), at OMGUS Legal Division, Legal Advice Branch, box 58, file "Property and External Property Commission—LA 64," RG 260, National Archives, Suitland, MD. This ITT memo reports that the company's properties included Conrad Lorenz (98.7 percent owned) and Lorenz's subsidiaries; Focke-Wulf aircraft (percentage of ownership not disclosed); Telegrafia Ceskoslovenská (acquired in 1940) and an unnamed electric tube factory at Vrchlabi, Czechoslovakia; Standard Elektrizitäts Gesellschaft AG (100 percent owned) and its subsidiaries—Ferdinand Schuchardt Berliner Fernsprech- und Telegraphenwerk (99.5 percent), Mix & Genest AG (94 percent), Suddeutsche Apparatefabrik GmbH (100 percent), Telephonfabrik Berliner (99 percent), Telefongyar r.t. (Budapest), total 75 percent ownership through two different ITT subsidiaries; and Gesellschaft für Telephon- und Telegraphenbeteiligungen (100 percent). James Stewart Martin of the OMGUS Finance Division reports that Conrad Lorenz owned 25 percent of Focke-Wulf and that the chairman of all three of ITT's major German subsidiaries was Gerhardt A.

Westrick, Heinrich Albert's partner in the Albert and Westrick law firm mentioned in the text; see James Stewart Martin, *All Honorable Men*. Boston: Little, Brown, 1950, p. 209.

13. U.S. Congress, Senate, Subcommittee on Antitrust and Monopoly, *The Industrial Reorganization Act: "American Ground Transport."* Washington, DC: USGPO, 1974, p. A–17; Alfred Sloan, *My Years With General Motors*. New York: Macfadden, 1965, pp. 321–29. On Fritz Opel as General Motors director: Moody's Investors Service, *Moody's Manual of Investments, American and Foreign Industrial Securities*. New York: Moody's, 1937, pp. 2192, 3204.

14. Moody's Investors Service, op. cit., 1936, pp. 1283–84.

15. Joseph Borkin, *The Crime and Punishment of IG Farben*. New York: Free Press, 1978, p. 51. See also: U.S. Congress, Senate, Subcommittee on War Mobilization, *Economic and Political Aspects of International Cartels* (report by Corwin Edwards, U.S. Department of Justice). Washington, DC: USGPO, 1944; Peter Hayes, *Industry and Ideology: IG Farben in the Nazi Era*, Cambridge: Cambridge University Press, 1987.

16. On General Electric: National Industrial Conference Board, *Rationalization of German Industry*. New York: National Conference Board, 1931, pp. 110–17. For footnote: the list here was developed from data presented in Mira Wilkins, *The Maturing of Multinational Enterprise. American Business Abroad from 1914 to 1917*. Cambridge, MA: Harvard Univ. Press, 1974. pp. 41, 67–68, 71–73, 103, 111, 143–45, 186–87. By 1940, the direct investments of Americans in Germany and Austria were estimated as approximately $225 million (book value) of branch plants of U.S. corporations and $400 million in U.S.-owned German bonds. Estimates of the value of U.S. ownership of shares in German companies were not immediately available. See Martin Domke, *Trading With the Enemy*. New York: Central Books, 1943, pp. 294–95.

17. The terms "business elite" and "financial and industrial elite," as used in this book, refer to the boards of directors and most senior management of the largest and most powerful banks and companies based in a given country, plus the senior partners in law firms that cater to such clients. A convenient listing of the names, addresses, and economic roles of about 600 German personalities meeting this description can be found in: U.S., Office of Military Government for Germany (US) [OMGUS], Finance Division, Financial Investigation Section, *Names of Persons and Industrial Groups Affected by the Application of the De-Nazification Program to Banks* (1946), box 54, RG 260, National Archives, Suitland, MD. No comparable consoli-

dated list for U.S. personalities is known to exist, but such individuals can be readily identified through their status as directors or senior management of the fifty largest U.S.-based banks and industrial corporations filing annual reports with the U.S. Securities and Exchange Commission (SEC). A small number of privately held companies and law firms based in the U.S. are not required to file annual reports with the SEC; personalities connected with such institutions can often be traced through the *Martindale and Hubble* law directories, *Who's Who in America*, press reports, and similar sources. See David Brownstone and Gorton Carruth, *Where to Find Business Information*. New York: Wiley-Interscience, 1979, for an extended presentation of informamtion sources for research into U.S.-based business affairs.

18. *Sale of Foreign Bonds* . . . op. cit., for a table of specific Dillon, Read loans, see pp. 501–506. See also: "Dillon, Read: Senate Inquiries Into the Formation and Operation of Two of the Firm's Trusts," *Newsweek*, October 14, 1933; "Easy Money," *The Nation*, October 18, 1933. Dillon, Read recently cooperated in the preparation of a high-quality, authorized history of the firm; see Robert Sobel, *The Life and Times of Dillon, Read*. New York: Dutton, 1991, pp. 92–118, for discussion of foreign banking activities in the 1920.

19. For data on postwar careers of senior Dillon, Read executives, see: "Oral History Interview with General William H. Draper," January 11, 1972, Harry S Truman Library, Independence, MO (on Draper); *Current Biography 1942*, p. 267, and *Current Biography 1948*, p. 223 (on Forrestal); *Current Biography 1962*, p. 322 (on Nitze); and *Current Biography 1942*, p. 230, and *Who Was Who*, vol. 5, p. 206 (on Eberstadt).

20. John Kouwenhoven, *Partners in Banking: Brown Brothers, Harriman & Co., 1918–1968*. Garden City, NY: Doubleday, 1968, 1983. Harriman and Lovett became two of the six so-called "Wise Men" widely regarded as the core of the U.S. foreign policy establishment from 1945 until the collapse of the U.S. campaign in Vietnam. Their colleagues in this role included John McCloy, Charles Bohlen, George Kennan, and Dean Acheson; see Walter Isaacson and Evan Thomas, *The Wise Men*. New York: Simon and Schuster, 1986. For a more critical analysis of the same phenomenon, see G. William Domhoff, "Who Made American Foreign Policy 1945–1963?" in David Horowitz (ed.), *Corporations and the Cold War*. New York: Monthly Review Press, 1969, pp. 25ff.

21. Pruessen, op. cit., pp. 76–152; Nancy Lisagor and Frank Lipsius, *A Law Unto Itself: The Untold Story of the Law Firm Sullivan and*

Cromwell. New York: William Morrow, 1988, pp. 77–159. On Sullivan & Cromwell representation of HAPAG: Eleanor Lansing Dulles interview, Columbia University Oral History Project, pt. 2, p. 57.

22. Pruessen, ibid., p. 66.

23. Ibid., pp. 69–72.

24. Dulles address, "The Power of International Finance," March 24, 1928, Dulles papers, Princeton University.

25. Paul Nitze with Ann Smith and Steven Rearden, *From Hiroshima to Glasnost.* New York: Grove Weidenfeld, 1989, p. xvii.

26. Martin Weil, *A Pretty Good Club: The Founding Fathers of the U.S. Foreign Service.* New York: Norton, 1978, p. 47.

27. Ibid., p. 48.

28. Daniel Yergin, *Shattered Peace. The Origins of the Cold War and the National Security State.* Boston: Houghton Mifflin, 1977, pp. 17–41.

29. Frederic Propas, "Creating a Hard Line Towards Russia: The Training of State Department Soviet Experts 1927–1937," *Diplomatic History,* Summer 1984, pp. 209–26.

30. Weil, op. cit.

31. John Foster Dulles, *War, Peace, and Change.* New York: Harper, 1939; Pruessen, op. cit., pp. 175–77; John Foster Dulles, *War or Peace.* New York: Macmillan, 1950, pp. 5–16. Forrestal and Nitze: Walter Millis (ed.), *The Forrestal Diaries.* New York: Viking, 1951, pp. 135–41; Nitze, *From Hiroshima to Glasnost,* op. cit., pp. xx–7; Wilson, Reed, and du Pont empire: Gerald Colby (Zilg), *Du Pont Dynasty. Behind the Nylon Curtain.* Secaucus, NJ: Lyle Stuart, 1984, pp. 291–451 passim. Also, following much the same ideological development as Kennan and other "Riga Axioms" advocates were W. Averell Harriman and Robert Lovett; see Walter Isaacson and Evan Thomas, op. cit.

32. Yergin, op. cit., p. 26.

33. On Albert's role at Ford: Moody's Investors Service, *Moody's Manual of Investments, American and Foreign Industrial Securities.* New York: Moody's, 1936, pp. 1283–84; and "The Right Men in the Right Places," *Prevent World War III,* no. 25, May 1948. For ITT role of Gerhardt Westrick, see U.S. Army Counter Intelligence Corps dossier "Westrick, Gerhardt" (file number has been suppressed), and OSS report "Request for Information about certain German business figures," May 2, 1945, available via Freedom of Information Act from U.S. Army INSCOM, Ft. Meade, MD. See also Martin, op. cit., p. 209; for Texaco role, see Anthony Sampson, *The Seven Sisters.* New York: Bantam, 1975, p. 98.

34. U.S. Army Counter Intelligence Corps dossier no. XE011561 I6D016

"Westrick, Ludger" available via Freedom of Information Act from U.S. Army INSCOM, Ft. Meade, MD.

35. *Das Deutsche Führerlexicon, 1934–1935.* Berlin: Otto Stollberg, 1935, p. 279. Lindemann's NSDAP membership record (no. 5453455) is available via the Berlin Document Center. See also: U.S. Congress, Senate, Committee on Military Affairs, *Elimination of German Resources for War*, pt. 5, July 2, 1945, pp. 819–20; and U.S. Army Counter Intelligence Corps (CIC) dossier no. XE000915 *Karl Lindemann* and USFET Military Intelligence Service Center, *Preliminary Interrogation Report: Karl Lindemann*, September 12, 1945, available through the Freedom of Information Act from U.S. Army Intelligence and Security Command, Ft. Meade, MD.

36. National Industrial Conference Board, *The Rationalization of German Industry.* New York: National Industrial Conference Board, 1931.

37. *Names of Persons and Industrial Groups Affected by the Application of the De-Nazification Program to Banks*, op. cit.

    The German system divides corporate boards into the *Aufsichtsrat*, which is roughly similar to a U.S.-style board of directors, and the *Vorstand*, or senior management committee. At Deutsche Bank, for example, the *Aufsichtsrat* was elected by the general stockholders' meeting, served four-year terms (and was frequently re-elected), met twice annually, and was responsible for overall bank policy. The *Aufsichtsrat's* working committees met monthly and provided much more direct supervision, including approval authority over all loans of 1 million RM or more. There were typically between twenty and thirty members of the *Aufsichtsrat* at Deutsche Bank, though most German corporations had much smaller boards. The *Aufsichtrat* appointed the *Vorstand*, which is similar to the president's committee or similar senior management body in many American companies. The *Vorstand* at Deutsche Bank typically had between seven and eleven members. It met almost daily and directed the day-to-day affairs of the bank. Deutsche Bank and many other German companies also created a *Bierat*, or advisory board, which facilitated greater input into decision-making by the bank's regional and district executives. At some companies, the *Bierat* included representatives of cartel partners, major suppliers or customers, the German government, or other outside groups. For details, see U.S., Office of Military Government for Germany (US) [OMGUS], Finance Division, Financial Investigation Section, *Report on the Investigation of the Deutsche Bank*, November 1946, pp. 21–27, in file: "Deutsche Bank," box 229, RG 260, National Archives, Suitland, MD. This is cited hereafter as *OMGUS Deutsche Bank*. For a German-language edition and commentary on this study, see OMGUS, *Ermittlungen gegen die Deutsche Bank.* Nordlingen: Greno, 1986.

38. *OMGUS Deutsche Bank,* ibid., p. 2.

39. The data concerning banking interlocks are calculated from *OMGUS Deutsche Bank,* ibid., table 11 (n.p.).

40. On interlocks with Allianz Insurance: ibid., table 10 (n.p.). See also: U.S., Office of Military Government (U.S.) [OMGUS], Finance Division, Financial Intelligence Section, *Report on the Investigation of Dr. Kurt Schmitt,* January 1948, file: "Investigation: Kurt Schmitt," box 233, RG 260, National Archives, Suitland, MD.

41. On interlocks with Daimler Benz, BMW, etc.: *OMGUS Deutsche Bank,* table 12 (n.p.). On ownership of company stock: ibid., pp. 108–109 and table 12.

42. On interlocks with Siemens group of companies: ibid., pp. 109–13. The relationship between Deutsche Bank and Siemens began in 1870, when Georg Siemens—already a major industrialist—helped found the bank and became its leading manager. Before two decades were out, Deutsche Bank became the Siemens empire's principal banking house and source of loans for new investment. Among its early projects was the establishment of Mannesman, a major manufacturer of the steel pipe used in the oil and natural gas industries. All three institutions have operated for decades as closely integrated branches of a single financial entity.

43. On Dresdner Bank, see: U.S., Office of Military Government for Germany (US) [OMGUS], Finance Division, Financial Investigation Section, *Report on the Investigation of the Dresdner Bank,* 1946, box 235, RG 260, National Archives, Suitland, MD, pp. 35–41, 71–75. This report is cited hereafter as *OMGUS Dresdner Bank.* A German-language edition and commentary is available: OMGUS (Hans Magnus Erzensberger, ed.), *Ermittlungen gegen die Dresdner Bank,* Nordlingen: Greno, 1986. Additional OMGUS studies in U.S. archives include profiles of Reichs-Kredit-Gesellschaft (RG 260, OMGUS Office of Economic Affairs, OMG Berlin Sector, Finance Division, box 461, National Archives, Suitland, MD), Baron Kurt von Schroeder (box 230—available as offset printing plates), Kurt Schmitt—Allianz Insurance (box 233), Hjalmar Schacht (box 236), among others.

44. *OMGUS Deutsche Bank,* op. cit., p. 79; *OMGUS Dresdner Bank,* op. cit., p. 41.

45. On Allen Dulles: Allen Dulles and Hamilton Fish Armstrong, *Can We Be Neutral?* New York: Council on Foreign Relations/Harper, 1936; reissued in an updated volume, 1939. On Warburg: Eric War-

burg, *Zeiten und Gezeiten*. Hamburg: Hans Christians Druckerei, 1982.

46. For Schippel comment, U.S. Army Counter Intelligence Corps dossier no. XE14864-16D044, *Hans Schippel*, document 27, available via Freedom of Information Act from U.S. Army INSCOM, Ft. Meade, MD.

47. Gabriel Kolko, "American Business and Germany, 1930–1941," *Western Political Quarterly*, December 1962, pp. 713ff.

48. United Fruit trade in strategic materials with Germany: Caspar Menke to Reichswirtschaftsministerium, "Betr.: Sonderkonto der United Fruit Comp., Boston." Records of the Reich Ministry of Economics, microfilm publication T-71, roll 79, RG 242, National Archives, Washington, DC, frames 580823-37. See related correspondence at frames 580731-88, 580808-10, 580926.

49. Sullivan & Cromwell role in attempted purchase of American Potash and Chemical, relations with IG Farben subsidiary GAF, Lisagor and Lipsius, op. cit., pp. 136–39. John Foster Dulles represents Metallgesellschaft: Borkin, op. cit., pp. 168–70. Chester Lane comment: Chester Lane, Oral History, New York: Columbia University, pp. 435–38. For a summary by John Foster Dulles of the scope of, and loopholes in, U.S. regulation of foreign businesses during wartime, see John Foster Dulles, "The Vesting Powers of the Alien Property Custodian," *Cornell Law Quarterly*, March 1943, pp. 245ff. On the seizure of corporate properties in U.S.-German relations, see Hans-Dieter Kreikamp, *Deutsches Vermogen in den Vereinigten Staaten*, Stuttgart: Deutsche Verlag-Anstalt, 1979, pp. 20–43.

50. Werner Link, *Die amerikanische Stabilisierungspolitik in Deutschland 1921–1932*. Düsseldorf: Droste Verlag, 1970, pp. 562–74.

51. See, for example, Charles Maier, Stanley Hoffman, and Andrew Gould, *The Rise of the Nazi Regime, Historical Reassessments*. Boulder, CO: Westview, 1986; Richard Evans, *In Hitler's Shadow. West German Historians and the Attempt to Escape from the Nazi Past*. New York: Pantheon, 1989; or the well-known controversy between David Abraham, *The Collapse of the Weimar Republic*, 2nd ed. New York: Holmes and Meier, 1986, and Henry Ashby Turner, *German Big Business and the Rise of Hitler*. New York: Oxford Univ. Press, 1985.

Chapter Five

The Profits of Persecution

1. "Gesetz zur Wiederbestellung des Berufsbeamtentums," *Reichsgesetzblatt* (Berlin), April 7, 1933, teil 1, p. 175; "Erste Berordnung

zur Durchfuhrung des Gesetz zur Wiederbestellung des Berufsbeam-
tentums," *Reichsgesetzblatt* (Berlin), April 11, 1933, tiel 1, p. 195.
Summaries and commentary available in English at: World Jewish
Congress et al., *The Black Book. The Nazi Crime Against the Jewish
People.* New York: Nexus, 1981, pp. 470–80.

2. For example, Raul Hilberg, *The Destruction of the European Jews.*
New York: Harper, 1961. pp. 285–89, 323–45, 586–600, and passim.

3. Ibid., p. 60.

4. Ibid., pp. 60–90.

5. Ibid., p. 60.

6. Interview with Benjamin Ferencz, July 9, 1988.

7. Anne Bloch, "The Law," in World Jewish Congress et al., op. cit., pp.
88–89.

8. *OMGUS Dresdner Bank,* op. cit., p. 78.

9. Ibid., p. 79.

10. Rasche became a defendant in the "Ministries Case" at Nuremberg;
see *Trials of War Criminals Before the Nuernberg Military Tribunals
Under Control Council Law No 10.* Washington, DC: USGPO, 1949,
vols. 12, 13, 14 *passim,* for extensive discussion of his case. On
Pleiger, see: U.S. Office of Military Government for Germany (US)
[OMGUS], Finance Division, Financial Investigation Section, *Names
of Persons and Industrial Groups Affected by the Application of the
De-Nazification Program to Banks,* box 54, RG 260, National Archives, Suitland, MD, entry for Paul Pleiger (n.p.).

11. "Industrielle Besitzverlagerungen," *Frankfurter Handelsblatt—
Handelsteil der Frankfurter Zeitung,* June 21, 1936.

12. Ibid. On Freudenberg, see *OMGUS Deutsche Bank,* op. cit., pp.
297–99.

13. "Industrielle Besitzverlagerungen," op. cit. On Siemens Aryanizations discussed in footnote, see *OMGUS Deutsche Bank,* op. cit., pp.
155–56. The sector of the Siemens empire specializing in various
aspects of electronics production is organized into two main divisions, Siemens & Halske AG and Siemens-Schuckert AG, which between them controlled at least twelve major subsidiaries during the
1920s and 1930s. On the Siemens companies' use of forced labor:
Max Stein, "Report on the Employment of Slave Work by the Siemens
Concern During World War II," February 1961, in Benjamin Ferencz
papers.

14. Moody's Investors Service, *Moody's Manual of Investments. American and Foreign Industrial Securities.* New York: Moody's, 1936, p.
3028.

15. "Industrielle Besitzverlagerungen," op. cit.

16. Simon Reich, *The Fruits of Fascism. Postwar Prosperity in Historical Perspective.* Ithaca, NY: Cornell Univ. Press, 1990, p. 113.

17. For an extensive discussion on Ford's complex activities in Nazi Germany, see ibid., pp. 111–46, with Diestel dismissal at p. 114. On directors of Ford Motor Company AG (Germany), see *Moody's Manual of Investments*, 1936, op. cit., pp. 1283–84. On Bosch Aryanization: "Industrielle Besitzverlagerungen," op. cit.

18. Reich, op. cit., pp. 113–14.

19. Mira Wilkins, *The Maturing of Multinational Enterprise. American Business Abroad from 1914 to 1970.* Cambridge, MA: Harvard Univ. Press, 1974. pp. 186–87.

20. *Moody's Manual of Investments,* 1939, op. cit., pp. 1798, 1800, 1801, 1804, a113–a117, "Six-Year Price Range of Foreign Industrials" (blue section).

21. On Draper, see James Stewart Martin, *All Honorable Men.* Boston: Little, Brown, 1950, p. 206; on German Credit and Investment Corps' role at Dillon, Read, see Robert Sobel, *The Life and Times of Dillon, Read.* New York: Dutton, 1991, pp. 89, 105–106.

22. Wilkins, op. cit., p. 187 & fn.

23. Ibid., p. 185; and U.S. Department of Commerce, *American Direct Investment,* op. cit.

24. *OMGUS Deutsche Bank,* op. cit., p. 151.

25. Erhardt Schmidt testimony, exhibit 148; *OMGUS Deutsche Bank,* op. cit.

26. For material quoted in footnote, see Hjalmar Schacht (Diana Pyke, trans.), *Confessions of the Old Wizard.* Westport, CT: Greenwood, 1974, pp. 325–26, 415; for related comments see p. 427. The U.S. Army Intelligence and Security Command has released a small collection of materials concerning Schacht; see INSCOM file 528H075/1381 "Schacht, Hjalmar," available via Freedom of Information Act. The released INSCOM material is fragmentary, however, and fails to report much that is on the record concerning Schacht's trial for war crimes and business activities. The available material is so scanty that it suggests that INSCOM's main collection of intelligence on Schacht has thus far been lost or suppressed.

27. U.S., Office of the U.S. Chief of Counsel for Prosecution of Axis Criminality, *Nazi Conspiracy and Aggression* (the "red" series). Washington, DC: USGPO, 1946, vol. 2, p. 739; for Schacht's defense, see supplement B, pp. 501–43. Schacht was eventually acquitted by the tribunal (over objections by the USSR) largely on the grounds that

his most important service to the Nazi state had predated the outbreak of war in 1939, and was thus regarded as largely outside the
purview of the tribunal.

28. Guenter Keiser, *Der Juengste Konzentrationsprozess*, vol. 2 of *Die Wirtschaftskurve*, published by *Frankfurter Zeitung*, 1939. Transla-tion is by Anne Bloch in *The Black Book*, op. cit., pp. 93–94. For a detailed recent discussion of the Aryanization process, including several case studies, see Johannes Ludwig, *Boycott Enteignung Mord*, op. cit.

29. Keiser, ibid.

30. Walther Funk speech as published in *Frankfurter Zeitung*, November 17, 1938; see Nuremberg document no. 3545-PS, RG 238, National Archives, Washington, DC.

31. "The Deutsche Bank served as the main collecting agency for a spe-cial levy imposed upon the Jewish population of Berlin after the November 1938 pogroms. This account held in the branch office 'H' of the Deutsche Bank was called 'Wiedergutmachungskonto für die Schaeden Berlins' (Compensation account for the damages of Berlin). This account was opened by Werner Waechter and Erwin Koehnen, who served as trustees of the Reich for the collection of this fine." *OMGUS Deutsche Bank*, op. cit., p. 154.

32. Nora Levin, *The Holocaust*. New York: Schocken, 1973, pp. 86, 90.

33. Military spending estimate is from Burton Klein, *Germany's Eco-nomic Preparations for War*. Cambridge, MA: Harvard Univ. Press, 1959, p. 14 (table 5, group I).

34. Moody's Investors Service, *Moody's Manual of Investments. Ameri-can and Foreign Banks*. New York: Moody's, 1940, p. 801.

35. Moody's Investors Service, *Moody's Manual of Investments. Ameri-can and Foreign Industrial Securities*. New York: Moody's, 1939, p. 1804.

36. Nuremberg document no. PS-5375, RG 238, National Archives, Washington, DC, cited in Levin, op. cit., p. 723, n6. For more detailed discussion of the economics of German rearmament, see Klein, op. cit., and Barton Whaley, *German Covert Rearmament 1919–1939: Deception and Misperception*. Frederick, MD: University Publica-tions, 1984.

37. Arthur Schweitzer, *Big Business in the Third Reich*. Bloomington, IN: Indiana Univ. Press, 1964, p. 86.

38. Henry Ashby Turner, *German Big Business and the Rise of Hitler*. New York: Oxford Univ. Press, 1985, p. 252.

39. Eric Warburg, *Zeiten und Gezeiten*. Hamburg: Hans Christians Druc-kerei, 1982, pp. 292–93.

40. Wilhelm Treue, "Widerstand von Unternehmern und Nationalokono- men," in Jürgen Schmadeke and Peter Steinback, *Der Widerstand gegen den Nationalsozialismus.* Munich: Piper, 1986, pp. 917–37.

41. Simon Wiesenthal Center (Los Angeles), "Wiesenthal Center De- mands Resignation of Hermann J. Abs, Hitler's Leading Banker, from Vatican Bank," press release with documentary exhibits, Decem- ber 29, 1982; copy in author's collection. For typical news coverage: Jay Mathews, "Vatican Advisor Accused by Center of Nazi Links," *Washington Post,* December 30, 1982. Abs was eventually barred by the U.S. Justice Department from traveling to the United States; see: "Abs darf nicht in die USA," *Frankfurter Abendpost,* May 7, 1990.

42. On Austrian measures as a model for Nazi persecution; see Hans Safrian and Hans Witek, *Und keiner war dabei: Dokumente des all- taglichen Antisemitismus in Wien 1938.* Wien: Picus Verlag, 1988, pp. 95–157 passim; Levin, op. cit., pp. 101–10; Christopher Simp- son, *Blowback.* New York: Weidenfeld and Nicolson, 1988, pp. 348– 49, sn22.

43. *OMGUS Deutsche Bank,* op. cit., p. 187. On Deutsche Bank's earlier attempts to take control of Creditanstalt, see David Kaiser, *Economic Diplomacy and the Origins of the Second World War.* Princeton, NJ: Princeton Univ. Press, 1980, pp. 35–41.

44. *OMGUS Deutsche Bank,* op. cit., pp. 189–90; *OMGUS Deutsche Bank Annex,* op. cit., pp. 23–25.

45. *OMGUS Deutsche Bank,* op. cit., pp. 189–93.

46. On ideological struggle: OMGUS, *Ermittlungen gegen die Dresdner Bank,* op. cit., pp. xlii–xlv; Klein, op. cit., pp. 35–55 passim; Arno Mayer, *Why Did the Heavens Not Darken?* New York: Pantheon, 1988, pp. 156–57.

47. *OMGUS Deutsche Bank Annex,* op. cit., p. 23; quotation is from the language of the report.

48. Loc. cit.; quotation is from Keppler.

49. Ibid., p. 24.

50. *OMGUS Deutsche Bank,* op. cit., pp. 53–54. One noteworthy new Creditanstalt director was Hans Fischböck, the German-appointed finance and economics minister of post-*Anschluss* Austria. Fischböck went on to make a career in expropriations in Austria and the Netherlands, where he was eventually charged with war crimes by the Dutch government. For background, see Safrian and Witek, op. cit., pp. 97–98; Dietrich Orlow, *The Nazis in the Balkans.* Pittsburgh, PA: Univ. of Pittsburgh Press, 1968, pp. 31–32, 187.

51. *OMGUS Deutsche Bank,* op. cit., pp. 53–54.

52. "Übersicht über die von der Kontrollbank durchgefuhrten Aris-ierungsfalle," reproduced in Safrian and Witek, op. cit., pp. 143–57. Thanks to Hans Safrian for bringing this document to my attention.

53. *OMGUS Deutsche Bank*, op. cit., p. 191; see also pp. 49–50, 171–74, 187–95. For data concerning Aryanizations in Vienna discussed in footnote, see "Übersicht über die von der Kontrollbank . . ." in Safrian, op. cit.

54. Cited in Levin, op. cit., p. 99.

55. Ibid., pp. 97–98.

Chapter Six

"Who Still Talks of the Armenians?"

1. Martin Weinmann (ed.), *Das nationalsozialistische Lagersystem.* Frankfurt a/M: Zweitausendeins, 1990, pp. xiii–xvi; Joachim Remak (ed.), *The Nazi Years, A Documentary History.* New York: Simon and Schuster, 1969, pp. 133–43; Nora Levin, *The Holocaust.* New York: Schocken, 1973, pp. 301–305.

2. Poland, Ministerstwo Informacji (Polish Ministry of Information, London), *The German New Order in Poland.* London: Hutchinson, 1942, pp. 71, 79–80.

3. Ibid., pp. 28–75, 219–21, 235–36. See also: Poland, Central Commission for Investigation of German Crimes in Poland, *German Crimes in Poland.* New York: Howard Fertig, 1982.

4. Biddle to Secretary of State, August 13, 1942, 740.00116 EW 1939/527, RG 59, National Archives, Washington, DC.

5. Richard Breiting (Edouard Calic, ed.), *Secret Conversations with Hitler. The Two Newly Discovered 1931 Interviews.* New York: John Day, 1971, p. 81.

6. U.S., Office of United States Chief of Counsel for Prosecution of Axis Criminality, *Nazi Conspiracy and Aggression*, vol. 3. Washington, DC: USGPO, 1946, p. 753.

7. Adolf Hitler, *Hitler's Secret Conversations 1941–1944.* New York: Farrar, Straus and Young, 1953, pp. 188, 317, 493.

8. Gerhard Hirschfeld, "Chronology of Destruction" in Gerhard Hirschfeld (ed.), *The Policies of Genocide. Jews and Soviet Prisoners of War in Nazi Germany.* London: Allen & Unwin/German Historical Institute, 1986.

9. Yehuda Bauer, "When Did They Know?" *Midstream*, April 1968, pp. 51–58.

10. John Mendelsohn (ed.), *The Holocaust: The Wannsee Protocol and a*

1944 Report on Auschwitz. New York: Garland, 1982, reproduces Nuremberg document no. NG-2586, a reporter's summary of the gathering.

11. Ibid.

12. For Eichmann's recollections of the Wannsee Conference: *Life*, November 28, 1960, pp. 24, 101.

13. See for example, "Terror Against Jews," *Times* (London) December 7, 1942, which reports in part that "In all parts of Europe the Germans are calling meetings, or issuing orders, to bring about what they call 'the final solution of the Jewish problem.' " The *Times* report is discussed in: Winant to Secretary of State, December 7, 1942, 740.00116 EW 1939/692, box 2917, RG 59, National Archives, Washington, DC. Eichmann discusses use of term "Final Solution" in Jochen von Lang (ed.), *Eichmann Interrogated.* New York: Farrar, Straus & Giroux, 1983, pp. 73, 131.

14. Nurenberg document no. NG-2586, RG 238, National Archives, Washington, DC.

15. Gerhard Hirschfeld, "Chronology of Destruction" op. cit., pp. 150–53.

16. Ibid.

17. Raul Hilberg, *The Destruction of the European Jews.* New York: Harper, 1961, p. 623.

18. Walter Lacqueur and Richard Breitman, *Breaking the Silence.* New York: Simon and Schuster, 1986, pp. 106–13.

19. Ibid., pp. 67, 72–73, 101.

20. "Memorandum of Conversation," September 7, 1942, 740.00116 EW 1939/543 (attachment), box 2916, RG 59, National Archives, Washington, DC.

21. Biddle to Secretary of State, August 13, 1942, 740.00116 EW 1939/527, RG 59, National Archives, Washington, DC. See also *The German New Order in Poland*, op. cit.

22. Harvey Sachs, "Der Ordinare," *New Yorker*, June 4, 1990.

23. Dietrich Eichholtz, *Geschichte der deutschen Kriegswirtschaft 1939–1945*, band II. Berlin: Akademie-Verlag, 1985, pp. 220–22; see also pp. 187, 189, 225.

24. Sachs, op. cit. There were reportedly about 8,000 prisoners in Auschwitz in late 1940, most of them Poles and Polish Jews. See Gerhard Hirschfeld, op. cit., pp. 150–51.

25. Albert Speer (Joachim Neugroschel, trans.), *Infiltration.* New York: Macmillan, 1981, p. 23. See also Eichholtz, op. cit., p. 225. See Joseph Billig, *Les Camps de Concentration dans l'Economie du Reich*

Hitlerien. Paris: Presses Universitaires de France, 1973, pp. 136–221, for an extensive report concerning SS economic enterprises. In addition to providing labor for the private sector, the SS in-house companies produced war materiel for SS troops and engaged in mining, heavy construction, brickmaking, and cement work associated with prisons, civil defense, and military installations. The SS companies also provided most of the labor for building the concentration camps, including the installation of gas chambers. For an excellent resource for locating forced labor centers, see Weinmann, *Das nationalsozialistische Lagersystem,* op. cit.

26. Rudolf Hoess (Auschwitz commandant) affidavit, March 12, 1947, Nuremberg document no. NI-4434-A, RG 238, National Archives, Washington, DC. Also available at Benjamin Ferencz, *Less Than Slaves.* Cambridge, MA: Harvard Univ. Press, 1979. pp. 202–204.

27. Eichholtz, op. cit., p. 225.

28. Ibid., pp. 225–26.

29. Karl Sommer affidavit, October 4, 1946, Nuremberg document no. NI-1065, National Archives microfilm collection T-301, roll 10, frames 001126ff.

30. U.S., Strategic Bombing Survey, *The Effects of Strategic Bombing on the German War Economy,* reports on the European War, no. 3. Washington, DC, October 31, 1945, p. 214, table 12; and Eichholtz, op. cit., pp. 245–47.

   For data in footnote, see Edward Homze, *Foreign Labor in Nazi Germany.* Princeton, NJ: Princeton Univ. Press, 1967, pp. 152–53. For an important early work on this subject, see John Fried, *The Exploitation of Foreign Labor by Germany.* Montreal: International Labor Office, 1945. Probably the most complete discussion of the subject thus far is Ulrich Herbert, *Fremdarbeiter: Politik und Praxis des 'Auslander-einsatzes' in der Kriegswirtschaft des Dritten Reiches.* Berlin: Verlag J.H.W. Dietz, 1985.

   For examples of corporate evasion and suppression of evidence concerning exploitation of forced laborers, see Karl-Heinz Roth and Michael Schmid, *Die Daimler-Benz AG 1916–1948. Schlusseldokumente zur Konzerngeschichte.* Nordlingen: Delphi, 1987, doc. no. 143, 145, 146, 147, pp. 374–91; and Hamburger Stiftung zur Foerderung von Wissenschaft und Kultur, *Industrie, Behoerden und Konzentrationslager 1938–1945. Reaktionen 1988–1989.* Hamburg: Hamburger Stiftung zur Foerderung von Wissenschaft und Kultur, 1989. In English, see Benjamin Ferencz, op. cit., for detailed discussion of efforts to obtain restitution for Jewish forced laborers, usually in the face of intense corporate opposition. IG Farben, which was particularly notorious for destroying records, was discovered to have pulped "tons of documentary evidence ... principally concerned with various phases of the administration of the Oswiecim (Auschwitz) concentration camp" when several IG Farben directors were on trial for war crimes and crimes against humanity in 1947; see John Alan Appleman, *Military Tribunals and International Crimes*. Westport, CT: Greenwood, 1971, p. 179.

31. Ferencz, op. cit., pp. 56–57.

32. Edward Zilbert, *Albert Speer and the Nazi Ministry of Arms*. London: Associated Univ. Presses, 1981, p. 111. See also Zilbert's study: RAND Corporation (Edward Zilbert), *The Development of Hauptausschusse und Ringe in the German War Economy*. RAND publication P 3649. Santa Monica, CA: RAND, 1967.

33. Ferencz, op. cit.

34. International Military Tribunal, *Trial of the Major War Criminals Before the International Military Tribunal*, Nuremberg: 1947, vol. 3, p. 440. This is cited hereafter as *International Military Tribunal*.

35. Bohdan Wytwycky, *The Other Holocaust*. Washington, DC: Novak Report, 1980, p. 49.

36. Arno Mayer, *Why Did the Heavens Not Darken? The Final Solution in History*. New York: Pantheon, 1988. pp. 310–12.

37. For a vivid example of this structure at the network of Krupp factories at Essen, see William Manchester, *The Arms of Krupp*. New York: Bantam, 1970, pp. 535–66. For contemporary German documentation in which Speer's ministry advertises the use of foreign labor in publications designed for German industrialists and economists, see Hauptausschuss Maschinen (ed.), *Einsatz von Östarbeitern in der deutschen Maschinenindustrie*. Essen: Bucherverlag W. Girardet, 1943; captured German records collection T-73 (Records of Reichsministerium für Rustung und Kriegsproduktion), roll 187, frame 3400898 ff. See Christa Rotzoll, "Östarbeiter im Lager und in der Fabrik," *Das Reich*, November 21, 1943, for a glowing presentation of "guestworkers" as they appeared in Nazi propaganda; contrast this with "Die Juden mussen arbeiten!" *Illustrierter Beobachter*, October 12, 1939, with photos depicting obviously sadistic penal labor for Jews in Poland in the wake of the Nazi invasion.

38. *International Military Tribunal*, vol. 3, p. 435.

39. For shipment of women, see *International Military Tribunal*, vol. 3, pp. 436–37. On murder of Ukrainian children, see Homze, op. cit., pp. 160–61. For material in footnote, see ibid., pp. 165–67, and Edgar Howell, *The Soviet Partisan Movement 1941–1944*. Department of the Army pamphlet 20-244, 1956, p. 107.

40. The estimate of casualties among forced laborers is the author's. No

complete statistics are known to exist, but some indication of the level of the carnage can be gleaned from the difference between the Sauckel and the Speer statistics discussed in the text. If they are roughly accurate, about three million forced laborers were "replaced" between 1942 and 1944 alone. Some of these workers escaped, and a small number were returned home or disappeared from government rolls in other ways. Considering, however, that particularly brutal forced labor had been under way in the occupied Eastern territories since 1939, and that the death rate among forced workers sharply escalated during the winter of 1944–45, the estimate of three million deaths among laborers seems conservative. For notes on sources for estimates, see Homze, op. cit., pp. 152–53.

41. Internationaler Suchdienst (International Red Cross), *Verzeichnis der Haftstatten unter dem Reichsführer-SS 1933–1945.* Geneva: International Red Cross, 1979, p. xx. An excellent and more easily available resource on this subject is Weinmann, op. cit. For a valuable study of forced labor in the Berlin region, with emphasis on the role of AEG, Siemens, and other electrical manufacturers, see Laurenz Demps and Reinhard Holzer, "Zwangsarbeiter und Zwangsarbeiterlager in der faschistischen Reichshauptstadt Berlin 1939–1945," *Miniaturen zur Geschichte, Kultur und Denkmalpflege Berlins*, no. 20/21, Berlin 1986.

42. Internationaler Suchdienst, ibid.; for Pohl report to Himmler on structure of the camp system, see Nuremberg documents no. NO-020(a) and NO-020(b), RG 238, National Archives, Washington, DC. For Pohl's April 1942 estimate of the number of prisoners in the six largest camps and his plans for further expansion, see Nuremberg document no. R-129.

43. Manchester, op. cit., pp. 535–664, with discussion of Krupp police at 538-40 and passim, and of numbers of camps at p. 553.

44. Ibid., p. 554.

45. Jaeger quote: *International Military Tribunal* vol. 3, p. 443.

46. Ian Kershaw, *Popular Opinion and Political Dissent in the Third Reich.* Oxford: Clarendon Press, 1983, pp. 368–70; "Nazis Blame Jews for Big Bombings," *New York Times*, June 13, 1942, p. 7; Joseph Goebbels, "Der Luft- und Nervenkrieg," *Das Reich*, (Berlin), June 14, 1942.

47. George Quester, *Deterrence Before Hiroshima. The Airpower Background of Modern Strategy.* New York: John Wiley, 1966, p. 142. Widely accepted estimates put German fatalities from Allied bombing at about 500,000; see James Taylor and Warren Shaw, *Dictionary of the Third Reich.* London: Grafton, 1987, p. 322.

48. Roosevelt statement: U.S. Department of State *Bulletin*, vol. 1, 1939, p. 181.

For discussion of the development of international law and custom concerning aerial warfare, see *Inquiry Handbooks*, vol. 3, *Selected Topics Connected with the Laws of Warfare as of August 1, 1914*, pp. 580–609, including excerpts from the Hague conventions of 1899 and 1907, with commentaries; "1923 Hague Rules of Aerial Warfare," in Adam Roberts and Richard Guelff (eds.), *Documents on the Laws of War*, 2nd ed. Oxford: Clarendon, 1989, pp. 121–35, with historical commentaries; J. M. Spaight, *Air Power and War Rights*. London: Longmans, Green, 1924; M. W. Royce, *Aerial Bombardment and the International Regulation of Warfare*. New York: Harold Vinal, 1928.

49. Jay Baird, *The Mythical World of Nazi War Propaganda, 1939–1945*. Minneapolis, MN: Univ. of Minnesota Press, 1974, pp. 101, 120–29, 134–35. Baird stresses German pledges to retaliate against Britain as such, but note Goebbels's use of British attacks to pledge extermination of Jews: Joseph Goebbels, "Der Luft- und Nervenkrieg," *Das Reich* (Berlin), June 14, 1942.

50. John Kenneth Galbraith lecture, "Sifting the Rubble: The Strategic Bombing Surveys." National Air and Space Museum, Washington, DC, September 6, 1990. Galbraith was the director of the economic aspects of the Strategic Bombing Survey research.

51. Ibid.

52. Comments by Ramsey Potts, Lord Solly Zuckerman, and David MacIsaac, "Sifting the Rubble . . . , op. cit.

53. Joseph Goebbels, "Der Luft- und Nervenkrieg," *Das Reich*, (Berlin), June 14, 1942; "Nazis Blame Jews for Big Bombings," *New York Times*, June 13, 1942, p. 7.

54. Ohlendorf, cited at Hilberg, op. cit., p. 695. Roughly similar defenses against Allied war crimes charges were offered by dozens of Nazis and SS men after the war but were consistently rejected by Allied tribunals.

55. See, for example, Nicolas Nazarenko speech quoted in Simpson, *Blowback*, op. cit., pp. 274–75.

56. Kershaw, op. cit., p. 369.

57. Loc. cit.

58. Ibid., pp. 369–70.

59. See, for example, Martin Gilbert, *Auschwitz and the Allies*. New York: Holt, Rinehart & Winston, 1981, pp. 299–311.

60. On air raid deaths among prisoners at Krupp: Manchester, op. cit., pp. 561–64; deaths at Heinkel: Gerhard Finn, *Sachsenhausen 1936–1950*. Bonn: Urheber, 1985, p. 22.

61. Martin Caidin, *The Night Hamburg Died*. New York: Ballantine, 1960, pp. 25–26.

62. Hamburger Stiftung zur Foerderung von Wissenschaft und Kultur, *Industrie, Behoerden und Konzentrationslager 1938–1945, Reaktionen 1988–1989*, op. cit.; Weinmann, op. cit., pp. 93, 492–94.

63. Weinmann, loc. cit.

64. Ibid., pp. 199–203, 223–29, 260, 564.

65. Ford plant at Cologne (Köln): *Bundesgesetzblatt*, September 9, 1977; and Karl Sommer affidavit, October 4, 1946, Nuremberg document no. NI-1065, National Archives microfilm collection T-301, roll 10, frames 001126ff. The GM-Opel plant at Russelsheim was converted to aircraft engine production for Junkers JU-88 bombers. Buchenwald supplied prison labor for all such production; see Weinmann, op. cit., pp. 923–24.

66. The GM-Opel plant at Brandenburg built three-ton "Blitz" trucks: see "American Ground Transport" and GM's reply, U.S. Congress, Senate, Committee on the Judiciary, Subcommittee on Antitrust and Monopoly, *The Industrial Reorganization Act, S, 1,167*, part 4A, 93rd Congress, 2nd session, 1974. Washington, DC: USGPO, p. A–21. The Sachsenhausen and Ravensbrück concentration camps appear to have supplied labor for the principal armament plants in Brandenberg; see Weinmann, op. cit., pp. 259, 576. On Ford's role in Germany: Simon Reich, *The Fruits of Fascism. Postwar Prosperity in Historical Perspective*, Ithaca, NY: Cornell Univ. Press, 1990, pp. 117–46, with discussion of use of POWs at pp. 121–22, 127.

67. Christian Streit, "The German Army and the Policies of Genocide," in Hirschfeld, *Policies of Genocide*, op. cit., pp. 15–29. The invasion of the USSR appears to have been the transit point where earlier Nazi policies of persecution and "cold pogroms" became a campaign of more direct and modern forms of extermination. It was here that the Nazis' ideology of extreme anticommunism became a seemingly acceptable rationale for tens of thousands of people to participate in the anti-Semitic mass murder programs that have come to be known as the Holocaust. "The infamous mobile execution units, the *Einsatzgruppen*, spearheaded the racial warfare in East Central Europe," writes Wolfgang Mommsen. At the same time, "the German Army allowed itself to become increasingly implicated in the sinister activities of the *Einsatzgruppen*. An important factor in this was that the military leadership in general accepted the National Socialist propaganda regarding the Soviet people . . . especially the radical anti-Semitic message that the Jews were largely responsible for communism. The *Wehrmacht* therefore put up little, if any, resistance to the idea that the war against Soviet Russia should be conducted as a racial war with the virtual annihiliation of

the enemy, or at least of its leadership cadres, as a 'legitimate' objective." See Wolfgang Mommsen, ibid., p. xii.

68. For discussion of attitudes of the "Riga Axioms" group toward the USSR, see Yergin, op. cit., pp. 17–41. For a sophisticated Western view of Soviet attitudes concerning international law during this period, particularly on war crimes and related issues, see T. A. Taracouzio, *The Soviet Union and International Law*. New York: Macmillan, 1935 (New York: Kraus Reprint, 1972), pp. 311–42. See also author's interview with John Hazard, June 7, 1991. In general, Taracouzio and other Western legal observers saw Soviet critiques and reservations on international law (which were based largely on Leninist doctrine) as indications of Soviet dishonesty, ill-intent, or at best unpredictability. Most Western commentators saw the reservations raised by the U.S. and other more conventional powers (which were based largely on contemporary versions of "realist" doctrines) as much less threatening—and, in fact, to be expected. Soviet commentaries suggest roughly parallel but opposite attitudes. See ibid., pp. 411–22. For similar Soviet arguments from a later period, see Ivan Artsibasov, *In Disregard of the Law*. Moscow: Progress, 1982, pp. 9–61.

69. Quoted at Daniel Yergin, *Shattered Peace: The Origins of the Cold War and the National Security State*. Boston: Houghton Mifflin, 1977, p. 40.

Chapter Seven
No Action Required

1. On Breckinridge Long: U.S. Department of the Treasury (Randolph Paul), *Report to the Secretary on the Acquiescence of this Government in the Murder of the Jews*, Jan. 13, 1944, Morgenthau *Diaries*, vol. 693, pp. 212–29 passim, Franklin D. Roosevelt Library, Hyde Park, NY; David Wyman, *The Abandonment of the Jews*. New York: Pantheon, 1984, pp. 80, 153, 190–98; David Wyman, *Paper Walls: America and the Refugee Crisis 1938–1941*. New York: Pantheon, 1985, pp. 146, 173–74; Arthur Morse, *While Six Million Died*. Woodstock, NY: Overlook Press, 1983, pp. 32–33, 38–42.

2. On James Clement Dunn: see Randolph Paul, ibid., p. 224. Harley Notter, *Postwar Foreign Policy Preparation, 1939–1945*. Department of State publication no. 3580. Washington, DC: USGPO, 1949.

3. Robert Murphy, *Diplomat Among Warriors*. Garden City, NY: Doubleday, 1964; on Murphy's rivalry with Morgenthau: John Morton Blum,

From the Morgenthau Diaries. Years of War 1941–1945. Boston: Houghton Mifflin, 1967, pp. 417–19 passim.

4. On Joseph Grew: Daniel Yergin, *Shattered Peace: The Origins of the Cold War and the National Security State.* Boston: Houghton Mifflin, 1977, pp. 18, 87–96.

5. On Green Hackworth: for a biographical summary, see *National Cyclopedia of American Biography,* vol. 57, p. 110, *Current Biography 1958,* pp. 181–82, and the introductory notes to Green Hackworth, *Digest of International Law,* vol. 1, Department of State publication no. 1506, Washington, DC: USGPO, 1940; reprint, New York, Garland Publishing, 1973. For a critical assessment of Hackworth's role in the development of U.S. war crimes policy, see Herbert Pell, *Oral History,* Columbia University, 1951, pp. 584–603. For Hackworth's role in vetoing an OSS psychological warfare plan against Nazi atrocities, see Hackworth to Berle, February 10, 1943, and Berle to Wilson (OSS), February 11, 1943, 740.00116 EW 1939/794, box 2917; Stettinius to FDR, November 4, 1943, 740.00116 EW 1939/1143, with attachments, box 2920; both in RG 59, National Archives, Washington, DC.

6. On Loy Henderson: Yergin, op. cit., pp. 26–27, 29; Loy Henderson, *Oral History,* Columbia University, 1972, pp. 1–6.

7. On Matthews: Yergin, op. cit., pp. 170, 443, sn21; H. Freeman Matthews, *Oral History Interview,* Harry S Truman Library, Independence, MO, 1976.

8. On John Hickerson: see Randolph Paul, op. cit., p. 224; John Hickerson, *Oral History,* November 10, 1972, January 26, 1973, and June 5, 1973, Harry S Truman Library, Independence, MO; "John Hickerson, Ambassador to 2 Nations, Dies," *Washington Post,* January 19, 1989.

9. On R. Borden Reams: Reams to Hickerson, December 9, 1942, 740.00116 EW 1939/694, box 2917, RG 59, National Archives, Washington, DC; David Wyman, *The Abandonment of the Jews,* op. cit., pp. 73–75, 99, 112–13.

10. On Elbridge Durbrow: see Randolph Paul, op. cit., p. 224; Hull to Biddle, 740.00116 EW 1939/1052, box 2920, and Durbrow to Hackworth, December 14, 1943, 740.00116 EW 1939/1187, box 2921, RG 59, National Archives, Washington, DC; see also Elbridge Durbrow, *Oral History,* May 31, 1973, Harry S Truman Library, Independence, MO.

11. Harvey diary cited in Tom Bower, *Blind Eye to Murder.* London: Granada, 1983, p. 44.

12. *UNWCC and the Laws of War,* op. cit., pp. 87–88.

13. Ibid., pp. 89–92.

14. Ibid., p. 92.

15. Cited in Bower, op. cit., p. 46.

16. Wyman, *The Abandonment of the Jews,* op. cit.

17. Bower, op. cit., pp. 47–51.

18. Ibid.

19. Ibid., p. 46.

20. The account of the Riegner telegram that follows is indebted to studies by Walter Lequeur and Richard Breitman, *Breaking the Silence.* New York: Simon and Schuster, 1986, pp. 143–63; Arthur Morse, *Six Million,* op. cit., pp. 3–36; Bower, op. cit., pp. 46–52; David Wyman, *The Abandonment of the Jews,* op. cit., pp. 42–58.

21. Durbrow memorandum, August 13, 1942, 862.4016/2235, RG 59, National Archives, Washington, DC.

22. Winant to the President, August 5, 1942 (Secret), can be located as an attachment to December 9, 1942, Stanton memo, 740.00116 EW 1939/693, box 2917, RG 59, National Archives, Washington, DC.

23. Berle to Secretary of State, June 22, 1942, 740.00116 EW 1939/502, box 2916, RG 59, National Archives, Washington, DC.

24. Bower, op. cit., pp. 49–51. On Lippmann and Sweetser's earlier role: Walter Lippmann, "The Peace Conference," *Yale Review,* July 1919, pp. 711ff, and Walworth op. cit., p. 138, 69n; and Steel, *Walter Lippmann and the American Century,* op. cit., pp. 128–70.

25. Bower, op. cit., pp. 47–49.

26. Loc. cit.

27. "A Proposal for a United Nations Commission on Atrocities" (Secret), attached to December 9, 1942, Stanton memo, 740.00116 EW 1939/693, box 2917, RG 59, National Archives, Washington, DC. See also Aide Memoire, September 7, 1942, 740.00116 EW 1939/557, box 2916, RG 59, National Archives, Washington, DC.

28. Winant to Secretary of State, October 6, 1942, 740.00116 EW 1939/574, box 2916, RG 59, National Archives, Washington, DC.

29. *UNWCC and the Laws of War,* op. cit., pp. 105–106; Bower, op. cit., p. 58.

30. Bower, op. cit., p. 80.

31. Hilberg, op. cit., p. 266; Wyman, *The Abandonment of the Jews,* op. cit., p. 53.

32. Winant to Secretary of State, December 7, 1942, 740.00116 EW 1939/692, box 2917, RG 59, National Archives, Washington, DC.

33. "Wise Says Hitler Has Ordered 4,000,000 Jews Slain in 1942" and "Himmler Order Reported," *New York Herald Tribune,* November 25, 1942.

34. *UNWCC and the Laws of War,* op. cit., pp. 94–99.

35. Ibid. The doctrine of humanitarian intervention is a traditional exception to the exclusive domestic jurisdiction of states over their nationals that can be traced to the seventeenth-century legal theorist Hugo Grotius, among others. As a practical matter, however, by 1939 this precedent had been so widely abused as a pretext for military aggression that very few of the international-law experts of the day considered the doctrine to be sufficiently robust to provide an effective foundation for prosecution of the types of crimes central to Nazi rule. For background, see Raymond Robin, *Des Occupations Militaires en Dehours des Occupations de Guerre.* Paris, 1913, and Washington, DC: Carnegie Endowment, 1942. For examples of continuing controversy over the legal utility of theories of humanitarian intervention, see Ian Brownlie, "Humanitarian Intervention," and Richard Lillich, "Humanitarian Intervention: A Reply to Dr. Brownlie," in John Norton Moore (ed.), *Law and Civil War in the Modern World.* Baltimore: Johns Hopkins Univ. Press, 1974; and Richard Falk (ed.), *The International Law of Civil War.* Baltimore: Johns Hopkins Univ. Press, 1971.

36. Ibid., p. 99–104. For background on Glueck, see *Contemporary Authors,* vol. 5, pp. 445–46; Sheldon Glueck, *War Criminals. Their Prosecution and Punishment.* New York: Knopf, 1944, and *The Nuremberg Trial and Aggressive War.* New York: Knopf, 1964. In addition to his work concerning war crimes, Glueck's specialty was the study of juvenile delinquency.

37. *UNWCC and the Laws of War,* pp. 100–104; Glueck, op. cit., *Criminals,* pp. 11–18.

38. *UNWCC and the Laws of War,* pp. 100–104.

39. Loc. cit.

40. Ibid., p. 100.

41. Wyman, *The Abandonment of the Jews,* op. cit., p. 44; Hull to Bern August 17, 1942, 862.4016/2235, RG 59, National Archives, Washington, DC.

42. Wyman, *The Abandonment of the Jews,* op. cit., p. 51.

43. Loc. cit.; also, "Wise Says Hitler Has Ordered 4,000,000 Jews Slain in 1942" and "Himmler Order Reported," *New York Herald Tribune,* November 5, 1942.

44. McDermott (Division of Current Information) to Editor, *Christian*

Century, Chicago, November 25, 1942, 740.00116 EW 1939/656, box 2917, RG 59, National Archives, Washington, DC.

45. British record: British Foreign Office FO 371 30923/C11923, December 2, 1942, Public Record Office, London; and Bower, op. cit., p. 63. U.S. record: Clattenberg to Breckinridge Long, November 11, 1943, 740.00116 EW 1939/1249 (cover note), box 2921, RG 59, National Archives, Washington, DC.

46. Reproduced at Bower, op. cit., p. 64.

47. Reams memorandum to Hickerson and Atherton, December 9, 1942, 740.00116 EW 1939/694, with attachments, box 2917, RG 59, National Archives, Washington, DC.

48. Reams memorandum to Hickerson and Atherton, December 10, 1942, attached to ibid.

49. Reams to Hickerson and Atherton, ibid.

50. "Practical measures": *UNWCC and the Laws of War*, op. cit., p. 111.

51. Achilles comment: Stanton memo, December 9, 1942, 740.00116 EW 1939/693, box 2917, RG 59, National Archives, Washington, DC. See also Theodore Achilles, *Oral History*, November 13 and December 18, 1972, Harry S Truman Library, Independence, MO.

Chapter Eight

Katyn

1. See, for example, Sergo Mikoyan comments to Smithsonian Institution Wilson Center Colloquium, June 10, 1991; or Eva Seeber, *Die Machte der Antihitlerkoalition und die Auseinandersetzung um Polen und die CSR 1941–1945*. Berlin: Akademie-Verlag, 1984, pp. 35–43. A similar trend is clearly manifest in the Anglo-Russian agreements of June 1942; see "Text of British White Paper, Including the Anglo-Russian Twenty-Year Treaty," *New York Times*, June 12, 1942.

2. Germany, *Massenmord in Winniza*, n.d.; Alfred de Zayas, *The Wehrmacht War Crimes Bureau*. Lincoln, NE: Univ. of Nebraska Press, 1989, pp. 162–80, 240–44.

3. Turner Catledge, "Our Policy Stated in Nazi-Soviet War," *New York Times*, June 24, 1941. For *Wall Street Journal* editorial cam paign opposing aid to the USSR in the wake of the German invasion: "When Thieves Fall Out" (June 24), "Tweedledum and Tweedle-dee" (June 25), "Aid for the Comrades" (June 26), "Here We Can Be Practical" (June 28), "Tweedledum and Tweedledee" (July 2), all in 1941.

4. Henderson to Secretary of State, October 20, 1942, 740.00116 EW 1939/616, box 2917, RG 59, National Archives, Washington, DC.

5. See, for example, Henderson to Secretary of State, November 26, 1942, 740.00116 EW 1939/655, box 2917, RG 59, National Archives, Washington, DC.

6. Loc. cit.

7. Loc. cit.

8. For the "official" version of the Darlan affair, see Murphy, op. cit., pp. 109–43. For a more critical perspective, see Gabriel Kolko, *The Politics of War*. New York: Random House, 1968, pp. 64–69. On the psychological warfare aspects of the Darlan affair, the unconditional surrender pledge, and their linkage to East-West confidence building, see Richard H. S. Crossman, "Supplementary Essay," in Daniel Lerner, *Psychological Warfare Against Nazi Germany*, Cambridge: MIT Press, 1971 (reissue of 1949 text titled *The Sykewar Campaign*).

9. Richard Harris Smith, *OSS*. Berkeley, CA: Univ. of California Press, 1972, pp. 36–67 passim.

10. Kolko, op. cit., p. 110.

11. Richard Harris Smith, *OSS* op. cit., p. 214.

12. Ibid., p. 213.

13. "Aufzeichung über Aussprachen mit Mr. Bull [Dulles] und Mr. Roberts [Edmond Taylor]," National Archives microfilm of captured German records T-175, reel 458, frames 2975007-2975043.

   Western historians have typically ignored or played down the significance of the Dulles/Hohenlohe encounters. A copy of Hohenlohe's reports was captured and eventually made public by the Soviets in an effort to discredit Dulles after the war, and for that reason it has been occasionally denounced in the West as a forgery. In fact, however, the Hohenlohe reports are authentic; the U.S. Army captured its own set of the same documents, and those papers are today available in U.S. archives at the citation above.

14. Ibid.

15. Edmond Taylor, *The Strategy of Terror*. Boston: Houghton Mifflin, 1940. See pp. 40–41 for Taylor's published views on anti-Semitism and pp. 111–13 on German use of "peace offensive" tactics. Taylor's book was republished in an updated version in 1942 by Pocket Books; see pp. 270–71 for Taylor's views on factions within U.S. government.

16. Dulles's claim of splitting tactics: OSS Headquarters to Bern, April 26, 1943 (Secret), file "D27 Bern Out June 42–Oct. 43," Wash Reg. R&C-56, box 165, entry 134, RG 226, National Archives, Washington, DC. Hohenlohe and Schellenberg's claims: "Aufzeichung über Aus-

sprachen mit Mr. Bull [Dulles] und Mr. Roberts [Edmond Taylor]," op. cit., and Walter Schellenberg, *Hitler's Secret Service* (originally titled *The Labyrinth*). New York: Pyramid, 1958, pp. 369–83 passim.

17. See, for example: Dulles to OSS Headquarters and to Secretary of State, April 7, 1943 (Secret), IN D27 #1 June 42–July 43, box 171, entry 134, RG 226, National Archives, Washington, DC. Dulles's most frequent argument was that if the U.S. failed to act, there were "powerful elements" among the Nazis who "are prepared to cast their lot with Russia on the theory that a Communist Germany eventually could reestablish itself as a great power by aligning itself temporarily with Russia, whereas were Germany to be defeated and be subjected to occupation by the powers of the West, it would, for generations to come, be reduced to a power of secondary position" (loc. cit.).

18. OSS Headquarters cabled to Bern on March 10, 1943: "In reference to the [Hohenlohe] situation, your discussions and contacts have been brought to Adolf's attention [Adolf Berle, then in charge of special war problems at the State Department]. Adolf is taking them across the street [to the White House]. . . . The general reliability of the Max [Hohenlohe] referred to in our cable . . . has been confirmed through further information from Zulu sources [British intelligence]. Perhaps you will want to investigate this contact should we decide to begin the negotiation phase"; file "To Bern June 23, 1942—October 30, 1943, CD 1366-out 4438," box 165, entry 134, RG 226 National Archives, Washington, DC. See also OSS to Bern, March 15, 1943 (Secret), loc. cit.

19. See, for example, Dulles writing on November 21, 1943: "There is a high degree of possibility that Himmler might use Max [Hohenlohe] for feelers of major importance . . . he can be of use to us. . . . His property interests are his main concern. He is aware that these interests are better guarded if he plays with our side than if he is too closely identified with the Nazis"; in Bern to OSS Headquarters, November 21, 1943 (Secret), Wash RG-RC-60-61, box 170, entry 134, RG 226, National Archives, Washington, DC.

20. OSS Headquarters to Bern, April 26, 1943 (Secret), file "D27 Bern Out June 42–Oct. 43," Wash Reg. R&C-56, box 165, entry 134, RG 226, National Archives, Washington, DC.

21. Heinz Hohne (Richard Barry, trans.), *Order of the Death's Head*. New York: Ballantine, 1971, pp. 591–609 passim; Schellenberg, op. cit., pp. 369–83 passim.

22. See, for example, Harry Rositzke, *The KGB*. Garden City, NY: Doubleday, 1981; or more recently, Phillip Knightly, *The Master Spy; The Story of Kim Philby*. New York: Knopf, 1989.

23. The Hungarian secret service, for example, is said to have succeeded

in intercepting and decrypting Dulles's radio transmissions; see Wilhelm Hoettl, *The Secret Front*. New York: Praeger, 1954, p. 285.

24. Ministry of Foreign Affairs of the USSR, *Correspondence*, op. cit., pp. 198–214.

25. Ingeborg Fleischhauer, *Die Chance des Sonderfriedens; Deutsch-sowietische Geheimgesprache 1941–1945*. Berlin: Siedler Verlag, 1986.

26. A. Poltorak, *Retribution; Notes of an Eye-witness of the Nuremberg Trial*. Moscow: Novosti, 1976.

27. *UNWCC and the Laws of War*, op. cit., p. 123. My special thanks to the United States Holocaust Memorial Museum for permitting me access to their microfilm collection of records from the Extraordinary State Commission.

28. Matthews to Secretary of State, March 5, 1943, 740.00116 EW 1939/813, RG 59, National Archives, Washington, DC; Hackworth to Welles, March 16, 1943, 740.00116 EW 1939/817, RG 59, National Archives, Washington, DC.

29. U.S. hears of German charges: Harrison to Secretary of State, April 15, 1943, 740.0011 EW 1939/29008, RG 59, National Archives, Washington, DC. For data on Katyn from the point of view of German propaganda and war crimes investigators, see de Zayas, op. cit., pp. 228–39, or Felix Lutzkendorf, "Das Waldchen von Katyn," *Das Reich*, May 2, 1943.

30. J. K. Zawodny, *Death in the Forest. The Story of the Katyn Forest Massacre*. Notre Dame, IN: Univ. of Notre Dame Press, 1962, pp. 3–28. For later Soviet reversal discussed in footnote, see "Soviets Admit Blame in Massacre of Polish Officers in World War II," *New York Times*, April 13, 1990.

31. Zawodny, ibid.

32. Ibid., pp. 31–41. For accounts of the complexities of Soviet-Polish relations during this period, see also Alexander Werth, *Russia at War, 1941–1945*. New York: Avon, 1964, pp. 582–612, and Gabriel Kolko, op. cit., pp. 99–122.

33. Zawodny, op. cit., pp. 34–41.

34. *UNWCC and the Laws of War*, op. cit., pp. 112, 158–59; Durbrow to Hackworth, December 14, 1943 (with attachment), 740.00116 EW 1939/1187, box 2921, RG 59, National Archives, Washington, DC.

35. Robert Conquest, *The Harvest of Sorrow*. New York: Oxford Univ. Press, 1986; U.S., Commission on the Ukrainian Famine, *Investigation of the Ukrainian Famine 1932–1933*. Washington, DC: USGPO, 1988.

36. FDR to Secretary of State, April 9, 1943, 740.00116 EW 1939/994, box 2919, RG 59, National Archives, Washington, DC. Pell's letter to FDR concerning the lunch is attached to this note.

37. FDR to MacIntyre, December 14, 1942, and Welles to MacIntyre, December 17, 1942, FDR papers, Pell file, Franklin D. Roosevelt Library, Hyde Park, NY; Kenneth Schwartz, "The United States and the War Crimes Commission: Stalemate and Checkmate," April 1977, p. 16, now in the Herbert Pell papers, collection of Senator Claiborne Pell.

38. Hackworth to Secretary of State, March 16, 1943, 740.00116 EW 1939/817, box 2918, RG 59, National Archives, Washington, DC; Hull to FDR, May 21 1943, 740.00116 EW 1939/949A, box 2919, RG 59, National Archives, Washington, DC.

39. Dunn's action: FDR to Secretary of State (with attachments), April 9, 1943, 740.00116 EW 1939/994, op. cit. Pell's appointment: FDR to Pell, June 14, 1943 740.00116 EW 1939/1275, box 2922, RG 59, National Archives, Washington, DC.

Chapter Nine

Silk Stocking Rebel

1. For background on Herbert Pell, see Leonard Baker, *Brahmin in Revolt*. Garden City, NY: Doubleday, 1972; Michael Blayney, *Democracy's Aristocrat: The Life of Herbert Pell*. Lanham, NY: University Press, 1986; Herbert Pell, *Oral History* (1951), Columbia University, NY; Herbert Pell, *Commission and Omission* (1945), unpublished manuscript, Pell papers, collection of Senator Claiborne Pell. I am grateful to Senator Pell for permitting me access to these papers and sharing with me his recollections of his father.

2. Arthur M. Schlesinger, jr. *Crisis of the Old Order, 1919–1933*. Boston: Houghton Mifflin, 1957, p. 397; and E. Digby Baltzell, *The Protestant Establishment: Aristocracy and Class in America*. New York: Random House, 1964, p. 241. For similar sentiments, see Herbert Pell, "The Bankers Have Failed" *Plain Talk* magazine, December 1932, or Herbert Pell, "Muzzling the Ox," *Yankee* magazine, both republished in pamphlet form in Pell papers.

3. Herbert Pell, *Oral History*, op. cit.; Baker, op. cit., pp. 176–237.

4. " 'Ah, Sweet Intrigue!' Or, Who Axed State's Prewar Soviet Division?" *Foreign Intelligence Literary Scene*, October 1984, p. 1; see also Frederic Propas, "Creating a Hard Line Towards Russia: The Training of State Department Soviet Experts 1927–1937," *Diplomatic History*,

Summer 1984, pp. 209–26; Daniel Yergin, *Shattered Peace: The Origins of the Cold War and the National Security State.* Boston: Houghton Mifflin, 1977, pp. 17–41.

5. Herbert Pell, *Oral History,* op. cit., p. 587.

6. On Green Hackworth: for a biographical summary, see *National Cyclopedia of American Biography,* vol. 57, p. 110, *Current Biography 1958,* pp. 181–82, and the introductory notes to Green Hackworth, *Digest of International Law,* vol. 1, Deparatment of State publication no. 1506, 1940; Washington DC: USGPO; reprint, New York: Garland Publishing, 1973.

7. Hackworth, ibid.

8. Ibid., vol. 6.

9. Pell, *Oral History,* op. cit., pp. 584–85. Hackworth suggested Preuss, a professor in international law, to Pell sometime in June 1943. Pell formally requested Preuss later that month, and evidently only later concluded that Preuss was cooperating with Hackworth in opposition to Pell; see Hackworth to Welles, June 29, 1943, 740.00116 EW 1939/1003, box 2919, RG 59, National Archives, Washington, DC.

10. Herbert Pell, *Commission and Omission,* op. cit., pp. 2–3. For State Department correspondence on this issue: Pell to Welles, July 3, 1943, 740.00116 EW 1939/1083; Shaw to Pell, July 10, 1943, 740.00116 EW 1939/1004; Winant to Secretary of State, July 13, 1943, 740.00116 EW 1939/991; Hull to U.S. Embassy London, July 17, 1943, 740.00116 EW 1939/991; Hull to U.S. Embassy London, August 5, 1943 (draft), 740.00116 EW 1939/991; Kelchner to Shaw, August 12, 1943, 740.00116 EW 1939/1036; all in RG 59, National Archives, Washington, DC.

11. Gerhard Hirschfeld, "Chronology of Destruction," in Gerhard Hirschfeld, *The Policies of Genocide. Jews and Soviet Prisoners of War in Nazi Germany.* London: Allen & Unwin/German Histsorical Institute,1986, pp. 153–55.

12. Schwartz, op. cit., p. 18.

13. FDR to Secretary of State, September 2, 1943, 740.00116 EW 1939/1084, box 2920, RG 59, National Archives, Washington, DC.

14. Kelchner to Hackworth, September 10, 1943, 740.00116 EW 1939/1079, box 2920, RG 59, National Archives, Washington, DC.

15. Schwartz, op. cit., p. 20.

16. Ibid. For details concerning the personnel and administrative structure of the UNWCC established at this time, see *UNWCC and the Laws of War,* op. cit., pp. 113–27.

17. *UNWCC and the Laws of War,* p. 113.

18. Memorandum of conversation, November 9, 1943, 740.00116 EW 1939/1178, box 2921, RG 59, National Archives, Washington, DC.

19. Pell to Secretary of State, November 11, 1943, 740.00116 EW 1939/1218, box 2921, RG 59, National Archives, Washington, DC.

20. Hans Frank diary, Nuremberg document no. PS-2233, National Archives, Washington, DC.

21. Wilson (OSS) to Berle, February 4, 1943, 740.00116 EW 1939/794, box 2917, RG 59, National Archives, Washington, DC.

22. David Wyman, *The Abandonment of the Jews.* New York: Pantheon, 1984, p. 44.

23. For State's vetoes of OSS psychological warfare plan against Nazi atrocities, see Hackworth to Berle, February 10, 1943, and Berle to Wilson (OSS), February 11, 1943, 740.00116 EW 1939/794, box 2917, and Stettinius to FDR, November 4, 1943, 740.00116 EW 1939/1143, with attachments, box 2920; both in RG 59, National Archives, Washington, DC.

24. Herbert Feis, *Churchill, Roosevelt, Stalin.* Princeton, NJ: Princeton Univ. Press, 1957, pp. 206–34.

25. Churchill to Eden, October 21, 1943, British Foreign Office 371 34376/C12918, Public Record Office, London.

26. Quoted in Martin Gilbert, *Auschwitz and the Allies.* New York: Holt, Rinehart & Winston, 1981, p. 159.

27. Anthony Eden, Prime Minister's papers, October 9, 1943, PREM 4 100/9, Public Record Office, London.

28. *UNWCC and the Laws of War,* op. cit., pp. 107–108.

29. Feis, op. cit.

30. Ibid., pp. 220–21.

31. Harriman to Secretary of State, November 16, 1943, 740.00116 EW 1939/1157, box 2921, RG 59, National Archives, Washington, DC.

32. Tom Bower, *Blind Eye to Murder.* London: Granada, 1983, p. 70.

33. Algiers to Secretary of State, November 23, 1943, 740.00116EW 1939/1169, and Secretary of State (vis. Bernard Guffler) to Amrep. Algiers, November 26, 1943, 740.00116EW 1939/1159, RG 59, National Archives, Washington, DC.

34. Ibid.

35. Randolph Paul, *Report to the Secretary on the Acquiescence of This Government in the Murder of the Jews,* Jan. 13, 1944, Morgenthau Diaries, vol. 693, Franklin D. Roosevelt Library, Hyde Park, NY, pp. 212–29.

36. Morgenthau *Diaries*, op. cit., vol. 688–II, pp. 156–57; Wyman, op. cit., p. 185.

37. Wyman, op. cit., pp. 179–80ff.

38. Saul Friedman, *No Haven for the Oppressed*. Detroit: Wayne State Univ. Press, 1973, pp. 115–16.

39. Wyman, op. cit., p. 182.

Chapter Ten

"The Present Ruling Class of Germany"

1. Author's interview with Bernard Bernstein, February 24, 1989.

2. Ibid.

3. Charles Burdick, *An American Island in Hitler's Reich. The Bad Nauheim Internment*, Menlo Park, CA: Markgraf, 1987.

4. George F. Kennan, *Memoirs 1925–1950*. Boston: Little, Brown, 1967, pp. 175, 179.

5. Loc. cit.

6. Ibid., pp. 175–77.

7. On Durbrow, Hickerson, and Reams: David Wyman, *The Abandonment of the Jews*. New York: Pantheon, 1984, p. 81; on Durbrow and Hickerson: Daniel Yergin, *Shattered Peace*. Boston: Houghton Mifflin, 1977, pp. 28–29, 301; and Weil, *A Pretty Good Club*. New York: Norton, 1978, op. cit., pp. 53–54, 84, 120 and passim.

8. Algiers to Secretary of State, November 23, 1943, 740.00116EW 1939/1169, and Secretary of State (vis. Bernard Guffler) to Amrep. Algiers, November 26, 1943, 740.00116EW 1939/1159; both in RG 59, National Archives, Washington, DC. See also P. H. Gore-Booth to Hackworth and attached documents, in Committee on Europe, box 138, SWNCC/SANACC Committee files, RG 353, National Archives, Washington, DC (rejection of prosecutions for crimes against humanity, or for offenses against Jews inside Axis countries); Le 740.00116EW/4-1945 in file: "Surrender," box 1, lot 61 D 33, RG 59, National Archives, Washington, DC (refusal to turn over war crimes suspects); "For Springer": November 21, 1946, 740.00116EW/11-1446 and attachment (Aryanizations in Belgium not a war crime).

9. See Kennan's comments, for example, in *Memoirs*, op. cit., pp. 176–77.

10. Ibid., p. 118.

11. For example, ibid, p. 123.

12. US Army Counter Intelligence Corps dossier XE000318-I6A009 *Henschel, Oscar R.*, available via Freedom of Information Act from U.S. Army Intelligence and Security Command, Ft. Meade, MD.

13. Oswald Pohl affidavit, October 7, 1946, Nuremberg document no. NI-1064, National Archives microfilm T-301, roll 10, frame 001112; Kranefuss to Himmler, April 21, 1943, at Berlin Document Center; copy in author's collection.

14. Ibid.

15. Eichholtz, *Kriegswirtschaft*, op. cit., p. 221.

16. Ludolf Herbst, *Der Totale Krieg und die Ordnung der Wirtschaft.* Stuttgart: Deutsche Verlag-Amstalt, 1982, pp. 383–409; Wolfgang Schumann, "Politische Aspekte der Nachkriegsplanungen des faschistischen deutschen Imperialismus in der Endphase des zweiten Weltkrieges," *Zeitschrift für Geschichtswissenschaft,* 1979 no. 1, pp. 395–408; Wolfgang Schumann, "Nachkriegsplanungen der Reichsgruppe Industrie im Herbst 1944, Ein Dokumentation," *Jahrbuch für Wirtschaftsgeschichte.* Berlin: Akademie, 1972, pp. 259–96.

17. Lindemann, in a postwar interrogation by U.S. intelligence, discusses a factional split in the *Himmlerkreis* over these issues, apparently leading to the establishment of the industry planning groups discussed in the previous source note. See "Preliminary Interrogation Report: *Lindemann, Karl*," September 12, 1945, in Lindemann INSCOM dossier.

18. Tabitha Petran, "Key Names in Nazi Peace Plot and British Banking Contacts," *New York Post,* February 3, 1944; Heinz Pol, "IG Farben's Peace Offer," *The Protestant,* June–July 1943, p. 41; Jonathan Marshall, *Bankers and the Search for a Separate Peace During World War II,* unpublished monograph, 1981; Nancy Lisagor and Frank Lipsius, *A Law Unto Itself: The Untold Story of the Law Firm Sullivan and Cromwell.* New York: William Morrow, 1988, p. 144.

   Schumann reports that German industrialists placed special emphasis on contacts through the Bank for International Settlements; see Wolfgang Schumann, "Die Wirtschaftspolitische Überlebensstrategie des deutschen Imperialismus in der Endphase des zweiten Weltkrieges," *Zeitschrift für Geschichtswissenschaft,* no. 6, 1979, p. 508.

19. Richard Harris Smith, *OSS.* Berkeley, CA: Univ. of California Press, 1972, pp. 204–41; Anthony Cave Brown (ed.), *The Secret War Report of the OSS.* New York: Berkeley, 1976, pp. 250–55.

20. Ingeborg Fleischhauer, *Die Chance des Sonderfriedens; Deutschsowietische Geheimgesprache 1941–1945.* Berlin: Siedler Verlag, 1986.

21. On terms of the "peace" offers, see Heinz Hohne, *The Order of the Death's Head*. New York: Ballantine, 1969, pp. 591–99 (in original German as *Der Orden unter dem Totenkopf*. Hamburg: Verlag der Spiegel, 1966). See also Bernd Martin, "Deutsche Oppositions- und Widerstandkreise und die Frage eines separaten Friedensschlusses im zweiten Weltkrieg," in Klaus-Jürgen Müller (Hrsg.), *Der deutsche Widerstand 1933–1945*. Paderborn: Ferdinand Schoningh, 1986.

22. Gabriel Kolko, *The Politics of War*. New York: Random House, 1968, p. 110.

23. Turner Catledge, "Our Policy Stated in Nazi-Soviet War," *New York Times*, June 24, 1941.

24. Raymond G. O'Connor, *Diplomacy for Victory; FDR and Unconditional Surrender*. New York: Norton, 1971, pp. 33–35, 41–43, 50–54; Feis, *Churchill, Roosevelt, Stalin*, op. cit., pp. 217–34.

25. Albert Speer, *Infiltration*. New York: Macmillan, 1981, pp. 117–32.

26. Weinmann, *Das nationalsozialistische Lagersystem*, presents data in tabular form concerning the liquidation of hundreds of business projects in the East in which the surviving prisoners were transferred to extermination camps.

Chapter Eleven

The Trials Begin

1. On Krasnodar trials and filming of executions: Standley to Secretary of State, September 9, 1943, 740.00116 EW 1939/1086, box 2920, RG 59, National Archives, Washington, DC. On gas vans: Raul Hilberg, *The Destruction of the European Jews*. New York: Harper, 1981. p. 219; Ohlendorf affidavit, November 5, 1945, Nuremberg document no. PS-2620; Alexander Werth, *Russia at War, 1941–1945*. New York: Avon, 1964 pp. 641, 669–70.

2. *The People's Verdict, A Full Report of the Proceedings at the Krasnodar and Kharkov German Atrocity Trials*. London, 1944, pp. 45–124; "Gallows for Germans Are Raised in Kharkov," *Daily Express* (London), July 6, 1944.

3. *UNWCC and the Laws of War*, op. cit., pp. 107–108.

4. Harriman to Secretary of State (reporting Morgenthau comments), November 16, 1943, 740.00116 EW 1939/1157, with attached notes by Dunn and Stettinius, box 2921, RG 59, National Archives, Washington, DC.

5. "USA.-Luftgangster nennen sich selbst 'Mordverein'," *Völkischer Be-*

obachter, December 21, 1943. See also Office of U.S. Chief of Counsel for Prosecution of Axis Criminality, *Nazi Conspiracy and Aggression*, Washington, DC: USGPO, 1946, vol. 8, pp. 539–45. For Western intelligence analysis of German announcements concerning Allied war crimes, see Alexander L. George, *Propaganda Analysis*, White Plains, NY: Row Peterson & Co., and Rand Corporation, 1959, pp. 161–70. For captured World War I–era German documentation concerning war crimes issues, see U.S. Department of State, *Documents on German Foreign Policy 1918–1945 from the Archives of the German Foreign Ministry*, Washington, DC: USGPO, 1949, p. 1025, entries 47, 48, and 49.

6. Hull to American Legation Bern, December 24, 1943, attached to 740.00116 EW 1939/1159, box 2921, RG 59, National Archives, Washington, DC. The cover note clearly links the announcement to the Kharkov trial: Hull "refers to press and radio reports that German authorities intend to try as war criminals American aviators held as prisoners of war by Germany, allegedly upon a basis of a precedent established by the Soviet authorities. Request Swiss [government] to report fully by telegraph regarding this matter. You may assure Swiss that this [U.S.] Government is not (repeat not) proceeding against German prisoners of war along lines similar to above reports. . . ." The Swiss government was serving as an intermediary between the U.S. and German governments, and was expected to pass this message to Berlin.

7. Hull to American Embassy Moscow, December 31, 1943, 740.00116 EW 1939/1249A, and Hull to American Embassy London, January 4, 1944, 740.00116 EW 1939/1249B, both in RG 59, National Archives, Washington, DC.

8. Stettinius to Dunn and Matthews, January 28, 1944, and Dunn to Stettinius, February 1, 1944; attachments to Harriman to Secretary of State, November 16, 1943, 740.00116 EW 1939/1157, box 2921, RG 59, National Archives, Washington, DC.

9. Algiers to Secretary of State, November 23, 1943, 740.00116 EW 1939/1169, and Secretary of State (via. Bernard Guffler) to Amrep. Algiers, November 26, 1943, 740.00116 EW 1939/1159, both in box 2921, RG 59, National Archives, Washington, DC.

10. Ibid. 740.00116 EW 1939/1249B. For materials on death of Stalin's son, see "Abschrift an den Lagerkommandant," April 14, 1943 (reporting on incident, with photos and accompanying German correspondence), now at 840.414/8-145, RG 59, National Archives, Washington, DC; Svetlana Alliluyeva (Priscilla Johnson McMillan, trans.), *Twenty Letters to a Friend*. New York: Harper, 1967, pp. 157–63.

11. Herbert Pell, *Oral History* (1951), Columbia University, pp. 538–39.
12. Loc. cit.
13. Ibid., pp. 569–70.
14. Gallman to Secretary of State, October 26 1943, 740.00116 EW 1939/1150, box 2921, RG 59, National Archives, Washington, DC, reports on a British Institute of Public Opinion poll released on October 25. In response to the question, "At the end of the war, what do you think should be done with the Axis leaders?" respondents answered:

	Percent
Let them go, ignore them	1
They won't be found	1
Leave them to their own peoples	1
They should be put on trial	18
Exile them, imprison them, put them in solitary confinement	11
Hand them over to the Jews, the Poles and others who have suffered	4
Shoot them	40
Nothing is horrible enough, torture them	15
Miscellaneous or no opinion	9
	100

15. Pell to FDR, January 27, 1944, with a cover note from Roosevelt to Hull requesting that State draft a reply for FDR's signature, 740.00116 EW 1939/1305, box 2922, RG 59, National Archives, Washington, DC.
16. Pell to Hull, January 28, 1944, 740.00116 EW 1939/1306, box 2922, RG 59, National Archives, Washington, DC.
17. FDR to Pell, February 12, 1944, attached to 740.00116 EW 1939/1305 (ibid.).
18. Pell, *Oral History,* op. cit., passim.
19. FDR to Pell, February 12, 1944, attached to 740.00116 EW 1939/1305 (ibid.).
20. See Hull to Pell, February 10, 1944 (Hull's reply to Pell's January 28 letter), attached to 740.00116 EW 1939/1306 (ibid.); Stettinius to Pell, February 15, 1944, 740.00116 EW 1939/1299; FDR to Pell March 1, 1944, attached to 740.00116 EW 1939/1340; and Hull to

Pell, March 15, 1944, 740.00116 EW 1939/1315; all at box 2922, RG 59, National Archives, Washington, DC.

21. *UNWCC and the Laws of War*, op. cit., p. 141.

22. Stettinius to Pell, February 15, 1944, 740.00116 EW 1939/1299; and Hull to Pell, March 15, 1944, 740.00116 EW 1939/1315; both at box 2922, RG 59, National Archives, Washington, DC.

23. Pell, *Oral History*, op. cit., p. 584.

24. Pell, *Omission and Commission*, op. cit., (see Chap. 9), pp. 15–17, 27; Schwartz, op. cit., pp. 31–33; Tom Bower, *Blind Eye to Murder*. London: Granada, 1983, p. 81.

25. Bower, ibid., p. 78.

26. British Foreign Office, Hurst to Simon, April 1, 1944, FO 371 38993/ C4637, Public Record Office, London; Bower, op. cit., p. 78.

27. Gerhard Hirschfeld, "Chronology of Destruction," in Gerhard Hirschfeld (ed.), *The Policies of Genocide: Jews and Soviet Prisoners of War in Nazi Germany*. London: Allen & Unwin/German Historical Institute, 1986.

28. Bower, op. cit., pp. 84, 476.

29. Ibid., pp. 85–86.

30. Werth, *Russia at War*, op. cit., pp. 806–15.

31. Ibid., p. 814.

Chapter Twelve
Morgenthau's Plan

1. John Morton Blum, *From the Morgenthau Diaries. Years of War 1941–1945*. Boston: Houghton Mifflin, 1917, pp. 329–33, 338–40. For Kennan's version: George F. Kennan, *Memoirs 1925–1950*. Boston: Little, Brown, 1967, vol. 1, pp. 164–87.

2. Harley Notter (U.S. Department of State, Office of Public Affairs), *Postwar Foreign Policy Preparation, 1939–1945*. Washington, DC: USGPO/Department of State, 1950, pp. 207–27 passim. Policy slogan: Blum, ibid., p. 332. Kennan presents his point of view concerning war crimes as a direct response to Morgenthau's (and apparently Roosevelt's) "pipedreams of collaboration with the Russians" in postwar reconstruction of Germany; see Kennan, op. cit., p. 178.

3. Blum, op. cit., pp. 338–40.

4. Ibid., p. 346.

5. Fred Kaplan, "Scientists at War. The Birth of the RAND Corporation," *American Heritage,* June–July 1983, p. 53.

6. Blum, op. cit., pp. 333–43.

7. Ibid., pp. 340–41.

8. Schwartz, *The United States and the War Crimes Commission,* op. cit.

9. Bradley F. Smith, *Reaching Judgement at Nuremberg.* New York: New American Library, 1977, p. 22; Blum, op. cit., p. 334.

10. Smith, ibid., p. 23.

11. Franklin Roosevelt, "Memorandum for the Secretary of War," August 26, 1944. Lot: Central European Division, box 4, file "German Handbook—SHAEF," RG 59, National Archives, Washington, DC.

12. Ibid.

13. Henry Morgenthau, *Diaries,* vol. 768, pp. 157–65, Franklin D. Roosevelt Library, Hyde Park, NY.

14. Ibid.

15. Blum, op. cit., p. 343.

16. David Wyman, *The Abandonment of the Jews.* New York: Pantheon, 1984. p. 258; Schwartz, op. cit., p. 37.

17. Frederick Kuh, "War Crimes Group Lists But 350 Names: Hitler, Himmler, Other Nazi Bigwigs Omitted by Commission in London," *Washington Post,* September 17, 1944. Hull quickly (and inaccurately) denied the report: "Hitler on List of Criminals, Hull Declares," *Washington Post,* September 19, 1944; but see Drew Pearson column "Washington Merry-Go-Round," *Atlanta Journal* (and many other papers), October 8, 1944. See also "Nine Months Work on War Crimes: Case Against Hitler Not Yet Being Prepared," *Daily Telegraph* (London), August 31, 1944.

18. Kuh, "War Crimes Group . . . ," ibid.

19. Pell, *Oral History,* op. cit., p. 590.

20. Smith, op. cit., p. 26.

21. Ibid., pp. 12–19 and passim.

22. On Glueck and Roosevelt precedents prior to Bernays: Glueck, *War Criminals. Their Prosecution and Punishment.* New York: Knopf, 1944. pp. 37, 39; Franklin Roosevelt, "Memorandum for the Secretary of War," August 26, 1944. Lot: Central European Division, box 4, file "German Handbook—SHAEF," RG 59, National Archives, Washington, DC. For discussion of significance of conspiracy charges to Nuremberg prosection: Smith, loc. cit., and "War Crimes Prosecutions: Planning Memorandum" (Secret), May 17, 1945, 740.00116EW/S-2445, box 3599, RG 59, National Archives, Washington, DC.

23. Blum, op. cit., pp. 378–79.

24. Schwartz, op. cit., pp. 45–50; Michael Blayney, "Herbert Pell, War Crimes and the Jews," *American Jewish Historical Quarterly*, June 1976, pp. 347–49.

25. Schwartz, op. cit., p. 45.

26. Blayney, op. cit., p. 348.

27. P. H. Gore-Booth to Hackworth, with attachments, December 21, 1944, box 138, Committee on Europe, SWNCC/SANACC Committee files, RG 353, National Archives, Washington, DC. Combined Chiefs of Staff, "Obligations of Theater Commanders in Relation to War Crimes," CCS 705/1, December 17, 1944, attached to Gore-Booth; and enclosure A, p. 8.

28. For Department of Justice opposition and reversal, see Smith, op. cit., pp. 33–34.

29. Gore-Booth to Hackworth, op. cit.

30. Ibid.; and attachment, Combined Chiefs of Staff, "Obligations of Theater Commanders . . . ," op. cit.

31. Pell, *Oral History*, op. cit., pp. 589–90.

32. Blayney, op. cit., p. 351; Victor Bernstein, "Who Are the U.S. Officials Seeking to Sabotage Trial of Nazi Killers?" *PM*, January 28, 1945.

33. Blayney, op. cit., pp. 351–52.

34. Loc. cit.

35. Saul Padover, *Experiment in Germany. The Story of an American Intelligence Officer.* New York: Duell, Sloan and Pearce, 1946, pp. 222–25.

36. Loc. cit.

37. Loc. cit.

38. Cedric Belfrage, *Seeds of Destruction.* New York: Cameron & Kahn, 1954, p. 38. Belfrage, a dedicated man of the left who was also a U.S. military government officer in Aachen specializing in newspapers, propaganda, and public opinion, offers an anecdotal account of the same events discussed by Padover. He describes his account as "fact-based" fiction, so obviously this text can be used by historians only with great caution. The public opinion statistics are accurate, however. For more on Belfrage's important role in encouraging the German left during the early occupation years in Germany, see Emil Carlebach, *Zensur ohne Schere. Die Grunderiahre der 'Frankfurter Rundschau' 1945–1947.* Frankfurt: Roderberg-Verlag, 1985.

39. Padover, op. cit., pp. 249–52.

40. Loc. cit.

41. Loc. cit.

Chapter Thirteen

"This Needs to Be Dragged Out Into the Open"

1. Bern to OSS headquarters and division chiefs, December 26, 1944 (Secret); Bern November 1, 1944–January 31, 1945, Wash Sect R&C 78, folder 19, box 278, entry 134, RG 226, National Archives, Washington, DC.

2. Ibid.

3. See, for example, Robert Joyce (Central Intelligence Group) to Walter Dowling (State Dept.), "Subject: Former SS Colonel Dollmann," December 1, 1946 (Top Secret), 740.00116EW/12-146; or Robert Murphy to Secretary of State, August 11, 1947 (Top Secret), 740.00116EW/8-1147; both obtained via Freedom of Information Act. For details concerning Dulles's denials, see the source notes in chapter 14.

4. Robert O. Paxton, *Vichy France, Old Guard and New Order, 1940–1944.* New York: Knopf, 1972, p. 242.

5. John Morton Blum, *From the Morgenthau Diaries. Years of War 1941–1945.* Boston: Houghton Mifflin, 1967. p. 394.

6. Ibid., pp. 416–18.

7. Ibid. Robert Murphy helped sponsor General Lucius Clay's appointment as Dwight Eisenhower's chief deputy for military government in March 1945. Clay soon rose to become the military governor in the U.S. occupation zone of Germany and the commander of U.S. forces in Germany; see Lucius Clay, *Decision in Germany.* Garden City, NY: Doubleday, 1950.

8. *Washington Post,* January 31, 1945.

9. JCS 1067 4.c., quoted in "Statements of policies and directives relating to foreign and domestic cartels," file: "Cartels, Decartelization," box 55, Legal Advice Branch, OMGUS Legal Division, RG 260, National Archives, Suitland, MD.

10. Loc. cit.

11. For example, German banking had fewer structural restrictions on its activities than those provided for in the U.S. under the Banking Act of 1933 (Glass-Steagall Act), although theoretically the occupation government could have remanded any particular banking action. See "Removals of Officials from German Banks and Companies: [Legal] Opinion," n.d. (Spring 1945), in file: "Denazification," box 229, OMGUS/FINAD, RG 260, National Archives, Suitland, MD. For an overview of U.S. postwar banking policy in Germany up to 1952, see

U.S., Office of the High Commission for Germany [HICOG], Histori-
cal Division (Rodney Loehr), *The West German Banking System*
(Restricted), n.p. (HICOG Historical Division, Bad Godesberg-
Mehlem), 1952.

12. "Removal of Undesirable Personnel from the German Financial
System—Denazification," March 19, 1945 (Secret), and "Schedule of
Financial Personnel" (Secret), n.d., in file: "Denazification," box 229,
OMGUS/FINAD, RG 260, National Archives, Suitland, MD.

13. Ibid.

Chapter Fourteen

Sunrise

1. See, for example, Robert Joyce (Central Intelligence Group) to Walter
Dowling, "Subject: Former SS Colonel Dollmann" (Top Secret), De-
cember 1, 1946, obtained in sanitized form via the Freedom of Infor-
mation Act, 740.00116EW/12-146, RG 59, National Archives,
Washington, DC; copy in author's collection; Murphy to Secretary of
State, 740.00116EW/8-1147 (Top Secret, No Distribution), August 11,
1947, RG 59, National Archives, obtained via Freedom of Information
Act in 1990.

2. Ildefonso Cardinal Schuster, *Gli ultimi tempi di un regime.* Milan,
1946, p. 35, as reported in Eugen Dollmann (J. Maxwell Brownjohn,
trans.), *The Interpreter; Memoirs of Doktor Eugen Dollmann.* London:
Hutchinson, 1967, pp. 340–41.

3. For a discussion of the "dual containment" thesis, see Thomas Alan
Schwartz, *America's Germany; John J. McCloy and the Federal Republic of Germany.* Cambridge, MA: Harvard Univ. Press, 1991.

4. Dollmann, op. cit., p. 340.

5. Ibid., p. 241.

6. Ibid., p. 342. For Parilli's own account, see Ferruccio Lanfranchi, *La
Resa Degli Ottocentomila, con le Memorie Autografe del Barone
Luigi Parrilli.* Milano: Rizzoli, 1948.

7. Dollmann, op. cit., p. 342.

8. See Allen Dulles's self-congratulatory account, *The Secret Surrender.*
New York: Harper, 1966. For more reliable accounts, see Karl
Stuhlpfarrer, *Die Operationszonen "Alpenvorland" und "Adri-
atisches Kustenland" 1943–1945.* Wien: Verlag Bruder Hollinek/
Österreichischen Instituts für Zeitgeschichte, 1969 (based mainly on
German records); Jochen Lang, *Der Adjutant: Karl Wolff, Der Mann*

zwishen Hitler und Himmler, Berlin: Herbig, 1985, pp. 259–306; and particularly Bradley F. Smith and Elena Agarossi, *Operation Sunrise; The Secret Surrender.* New York: Basic Books, 1979, p. 190. Gabriel Kolko was among the first Western historians to recognize the pivotal importance to the Soviets of the Italian surrender negotiations; see Gabriel Kolko, *The Politics of War,* New York: Random House, 1978. pp. 375–79.

9. Nuremberg doc. no. 2207, cited in Smith and Agarossi, loc. cit; see also "Summary Prepared by W. M. Chase on 'The Role of the Wolff Group in Operation Sunrise,'" March 10, 1947 (Top Secret), 740.00116EW/11-1047, box 3625, RG 59, National Archives, Washington, DC.

10. Smith and Agarossi, op. cit., p. 91.

11. Molotov letter to Harriman, March 16, 1945, published in Ministry of Foreign Affairs of the USSR, *Correspondence,* op. cit., pp. 296–97, 78n.

12. "Personal and Top Secret for Marshal Stalin from President Roosevelt" (received March 25, 1945), ibid., pp. 198–99.

13. "Personal and Secret from Marshal J. V. Stalin to the President, Mr. F. Roosevelt," March 27, 1945, and second Stalin note of March 29, 1945, ibid., pp. 199–201.

14. Two notes marked "Personal and Top Secret for Marshal Stalin from President Roosevelt" (both received April 1, 1945), ibid., pp. 201–205.

15. "Personal, Most Secret from J. V. Stalin to the President, Mr. Roosevelt," April 3, 1945, ibid., pp. 205–206.

16. See, for example, German proposal outlined in OSS cable Suhling to Glavin and Ryan, March 6, 1945 (Top Secret), OSS Sunrise I-XXX, entry 110, folder e2, box 2, RG 226, National Archives, Washington, DC.

17. "Personal and Top Secret for Marshal Stalin from President Roosevelt," received April 13, 1945, Ministry of Foreign Affairs of the USSR, *Correspondence,* op. cit., p. 214.

18. Key observers convinced that Dulles offered de facto amnesty to the Wolff group: Murphy to Secretary of State, 740.00116EW/8-1147 (Top Secret, No Distribution), August 11, 1947, RG 59, National Archives, obtained via Freedom of Information Act. "Interrogation Report on SS Standartenfuehrer Rauff, Walter," May 15, 1945 (Confidential), in U.S. Army Counter Intelligence Corps file no. D-216719, *Rauff, Walter,* obtained via Freedom of Information Act

from U.S. Army INSCOM, Ft. Meade, MD. Soviet comments: Ministry of Foreign Affairs of the USSR, *Correspondence*, op. cit., pp. 198–99, 296–97, sn78.

19. Smith and Agarossi, op. cit., p. 145.

20. Ibid., p. 214, 103n.

21. Daniel Yergin, *Shattered Peace. The Origins of the Cold War and the National Security State*. Boston: Houghton Mifflin, 1977. op. cit., p. 89.

22. Ibid., pp. 90–91.

23. Loc. cit.

24. Loc. cit.

25. For a good summary of early Yugoslav requests, see Carmel Offie to Secretary of State, "Alleged Yugoslav War Criminals" (with attachments), August 28, 1945, 740.00116EW/8-2845, box 3602, RG 59, National Archives, Washington, DC.

26. For a partisan but nonetheless well-documented discussion, see Vladimir Dedijer, *Jasenovac, der jugoslawische Auschwitz und der Vatikan*. Freiburg: Ahriman-Verlag, 1988.

27. Vincent LaVista, "Illegal Immigration Movements in and Through Italy," with appendixes (Top Secret), FW 800.0128/5-1547, National Archives, Washington, DC.

28. For incident discussed in footnote, see Serbian Benevolent Society to Secretary of State, September 1, 1945, with attached routing slip to Military Intelligence Division, Office of Naval Intelligence, etc., 740.0016EW/9-145, box 3602, RG 59, National Archives, Washington, DC.

29. Supreme Commander Allied Forces, HQ Caserta, Italy, to War Department, July 27, 1945, in CCAC 193/4, Committee on Europe, SWNCC/SANACC Committee files, box 138, RG 353, National Archives, Washington, DC.

30. Combined Civil Affairs Committee, "Policy as to Disposition of War Criminals, Renegades, and Quislings," with enclosures, August 19, 1945, in CCAC 193/5, Committee on Europe, SWNCC/SANACC Committee files, box 138, RG 353, National Archives, Washington, DC.

31. Cabot to Secretary of State, June 12, 1947 (Top Secret), 740.00116EW/6-1147, box 3623, RG 59, National Archives, Washington, DC. For a second, similar Cabot protest, see 740.0016 EW/6-2547 in the same box.

32. State action: cover note attached to June 12 protest, ibid. Formal protests on related disputes to the U.S. State Department from

other governments include: 740.00116EW/12-547 (Netherlands), 740.00116EW/2147 (Poland), 740.00116EW/11-1447 (Czecho-slovakia), 740.00116EW/1-848 (Poland), 740.00116EW/10-3147 (France), 740.00116EW/12-1947 (Netherlands), 740.00116EW/6-2449 (France), 740.00116EW/6-16-49 (Belgium), all at RG 59, National Archives, Washington, DC.

33. "Yugoslav War Crimes Extradition Request: Dr. Nikola Rusinovic," September 9, 1947 (Secret), 740.00116EW/9-947, box 3624, RG 59, National Archives, Washington, DC. For a detailed and well-documented discussion of the problem of escaped Yugoslav war criminals, including their postwar role, see Mark Aarons, *Sanctuary. Nazi Fugitives in Australia*. Port Melbourne: Mandarin-Australia, 1989.

34. Nicholas Bethell, *The Last Secret*. New York: Basic Books, 1974.

35. Ibid., p. 4.

36. Ibid., p. 9.

37. Ibid., p. 20.

38. Ibid., pp. 23–27.

39. Loc. cit.

40. Bethell, op. cit., pp. 31–34.

41. Jackson to Byrnes, July 4, 1945, 740.00116EW/7-445 (Confidential), box 3600, RG 59, National Archives, Washington, DC.

42. Loc. cit.

Chapter Fifteen

White Lists

1. Bern to OSS headquarters and division chiefs, November 3, 1944 (Secret), Bern, November 1, 1944–January 31, 1945, Wash. Sect. R&C 78, folder 19, box 278, entry 134, RG 226, National Archives, Washington, DC.

2. Bradley F. Smith, *The Shadow Warriors: The OSS and the Origins of the CIA*. New York: Basic Books, 1983, pp. 222–26, provides what is perhaps the most balanced and thorough evaluation of Dulles's effectiveness as a source of intelligence. For internal OSS criticisms of Dulles cited in footnote, see OSS HQ to Bern, January 22, 1944 (Secret), Washington Register R&C 56, box 165; Ustravic (London) to OSS HQ and to Bern, May 26, 1944 (Secret), Bern-London May-October 1944 in B. L. London, box 157: both in entry 134, RG 226, National Archives, Washington, DC. For OSS War Diary

comment: European Theater of Operations, Secret Intelligence War Diary, Reports Division, p. 314, vol. 8, book 11, entry 91, box 14, RG 226, National Archives, Washington, DC. For Dulles's version, see Allen Dulles, *Germany's Underground*. New York: Macmillan, 1947, and *The Secret Surrender*. New York: Harper, 1966. For a well-informed eyewitness's reply to Dulles's claim that he was effective in bringing about a German surrender, see Max Corvo, *The OSS in Italy 1942–1945*. New York: Praeger, 1990, pp. 242–72 passim.

3. Probably the best overall source on the official aspects of the Bank for International Settlements' activities during this period is the Bank for International Settlements Annual Reports, 1938–1943. Basle: BIS.

4. Eleanor Lansing Dulles, *The Bank for International Settlements at Work*. New York: Macmillan, 1932.

5. For a careful dissection of the Dulles business ties to European companies, see Ronald Pruessen, *John Foster Dulles: The Road to Power*. New York: Free Press, 1982, pp. 123–32.

6. On McKittrick: see, for example, Robert Joyce to Lewis Gable (OSS commander for France, 1945), August 20, 1945, entry 148, folder 2046, box 119, "500 fides," RG 226, National Archives, Washington, DC.

7. Confidential source; author's collection.

8. See BIS, Annual Reports, 1938–1939, op. cit., Annex 1, "Central Banks or Other Banking Institutions Possessing Right of Representation and of Voting."

9. "World Bank [sic] to Release Gold Looted by Germany," *New York Times*, May 15, 1948; "The Case of Thomas McKittrick," *Prevent World War III*, September-October 1948.

10. United Nations War Crimes Commission case no. 7347 (Polish case No. 1366), *Poland v. Dr. Paersch, Reichsbank Berlin, et al.* A copy of this case is available at the UNWCC archives in New York, or at Springer to Secretary of State, February 27, 1948, 740.00116/EW 2-2748, box 3628, RG 59, National Archives, Washington, DC.

11. Ibid. On currency clearing, see Raphael Lemkin, *Axis Rule in Occupied Europe*. Washington, DC: Carnegie Endowment, 1944, pp. 58–63, 127–28; Thomas Reveille (Rifat Tirana), *The Spoil of Europe*. New York: Norton, 1941, pp. 89–101, 121–29, 138–47; Henry Bloch and Bert Hoselitz, *Economics of Military Occupation*. Chicago: Univ. of Chicago Press,, 1944, pp. 5–27.

12. Reveille, loc. cit.; Bloch and Hoselitz, loc. cit.

13. UNWCC case no. 7347, *Poland v. Dr. Paersch, Reichsbank Berlin,*

et al, op. cit. For estimate of German war budget: Klein, op. cit., p. 256, table 65.

14. For British estimate of scope of looting: "Big Sums Exacted of Occupied Lands," *New York Times,* October 29, 1943. The estimate is based on wartime exchange rates.

15. The indictment's extended discussion of the complex clearing process in Poland has been simplified slightly here for clarity's sake. German Finance Minister Funk eventually admitted his role in the expropriation via the clearing system, then retracted this confession. See "Testimony of Walter Funk," October 22, 1945, pp. 19–22, Nuremberg doc. no. PS-3545, RG 238, National Archives, Washington, DC. "World Bank [sic] to Release Gold Looted by Germany," *New York Times,* May 15, 1948.

16. Allen Dulles to Joseph M. Dodge, September 20, 1945, file: *"Johannes Tuengeler,"* OMGUS-FINAD, box 237, RG 260, National Archives, Suitland, MD.

    Also on Dulles's list was Robert Pferdemenges, a Cologne banker with a reputation for hostility to Nazism who ended up as German Chancellor Konrad Adenauer's most powerful advisor and confidant. Dulles said that Pferdemenges had "made such compromises during the Nazi regime as were necessary to maintain his business" and ran an Aryanized banking house, but he had helped Jewish friends at the time he took over their businesses. The most important of these appears to have been Eric Warburg, who eventually reentered a banking partnership with Pferdemenges after the war.

17. "Victor Over Inflation; Dr. Karl Blessing," *New York Times,* January 3, 1970.

18. Affidavit of Oswald Pohl, October 7, 1946, Nuremberg document no. NI-1064, National Archives microfilm T-301, roll 10, frames 001112-001114.

19. Kranefuss to Himmler, April 21, 1943, Berlin Document Center; copy in author's collection.

20. Karl Blessing, *Fragebogen,* August 31, 1946, in U.S. Army CIC dossier no. XE 170459 89291-3410, *"Blessing, Karl,"* obtained via Freedom of Information Act, U.S. Army INSCOM, Ft. Meade, MD. Blessing's NSDAP record is in the Berlin Document Center, no. 5917306.

21. Ibid.

22. Ibid.

23. Berthold Gerber, *Staatliche Wirtschaftslenkung in den besetzten und annektierten Östgebieten waehren des zweiten Weltkrieges.*

Tübingen: Institut für Besatzungfragen, 1959, pp. 118–20; Alexander Dallin, *German Rule in Russia*, 2nd ed. Boulder, CO: Westview, 1981, pp. 242–43; Timothy Patrick Mulligan, *The Politics of Illusion and Empire. German Occupation Policy in the Soviet Union 1942–1943*, New York: Praeger, 1988, p. 29; Reveille, op. cit., pp. 250–53; Eichholtz, *Geschichte der deutschen Kriegswirtschaft*, op. cit., pp. 407–11, 477–87, with table of Kontinentale Öl subsidary companies at p. 480; Peter Hayes, *Industry and Ideology: IG Farben in the Nazi Era*, Cambridge: Cambridge Univ. Press, 1987, pp. 253–65. For the role of Hermann Abs in Kontinentale Öl, see *OMGUS Deutsche Bank*, pp. 246–51; for an account of Hitler's direct sponsorship of the enterprise, see *OMGUS Dresdner Bank*, pp. 66–70. For an overview of the significance of petroleum in German war strategy, see Robert Goralski and Russell Freeburg, *Oil and War*. New York: William Morrow, 1987; Nahostliches Erdöl, zur Geopolitik der Europaischen Erdolversorgung," *Das Reich*, September 1, 1940; Walter Greiling, "Öl—Mettgesetzte Weltmacht," *Das Reich*, June 23, 1940.

24. Dallin, op. cit., p. 243.

25. International Tracing Service, *Verzeichnis der Haftstatten unter der Reichsführer-SS 1933–1945*. Geneve: Red Cross International Committee, 1979; copy in author's collection. For an excellent and easier-to-access source, see Martin Weinmann with Anne Kaiser and Ursula Krause-Schmitt (eds.), *Das nationalsozialistische Lagersystem*. Frankfurt: Ausgabe bei Zweitausendeins, 1990.

26. "Re: Solution of the Jewish Question in Galicia," June 30, 1943, with enclosed report, translated as International Military Tribunal prosecution document no. L-18, U.S. Chief of Counsel for Prosecution of Axis Criminality, *Nazi Conspiracy and Aggression* (red series), vol. 7. Washington: USGPO, 1946, pp. 755–70. See particularly Hoffman correspondence concerning terms for use of Jews in forced labor, October 23, 1942 (Secret), pp. 761–63; quote in text is from p. 762.

27. Bohdan Wytwycky, *The Other Holocaust*. Washington, DC: Novak Report, 1980, p. 49. The Nazis eventually executed many of the laborers who survived the camps. According to International Red Cross reports, for example, of about 800 prisoners surviving at Kontinentale Öl's Borisow camp when it closed in March, 1943, "about 80 men and 20 women were evacuated to Smolensk, the rest were shot." The Smolensk center was also a forced labor camp. See International Tracing Service, *Catalogue of Camps and Prisons in Germany and German-Occupied Territories, 1939–1945*, (first issue). Arolsen: International Tracing Service Records Branch, 1949; reproduced in *Das nationalsozialistische Lagersystem*, op. cit., p. 699.

28. Nuremberg doc. no. NG-2586, op. cit.

29. Spezial-Archiv der Deutschen Wirtschaft, *Wer Leitet? Die Männer der Wirtschaft und der einschlagien Verwaltung 1941–1942.* Berlin: Hoppenstedt, 1942, p. 77; see also Karl Blessing, *Fragebogen,* August 31, 1946, in U.S. Army CIC dossier no. XE 170459 89291-3410, "*Blessing, Karl,*" obtained via Freedom of Information Act, U.S. Army INSCOM, Ft. Meade, MD.

30. See Kontinentale Öl's 1943 correspondence with the SS's Deutsche Wirtschaftsbetriebe GmbH on this project, National Archives microfilm T-976, roll 6, frames 001080-001110.

31. "Karl Blessing Is Dead at 71; Led West German Central Bank," *New York Times,* April 27, 1971, and "Who's Who in Foreign Business," *Fortune,* February 1958.

32. Ibid.

33. Ibid. For data in footnote, see Blessing, *Fragebogen,* op. cit. Not all of Dulles's interventions on behalf of favored Germans were so successful, particularly when outsiders raised questions about his judgment. Several of his key agents fell afoul of postwar denazification authorities. See Laqueur and Breitman, *Breaking the Silence,* op. cit., pp. 231–39.

34. John Alan Appleman, *Military Tribunals and International Crimes.* Westport, CT: Greenwood, 1971, pp. 177–83.

35. Bradley F. Smith, *Reaching Judgement at Nuremberg.* New York: New American Library, 1977, pp. 266–84.

36. Murphy to Secretary of State, December 10, 1945, Harrison to Secretary of State, December 13, 1945; both at file "War Crimes— International Military Tribunal, folder a#1," lot 61 D 33, box 1, RG 59, National Archives, Washington, DC.

37. On Gisevius's role, see Smith, op. cit., p. 271.

38. On Gafencu's role; see Davidson, *Trial of the Germans,* op. cit., p. 34.

39. Smith, op. cit., pp. 270–72. Schacht's attorney told the media that U.S. Consul Sam Woods (who also played a role in the later Horthy affair) offered Schacht a deal in 1939 under which the banker would resign from Hitler's government "with a promise he would be restored to power as post-war German official"; see Acheson to U.S. Legation, Bern, May 7, 1946 (Top Secret), 740.00116 EW/5-746, box 3615, RG 59, National Archives, Washington, DC.

40. See, for example, Robert Conquest, *The Harvest of Sorrow.* New York: Oxford Univ. Press, 1986.

41. For documentary background concerning Horthy's role in aggression

and war crimes, see Lemkin, *Axis Rule in Occupied Europe*, op. cit., pp. 361–67.

42. Hodgson (UNWCC) to Secretary of State transmitting copy of the Yugoslav case against Horthy, January 15, 1946, in file "War Crimes—Horthy," lot 61 D 33, box 4, RG 59, National Archives; and Schoenfeld to Secretary of State, September 10, 1945 (Secret), in file: "War Crimes—Horthy," lot 61 D 33, box 4, RG 59, National Archives. For U.S. agreement concerning return of criminals, see *UNWCC and the Laws of War*, op. cit., pp. 107–108.

43. Unsigned U.S. Embassy message to Secretary of State, November 29, 1945 (Secret), in file: "War Crimes—Horthy," lot 61 D 33, box 4, RG 59, National Archives, Washington, DC.

Chapter Sixteen

Prisoner Transfers

1. Lucy Dawidowicz, *The War Against the Jews*. New York: Bantam, 1975, pp. 512–17. For the events surrounding Horthy's belated order halting deportations to Auschwitz after some 430,000 Jews had been shipped to the camp, see Martin Gilbert, *Auschwitz and the Allies*. New York: Holt, Rinehart & Winston, 1981, pp. 262–66. For an unusually detailed, Ceauşescu-era indictment of Horthy drawn from what would otherwise be unavailable Romanian documentation, see Mihai Fatu and Mircea Musat (eds.), *Horthyist-Fascist Terror in Northwestern Romania 1940–1944*, Bucharest: Meridiane, 1986.

2. Murphy to Secretary of State, with attached reply, September 1, 1945 (Secret), 740 00116 EW/9-145, box 3602, RG 59, National Archives, Washington, DC.

3. AE Donovan (Legal Advisor's staff) to U.S. Embassy, Moscow, October 31, 1945, 740.00116EW/10-3145, box 3606, RG 59, National Archives, Washington, DC.

4. Murphy to Secretary of State, with attached reply, September 1, 1945 (Secret), 740.00116 EW/9-145, box 3602, RG 59, National Archives, Washington, DC. Note role of Army intelligence (G-2) in this exchange. Schoenfeld to Secretary of State, September 10, 1945 (Secret), in file "War Crimes—Horthy," lot 61 D 33, box 4, RG 59, National Archives, Washington, DC.

5. Schoenfeld to Secretary of State, September 10, 1945; ibid.

6. Murphy to Secretary of State, January 8, 1946 (Secret), 740.00116EW/1-845, box 3610, RG 59, National Archives, Washington, DC.

7. U.S. Political Advisor for Germany, "Surrender of Nicholas Horthy to Yugoslavia for Trial as a War Criminal" (Secret), January 22, 1947, 740.00116EW/1-2247, box 3621, RG 59, National Archives, Washington, DC.

8. Fite to Fahy, October 11, 1946, in file: "War Crimes—Horthy," box 4, D 33 lot 61, RG 59, National Archives, Washington, DC.

9. Medical report attached to U.S. Political Advisor for Germany, "Surrender of Nicholas Horthy to Yugoslavia for Trial as a War Criminal" (Secret), January 22, 1947, op. cit.

10. Hodgson to Secretary of State, March 6, 1946 (report on February UNWCC activities), 740.00116EW/3-646, box 3613, RG 59, National Archives, Washington, DC. For material in footnote, see, for example, Fite to Fahy, October 11, 1946, in file: "War Crimes—Horthy," box 4, lot 61 D 33, RG 59, National Archives, Washington, DC.

11. U.S. Political Advisor for Germany, "Surrender of Nicholas Horthy to Yugoslavia for Trial as a War Criminal" (Secret), January 22, 1947, op. cit.

12. Embassy of the Federal Peoples Republic of Yugoslavia to U.S. Secretary of State, March 3, 1948, with State's reply of March 15, 740. 00116EW/3-348, box 3628, RG 59, National Archives, Washington, DC.

13. Ibid.

14. OSS reports quoted in Bradley F. Smith and Elena Agarossi, *Operation Sunrise*. New York: Basic Books, 1979, p. 188.

15. Murphy to Secretary of State, 740.00116EW/8-1147 (Top Secret, No Distribution), August 11, 1947, obtained via Freedom of Information Act, RG 59, National Archives, Washington, DC.

16. For a summary, see Simon Wiesenthal Center (Los Angeles), *SS Col. Walter Rauff. The Church Connection, 1943–1947*—the first to plausibly link Dulles and Bicchierai to Rauff's escape. Despite the overall good quality of this study, it erroneously concluded that Dulles had been Rauff's U.S. interrogator on the basis of the initials "A.J.D." appearing in an Army Counter Intelligence Corps report. Dulles's initials are A.W.D. See particularly "Interrogation Report on SS Standartenfuehrer Rauff, Walter," May 15, 1945 (Confidential), in U.S. Army Counter Intelligence Corps file no. D-216719, "*Rauff, Walter*," obtained via Freedom of Information Act from U.S. Army INSCOM, Ft. Meade, MD.

17. Smith and Agarossi, op. cit., p. 189.

18. Loc. cit.

19. For correspondence concerning Jackson's resignation and Taylor's

appointment, see *SWNCC 237: Further Proceedings Against Axis War Criminals,* December 1945–January 1947, State-War-Navy Coordinating Committee Records, available via microfilm from Scholarly Resources.

20. John Alan Appleman, *Military Tribunals and International Crimes.* Westport, CT: Greenwood, 1971.

21. Ibid., data summarized.

22. Robert Joyce (Central Intelligence Group), to Walter Dowling, "Subject: Former SS Colonel Dollmann" (Top Secret), December 1, 1946, obtained in sanitized form via Freedom of Information Act, 740.00116EW/12-146, RG 59, National Archives, Washington, DC.

23. Rauff version: "Interrogation Report on SS Standartenfuehrer Rauff, Walter" May 15, 1945, op. cit. Dulles's version: Allen Dulles, *The Secret Surrender.* New York: Harper, 1966. pp. 66, 83, 102, 107, 158, 188, 192–93.

24. For Rauff's testimony on this point to a Chilean immigration court, see Simon Wiesenthal Center, *SS Col. Rauff,* op. cit.

25. Ibid.

26. Ibid.

27. Leghorn to Secretary of State, 740.00116EW/5-1547 (Top Secret), May 15, 1947, obtained in sanitized form via Freedom of Information Act, RG 59, National Archives, Washington, DC.

   Wenner, it should be noted, also often served as Wolff's personal representative in negotiations between major German companies and the SS; see "Geschaftsanweisung" (an SS-Dresdner Bank contract regarding Ostindustie accounts, July 9, 1943), National Archives microfilm no. T-976, reel 6, frame 001074.

28. Leghorn to Secretary of State, ibid.

29. Murphy to Secretary of State, 740.00116EW/8-1147 (Top Secret, No Distribution), August 11, 1947, RG 59, National Archives, Washington, DC.

30. Jack Neal, "Memorandum for the Files" (Top Secret), September 16, 1947, found at 740.00116 EW/8-1147, RG 59, National Archives, Washington, DC. This record, which had previously been withheld from the State Department files in the National Archives, was obtained by the author via the Freedom of Information Act.

31. Ibid.

32. Smith and Agarossi, op. cit., pp. 189–90.

33. Loc. cit.

34. Loc. cit.

35. Loc. cit.

36. "SS-General Wolff gestorben," *Franfurter Allgemeine Zeitung*, July 17, 1984; Jochen Lang, *Der Adjutant; Karl Wolff: Der Mann zwischen Hitler und Himmler*, Munchen: Herbig, 1985.

37. For an overview of Grombach's employment by, and rivalry with, the CIA, see Christopher Simpson, *Blowback*. New York: Weidenfeld and Nicolson, 1988. pp. 235–38.

38. John Valentine Grombach, "The Case of Dr. Eugen Dollmann"; (Annex "D") in *The Otto John Case*, unpublished manuscript, n.d. (1954?); copy in author's collection.

39. Eugen Dollmann, *The Interpreter: Memoirs of Doktor Eugen Dollmann*. London: Hutchinson, 1967.

40. On Bicchierai's work with U.S. intelligence, see Simpson, op. cit., pp. 92–94.

41. "Protocol of the Proceedings of the Berlin (Potsdam) Conference, August 1, 1945," in U.S. Department of State, Office of the Historian, *Documents on Germany, 1944–1985*. Department of State publication no. 9446. Washington, DC: USGPO, pp. 54–65.

Chapter Seventeen

Double-Think on Denazification

1. "Protocol of the Proceedings of the Berlin (Potsdam) Conference," op. cit. For an orthodox Soviet collection of documents from the same conference that reveals important differences in tone and interpretation from the latter-day official U.S. position, see Ministerium für Auswartige Angelegenheiten der UdSSR, *Die Potsdamer (Berliner) Konferenz der hochsten Reprasentanten der drie alliierten Machte*. Moskau/Berlin: Verlag Progress (DDR state publishing house), 1984, pp. 375–98.

For a detailed discussion of the often-pivotal role of the reparations issue in U.S.-Soviet relations of the period, see Bruce Kuklick, *American Policy and the Division of Germany*. Ithaca, NY: Cornell Univ. Press, 1972; and Thomas Peterson, *Soviet-American Confrontation*, Baltimore: Johns Hopkins Univ. Press, 1973, pp. 235–67. See also Inter-Allied Reparation Agency, *Report of the Assembly of the Inter-Allied Reparation Agency to its Member Governments*. Brussels: Inter-Allied Reparation Agency, 1951. For an overview of the reparations issue at the Potsdam Conference, see Herbert Feis, *Between War and Peace: The Potsdam Conference*. Princeton, N.J.: Princeton Univ.

Press, 1960, pp. 56–61, 232–44, 253–65, with a text of the treaty at pp. 338–54.

For a good summary of the legal implications for war crimes enforcement of the Potsdam agreements as seen by contemporary observers, see Joseph Hodgson (then U.S. Commissioner on the UNWCC) to Secretary of State, "Forwarding Data Concerning the United Nations War Crimes Commission" (Confidential), August 6, 1945, 740.001166EW/8-645, box 3601, RG 59, National Archives, Washington, DC.

2. "Protocol of the Proceedings . . . ," ibid.

3. Ibid.

4. Ibid.

5. Ibid. There is no single list of those who were to be regarded as "key men" in the German economy in the sense that this term was used at Potsdam. Hodgson of the UNWCC refers to the UNWCC lists no. 7 and no. 9 as models; copies of each of these are today available at the United Nations archives in New York. But the UNWCC's early effort was never viewed as comprehensive, and the Western adherence to this aspect of the Potsdam agreement collapsed before any serious effort was made to prepare a complete list of "key men." One of the more comprehensive efforts along these lines was "Names of Persons and Industrial Groups Affected by the Application of the Denazification Program to Banks," n.d. (1947?), box 54, OMGUS/FINAD, Finance Division/Investigations, RG 260, National Archives, Suitland, MD.

6. "Criticism of Denazification Program," August 25, 1945, file: Special Reports, box 237, OMGUS/FINAD, RG 260, National Archives, Suitland, MD.

7. Gabriel Almond and Wolfgang Kraus, "The Social Composition of the German Resistance," in Gabriel Almond (ed.), *The Struggle for Democracy in Germany*. Chapel Hill, NC: Univ. of North Carolina Press, 1949, pp. 65–67.

8. U.S. Government, OMGUS, Internal Affairs and Communication Division, Public Safety Branch (Berlin), *Report on Effect of Denazification upon Industry in US Zone of Occupation, Germany*, with exhibits and company reply forms, October 9, 1947, in file: "Survey of the Effects of Denazification on Industry," Public Safety Branch S-17, box 334, RG 260, National Archives, Suitland, MD. For a detailed and sophisticated discussion of the complex evolution of the *Betriebsrats*, see Michael Fichter, *Besatzungsmacht und Gewerkschaften*. Berlin: Westdeutscher Verlag, 1982; and Michael Fichter, *Von Stalingrad zur Wahrungsreform*. München: Oldenbourg Verlag, 1988.

9. Almond and Kraus, op. cit., p. 68.

10. James Stewart Martin, *All Honorable Men*. Boston: Little, Brown, 1950, p. 206.

11. The Drapers have been leading Republican party fund-raisers for at least four generations, and remain so today. On Draper family and Draper mills history: Orra Stone, *History of Massachusetts Industries*, vol. 2. Boston: S. J. Clarke, 1930, pp. 1910–16; John Garner, *The Model Company Town*. Amherst, MA: Univ. of Massachusetts Press, 1984, pp. 183ff; "Strikers' Demands Today Not Granted by Draper Company," *Milford Daily Journal*, April 3, 1913. I am grateful to the Museum of American Textile History, North Andover, MA, for their assistance in researching Draper Mills.

12. General William H. Draper, Jr., *Oral History Interview*, January 11, 1972, Harry S Truman Library, Independence, MO., pp. 32–33.

13. Martin, op. cit., passim; Draper, ibid., pp. 40–42.

14. Martin, op. cit., pp. 164, 173.

15. Draper, op. cit., pp. 40–42.

16. Lucius Clay, *Oral History Interview*, July 16, 1974, Harry S Truman Library, Independence, MO, pp. 15–16 (on JCS 1067) and p. 13 (on Truman); see also "Was the Decartelization Program Sabotaged? Profile No. 3: General Lucius D. Clay," *Prevent World War III*, no. 38 Summer 1951. Elsewhere, Clay has commented that he regarded the JCS 1067 order as having had a "devastating effect" on the morale of his supporters in the U.S. Group Control Council, apparently as early as the summer of 1945; see Lucius D. Clay, *Decision in Germany*. Garden City, NY: Doubleday, 1950, p. 8.

17. U.S. Congress, Senate, Committee on Military Affairs, *Elimination of German Resources for War*, Part 11 (Russell Nixon testimony), pp. 1545–46. Senator Kilgore's intervention ensured that a limited study of the German financial elite did take place, despite considerable harassment from Draper and his supporters. In the end, Draper succeeded in pushing the rebellious aides out of his administration and in burying the reports of their investigations in classified files, where they have lain undisturbed and largely unread for more than forty years. They were finally published in 1986 in German translation by the Hamburger Dokumentationsstelle zur NS-Sozialpolitik; they have never been published in English.

    On "double-think" phenomena and its treatment in U.S. historical accounts, see Gabriel Kolko, "American Business and Germany, 1930–1940," *Western Political Quarterly*, vol. 15, no. 4, December 1962, pp. 713ff.

18. Martin, op. cit., pp. 163–64.

19. "Potsdam Mandate Is Seen Softened," *New York Times*, November 25, 1945, p. 32. On Kilgore's efforts, see also C. P. Trussell, "German Industry Grew Under Raids," *New York Times*, August 8, 1945, p. 15; Harley M. Kilgore, "Germany Is Not Yet Defeated," *New York Times Magazine*, August 12, 1945, pp. 10ff; "Kilgore Criticized U.S. Reich Chiefs," *New York Times*, October 4, 1945, p. 7; "AMG in Germany Scored by Kilgore," *New York Times*, December 22, 1945, p. 7. For Allen Dulles's economic analysis of Germany during the first years after the war, see Allen Dulles, "Alternatives for Germany," introduction to Hoyt Price and Carl Schorske, *The Problem of Germany*, New York: Council on Foreign Relations, 1947.

20. On Clay and Draper: their oral histories, cited above. On FTC investigation: U.S. Government, Federal Trade Commission, *Report of the Committee Appointed to Review the Decartelization Program in Germany to the Honorable Secretary of the Army*, April 15, 1949, (often known as the Ferguson Committee Report), box 1, entry 131, RG 335, National Archives, Suitland, MD. See also: U.S. Government, OMGUS, Economics Division, Decartelization Branch, *Report on Progress of the Decartelization Branch*, June 14, 1947, and *Report to the Secretary of War on the Decartelization Program in Germany*, September 24, 1947, and *Decartelization in the U.S. Zone of Germany*, December 1948, each of which is found at box 1, entry 131, RG 335, National Archives, Suitland, MD. The December 1948 report is also available in more accessible form at the Law Library of the Library of Congress, Washington, DC.

Chapter Eighteen

"It Would Be Undesirable if This Became Publicly Known"

1. See, for example, Matthews memorandum, February 28, 1946, 740.00116EW/2-2846, and Riddleberger to Matthews, February 28, 1946, 740.00116EW/2-2846; both at box 3612, RG 59, National Archives, Washington, DC.

2. Loc. cit.

3. Hodgson to Secretary of State, November 2, 1945, 740.00116EW/11-245, box 3607, RG 59, National Archives, Washington, DC.

4. War Department Adjutant General to Department of State, February 18, 1946, 740.00116EW/2-1846, box 3612, RG 59, National Archives, Washington, DC. See also Byrnes (Fite) to Hodgson, March 21, 1946,

740.00116EW/3-2146, box 3613, RG 59, National Archives, Washington, DC.

5. Extract from Hodgson letter to Hackworth, which appears as an attachment to Matthews memorandum, February 28, 1946, ibid., Wolff to Secretary of State, April 25, 1946, 740.00116EW/4-2546, box 3614, RG 59, National Archives, Washington, DC.

6. Matthews memorandum of February 28, 1946, ibid.

7. Riddleberger to Matthews, February 28, 1946, 740.00116EW/2-2846, op. cit.

8. Eugene Davidson, *The Trial of the Germans*. New York: Macmillan, 1966, pp. 553ff.

9. Leon Friedman (ed.), *The Law of War. A Documentary History*, vol. 1. Westport, CT: Greenwood, 1972, pp. 908–909.

10. U.S., OMGUS, "Report of the Denazification Policy Board to the Deputy Military Governor" (Restricted), January 15, 1946, pp. 6–7, in file: "Denazification Publications," box 326, entry S-17, OMGUS Public Safety Branch, RG 260, National Archives, Suitland, MD.

11. Ibid., p. 12.

12. Ibid., pp. 5–6.

13. Loc. cit. For recent scholarship concerning the number and treatment of German POWs in Western hands at the end of World War II, see two papers presented at the Society for Historians of American Foreign Relations, 1992 Conference (Vassar College and Franklin D. Roosevelt Library, New York): Gunter Bischof, "American Treatment of German POWs During and After World War II in Light of Recent Historiography" (1992), and Richard Wiggers, "The United States and the Denial of Prisoner of War Status at the End of the Second World War" (1992). For prosecutors estimates of "Number of (Nazi) Politische Leiter Being Prosecuted Compared to Number of Nazi Elements in Germany and Entire German Population," see Office of U.S. Chief of Counsel for Prosecution of Axis Criminality, *Nazi Conspiracy and Aggression*, Washington, DC: USGPO, 1946, vol. 8, chart 14.

14. See, for example, the various "schedules" of financial personnel listing specific companies, offices, enforcement priorities, etc., found at file: "Denazification," box 229, OMGUS/FINAD, RG 260, National Archives, Suitland, MD.

15. U.S., OMGUS, "Report of the Denazification Policy Board," op. cit., pp. 8–11.

16. Ibid., p. 10.

17. U.S., OMGUS/FINAD, Financial Intelligence and Liaison Branch

Field Investigation Section, *Report on the Investigation of Law 52 in the US Zone* (Restricted), May 1946; copy in author's collection. My special thanks to Louis Madison for his comments concerning denazification, and for bringing these records to my attention. See also: U.S., OMGUS, "Law No. 52: Blocking and Control of Property," (n.d.), four pages, in the same collection.

18. U.S., OMGUS, "Report of the Denazification Policy Board," op. cit., p. 1.

19. James Stewart Martin, *Honorable Men*. Boston: Little, Brown, 1950, pp. 184–85.

20. Lewis H. Brown, *A Report on Germany*. New York: Farrar, Straus, 1947.

21. Milton Moskowitz, Michael Katz, and Robert Levering. *Everybody's Business*. San Francisco: Harper & Row, 1980, pp. 163–65.

22. Brown, op. cit., p. ix.

23. Ibid., pp. v–xii passim.

24. Ibid., pp. 17–18, with quote from p. 18.

25. Ibid., p. x.

26. Martin, op. cit., pp. 193–94, 223.

27. Ibid., pp. 226–27.

28. National Industrial Conference Board, *Rationalization of German Industry*, op. cit., pp. 110–11.

29. Ferdinand Lundberg, *The Rich and the Super-Rich*. New York: Bantam, 1969, pp. 141–44. For a recent example of somewhat similar behavior by General Electric, see Steven Pearlstein, "GE Told to Toughen Fraud Case Penalties," *Washington Post*, June 3, 1992, p. F-1.

30. Martin, *All Honorable Men*, op. cit., p. 185.

31. Harley M. Kilgore, "Germany Is Not Yet Defeated," *New York Times Magazine*, August 12, 1945, pp. 10ff.

32. Ibid.

33. Michael Wala, "Selling the Marshall Plan at Home: The Committee for the Marshall Plan to Aid European Recovery," *Diplomatic History*, Summer 1986, pp. 221ff. On Dubinsky, see p. 261. On James Carey, see *Blowback*, p. 126. Carey, who also served on the board of the National Committee for a Free Europe and a number of similar organizations with unacknowledged ties to the CIA, told the *New York Herald Tribune* in June 1950 that "in the last war we joined with the Communists to fight the Fascists. [In the next], we will join the Fascists to defeat the Communists."

34. Wala, ibid., p. 252.

35. Lucius D. Clay, *Oral History Interview*, op. cit., pp. 25–26. Abs's name is mistranscribed in this publication as Hermann Epps, though it is in fact Abs that Clay is discussing.

36. "International Outlook," *Business Week*, February 1, 1947, pp. 99–100.

37. Wala, op. cit., pp. 253–58, with Plumley quote on p. 264.

38. Ibid., p. 264.

Chapter Nineteen

The End of the War Crimes Commission

1. *OMGUS Deutsche Bank*, op. cit., p. 1; "Hermann J. Abs," in file: *Nazis Dismissed from German Banking*, n.d. (1946?), OMGUS/FINAD, box 234, RG, 260, National Archives, Suitland, MD. Abs was eventually barred from entry into the United States; see "Abs darf nicht in die USA," Reuter news dispatch, May 7, 1990.

2. For an excellent and convenient summary of the Nuremberg Subsequent Proceedings, see John Alan Appleman, *Military Tribunals and International Crimes*, Westport, CT: Greenwood, 1971; Frank Buscher, *The U.S. War Crimes Trial Program in Germany, 1946–1955*. Westport, CT: Greenwood, 1989; Telford Taylor, *Final Report to the Secretary of the Army on the Nuernberg War Crimes Trials*. Washington, DC: USGPO, 1949.

3. See U.S. filings now held at the United Nations War Crimes Commission Archives, New York, NY.

4. Author's interview with Telford Taylor, July 14, 1988; see also author's interview with former Nuremberg prosecutor Benjamin Ferencz, July 9, 1988.

5. Ibid., and Appleman, op. cit., p. 174.

6. Ibid. For a concise presentation of how the defense of necessity was perceived prior to the Flick case, see "Exhibit B: In Connection with General MacArthur's Talk Before the War Policies Commission," War Policies Commission, *Hearings*, op. cit., pp. 474–75. The discussion there, prepared by the U.S. Department of War, indicates that the legal claim of "necessity" had up to that time been employed primarily by the government in cases stemming from military damage to private property and/or seizure of private goods during the course of a war. Further, the circumstances in which the defense could be raised were quite narrow: "The necessity must be immediate, imperative, and in

some cases extreme and overwhelming [in order to be accepted as a defense], mere expediency or utility will not suffice" (p. 475). The court's extension of this defense to Flick, a corporate officer, seems to have stood precedent on its head.

7. Office of U.S. High Commissioner for Germany, Office of Public Affairs, "Landsberg: A Documentary Report," *Information Bulletin,* February 15, 1950.

8. For a biographic summary, see *National Cyclopedia of American Biography,* vol. 57, p. 110, *Current Biography 1958,* pp. 181–82, and the introductory notes to Green Hackworth, *Digest of International Law,* vol. 1, Department of State publication No. 1506, 1940, reprinted by Garland Publishing (New York), 1973.

9. Walter Millis (ed.), *Forrestal Diaries.* New York: Viking, 1951; and Townsend Hoopes and Douglas Brinkley, *Driven Patriot, The Life and Times of James Forrestal,* New York: Knopf, 1992.

10. It has not been possible in this volume to discuss the postwar reconstruction of Japan's major business cartels during Draper's tenure there. However, Michael Schaller, *The American Occupation of Japan, The Origins of the Cold War in Asia.* New York: Oxford, 1985, pp. 107–140, makes an important contribution to understanding this subject. For reviews of the war crimes trials in Japan, see R. John Pritchard, *Overview of the Historical Importance of the Tokyo War Trial.* Oxford: Nissan Occasional Papers, 1987, or Richard Minear, *Victors' Justice. The Tokyo War Crimes Trial.* Princeton, N.J.: Princeton Univ. Press, 1971.

11. John Martin Blum, *From the Morgenthau Diaries. Years of War 1941–1945.* Boston: Houghton Mifflin, 1967.

12. Author's interviews with Senator Claiborne Pell.

13. See for example, John Gillingham, *Industry and Politics in the Third Reich.* London: Methuen, 1985 (re: Ruhr coal); Simon Reich, *The Fruits of Fascism: Postwar Prosperity in Historical Perspective.* Ithaca, NY: Cornell Univ. Press, 1990. (re: auto industry); Peter Hayes, *Industry and Ideology.* New York: Cambridge Univ. Press, 1987 (re: IG Farben).

14. United Nations War Crimes Commission Archives, New York, NY. Cases include, for example, Netherlands vs. Ludwig Nolte (formerly of the Netherlands-based Philips corporation), charged with murder and pillage; UNWCC vs. Ernst Poensgen (of Vereinigte Stahlwerke—United Steelworks); Luxembourg vs. Gunther Quandt (Akkumulatorenfabrik—batteries, Daimler Benz autos, and other companies), charged with complicity in arrests and deportations; France vs.

Dr. Karl Ritter (German Foreign Ministry), charged with murder; Poland vs. Alfons Wagner (prominent mining industrialist), for confiscation of property; UNWCC vs. Wilhelm Zangen (Deutsche Bank, AEG, etc.), for crimes against peace and crimes against humanity; and many others.

15. Benjamin Ferencz, *Less Than Slaves*. Cambridge, MA: Harvard Univ. Press, 1979. pp. 179–81; Ferencz interview.

16. Ferencz interview with author.

17. Reported in "The Suppressed Dulles Story," *In Fact* (New York), no. 472, October 24, 1949.

18. John Foster Dulles to Secretary of State, with attachment, March 10, 1948 (Confidential), 861 20211/3-1048, RG 59, National Archives, Washington, DC.

19. Quoted in Ronald Pruessen, *John Foster Dulles: The Road to Power*. New York: Free Press, 1982, p. 124. Pruessen presents what is probably the most complete and cautious examination of the evidence still extant on John Foster Dulles's business affairs in Germany; see particularly pp. 123–32. See also Nancy Lisagor and Frank Lipsius, *A Law Unto Itself: The Untold Story of the Law Firm Sullivan and Cromwell*. New York: William Morrow, 1988, pp. 119–59.

20. See Fite (legal advisor's office) to Secretary of State, with attachments, August 6, 1947, f/w 740.00116EW/6-1847; Henderson to Fite, June 18, 1947, 740.00116EW/6-1847; and Solly-Flood to Barbour, June 21, 1947, 740.00116 EW/6-2147; all in box 3623, RG 59, National Archives, Washington, DC.

21. Robert Patterson (Secretary of War) to Secretary of State, July 22, 1947 (Top Secret), 740.00116 EW/7-2247, box 3624, RG 59, National Archives, Washington, DC. "Exceptions" discussed in Fite memo to U.S. Political Advisor, Berlin (Murphy), June 9, 1947: "[State] does not consider that US constitutional definition treason can be accepted as standard for judging surrender requests ... more rigid standard should be required," in file: "US POLAD," lot 61 D 33, box 2, RG 59, National Archives, Washington, DC.

22. 740.00116EW/12-547 (Netherlands), 740.00116EW/11-2147 (Poland), 740.00116EW/11-1447 (Czechoslovakia), 740.00116EW/1-848 (Poland), 740.00116EW/10-3147 (France), 740.00116EW/12-1947 (Netherlands), 740.00116EW/6-2449 (France), 740.00116EW/6-16-49 (Belgium); all at RG 59, National Archives, Washington, DC.

23. U.S. diplomatic note to French ambassador, July 20, 1949, 740.00116 EW/6-2449, RG 59, National Archives, Washington, DC.

24. UNWCC case no. 7593, United Nations War Crimes Commission

Archives, New York, NY; or copy at 740.00116EW/2-2748, box 3628, RG 59, National Archives, Washington, DC.

25. UNWCC case no. 7347, *Poland vs. Dr. Paersch, Reichsbank Berlin, et al*, op. cit.

26. Alti Rodale, "Canadian and Allied Government's Policies with Regard to Nazi War Crimes," (unpublished paper, courtesy of Dr. Rodale).

27. "Israel Urges Public Access to U.N. War Files," *New York Times*, May 2, 1986; Ruth Marcus, "Nazi-Hunters Gain Access to U.N. Documents," *Washington Post*, November 23, 1987.

28. Alti Rodale, op. cit.

29. FBI file No. 100-380802, *Ivan Kerno*, and Department of State records on Kerno obtained via Freedom of Information Act.

30. Ibid., and Maney to Bender, Department of State, July 20, 1954, in Department of State FOI case no. 8901702.

31. Ibid.

Chapter Twenty

Money, Law, and Genocide

1. Sergo Mikoyan comments, June 10, 1991, Smithsonian Institution, Wilson Center Colloquium. Mikoyan is the son of Anastas Mikoyan, who played a prominent role in the foreign affairs of the Stalin and Khrushchev governments in the USSR. The younger Mikoyan, also a foreign policy professional from the former USSR, is editor of *Latinskaia Amerika*. See also Michael McGwire, *The Genesis of Soviet Threat Perceptions*. Washington, DC: Brookings Institution monograph, 1987 (contractor's report No. 800-5 to the National Council for Soviet and East European Research). For an example of contemporary Soviet writing about these issues, see Sovinformburo, *Falsifiers of History (Historical Survey)*. Moscow: Foreign Languages Publishing House, 1951.

   New evidence underlining Mikoyan's point arrived from recently opened Soviet archives as this book was in preparation. On September 27, 1946, Soviet ambassador to the United States Novikov sent a long dispatch to Stalin summarizing the factors that he saw as central to understanding U.S. intentions. The Novikov dispatch reads in part: "One of the most important elements in the general policy of the United States . . . is the policy with regard to Germany. . . . The American occupation policy does not have the objective of eliminating the remnants of German Fascism and rebuilding German political life on a democratic basis, so that Germany might cease to exist as an aggressive force. The United States is not taking measures to eliminate the monopolistic associations of German industrialists on which German Fascism depended ... neither is any agrarian reform being conducted. . . . One cannot help seeing that such [policies have] a clearly outlined anti-Soviet edge. . . ." (translation by Ken Jensen and John Glad). The point here is Novikov's *interpretation,* not whether or not he accurately portrayed U.S. intentions. Given the context of the time, Novikov's perception almost certainly mirrored Stalin's own. The Novikov telegram is widely regarded by historians today as "in some ways parallel," as Vladimir Shustov put it, to George Kennan's famous Mr. X telegram of roughly the same period in that it frankly summarizes the dominant interpretation of the actions of rivals. See Ken Jensen, U.S. Institute of Peace, "Memorandum," August 15, 1990.

2. United Nations, *Human Rights, A Compilation of International Instruments.* New York: United Nations, n.d.

3. Important exceptions to the usual silence concerning bombing include: Seymour Melman, *In the Name of America.* Annandale, VA: Clergy and Laymen Concerned About Vietnam, 1968, pp. 173–268; and Duffett, *Against the Crime of Silence,* op. cit. For discussion of the issue of war crimes and crimes against humanity during the 1991 "Desert Storm" bombardment of Iraq, see Middle East Watch, *Needless Deaths in the Gulf War. Civilian Casualties During the Air Campaign and Violations of the Laws of War.* New York: Human Rights Watch, 1991; William Arkin, Damian Durrant, and Marianne Cherni, *On Impact: Modern Warfare and the Environment.* Washington, DC: Greenpeace, 1991; San Francisco Commission of Inquiry, *High Crimes and Misdemeanors: U.S. War Crimes in the Persian Gulf.* San Francisco, International War Crimes Tribunal, 1991.

   For discussion of the use of atomic bombs as a prima facie war crime due to the indiscriminate destruction resulting from an atomic attack, see Leon Friedman, "The Shimoda Case," in *The Law of War. A Documentary History,* vol. 2. Westport, CT: Greenwood, 1972, pp. 1688–1702.

4. Thomas Buergenthal, *International Human Rights.* St. Paul, MN: West, 1988, pp. 213, 221–22, 230. For concise background on the Genocide Convention, see Vita Bite, *Genocide Convention,* Washington, DC: Congressional Research Service publication IB74129, 1987; and Barbara Harff, *Genocide and Human Rights: International Legal and Political Issues,* University of Denver School of International Studies, *Monograph Series in World Affairs,* vol. 20, book 3, 1984.

5. Neil Lewis, "Sorting Out Legal War Concerning Real War," *New York Times,* November 15, 1990, p. A-18. The comment from Acheson was reported by Harvard professor Abram Chayes, the legal advisor to President Kennedy during the 1962 Cuban missile crisis, who sat in on Acheson's session with Kennedy at the height of the crisis.

For a concise presentation of the various trends of thought in ongoing debates among specialists concerning international law and human rights, see Tom Farer, "Human Rights in Law's Empire: The Jurisprudence War," *American Journal of International Law,* January 1991, pp. 117ff.

6. For recent articles on U.S. lawlessness, see Noam Chomsky, "Letter from Lexington, December 8, 1991," *Lies Of Our Times,* January–February 1992, pp. 11ff; Richard Falk, "The Extension of Law to Foreign Policy: The Next Constitutional Challenge," in Alan Rosenbaum's (ed.) *Constitutionalism: The Philosophical Dimension,* Westport, CT: Greenwood Press, 1988; Richard Falk, "Preface," *Vietnam and International Law,* Northampton, MA: Aletheia Press, 1990; Marcus Raskin, "American Idealism, War Crimes, and a Law of Personal Accountability," in *Essays of a Citizen,* New York: M. E. Sharpe, 1991, pp. 139–66; Daniel Ellsberg, "The Responsibility of Officials in a Criminal War," in *Papers on the War,* New York: Simon and Schuster, 1971, pp. 275ff. For overviews, see Lori Damrosch (ed.) *The International Court of Justice at a Crossroads,* Dobbs Ferry, NY: Transnational Publishers/American Society of International L 1987; H. W. A. Thirlway, *Non-Appearance Before the Internati Court of Justice,* Cambridge: Cambridge Univ. Press, 1985.

7. United Nations Children's Fund (UNICEF), *The State of the Children 1989.* New York: Oxford Univ. Press/UNICEF, 1 nual); and Lori Heise, "Killing the Children of the Third Washington Post,* April 21, 1991, p. B-1.

Index

About the Author

Christopher Simpson teaches journalism at the American University in Washington, DC. His earlier book, *Blowback*, won the National Jewish Book Award for historical writing concerning the Holocaust, the Joel H. Cavior/Present Tense Literary Prize, the Investigative Reporters and Editors Prize for investigative reporting, and other awards. He served as Research Director for Marcel Ophuls's documentary *Hotel Terminus: The Life and Times of Klaus Barbie*, which won an Academy Award in 1989 and the International Critics Prize at the Cannes Film Festival. He has written for the *Washington Post*, *Atlanta Constitution*, *Boston Globe*, *Inquiry*, *Omni*, and many other magazines, newspapers, and television news programs. His work has been translated into German, French, Japanese, and other languages.